Ten Thousand Miles
Without a Cloud

SUN SHUYUN

Ten Thousand Miles Without a Cloud

HarperCollins*Publishers*

HarperCollins*Publishers*
77–85 Fulham Palace Road,
Hammersmith, London W6 8JB

www.harpercollins.co.uk

Published by HarperCollins*Publishers* 2003
1 3 5 7 9 8 6 4 2

Copyright © Sun Shuyun 2003

Sun Shuyun asserts the moral right to
be identified as the author of this work

A catalogue record for this book
is available from the British Library

ISBN 0 00 712964 5

Map by John Gilkes

Typeset in PostScript Linotype Minion with
Janson and Spectrum display by
Rowland Phototypesetting Limited,
Bury St Edmunds, Suffolk

Printed and bound in Great Britain by
Clays Ltd, St Ives plc

All rights reserved. No part of this publication may be
reproduced, stored in a retrieval system or transmitted,
in any form or by any means, electronic, mechanical,
photocopying, recording or otherwise, without the prior
permission of the publishers.

This book is sold subject to the condition that it shall not,
by way of trade or otherwise, be lent, re-sold, hired out or
otherwise circulated without the publisher's prior consent
in any form of binding or cover other than that in which it
is published and without a similar condition including this
condition being imposed on the subsequent purchaser.

*For Robert,
and my Chinese family*

PREFACE

Xuanzang, the subject of this book, could not have completed his epic journey without the help he received from kings, emperors and princes. I too have to thank a large number of people who made my journey possible; they helped me practically and intellectually. They include R. C. Agrawal, Daub Ali, Swati Barathe, Vasanta Bharucha, Bodhisen, Peter Coleridge, Joe Cribb, Mick Csaky, G. P. Deshpande, Toby Eady, Elizabeth Errington, Katie Espiner, Anthony Fitzherbert, Madhu Ghose, Richard Gombrich, Ruchira Gupta, Sue Hamilton, Hu Ji, Prem Jha, M. C. Joshi, Shah Nazar Khan, Robert Knox, Luo Feng, Philip Lutgendorf, Ma Shichang, Manidhamma, Robert Mason, Jean McNeil, Venerable Miaohua, Yumiko and Paul Mitchell, Vivek Nanda, Lolita Nehru, John Pell, M. C. Ranganathan, Harapasad Ray, Gowher Rizvi, Virginia Shapiro, Sarah Shaw, Romila Thapar, Judy and John Thompson, Uma Waide, Wang Qihan, Roderick Whitfield, Sally Wriggins, Zhang Jianhua, and many other friends and experts in China and elsewhere too numerous to list. I must single out Sally Wriggins, whose academic study of Xuanzang has been invaluable.

I owe an especially large debt to five people:

to Susan Watt, my editor at HarperCollins, who saw I had a book to write before I did, who had confidence in me before I acquired it myself and who led me through the new experience of writing with insight and assurance;

to Fang Xichen, who has been nothing less than an inspiration on the history and culture of my own people, a man of real wisdom and generosity;

vii

to Venerable Dr Jingyin, who has been my guide and teacher in the vast canon of Buddhist writings, and who, with immense kindness, has shared with me his broad understanding of his faith;

to Tapan Raychaudhuri, whom I have troubled again and again, yet have always been received with warmth. He has put at my disposal his great knowledge of Indian history, not to speak of his expertise in Pali, Sanskrit, Indian literature and much else besides;

and above all to my husband, who kept encouraging me to write the book in the first place, who tolerated with the mildest of complaints my long absences abroad and who remained calm, patient and supportive throughout. Of all the people I know he comes closest to having the qualities of a Buddhist.

SUN SHUYUN

AUTHOR'S NOTE

Spelling

I have used the pinyin system which is used in mainland China for transliterating Chinese. Xuanzang is known in older texts, and also to Indian readers, as Hiuen Tsang, or Hsuan-tsang.

Sanskrit and Indian words are Romanized, without diacritical marks.

Pronunciation

Q is pronounced 'ch' as in church, so the *Qin* (dynasty) is pronounced 'Chin', and *Qu* (as in *Qu Wentai*) is pronounced 'Chew'.

X is an aspirated 's', and Z before a vowel is 'dz' as in adze, so Xuanzang is pronounced 'Hswan-dzang', the two 'a's short as in gang – 'Shwanzang' is near enough if you cannot get your tongue round it.

Zh before a vowel is pronounced 'j' as in joke, so Zhao is pronounced 'Jao', rhyming with cow.

In Sanskrit words C is pronounced 'ch' as in church, so Yoga-cara is pronounced 'Yogachara'.

Place names

I use the most familiar forms, such as Khotan rather than the Chinese Hetian.

Translations

I have relied mainly on Samuel Beal's translations of Xuanzang's

Record of the Western Regions, and of Hui Li's biography of Xuan-zang, but I have taken the liberty of amending his versions without indication in some of the quotes, wherever I found them inaccurate or too archaic. I have sometimes done the same with other translations from the Chinese. (The title of Xuanzang's book also has various versions, but I have kept to the one mentioned here, or just his *Record*.)

Date of Xuanzang's birth

Xuanzang's date of birth is disputed. AD 602 is suggested by some historians; I have taken it to be AD 600, as most Chinese scholars now do.

Name of the Buddha

The Buddha was given this name only after his enlightenment. I have not made the distinction, and for simplicity refer to him as the Buddha throughout.

CONTENTS

	LIST OF ILLUSTRATIONS	xii
	MAP	xiv–xv
ONE	Bringing Back the Truth	1
TWO	Three Monks at the Big Wild Goose Pagoda	45
THREE	Fiction and Reality	73
FOUR	Exile and Exotica	111
FIVE	Land of Heavenly Mountains	145
SIX	Imagining the Buddha	179
SEVEN	Light from the Moon	209
EIGHT	Not a Man?	257
NINE	Nirvana	287
TEN	Battleground of the Faiths	329
ELEVEN	Lost Treasures, Lost Souls	363
TWELVE	Journey's End	407
	SELECTED READINGS	449
	INDEX	455

ILLUSTRATIONS

Chapter 1. Cultural Revolution Poster
Chinese Poster Collection, University of Westminster

Chapter 2. 'The sun rising from behind Chang'an Dayan Tower'
(Big Wild Goose Pagoda), China by Ikuo Hirayama,
2000
Ikuo Hirayama Museum of Art

Chapter 3. Caravan, little changed from Silk Road days
The British Library (Stein Collection, photo 392/26)

Chapter 4. Apsara, Kizil Caves, 3rd Century AD
© Reza/Webistan

Chapter 5. The Heavenly Mountains
The Royal Geographical Society

Chapter 6. Gandhara Buddha head, 4th–5th Century AD
The V & A Picture Library

Chapter 7. 'Yindu' – Chinese name chosen by Xuanzang for
India.
Calligraphy by Su Ping

Chapter 8. Worshipping the Bodhi Tree, Bharhut Stupa, early 1st
Century BC
Indian Museum, Calcutta

Chapter 9. Dhamekh Stupa, Sarnath, 5th Century AD. It marks
the spot where the Buddha first preached after his
Enlightenment.
The Hutchison Library

xii

Chapter 10. Ruined hall in Khotan
The British Library (Stein Collection, photo 392/27)

Chapter 11. Wutai Mountain, place of pilgrimage, Dunhuang
mural, 11th Century
Dunhuang Academy. Photo by Lois Conner

Chapter 12. Xuanzang with Emperor Taizong, painting on sillk
scroll, 14th Century
Fujita Museum of Art, Osaka

*While every effort has been made to trace the owners of copyright
material reproduced herein, the publishers would like to apologise for
any omissions and will be pleased to incorporate missing
acknowledgements in any future editions*

Endpapers; Map: Five Provinces of India, dated 1749, *courtesy of Kobe
City Museum*; Scrolls (front and back): 'Illustrated hand scrolls of
the monk Xuanzang', 14th Century, *courtesy of Fujita Museum of
Art, Osaka*; Pagoda: 'The sun rising from behind Chang'an Dayan
Tower' (Big Wild Goose Pagoda), *China* by Ikuo Hirayama, 2000,
courtesy of Ikuo Hirayama Museum of Art.

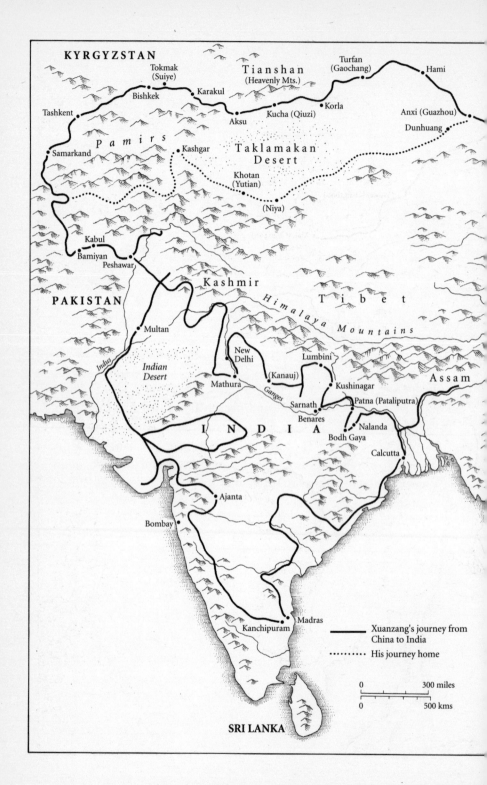

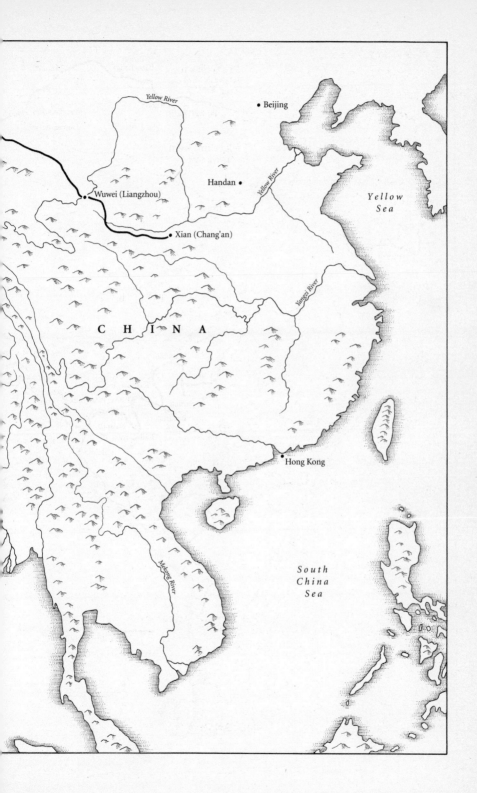

ONE

Bringing Back the Truth

I GREW UP in a small city in central China, in a time that now seems remote and strange. It was the 1960s. Life went by like scenes in a play I could not understand.

At first it was much the same every day, just Mother, Father, Grandmother and my two older sisters in our house in a military compound; nobody smiled much, never any treats. Things only livened up for the few days of the Chinese New Year. We ate sweets, and dumplings with meat in them; we had new clothes and a few pennies of pocket money; we bought firecrackers, watched puppet shows, put bright red posters on the front door and beautiful paper cut-outs in the windows.

Suddenly everything changed, and the streets were alive, as if every day was the New Year. There were posters, red, green, pink and yellow, waving in the wind, or blown along the road; flags flew on top of houses and workplaces; walls were painted with portraits of Mao. Loudspeakers blared out revolutionary songs from morning till night. Young men and women from Mao's propaganda teams recited from his *Little Red Book*, twirled about in 'loyalty dances', and struck revolutionary poses – they never seemed to tire, but sometimes they fainted and had to be carried away. Some of them even pinned Mao's portrait on their chests, and their blood dripped down. The Cultural Revolution was on the way.

Often the whole city turned out in force. People walked in ranks, some holding little paper flags, others carrying huge banners, everyone shouting slogans, young girls and women jumping up and down to the sound of cymbals and drums, with firecrackers sounding off. It was like the pageant shows during the New Year, with farmers walking on stilts, acting pantomime lions and donkeys, and dressing up as popular characters from folklore. When I asked my parents why they were marching today, the answer was nearly always the same. There was a new dictum from Mao! People stopped whatever they were doing and took to the streets, pledging their loyalty.

Another popular event was the frequent parading in the streets of what we called the 'enemies' of the people. They all wore dunces' caps, and had huge placards hanging from their necks, the black characters of their names cancelled by big red crosses. There were landlords in their silk jackets, and their wives with painted faces and heads half-shaved; teachers had their shirts splashed with ink, black, blue and red; some women carried their shoes round their necks – these were bad women who had cheated their husbands; old monks with grey hair and beards wore their long robes torn and smeared with cow-dung. They were all like circus clowns with their make-up; I ran after them, shouting and laughing.

When they came to a big space, they would stop for struggle meetings, like public entertainments, drawing huge crowds. One day I dragged my grandmother along to watch. The 'cow demons' and 'snake spirits', as they were called, walked slowly round in a circle; they were reviled and spat on and a Red Guard whipped them with a belt. Some of the dunces' caps fell off. The wires of their heavy placards cut into their flesh.

4

The loudspeakers on the truck shouted: 'Down with the reactionaries! Let them taste the strength of the proletarian dictatorship! And let them be trampled on for eternity!' We were informed they were the agents of feudalism, capitalism, American imperialism and Soviet revisionism, who dreamed of toppling the dictatorship of the proletariat. So everyone must be on guard and think of class struggle hourly, daily, weekly, monthly – never forget it! I was hopping up and down, trying to get a better view. Grandmother was leaning on an electricity pole, her face white as ashes. She turned to me, looked me in the eye and said I would go to hell if I ever treated people like that. 'Don't frighten me. There is no hell,' I answered back. When it was getting dark, the Red Guards marched off, the 'enemies' gathered up their caps and placards, and with their heads lowered, walked slowly back home. Tomorrow they might be paraded again.

I remember asking Grandmother, how could those people possibly topple the government? I did not understand. The old, bald priests in their long dirty robes looked so frail, as if they could collapse any minute under their heavy placards. My grandmother said they were the gentlest of men – they walked very carefully so they would not tread on ants; and in the old days, when they lit a lamp, they would cover it with a screen so that moths could not fly into it. But my father said I should not be fooled by appearances. 'Even a dying cobra can bite,' he warned me.

It was a fun time for kids. Schools were often closed, and all the children from the compound I lived in played together; we made up a unit of our own and my older sisters joined in. We wore mini-versions of military tunics – Mother sewed them from an old uniform of Father's, and put a belt round the waist. She said, 'If they ask you, just say your father is in the army and you will be safe; nobody will dare to touch you.'

My sisters did not study much when they did go to school. Reading and writing, addition, subtraction – there was not too much of these. Books were burnt, school libraries set on fire. Students who rebelled against their teachers were good, they were role models. Handing in a blank exam paper was heroic. The teachers' job was to groom the successors of Communism. If they did not, they were sent away to be 're-educated'. They had to instil the right ideas from day one. Better socialist weeds than capitalist seeds, illiterate rebels rather than educated pupils bent on scholastic achievement. What was the point of a brilliant mind that could not tell grass from wheat?

It was the same when I started school. We did not have many normal lessons; instead we learned from peasants and workers. 'Eat with them, sleep with them, work with them.' We served apprenticeships in factories, making simple tools, such as hammers and chisels – half the things we made were useless, but it did not matter. We were learning the right attitude. We went to the countryside at harvest-time, helping the farmers to bring in the wheat. At least we thought we were helping: in fact, we were in the way and the farmers worried they would be in trouble if we cut ourselves on their sickles; they had to feed us; and when they were worn out at night, they had to stay up lecturing us about the bitter past and the sweet life that the revolution had brought. We did reward them: every day we went out after lunch to collect animal droppings for them, and we took night-soil from the school cesspit to their fields. That taught us something.

Then life on the streets became fiercer. The Cultural Revolution had taken on a more sinister twist. It was 'Smash the Old' time. The Red Guards were in full spate, storming temples, demolishing pagodas, removing traces of capitalism – old shop signs, neon lights on top of department stores, even the rotating lights outside barber shops. They took down the old street signs, which normally had auspicious names in one form or another, and replaced them with 'struggle' themes. They patrolled the roads and stopped anyone with curly hair, high heels or tight trousers – they shaved their heads, broke the heels and cut the trousers open. There was a small temple near home: it was very familiar – Grandmother used to take me there. I liked it; at festival times there were paper lanterns and paper animals to entertain us. Now the temple was broken up and sealed off. Then the Red Guards began ransacking people's homes, throwing out posters, record players, clocks, antique furniture, any books that were not by Mao or Marx and Lenin – everything was piled in the streets and sent up in flames.

In one of the piles Grandmother found something special for me. I was thrilled – it was a comic-strip version of a novel, *The Monkey King*. The front cover was gone and some pages were missing.

The Monkey King tells the epic story of a monkey, a pig and a novice accompanying a monk to India to seek sutras, sacred writings. The monk is utterly useless. He is kind and pious, but weak, bumbling and, as the Chinese say, with a mind as narrow as a chicken's intestine. He cannot tell right from wrong. But it is reputed that eating his flesh will guarantee immortality, so demons and vampires are all out to get him. He is in luck though: soon after he sets off, he runs into the monkey, sent to help him by the Goddess of Compassion. Without the monkey, he would not stand a chance of saving his skin, let alone getting his job done. The monkey looks like any other, but he is far from ordinary. His eyes are the sun and the moon. He appeases his hunger with iron-pills and slakes his thirst with copper-juice. In one somersault he covers 180,000 leagues. Reciting a spell, he can turn himself into anything he desires: a cloud shrouding everything in darkness, an insect hidden in a peach, a giant so big that even hurricanes cannot blow him away. No weapon can harm him, and a contingent of 100,000 heavenly troops fails to catch him. Even alchemical fire cannot burn him. He is inviolable and he gives himself a fitting title – 'The Great Sage, Equal to Heaven'. He is submissive only to the Buddha and the monk – whenever the monk recites a spell from a sutra, the monkey curls up and cries with unbearable pain. After eighty-one titanic battles the monkey finally finds the sutras and brings them back with the monk on a magic wind. The monk, the monkey, the pig and the novice all became Buddhas.

I showed the book to my father when he came back from work. 'It is a good book,' he said. 'Chairman Mao loves it. He even wrote a poem about it: "The monk is confused but can be reformed; the vampire is vicious and must be killed. The golden monkey strikes with his cudgel, and Heaven is cleared of all evil. Welcome, welcome, Monkey King, for the battle against new demons."'

'What are the sutras? Why did the monkey go all that way to get them? Are they like Chairman Mao's *Little Red Book*?' I asked. I had heard adults use the word 'sutra' to describe the latest instruction from Chairman Mao.

'Sutras are the words of the Buddha,' my father told me.

'Who is the Buddha? Is he like Chairman Mao, very important?'

Father was suddenly very irritated. 'These are not things for children. You cannot understand them. And you mustn't talk about them outside this house.'

8

Many Red Guards took Mao's poem as their cue and called their factions 'The Magic Cudgel' or 'The Golden Monkey'. Little did I know that they created more havoc and unleashed more terror than the monkey could have done.

As it went on, the Cultural Revolution became ever more extreme. There was no more singing and dancing, no parading. It progressed to blows, bloody noses and bruised eyes; from debates to vituperation and violence. I often ran home, scared. Then barricades began to appear in the streets, and rifles and cannons. I was no longer allowed out of the house, which was almost like a fortress, with sandbags at the door and all the windows boarded up. Only my father could sneak off in his officer's uniform and buy groceries. At night we huddled together in the dark, listening to the gunshots snapping like fireworks. Grandmother was confused. 'Are the Japanese invading us again?' she asked my father. 'Why are people killing each other?' He did not answer. It was no circus any more.

I retreated to my book. I still remember reading *The Monkey King* for the first time. It was sheer magic: every step of the way was an adventure, replete with hordes of gods and goddesses, fairies and spirits, humans and demons. I felt transported to another world where nothing was impossible.

But I felt irritated too. I could not see why the monkey wanted to protect a hopeless, feeble monk. He had to go through 'mountains of knives and seas of flame' to find the sutras. What were they for? Why did he not just forget about them? Besides, how could the powerless monk have control over the almighty monkey simply by reciting a spell? Who was the Buddha anyway?

In the evening, I raised these questions with Grandmother.

She hesitated, but I insisted. She asked me to close the door. 'Sutras are very important. That's why the monk risked his life getting them.'

'But the monkey found them for him, really,' I protested.

'That is the story. In real life, the monk went on his own,' Grandmother said quietly.

'How do you know so much?' I asked Grandmother.

'Oh, a monk in our temple in the village was a great fan of Master Xuanzang. He told us a lot about him.'

'It isn't possible. Devils were waiting for him every step of the way. He would have been dead a hundred times over. He was so useless.'

While Grandmother was explaining to me what the monk really did, I felt my eyes were closing. I slept, and dreamed I was very thirsty, as if I were struggling in the desert and could not find the way. For a long time afterwards, I saw the monkey and the monk in my dreams.

They remained vividly in my memory. But it was no more than that until many years later, when I met an Indian history student in my college's common room in Oxford.

'I know about someone from China.'

'You have friends there?'

'No.'

'Do you mean Mao?'

He shook his head. There was a look of disappointment on his face, as if it was obvious and I ought to know. He straightened up, and put down his drink. 'It is Xuanzang. You must know about him.'

'Of course, he is the monk in *The Monkey King*. It's one of the most popular Chinese novels,' I explained.

'He is India's great friend. We love him. He was an extraordinary man. He preserved a large part of our history for us.'

I must have looked surprised, and I felt embarrassed. 'I know who you mean,' I said.

But I was puzzled. Could this be the same Xuanzang? I dimly remembered from school that Xuanzang had written about his journey, but we were never taught about him, nor did we read his book, *The Record of the Western Regions*. The next day I went to the Bodleian Library to see if I could find it. It was there, of course, and also *The Life of Xuanzang*, the biography written by his disciple, Hui Li, both in English. I sat down at once in the Upper Reading Room and began to read.

I became completely absorbed. For the next three days I hardly did anything else. I felt I was on a treasure hunt, each page its own reward, but giving me a clue to the next discovery. I could not believe the wealth of information contained in the two books. The sheer number of cities and towns he visited, the history and legends associated with each place, the kings who ruled with righteousness, the Buddhist masters and their luminous wisdom – his *Record* is an encyclopaedia of the history and culture of the time; it is the testimony to a lost world. I wondered how much of it remained to be rediscovered.

The *Record* gives you no impression of Xuanzang himself nor of his adventures on the journey; those you find in the biography. It was a total revelation. Xuanzang was lost in the desert for four days without water. He was robbed many times – once pirates even threatened to throw him into the river as a sacrifice to the river goddess. He was almost killed by an avalanche in the Heavenly Mountains. At one point he even had to go on hunger strike to be allowed to continue his journey. The monk whose biography I was reading bore no relation to the one I had known from childhood. In fact, he was the very opposite of the helpless man in *The Monkey King*. He embodied determination, perseverance and wisdom. They were both monks, and both went to India in search of sutras – but there the resemblance ended.

Grandmother was right after all. There was a real Xuanzang. He was born into a scholarly Confucian family in 600 AD, in Henan Province, the cradle of Chinese civilization. He was the youngest of four sons and lost his parents when he was an infant. A serious child, he did not want to play with other children; even at festival times he stayed in and read. He soon became fascinated by monastic life – one of his brothers was initiated as a monk early in his life, and Xuanzang often went to stay with him in his monastery.

When he was thirteen years old, an imperial decree announced that fourteen monks were to be trained and supported by the state at his brother's monastery. Several hundred candidates applied. Xuanzang was too young to qualify but he had set his mind on it. He lingered round the examination hall all day until the imperial invigilator noticed him and called him in. When asked why he was so keen on becoming a monk, he replied: 'I wish to continue the task of the Buddha and glorify the teachings he bequeathed.' The invigilator was surprised by this answer from a young boy who seemed to know his mind so well. He made an exception for him.

Xuanzang took to monastic life like a fish to water. He studied day and night, with little sleep or food. After hearing a sutra only twice, he could remember every word. But his studies were soon interrupted by a major peasant uprising. 'The capital has become a nest of bandits,' as he later told Hui Li. 'Law and order has broken down completely. The magistrates have been killed and the priests have perished or taken flight. The streets are filled with bleached bones and the rubble of burned buildings.'

He and his brother fled first to the capital, Chang'an, today's Xian, but there were few monks there: most had gone to Sichuan in the southwest, where, isolated by high mountains and the Three Gorges of the Yangzi River, life was unaffected by the war. Xuanzang followed them and was able to learn from monks from all over the country who had taken refuge there. Within two or three years, he mastered all the Buddhist scriptures of different schools and soon made a reputation for himself. He and his brother preached with an ease and eloquence that the local people had never heard before. And Xuanzang in particular made a strong impact. He was almost six feet tall, with bright eyes and a clear complexion, and he cut an impressive figure in his Buddhist robe, graceful, serious and dignified. When he spoke, his sonorous voice had a hypnotic effect. His loftiness of mind, his lack of attachment to worldly things, his insatiable curiosity about the metaphysical aspects of the cosmos, and his ambition to clarify the meaning of life left a deep impression on everyone who came into contact with him.

But Xuanzang was far from content. The more he studied, the more dissatisfied he felt. *Chan* masters, or Zen as the world now calls the school, would tell him that we all had in us the purest, unspoiled mind, the Buddha-nature, but it was defiled by erroneous thoughts; if only we could get rid of them, we would experience awakening. This could happen any time, at any place – while you were drinking tea, hearing a bell ring, working in the field, or washing your clothes. But Zen placed much emphasis on meditation that enabled one to go beyond logic and reason, the stumbling-blocks to enlightenment. How do you get a goose out of a bottle without breaking the bottle?

This was the sort of question, or *koan*, that Zen masters would ask their disciples to jolt them out of their analytical and conceptual way of thinking, and to lead them back to their natural and spontaneous faculties. Reciting the sutras – the teachings of the Buddha – and worshipping his images were no use at all. As a famous Zen master said, 'If you should meet the Buddha, kill the Buddha.'

But Xuanzang was told by masters of the Pure Land School that practising Zen was difficult and laborious, like an ant climbing a mountain. Instead he should simply recite the name of Amitabha Buddha, who presided over the Pure Land of the Western Paradise. The Bodhisattva of Compassion, Guanyin, is his chief minister. Often portrayed in Chinese temples with ten thousand hands and eyes, Guanyin is ever ready to go anywhere and lead the faithful to the land of purity and bliss. Once there, in the company of Amitabha, anyone can swiftly achieve enlightenment. Guanyin became Xuanzang's favourite deity and he would pray to her whenever he was in difficulty. She was also Grandmother's favourite, and that of all Chinese Buddhists.

The followers of the Tiantai School, based in the Tiantai Mountains in eastern China, claimed, however, that they had found the true way. Buddhism was introduced into China in the first century A D and with the help of Indian and Central Asian monks, most of the major sutras had been translated into Chinese by Xuanzang's time. The Tiantai School made the first comprehensive catalogue of the large number of sutras and synthesized all the various thoughts and ideas. They came to the conclusion that the entire universe was the revelation of the absolute mind, that everyone possessed the Buddha-nature, and that all truth was contained in the Lotus Sutra alone. You could forget about all the others.

Xuanzang never ceased to examine the different schools, but he told Hui Li that despite all his efforts, he was never free from doubts. Each of the schools claimed to know the quickest way to enlightenment, but he found them wildly at odds with each other. Was it because the sutras they read were in different translations? The early Indian and Central Asian monks did not speak Chinese and the sutras they had translated were not always accurate. But what troubled him even more was whether all the schools were authentic. The Chinese were very practical and down-to-earth, not given to abstract concepts and metaphysical speculation, and had no time for abstruse doctrines and convoluted logical debates. This was why they preferred the instant enlightenment of *Chan* or winning a place in paradise through recitation. It seemed all too easy. Xuanzang knew well that the Buddha's path to enlightenment was long and arduous. He was far from sure that everyone had the Buddha-nature, and he could not believe enlightenment was to be reached without fundamental understanding of the nature of reality and the mind.

Xuanzang decided to go back to Chang'an where the head of the rebels, Li Yuan, had crowned himself the emperor in 618 and established a new dynasty, the Tang. He thought he might find some masters there who would help him clear the doubts in his mind. He was particularly keen on Yogacara, the most abstract and intellectual school of Buddhism which held that everything in the world was created by the mind. But no one could shed light on it. His brother did not want to leave: they had already acquired a reputation for themselves and he thought they should stay put. So without telling him, Xuanzang left with some merchants.

Back in the capital, he studied with two masters 'whose reputation spread beyond the sea and whose followers were as numerous as the clouds'. But even their interpretations differed and he told Hui Li that he was at a loss to know whom to follow. One day he met an Indian monk, who told him that Yogacara was very popular in India, particularly in Nalanda, the biggest monastic university. Xuanzang's interest was aroused. He had long sensed there was a vast ocean of Buddhist wisdom, which he could perceive only dimly. A pilgrimage to India would give him direct knowledge of Buddhism and clear all his doubts. Once he set his mind on the journey, he started making preparations: taking Sanskrit lessons from Indian monks, gathering information about the countries along the way from the Silk Road merchants in Chang'an, reading accounts of early pilgrims to India, looking for fellow-travellers, and exercising to make himself fit. Meanwhile he sent a request to the imperial court for permission to go abroad, but in vain. There was a coup in the imperial palace: the young Emperor Taizong had just come to the throne after killing his brothers and forcing his father to abdicate. People were not happy; there was the threat of more rebellions. Everything was in flux and nobody was allowed to travel.

But Xuanzang had to leave, imperial approval or not. One day he had a dream in which he saw Mount Sumeru, the sacred mountain at the centre of the universe in Indian and Buddhist mythology. It was surrounded by sea but there was neither ship nor raft. Lotus flowers of stone supported him as he crossed the waters, but so slippery and steep was the way up the mountain that each time he tried to climb he slid back. Then suddenly a powerful whirlwind raised him to the summit where he saw an unending horizon. In an ecstasy of joy he woke up; he believed he had been shown a vision of what he must do – he must go to India and learn the teaching of the Buddha at its source.

I returned again and again to reading about Xuanzang. It was as if a new person was entering my life, someone to whom I was strongly drawn, wise and calm, brave and resourceful. He did go to India, but on his own, with no magical protector. The more I learned about him, the more extraordinary I found him, and the more puzzled I was. Why had I known so little about him? After all, my education was full of the emulation of one hero after another. What was it that had kept him away from me, and from most Chinese? I had to find out. I had to separate fact from fiction. Gradually I realized all the clues were in my own family. Only I was part of it, and could not see them.

My father was an ardent Communist. He joined the People's Liberation Army in 1946, when he was sixteen, and marched from northern China to the southern coast, helping to bring the whole country under Communist control. Then he saw duty in Korea for eight years. In the process, he joined the Communist Party, rose through the ranks and became a firm believer in Marx, Lenin and Chairman Mao. When he came back from Korea in 1958, he divorced the wife arranged by his parents, and fell in love with and married my mother, a beauty twelve years his junior.

My maternal grandmother was a Buddhist, the only one in our family. Most men and women of her generation believed in Buddhism one way or another. Mao's own mother did, and under her influence the young Mao worshipped the Buddha too, even attempting to convert his father. Ever since Buddhism spread to China in the first century AD, it had struck a chord in the hearts of the Chinese. They had their indigenous beliefs, Confucianism and Daoism. While Confucianism emphasized the order and harmony of society where everyone had their place, with the emperor at the apex, Daoism concentrated on the search for the eternal, unchanging nature that unifies the individual with the universe, with the ultimate goal of achieving immortality in this world. Neither said anything about the question most of us wanted answered: what would be waiting for us after we departed from this world? The Buddhist doctrine of karma and paradise allayed Chinese anxieties about the afterlife, and satisfied their desires for longevity, for justice, and also for compassion. In the end, in this land already possessed of a long history and strong culture of its own, Buddhism adapted, survived and blossomed, despite opposition and frequent persecution.

Father had a deep affection for Grandmother. He never talked about it but he was full of regret and remorse about abandoning his own parents – he never saw them again after he joined the army; his mother went mad missing him and drowned herself, and his father died too while he was in Korea. He treated Grandmother with enormous respect and kindness. She had bound feet and it was very hard to buy shoes for her. Every time he went on a work trip somewhere, he would search all the department stores and always came back with a few pairs. Grandmother was very grateful; she would say to my mother: 'How lucky you are to have such a wonderful husband! Kindness and prayer do pay.'

For all his affection, Father found Grandmother's behaviour embarrassing. She made no secret of her faith and was kind to people who were in political trouble and shunned by everyone else. Father asked my mother to talk to her about the matter. My mother worked in the nursery of my father's regiment and she was very aware of the political pressures. She had seen too many people being denounced for an innocent remark or for no reason at all. Grandmother was a potential threat to Father's career in the army. The Party had its eyes and ears in the neighbourhood committees, which knew exactly what went on in every household. Father could get into trouble for not 'keeping his house in order' and not taking a firm stand against feudal practices and the enemies of the people. Long before I was born, my parents had persuaded Grandmother not to go to the temples, or burn incense at home. My father even sold her 'superstitious article' – a little bronze statue of Guanyin and her most precious possession – to the rag-and-bone man.

Grandmother was deeply hurt. The statue was her amulet. She thought her prayers had been effective: her children and grandchildren were healthy; her daughter was lucky to have found a good husband; her son-in-law was safe from political persecution. Perhaps she got the point from my mother's explanation. Particularly at that time, when my father's job in military supply was keeping the family fed while so many were going hungry. The great famine which began in 1959 and claimed over thirty million people was coming to an end, but the country was still suffering. Farmers back in Grandmother's village were too weak to plough the fields; factories were shut down; very few children were born – starvation had made women infertile. On top of everything, parts of China were going through appalling drought, while others were afflicted by severe floods.

Reluctantly, in the face of all the misery the Party relaxed its grip, not only in its economic policy but also in its ideological control. But what followed took Mao and the Party by surprise: the masses who had survived the hunger immediately returned to their old gods and goddesses for solace and divination – they even built new temples. They were not just old ladies like Grandmother, but even Party members. Mao must have found this very discouraging, particularly after thirteen years of intensive campaigns to educate the masses and implant socialist ideas. He had lost confidence in the Marxist-Leninist 'law' that religion would fade as socialism developed – it was on this basis that a guarantee of freedom of religious belief had been included in the Constitution. Mao resorted to his old method, mass campaigns. The Campaign against Superstitious Activities and the Socialist Education Campaign began in 1963, the year I was born.

They were some of the biggest programmes Mao launched prior to the Cultural Revolution. Hundreds of thousands of civil servants, teachers, doctors, artists, engineers and soldiers were sent to the rural areas to reinforce the Communist ideology. My father went to a commune near his military base. For four months he helped the farmers with their work, ate with them, and slept in their huts to gain their confidence. He spent days and nights persuading the activists of the village to target what the Party regarded as the residue of feudalism: traditional Chinese medicinal practice and funeral customs, fortune-telling and arranged marriage, and visiting local temples. Father lectured them not to put their faith in God, but in the Party, echoing a verse of the time written by a loyal farmer:

> God, O God, be not angry,
> Step down as quickly as you can.
> I revered you for a long time,
> And yet you changed nothing
> And our farms were still ploughed by the ox.
> Mechanization is now being carried out,
> I request you to transform yourself.

But instead of helping him root out the die-hard believers, the locals took advantage of the struggle meetings he organized to voice their grievances. They told him about the suffering and deaths in their villages during the recent famine – the worst they could remember. They begged him to go back and tell the Party the real problems in the countryside. Superstition was not on their minds – survival was.

Father had a frustrating four months, and he was even more disappointed when he returned home. I was born, his third daughter. Despite Mao's claim that women were half the sky and the absolute equal of men, my father desperately wished for a son to keep the Sun family line going. A veteran Communist, he none the less believed in a dictum of Confucius, as all Chinese had done for more than two thousand years: the biggest shame for a family is to fail to produce a son. Now my mother had borne yet another girl, instead of the much-wanted boy. Father was so disappointed he did not even visit Mother and me in hospital. We were left there for three days and it was Grandmother who brought us food and took us home. Years later Grandmother told me what happened – the only fight she ever had with Father.

She prepared a special meal to welcome Father, Mother and me home. But Father, even while he was gulping down the dishes that Grandmother conjured up, could talk about nothing but his headaches and successes during the campaign. 'They were really backward in the villages. Even the cadres weren't good Communists. They allowed temples and family shrines to be rebuilt. We had a good go at them. We banged away at the village officials, then we asked them to identify the most superstitious people. If they didn't cooperate, we would take away their jobs. There were some really stubborn ones; you can guess where they ended up.'

When Father had finished his meal, he cast a casual glance at me in the pram, shook his head, and sighed. He turned to my mother. 'Why didn't you give me a son?'

My mother was very apologetic. Back in her village, there was a saying: 'A hen lays eggs. A woman who cannot produce a son is not worth even a hen.' Years ago Father could simply have taken a concubine to give himself another chance. He could not do that now but he had other ways of showing his displeasure. And I, the unwanted girl, could not be drowned as in the bad old days; instead I would bear the brunt of his disappointment.

Then Grandmother made a rare intervention; 'It wasn't her fault. You should blame me.'

'What has it got to do with you?' Father asked impatiently.

Grandmother said she felt responsible for my birth. In the Lotus Sutra there is a passage which many Chinese, Buddhist and even non-Buddhist, passionately believe: 'If there is a woman who desires to have a son, then she should pray to Guanyin with reverence and respect, and in due time she will give birth to a son endowed with blessings, virtues and wisdom.' My mother desired a son as much as my father and grandmother, but she was a Communist and would never think that praying, even to Chairman Mao, let alone to anyone else, would get her a son. So Grandmother decided it was her job to do the praying for our family. But she could only say her prayers at home, silently and late at night. She could not go to the temples and bow in front of the statue of Guanyin; she could not offer incense to send a message to her – Mao had all the incense factories switched to making toilet paper in 1963. Grandmother thought it was unpropitious: if the goddess did not hear her prayers or receive her message, how could she ensure a much-desired son for our family? That was why my parents were given a girl, an inferior being.

Father looked at her in disbelief, apparently wondering whether Grandmother was serious. He had been fighting superstition in the countryside, but here it was, rampant in his own home. Suddenly he thumped the table.

'What nonsense are you talking?' he yelled. 'To hell with all your superstitious crap. What is so good about your gods up there? If they're as good as you boast, how come they let people live in such misery before? How come they were so useless in protecting your children? You know what? They are not worth a dog's fart.'

Grandmother was shocked by the anger in Father's voice – they were the harshest words she ever heard from him. She picked me up and went quietly back to our room.

From very early years, I had felt I was the unwanted daughter in my family. The one person who always cared for me was Grandmother. I shared a bed with her, head to toe, until I went away to university. My earliest and most enduring memory was of her bound feet in my face. The first thing I learned to do for her, and continued doing right up to my teens, was to bring her a kettle of hot water every evening to soak her feet. The water was boiling and her feet were red like pigs' trotters, but she did not seem to feel it – she was letting the numbness take over from the pain, the pain that had never gone away since the age of seven when her mother bound her feet. It was done to make her more appealing to men. The arch of her foot was broken, and all her toes except for the big one were crushed and folded underneath the sole, as if to shape the foot like a closed lotus flower. On these tiny, crippled feet, she worked non-stop every day from five o'clock in the morning: making breakfast, washing clothes in cold water, cleaning the house and preparing lunch and supper seven days a week – both my parents were too busy with their work and the endless struggle meetings they had to attend. The only time she gave to herself was this daily ritual of foot-soaking to soothe the pain, restore her strength and prepare her for another day. She took her time. She massaged her feet gently and slowly, unbent the crushed toes one by one, washed them thoroughly, and carefully cut away the dead skin. After I took away the dirty water she would lie down and we would chat for a while. She would say to me sometimes, pointing at her feet: 'It is tough to be a woman. I'm glad you did not have to go through this.' Then she would add: 'Life will be hard for you too. But if you can take whatever life throws at you, you will be strong.'

I was not sure what she meant. Father was very harsh with me; he would slap my face if I reached for food at table before everybody else, or had a fight with my sisters. I thought she was sympathizing with me for what he did; she was powerless to protect me, however much she wanted to. I was too young then to be able to imagine the trials life might hold – I knew no real pain, nothing like that Grandmother had suffered.

She was born in 1898 in a small village in Shandong, a great centre of Buddhism on the eastern coast. There were three temples in her village; the biggest one, the temple of Guandi, the God of Fortune, was only a hundred metres from her house. She saw it every morning when she woke up. It was tall; the statue alone was three metres high, carved by the village men in stone from the nearby mountain. It was always bustling with people who came to pray that Guandi, with his indomitable power, would help them to make a fortune. But it had no place for women; the temples for the God of Earth and for Guanyin were where Grandmother went and prayed, for rain and sunshine, for a good harvest, for sons instead of daughters, and for evil spirits to stay away. April, October and the third day of the Chinese New Year were particularly busy in these two temples. People came with clothes, carts, horses, cows, boats, money and anything else you could think of, all made of paper. They were burned to commemorate the dead. In April you changed your summer clothes and in October your winter outfit; and nobody should go without money for the New Year, particularly the dead.

Grandmother was married at the age of seventeen to a boy of thirteen; such was the custom in that part of China. The boy's family gained a daughter-in-law, a servant, a labourer and a child-minder all at once. Grandmother cooked for the whole family, did all the chores in the house and helped with work in the field. She took over from her mother-in-law the responsibility of looking after her child-husband. She dressed him in the morning, took him to school, washed his feet in the evening and made sure he did not wet the bed. She cuddled him at night and told him about things between men and women. Occasionally he tried to put this information into practice but it did not come to much. In Grandmother's words, 'It was more water than sperm.' But she was not annoyed because her husband really was a child. Bringing him up and making him a man was expected of every woman in Grandmother's world. And then, when their husbands were in their prime, the women were often old and exhausted, which gave the men the perfect excuse to take concubines. It was a rotten deal for women but Grandmother did not feel it that way. She accepted it. When her young husband finally acquired the knack of lovemaking at the age of sixteen, they had their first child, and then eight more in the next seven years. With one acre of land, two donkeys and a mule, nine children and one 'big child' – her nickname for Grandfather – life, as Grandmother said, was 'sweet as moon-cake'.

Then terror struck. Within a week, three of her children caught smallpox. There was no doctor, and an old woman in the village told Grandmother to mix ashes with cow's urine as a medicine. The eldest son and two of his sisters died, choking on the mixture. The village had a custom that if you placed mirrors on your roof, the devils would be too dazzled by the light to come in and trouble your family. She did that and also put peach branches under her children's pillows to ward off any hungry ghosts. But none of it worked. In the following two years, dysentery took away another four of her children. She cried for days on end; her hair turned white and she became almost blind. She wanted to take her own life but she had to live on for her remaining two children. She was so scared of losing them that she had them adopted. My uncle went to a family of eight boys and three girls, and my mother to a family of five girls and two boys. Grandmother hoped that the sheer number of healthy children in those two households would give her son and daughter some protection. If the others could survive, hers would too. Her children spent most of their time with their adoptive families, playing, eating and sleeping in their houses and giving a hand in their fields. They were hardly hers any more. She was heartbroken, but they were alive and she was happy for them.

As if she had not suffered enough, my grandfather died of an unknown disease, probably stomach cancer, when Grandmother was still young – she lived well into her nineties. A good-looking woman with seven dead children and a dead husband could not be a good omen. People in the village began to shun her, as if contact with her would bring them bad luck. They would go the other way when they saw her coming; the foster-parents of my uncle and mother forbade their children to visit her house; even farm labourers did not want to work on her land. She was half blind; now she hardly spoke.

Grandmother was desperate to know what crimes she had committed to deserve such harsh punishment and what she should do now to make sure her son and daughter would survive. One day she met an itinerant monk who was passing through her village. He told her that she must have done something terrible in her previous life and now it had caught up with her. He took out a small statue of Guanyin and gave it to her. If she prayed hard and recited the name of Amitabha, her son and daughter would be safe and she would unite with all her children in the Western Paradise. From that day on, Grandmother was a changed woman. She no longer burst into tears when she saw children playing in the street. She stopped reminiscing about the deaths in her family to anyone who cared to listen. To support herself and her children, she spun silk from cocoons for a local middleman who sold it to the big cities. And she prayed and recited Amitabha's name day and night.

Even today, I can remember clearly the night when Grandmother told me all this. Grandmother did not sleep very much. Whenever I woke up in the middle of the night, I always found her sitting there. Most of the time it was too dark to see her but occasionally her face hovered above me in the faint light of the moon. She looked serene; her eyes, almost blind, looked up as if searching for something; her white hair glowed in the moonlight; her lips were moving quickly but silently while she dropped things continuously into a bowl in front of her. Once I asked her what she was doing and she said she was counting beans to pass the time because she could not sleep. I said I could ask my parents to get some sleeping pills for her. 'Don't bother. Old people don't need much sleep,' she told me with a gentle smile. 'Please don't tell your father about it. He has quite a lot to worry about as it is.'

I thought nothing of Grandmother's sleepless nights until one day in the early 1980s. When life resumed its normality after the tumult of the Cultural Revolution, *The Monkey King* was the first classic Chinese novel adapted for television – an ideal medium for bringing alive its colourful characters, fantastic stories and magical elements. It was an astonishing success. I, like the whole country, was glued to the box for two months. Every boy in our neighbourhood had a plastic cudgel; everyone could sing the theme song; adults talked about nothing but last night's television. Even Grandmother, who was half-blind, joined us. The magic was still there, and I was lifted once again out of the mundane world.

One night I woke up to find Grandmother in her usual position and counting the beans. Her posture and expression struck me at once as familiar, not because I had seen them so many times but because they reminded me of something. But what? Then it occurred to me that the monk in *The Monkey King* sat like this to pray whenever he was in trouble, with the same concentration and calmness; the only difference was that he had a long string of beads round his neck, which he never stopped counting. Was Grandmother praying? I asked her; she nodded. She was counting the beans to remember how many prayers she had said. I asked her what she was praying for. She said for her dead children and husband, for her to join them in paradise, for me not to suffer too much as the unwanted daughter, for my brother, for us all to be healthy, for us to have enough to eat, and for Father not to be a target in the endless political campaigns.

I was astonished. I did not know whether to laugh or to cry. Looking at her, fragile as a reed and with deep lines of sorrow on her face as though carved by a knife, I felt immensely sad. I wanted to shake her by her slender shoulders and wake her up. How could she be so stupid? How could she be sure there was a god up there who would answer her prayers? How could she bank all her hopes on the next world that did not even exist? Why did she blame herself for my being a girl instead of a boy? Why had I never heard her claiming credit for the birth of my brother born four years after me? Besides, what was the point of having gods and goddesses who did nothing for her but made her feel she never did enough to please them? Somehow, though, I knew I would never convince her. My father did not succeed. Those beliefs sustained her all her life. They were her life, her very being. We were worlds apart.

Grandmother must have felt very lonely among us. Despite her love and affection for me, I and my sisters always sided with Father and made fun of her Buddhas and Bodhisattvas. The relentless political drill that ran throughout my education had turned me, like most Chinese born after 1949, into a complete atheist. Buddhism was not only bad, it was dead, part of the old life, like the last emperor. As the *Internationale* says: 'There is no saviour, nor can we depend on gods and emperors. Only we can create happiness for ourselves.' The teachers told us that the only Heaven would be a Communist one and we must work for it. China had suffered centuries of wretchedness with no help from the Buddha. Chairman Mao changed our lives. We memorized a verse that was supposed to have been composed by Mao after he took up Communism:

What is a Buddha?
One clay body,
With two blank eyes,
Three meals a day are wasted on him,

With four feeble limbs,
He cannot name five cereals,
His six nearest relatives he does not know . . .
What should we do with him?
Smash him!

I recited the poem to Grandmother one night when we were following her foot-washing ritual. She did not say anything; instead she asked me if I wanted to hear a story. I nodded for I always liked her stories; some were as magical as those in *The Monkey King*.

A long, long time ago, Grandmother said, a pigeon was flying about searching for food. Suddenly it saw this huge vulture hovering over it. Frightened, it began to look for a place to hide but could find none. It could see no trees, no houses, just a group of hunters on their way to the forest. In desperation, the pigeon dropped in front of a handsome prince in the hunting party, begging for protection. The vulture descended too and asked for its prey back. 'I am hungry,' it pleaded. 'I have had no luck for days and if I don't eat some-thing, I will die of hunger. Please have pity on me too.' The prince thought for a while and said to the vulture: 'I cannot let you starve. Let's weigh the pigeon. I will give you the same amount of flesh from my own body.' His courtiers were shocked, but the prince insisted and sent one of his ministers for a set of scales. Meanwhile he had a knife sharpened. The pigeon was put in one scale, and the prince's flesh in the other. But no matter how much of himself the prince put on the scale, the pigeon was always heavier. The vulture was so moved by the noble prince he decided not to eat the pigeon.

'What happened to the handsome prince? Did he die of bleeding?' I asked Grandmother impatiently, forgetting all about the poem and the clay Buddha. 'He did not die,' she said. 'He was the Buddha in disguise.' I was so relieved, and got up to take the basin of water away. Grandmother told me many stories like this. At the time I thought that was all they were, tales of animals and heroes. But she was teaching me humility, self-sacrifice, kindness, tolerance: looking back, I can see now how much she influenced me.

My father left the army in early 1966, when I was three, and the whole family moved with him from Harbin in the far north, where I was born, to Handan. It is a small city, with a history going back to the sixth century BC – the remains of the ancient citadel are still at its heart. It is most famous among the Chinese for the numerous idioms which permeate our language. Everyone knows the phrase 'Learn to walk in Handan' – it means if you learn something new, learn it properly, otherwise you are just a dilettante. Father said we were lucky to live in this old, civilized place.

Father was made head of production in a state timber factory employing 400 people – but there was no production. Hardly had he settled down in his new job, when the Cultural Revolution began. It was to purge the Communist Party of anyone who was not sufficiently progressive, to shake the country out of its complacency, and to revive enthusiasm for the Communist cause. The Red Guards were the front-runners but the real players were the workers. My father's workforce was busy grabbing power from the municipal government; people fought each other, armed with guns stolen from military barracks. The city and the timber plant were divided into two factions, the United and the Alliance, with the former in control and the latter trying to oust them. My father tried to persuade the two sides to go back to work but nobody listened to him. 'Chairman Mao says revolution first, production second. How dare you oppose our great leader?' one of his workers warned him. Eventually, Father joined the United faction: nobody could sit on the fence or they would be targets themselves. All our neighbours were United members.

My father often told us how much he regretted leaving the army. At least we would have felt safe inside the barracks. Our new home town reminded him of a battlefield, with machine-guns, cannons and explosives going off day and night. In this escalating violence, my mother was about to give birth to her fourth child. Grandmother was happy, her face all smiles. She told Father that all the signs of the pregnancy indicated that Mother would produce a son this time: her reactions were very strong, unlike the previous three times; she insisted on vinegar and pickled cabbage with every meal; her stomach was pointed but not very big; most importantly, two pale marks like butterflies had appeared on her cheeks. My father could not conceal his delight – he did not lose his temper as often as before. He spent many months deliberating on a suitable name and in the end he chose Zhaodong, 'Sunshine in the East'. To him, a son would be as precious as the sun – but it had a double meaning: all Chinese had been singing 'East is Red' in praise of the Great Leader, Chairman Mao, who was like the sun rising in the east to bring China out of darkness.

The birth was complicated. Almost all doctors had been labelled 'Capitalist experts' and sent to the country or to labour camps for re-education; hospitals were taken over by the Red Guards, who were more interested in saving people's souls than their lives. The constant fighting in the streets and the blockades put up by all the factions made the journey to the hospital impossible. Mother consulted with Father and decided it would be better to use the woman from a nearby village who served as a midwife – experienced if not trained. Unfortunately the baby's legs came out first and the midwife panicked. She asked Mother to breathe deeply and push hard. The baby reluctantly showed a bit more of itself: it was a boy indeed but there he stuck, seemingly unwilling to come into this turbulent world.

Then Mother started bleeding heavily. Father was frightened to death and kept asking Grandmother what to do. Grandmother tried to calm him down but her teeth were chattering like castanets. While Father was pacing about like a caged animal, Grandmother knelt down and began to pray loudly to Guanyin, holding tight to Mother's hand. 'I have been praying to you for more than fifty years,' she pleaded urgently. 'If you have too much to do and can only help me once, please do it now. I need you more than ever. I am begging you.' She promised she would do anything if the boy was delivered safely: she would produce a thanksgiving banquet for Guanyin for seven days; she would go on a pilgrimage to her place of abode in southern China even if she had to pawn her bracelet, her only piece of jade; she would tell her grandchildren to remember the loving kindness of the Bodhisattva for ever. While Grandmother was praying fervently, the midwife was pulling hard, as if it did not matter if a limb was broken as long as the boy was alive. When he was finally dragged out, he had his arms above his head, looking as though he had surrendered to the world.

With the baby's first cry, Father fell on his knees beside Grandmother, thumping the floor with his fist and murmuring softly. He did not stand up until the midwife handed his son to him. He was beside himself: at last he had an heir. He was overcome with gratitude – but to whom? To Heaven, to earth, to Grandmother's deity, to the midwife? Grandmother was still on her knees, praying. Tired or overwhelmed, Father knelt again beside her, praying too, or at least appearing to.

Of course Father did not believe for a moment it was the Bodhisattva Guanyin who saved his wife and son. But he was very grateful to Grandmother. Perhaps her prayer did help him psychologically: it gave him a gleam of hope when everything else seemed to have failed; it kept him calm and it had a soothing effect on my mother and the midwife. Some time later when I reported to my parents that Grandmother was muttering her prayer again in our room, my father told me not to tell anybody else. Then he said to my mother: 'I guess praying is better than killing people and burning factories.'

After the birth of my brother, my father changed into a different person. He was not as enthusiastic about his job as before. He used to work really hard, going out before I got up and coming home when I was asleep. Now he often drank on his own. He even had time to play with us. He seemed to have lost interest in the revolution that was going on. As a soldier he had killed his enemies, but that was to liberate the country. In the land reform of 1950, tens of thousands of landlords and rich farmers were executed because they were the enemies of the people, threatening the stability of the new China. He did not think twice even when his own father was labelled a landlord, though his family had hardly more than four acres of land and employed only two labourers. He could understand why Mao sent half a million intellectuals to labour camps in 1957 after they had criticized the Party openly and fiercely. But what was it all for now?

My father often said that in the thirty years of his revolutionary career, he had never seen so much harm done in the name of a cause. He could not understand how an ideal that had inspired so much devotion in him had gone so terribly wrong. He never said much but it was obvious he was losing heart. He did not mind Grandmother praying at home; he even bought her candles for the Day of Ghosts.

After I entered middle school, my teacher encouraged me to join the Communist Youth League, as an induction into the Party: it was not good enough simply to get good marks; the most important thing was to have the right political attitude – only then could our knowledge be truly useful. Father had insisted that my two sisters join. But when I asked him whether I should follow them, he was vague. 'There is no hurry. You should concentrate on your studies,' he told me. I never did join the Youth League.

In 1982, I gained a place in the English Department in Beijing University. I felt like the old Confucian scholar I read of in the Chinese classics, who finally made it in the imperial exams and wanted to tell the whole world about his happiness. Out of millions, only a few hundred were chosen. I had heard of Oxford and Cambridge, both of which were considerably older, but perhaps no university occupied the unique position of Beijing University, absolutely the academic and spiritual nerve of the country. Perhaps only a Chinese would fully appreciate my good fortune. It was students of Beijing University in 1919 who first created the slogan 'Democracy and Science', as the cure for the ills of a China at the mercy of all the Western powers. It was two professors from Beijing University who started the Communist Party of China. Mao went there to study at their feet. It was one of the fiercest battlegrounds in the Cultural Revolution, and again it was there that the deepest introspection on the Cultural Revolution took place, just when I arrived.

Self-searching was rampant throughout the country: its

most public form was the Scar Literature, the outpouring of novels and memoirs describing the unbelievable cruelty of the Cultural Revolution, suffered by individuals as well as the whole nation. The students went a step further. What caused this suffering, unprecedented in Chinese history? Never before was the whole nation, hundreds of millions of people, allowed to think only one thought, speak with one voice, read only one man's works, be judged by one man's criteria. Never before were our traditions so thoroughly shaken up, destroying families, setting husbands against wives, and children against parents. Never before was our society turned so completely upside down. The Party was barely in control, with all its senior members locked up or killed. Workers did not work; farmers did not produce; scientists and artists were in labour camps; not criminals, but judges, lawyers and policemen were in prison; and young men and women were sent to the countryside in droves for re-education. On top of the physical devastation, the psychological impact on everyone was even more poisonous. The Cultural Revolution brought out the worst in people. They spied on, reported, betrayed and murdered each other – strangers, friends, comrades and families alike – and all in the name of revolution. So much hope, so much suffering and sacrifice, and for what?

There were heated debates in our dormitory, in the lecture halls, in the seminars after class, and in a tiny triangular space right in the heart of the campus. Freedom to think and openness to all schools of thought – the ethos of Beijing University from its very birth – were in full flower. Coming from a small sleepy city, I was like Alice in Wonderland, bewildered and exhilarated at the same time. Thoughts and ideas flooded in with the opening up of China to the outside world, after decades of isolation – we breathed them in like oxygen.

'Democracy and Science', the slogan raised seventy years earlier, came to the forefront again. Could this be the solution for China? Certainly it seemed time to try something new.

When I described to my parents the stimulating life on campus, my father wrote back immediately, warning me not to follow the crowd. 'You're still young,' he said, 'and have just begun your life in the wider world. You have no idea how politics work in China. I've been through it all. Liberal thinking is never a good thing. The crushing of the intellectuals in 1957 is a lesson. Find some books in the library and read them, you will see what I mean. As Mao said, students should study. I think you should talk to the Party Secretary in your department, reporting to him your wish to be educated, judged and accepted by the Party. You perhaps know that being a member will be of great help to you if you want to stay in Beijing and get a job in government departments after your graduation.' He ended the letter with 'These are words from my heart. I hope you remember them.'

While the students in Beijing University were busy exploring how democracy could be adapted to suit Chinese conditions, I was given the chance to go to Oxford. It was 1986. When Grandmother heard the news, she could not sleep for days: 'You are just like the monk, going to the West for new ideas,' she enthused. 'It won't be easy but if you are determined to do good, you will have people helping you. You will get there in the end. When you come back, you can help the country.'

Father was very happy for me too. He had learned that the West was not a dungeon as he had been made to believe. Nevertheless he still warned me, in the only language he knew – that of Communist jargon: decaying capitalist society was no Heaven, and I should be vigilant and not allow decadent bourgeois thoughts to corrupt me. He insisted on coming to Beijing to see me off. I thought it was unnecessary: his health was poor and the train to Beijing was slow and crowded and anyway I would be back in one year. Then he said something that made me understand. Just before I boarded the plane, I gave him a hug and asked him to take care of himself. For only the second time in my life I saw tears in his eyes – the first was when my brother was born. 'Don't worry about me. This is your big chance, you've got to take it. Look at me, look at your sisters, look at what society has come to. Don't get homesick. There is nothing here for you to come back to.' When I turned around and waved him goodbye, I was shocked, and sad. As someone who had devoted his entire life to the revolution, he must have been in total despair.

My father died in 1997. He was strong and had never taken a day's sick leave. But his depression ruined his health. He came down with diabetes, and soon was paralysed and became blind. His old work unit, which was supposed to look after him, could not afford to pay his medical bills and he refused to let me do it for him. His last wish was to be buried not in a Western suit I had bought for him, nor a traditional Chinese outfit, but in a dark blue Mao suit. It was a difficult wish to gratify – nobody wore one any more. We searched for three days before we finally found one in a little shop on the outskirts of the city. We wanted him to be buried in it because it embodied his lifelong hopes, his ideals and unbounded faith, even though he had died a broken man.

Many of my father's friends, colleagues and comrades from the army came to his funeral. The occasion, the gathering, brought out their own anger and frustration. I could understand their feelings; they were just as my father's had been.

They had sacrificed so much, gone through so much suffering and deprivation for the revolution – and now they were told what they had done was wrong. They must embrace this new world of markets and reform – but they could not; they felt they had no place in it; it was against all the beliefs they had held throughout their lives. Their whole *raison d'être* had been taken away. They were betrayed; they were even being blamed for what had gone wrong. The bitterness of loss was crushing and the void left in their hearts was deep. They found it impossible to cope with a past that had been cancelled and a future so uncertain.

As is the custom, my mother and my sisters prepared a meal with several dishes to thank the visitors for their sympathy and support – they had all brought presents, and gifts of money that was later used to pay off my father's medical bills. Mother was moved – their lives were not easy either. To her surprise, many of them left the meat dishes and ate only the vegetables. These were people who used to drink with my father, and feast on all kinds of delicacies such as pig's trotters and ox tails. 'How come you have all turned into monks?' she joked with them.

'We can't be monks. We are old Communists,' one of them laughed, and then added, 'it's good for our health. And it's better not to kill anything.'

I wanted to ask the old men about what they believed. In his last years my father often reminisced about Grandmother, and regretted his harshness towards her, especially selling her little statue of Guanyin. He did not become a Buddhist but in the twilight of their lives, I knew some of his oldest friends had actually turned to Buddhism, the very target of their earlier revolutionary fervour.

But before I had a chance to question them, they asked me

if I had become a Christian. I shook my head, telling them I still did not know what to believe. 'Many Chinese are going to church. You live in England and you don't go to church?' one of them said. 'She should be a Buddhist,' another one interrupted him. 'She is Chinese after all. Buddhism is the best religion.'

Buddhism was making a come-back in China. In the early 1980s, the government had issued a decree allowing a limited revival of religion. As a Marxist would put it, the base had changed so the superstructure had to change too. The decree allowed for the 142 most important Buddhist monasteries damaged or destroyed in the Cultural Revolution to be restored or rebuilt. Monks and nuns in their orange and brown robes once more became a regular sight in towns and villages. In the cinema and on television, young people watched for the first time the lives of great Buddhist masters, albeit all kung fu wizards or martial arts heroes, who used their fantastic skills to save a pretty woman or impoverished villagers. The faithful could go to the temples, make offerings to the Buddha, draw bamboo slips to tell their families' fortunes, and join monks and nuns in their chanting of the sutras and other Buddhist rituals. In a way, it resembled the old days when Buddhist monasteries were among the most important centres of Chinese life. They were a source of spiritual comfort but also of practical help with birth, illness, death and other crucial events in life. They received the infirm and the insane who were abandoned by their families and reviled by society. They gave the disillusioned and the discontented the perfect retreat, where they were asked no questions and given the space they needed. Many Communists, including senior Chinese leaders, had been sheltered in monasteries when they were hunted by the Nationalist government.

Observing these changes, I found myself thinking more and more about Grandmother. When I visited a temple, I would light incense for her; in the swirling smoke, the image of her counting beans in the night came back to me again and again. Sometimes I read a sutra and found the stories in it very familiar – they were among those she had told me in our long foot-washing sessions. The forbearance, the kindness, the suffering, the faith and the compassion were what she embodied. I felt many of the elements she had tried to instil in me were slowly becoming part of me. I began to see how extraordinary her faith was. She had suffered so much, enough to crush anyone, let alone such a frail person. Her faith kept her going, even though all she could do was to pray on her own in the dark, without temples and monks to guide her, and derided by her own family. Her beliefs made her strong despite her lifelong privations. She was illiterate but she knew the message that lies at the heart of Chinese Buddhism, the certainty and the solace. That is why she wanted me to follow her faith and acquire the strength it gave her. I never gave it a chance, rejecting it early on without really knowing what it was. Now I wished *I* could believe something so profoundly.

It was about the time of Father's death that I decided to go on my journey and follow Xuanzang. I had been inspired through my early education by the idealism of Communism, but the intellectual ferment and questioning I was exposed to at Beijing University stayed with me. With Father's death and the collapse of his world I lost all that remained of my attachment to the cause he gave his life to. I knew I was lucky, I was free and I had not suffered like my forebears and my fellow-countrymen. But like so many Chinese, I felt strongly that something was missing. The idea of a confirming faith dies hard. I was increasingly unsure of where I was going, why

I was doing the things I did; I was at a loss, and pondering. Probably when I made the decision to go I wanted some clarity in my life, and the journey would give me a very clear objective.

Of course, I could have just sat in libraries and read about Xuanzang. But I knew that would not be enough. I did not think I could find a different outlook just by reading. The Chinese have a saying: 'Read ten thousand books; walk ten thousand miles.' I wanted to explore for myself, to make sense of everything I had been reading about Xuanzang and about Buddhism. He found his truth by going in search of the sutras – I had to go and look for mine.

It would be a spiritual journey for me but physically demanding too. Travelling along Xuanzang's route would not be easy. In his time, covering those 16,000 miles through some of the world's most inhospitable terrain, not knowing what he would encounter, required enormous courage and strength of will. What inspired him to brave the unknown and keep going for eighteen years, and what did he inspire in others? Was it the same faith that had sustained Grandmother? How did he maintain his equanimity and remain indifferent to flattering royalty and aggressive bandits? How did he manage to achieve so much? If I followed him, perhaps I would come to understand his life, his world and the tenets of Buddhism. I would also learn how much Buddhism has contributed to Chinese society, a fact well hidden from me and my fellow-countrymen. And perhaps I would find what I was missing.

When I told my mother about my plan, she exploded. Why was I going alone to those God-forsaken places in search of a man who died more than a thousand years ago? I must be out of my mind. Was I unhappy living in England? What was it for anyway? But she knew she could not stop me. I told her I would not be away for eighteen years. Many of the places

Xuanzang visited no longer exist, or at least no one knows where they are; some, like Afghanistan, I could not visit. I would go only to the key places that mattered to him personally, and were important for the history of Buddhism. I would be travelling for no more than a year.

My little nephew Si Cong was also concerned. He had been completely gripped by yet another cartoon series of *The Monkey King* on television. It looked magnificent with the latest computer graphics and special effects. It was on every day at five o'clock when children came back from school. Would I have someone like the monkey to protect me? he asked me, while his eyes were fixed on the television. I said no. He quickly turned around. 'What happens if you run into demons? They're everywhere. Even the monkey can't always beat them. You'll be in big trouble.' I told him the demons would not eat me because my flesh was not as tasty as the monk's and it would not guarantee their longevity. He seemed relieved and went back to the magical world of *The Monkey King*.

It set me thinking, watching with him and looking at the steep mountains clad with snow, the deep turbulent rivers, the sandstorms that swept away everything in their path. Soon I would have to encounter them myself, not in fiction but in real life. I would pass through dangerous and strife-torn places; I might be robbed, or put in situations beyond my control. Whatever might happen, I would try to face it. Xuanzang would be my model and my guide.

TWO

Three Monks at
the Big Wild Goose Pagoda

I N A U G U S T 1999 I took a late-afternoon train from Handan, my home town, to Xian, the capital of the early emperors for much of the first millennium. It was where Xuanzang began and ended his travels. I was conscious that I was starting the most important journey of my life. But for the other people in my hard-sleeper compartment, the first order of business was food. As soon as the train started moving, the man opposite me produced a big plastic bag and unwrapped the contents. An amazing banquet slowly appeared: roast chicken, sausages, pot noodles, pickled eggs, cucumbers, tomatoes, melons and dried melon seeds, apples, pears, bananas and six cans of beer. The Chinese have suffered so much from starvation and famine that eating is rarely far from their minds. Everyone followed suit. Before long, they were sharing food, finding out each other's names, where they were going, and why.

Privacy is not a concept we understand in China. We have lived far too long on top of each other, as in this six-bunk compartment, off a narrow corridor without doors. Conversation reduces the tension and makes life tolerable, but it is not small talk; more like an interrogation. After ten years in England where you can choose to live and die without knowing your neighbours, I was uncomfortable with the intrusion. I took out a book about Xuanzang and tried to read, but that was no protection. A single woman travelling on her own makes her fellow-passengers curious. Whether for business or pleasure, the Chinese like to do it in groups. Xuanzang tried very hard to find companions, but in vain, owing to the emperor's prohibition against travelling abroad. I had also asked several monks myself. They were over the moon; pilgrimage to the land of the Buddha was the dream of every Buddhist – they would even gain merit from it should they need it for their rebirth in the Western Paradise. And to follow in the footsteps of Master Xuanzang! He was a model for them. His indomitability was an inspiration for them in their struggle for enlightenment. Many of the sutras they read every day, their spiritual sustenance, were his translations. His selflessness in giving his life to spreading Buddhism, not seeking his own salvation, was the ideal of the Bodhisattva, and of all Chinese monks. And for me, to see their reactions, to hear their thoughts, to ponder their reflections and to ask them questions – I would have learned so much more and understood Xuanzang better. I was not so fortunate, oddly enough for the same reason as Xuanzang: Chinese monks were not allowed to go abroad, unless they were on an official mission.

The men and women in my compartment quickly determined they were all going to Xian for business: the men were in engineering and the women in quality control. Then they turned to quizzing me, firing rapid questions like well-trained detectives. Who are you? Where are you going? Why? I told them I was following Xuanzang. They fell silent for a moment, then erupted into questions.

'You mean you are really following that monk in *The*

Monkey King, the one who went to India? Are you really going all that way?'

I nodded.

'Why? Are you a Buddhist?'

I had hardly finished answering him when the man sitting next to me put his hand on my forehead. I stiffened. 'I want to see if you are running a fever,' he said. His colleagues laughed and I relaxed.

'If you really want to travel, why don't you go to Europe, or America or Australia? I wouldn't go to India if you paid me! It is so dirty, so poor, worse than China.'

'If you want to write about Xuanzang, why don't you talk to some academics in Xian and make it up? Do you really think all the scholars do such hard work? You must be joking.'

They went on for some time, trying to dissuade me. After the lights were switched off the woman above me knocked on the edge of my bunk. 'You really shouldn't make this trip,' she said. 'It's too dangerous. Why don't you join our group and have a good time in Xian?'

We arrived in Xian early next morning, by which point my companions seemed to have become used to the idea that I really was going on my journey. Perhaps they thought I was a bit crazy. The men all helped me with my luggage. I told them I could manage on my own. 'Save your energy. You have a long way to go. You don't have the Monkey King to help you. You must take care of yourself,' they said, smiling and waving from the platform.

Just outside the railway station stands the old city wall. I asked the taxi-driver to take me first alongside the wall to the main North Gate. I sat in the front seat, keen to see everything. The wall is weighty and ancient, towering high above the car, and made me feel that once inside it, I would be safe, but also in a place of mystery, full of the secrets of the past. Most of the wall is seven hundred years old, part of it even older, going back another six hundred years to Xuanzang's time. No other large Chinese city has anything comparable. Beijing's, for example, was completely destroyed on Mao's orders, to make way for a new ring-road.

The North Gate is vast, surmounted by a three-eaved tower. It was dark going through it; because of its dense traffic it took some minutes to emerge into the light, into the modern city. A wide boulevard leads to the Bell Tower at its centre. Every old Chinese city has one, or used to have one. From it the ancient city received its wake-up call at sunrise. It is an imposing sight, over a hundred feet high with its three flying rooftops and an arch at its base. But it was not what Xuanzang would have seen. Then, the imperial city stood within these walls, and extended well to the north, with all the palaces and buildings of government. He would have come here to ask for travel passes for his journey to India, but his monastery was beyond the southern wall, where the rest of the city lay.

Even the commoners' city was spacious and grand in those days. Wide avenues ran north to south, crossed by boulevards east and west, dividing the capital into geometrical wards, which bore propitious names: Lustrous Virtue, Tranquil Way, Eternal Peace. Xian, or Chang'an as it was called back then, was neither tranquil nor peaceful when the young Xuanzang arrived here in 625 A D. The new dynasty, the Tang, was founded at a great cost. Over twenty million people, two-thirds of the population, perished in the uprisings, famines and epidemics that followed. Xuanzang was deeply affected. He remembered how his old monastery had been razed to the ground, and when he was fleeing from it, skeletons were everywhere on the roads and deserted villages and devastated fields stretched for hundreds of miles. Old people told him that no turmoil and destruction like it had happened since the First Emperor eight hundred years before. In Chang'an, people came to his monastery – each ward would have one – fervently praying for certainty, for the calamities to go away, and for the return to a peaceful life. Buddhism was supposed to save people from all this suffering. Why was it so rampant? Was there something wrong with the doctrines the Chinese believed? Were they the true teachings of the Buddha? As he said, he 'desired to investigate thoroughly the meaning of the teachings of the holy ones, and to restore the lost doctrines and give people back the real faith'.

Very little remains of the old Chang'an beyond the South Gate. The imposing avenues have shrunk, through the centuries, to narrow streets lined with restaurants, shops and government offices. One of them brought me to the Monastery of Great Benevolence, where the Big Wild Goose Pagoda stands. This is Xuanzang's monastery, where he spent many years of his life. This was where I wanted to be in Xian, to learn as much as possible about him.

It was much smaller than I expected, containing little more than the pagoda, a single shrine hall, and the monks' quarters, surrounded by village houses and fields. Clouds of smoke wafted up from the altar in front of the main temple. Long queues of people were waiting to light candles and burn incense. The hypnotic sound of monks chanting sutras reached me from the loudspeakers in the temple shop. Busloads of tourists, foreign and Chinese, poured through the gate and rushed to get their pictures taken: this is Xian's second most popular tourist attraction, after the famous Terracotta Army. The pagoda is what they come to see, and there is a good view of the city from the top. Xuanzang designed it himself in a graceful and slightly austere style, reminiscent of India.

Sixty-four metres up, from the topmost of its imposing seven storeys, I could see the whole of Xian – low houses lining the street leading to the pagoda, streams of people and cars moving at a snail's pace, high-rise buildings dwarfing the magnificent city wall, and vast stretches of fertile land to the south that have nourished the city for more than two thousand years. No wonder that after the pagoda was built in the seventh century, young men used to climb up here to celebrate when they had passed the imperial exam and joined the ruling class. They must have felt the world was at their feet and their ambition could soar into the sky. Even today, the Big Wild Goose Pagoda is one of the tallest structures in Xian, dominating the scene – in fact it is the city's symbol.

I used to go to monasteries as a tourist myself, enjoying the quietness, the chanting and the old trees in the courtyards. I would look around, take a picture or two, and then go away, vaguely comforted. Now, having learned something of Grandmother's faith and Xuanzang's, I began to understand what it was to feel reverence for this place. There are three treasures of Buddhism: the Buddha; the Dharma, the Buddha's teachings; and the Sangha, the community of monks who make up the monastery. The monastery is the outward symbol of Buddhism. It tells the world a different way of life does exist – we crave love, fortune and fame; the monks and nuns live happily without them. As Grandmother used to say, it was the centre of our life. I had to try and find out what that means.

From a row of traditional courtyards on the left, one or two monks appeared now and then and disappeared quickly back inside. That was where they ate, slept, prayed and meditated, and where they could not be disturbed. I decided to be bold, and the next time I saw one, I went up to him and greeted him. I asked him where the abbot's office was. He pointed to one of the courtyards on the left. But the abbot was away, he told me and he asked if he could help me. I told him I wanted to find out more about the monastery and Xuanzang. 'You definitely should go and talk to an old man in the village outside. His name is Mr Duan,' he said. How would I find him? 'No problem, if you ask for the ex-monk.'

It was indeed very easy to find Duan's house, barely a hundred yards from the monastery, down a small lane. Casual workers were squatting on the ground. They had just finished their lunch and were washing out their bowls in a bucket of grey water and emptying the bowls on to the hard-baked road. Dogs and chickens came up looking interested. Mothers were screaming at their children and shouting threats of punishment. It was just the kind of hectic scene which Duan must have become a monk to get away from. I asked an old lady who was busy chatting with her neighbour and she said Mr Duan was meditating. She was his wife. Did I mind waiting? Or could I come back in an hour?

I asked her if she knew the monastery well. 'My family has been living here for almost a hundred years,' she said, 'and I am married to one of its monks.' We went off and sat on a bench. She pointed to the dusty square in front of the monastery and the fields in the distance. 'All this area used to be the monastery's land. We leased it from them and gave them grain as rent after the harvest. The monks were really kind – they let us use their mills for free and take water from their well. There weren't many of them, only six or seven.'

The land became the villagers' in the Land Reform of 1950. Monasteries used to be among the biggest landowners in China and so were the first targets. Monks were told to give up their 'parasitic' life and work just like everyone else, growing what they ate and weaving what they wore. Mrs Duan found the turn of events puzzling. 'Their job was to pray, meditate and perform ceremonies for the dead and the living. How could they know about growing soya beans?' She shook her head. 'We wanted to help them, but the village Party Secretary told us we were masters of the new China and shouldn't allow ourselves to be exploited by them any more.'

I asked Mrs Duan what happened to the monks. She said that her husband would know more about it. He should have finished his midday meditation. 'Eight hours a day he does it. Three in the morning, two around now and three in the evening. He might just as well be in another world. But it's what keeps him going,' she sighed.

Just then I saw a man walking slowly towards us from across the street. I told Mrs Duan her husband was coming. She looked over her shoulder. 'Yes, that's my old man.' She turned back to me. 'How did you know it was him? Have you seen him before or seen his picture?' I didn't know what to say, but I just knew it was him. He was thin, even stick-like. Behind a pair of dirty glasses were sunken eyes in a wizened face, and his straggling hair came down to his neck. He had on a threadbare blue Mao suit, faded from what must have been hundreds of washings, and an ancient pair of soldier's shoes, which he wore without socks. He looked as if he were sleep-walking – perhaps he was still meditating. 'Come on, hurry up!' his wife shouted. 'This lady wants to talk to you about Xuanzang and the monastery.'

He ambled up to us murmuring, 'I am a sinner. I am a sinner. What is there to talk about?' As we walked back to their house, I asked him if he would tell me about his meditation.

'He's been doing it for thirty years,' Mrs Duan said

petulantly, pulling at Duan's sleeve until he sat down next to her. 'Nothing distracts him. Even if a bolt of lightning dropped on his head he still wouldn't move.'

'She's exaggerating,' Mr Duan said, looking at his wife fondly. 'I am just a worldly man distracted by mundane thoughts. So you want to know about Xuanzang?' He paused, then continued, his voice becoming more animated at the sound of the monk's name. 'Now there was a great man. He was above it all. When I worked in the monastery I used to walk around the pagoda whenever I had problems. But really, they were so trivial. Master Xuanzang was very brave to go on that journey, risking his life. He never gave up, he came back with the sutras. All *I* have to do is to sit and meditate in a comfortable room – I don't call that difficult.'

I told him I was surprised that he loved the monastery so much, yet he had given it up and returned to secular life.

'It is a long story. You are too young to understand,' Duan said, his voice suddenly sombre.

After the Land Reform in 1950, the monasteries were left with very little land, barely enough for the monks to live on. Donations and fees for religious rituals – a considerable proportion of the monastic income in the old days – were drying up. Monks were warned against 'making a business out of superstition'. In a monastery in northeastern China they were forced to put up this poster:

Do not think that through the Buddhas and Bodhisattvas you can obtain good fortune, cure disease or avoid disaster. No matter how big a donation you make, they cannot grant you such requests. Keep your good money for buying patriotic bonds and you can create infinite happiness for society.

Hunger made many monks return to secular life. By 1958, nine years after the revolution, ninety per cent of Chinese monks and nuns had left their monasteries for the world outside, or had died of starvation. The abbot of the Big Wild Goose Pagoda was forced to leave the monastery and had to make a living selling coal from a handcart. Duan was an orphan and had nowhere to go, so he stayed on where he was, barely surviving on cornflour porridge and vegetable leaves.

His old monastery was shut down in the 1960s and the government Religious Bureau assigned him to the Big Wild Goose Pagoda. There were three other monks and also four cadres from the Xian Municipal Cultural Bureau, ostensibly to protect the pagoda but also to keep an eye on the monks. They forbade them to shave their heads, wear their robes, make offerings to the Buddha and Bodhisattvas, or conduct the morning and evening services in the shrine hall. In fact the shrine hall could be used only for political study sessions or struggle meetings. They did allow the monks to say prayers in their own rooms, but not too loudly – that would disturb other people working in the monastery.

Normal religious life was resumed, however, when there were foreign Buddhist delegations. Buddhism helped China to develop friendly foreign relations, especially with Japan, Sri Lanka, Burma, Cambodia, Vietnam and Laos. The monks' presence would show that the Communist Party, though not religious itself, respected religious freedom for its people. When there was an important visit, the cadres would collect monks from all over Xian to simulate the appearance of a functioning monastery. The monks were carefully rehearsed in the questions that might be asked.

Duan was even trained at the Chinese Buddhist Seminary in Beijing to answer every kind of question. 'That was when

I learned a lot about Xuanzang and how important he is, not just for us monks, but for Buddhists throughout Asia,' he remembered. 'They told us Master Xuanzang was a trump card, very important. In fact he was our only card. We were not allowed to talk about anything but him. I guess there was nothing to say about our religious observance – we did not have any. So all we could do was to show the delegates the sutras that Xuanzang translated, which we were not allowed to read. Then we brought them to the pagoda and told them how we remembered the great man on his anniversary with special ceremonies – which of course we could not hold. Before they left, we gave them a portrait of Xuanzang from a rubbing and told them how we were carrying forward his great legacy. All the time Party officials watched us. Then the delegation left, convinced of our freedom of worship, and we returned to our so-called normal life.'

Much of Duan's life was taken up by relentless political studies. 'We were asked to surrender our black heart in exchange for a red heart faithful to the Communist Party,' Duan said. Week after week, sometimes for months on end, they studied the works of Mao and editorials in the *People's Daily*. Then they had to hand in reports of what they learned from their studies.

I asked how much he had really taken on board.

'A lot of it was beyond me,' he said. 'I couldn't see why we should spend weeks studying the new marriage law. It had absolutely nothing to do with us. Perhaps they knew all along we were going to be sent home and get married so it would do us good to know what our rights were as husbands.' He gave an awkward laugh.

Was there a lot of pressure for him to marry?

'Plenty,' he sighed. 'Sometimes monks and nuns were put

in a room together and were told they couldn't leave until they agreed to marry.' There was a nunnery on the outskirts of Xian. One day the abbess came to see Duan and asked if he would take care of one of the novices. 'The nuns suffered more than us monks. Officials spread rumours about them, saying the nunnery was a den of vice and the nuns were prostitutes. Many could not bear it and left, and the nunnery had only two novices and the old and weak staying on,' Duan said. He told the abbess that he would think about it, and eventually he agreed. But then the girl died suddenly. He thought it might have been suicide. 'I felt very guilty; maybe if I had agreed sooner, I would have saved her life.'

Under the unremitting pressure from the government, two of Duan's fellow-monks finally gave in and got married. Then officials badgered him daily, asking him when he would make up his mind. There was a woman, a water-seller outside the monastery, whom Duan had seen around for ages. She was a widow from the village, with four children to support. He thought, why not?

By then he had been a monk for nearly thirty years. That was the only life he knew: simple, quiet living, with just enough to eat and three items of clothing; content and secure, sheltered by the high monastic walls. Now the routine and the structure were gone – no drum to wake him up in the morning, no services and prayers to shape his day, and no beautiful chanting and great masters to reinforce his belief. He must have found it terribly hard in the real world. I looked round the room we were sitting in – it was antiquated, as if it had not been touched for decades. There was practically no furniture, just a saggy, torn sofa and a refrigerator standing in a corner. Next to it, a small rickety altar with a tiny statue of Guanyin. The bare walls held only a huge Mao portrait dominating the room.

'He was born to be a monk,' Mrs Duan interjected before her husband had a chance to say anything more. 'When we got engaged, a dreadful woman in the village started slandering us, saying we weren't really man and wife because monks are like eunuchs. I begged him to do something.'

'What did you do?' I asked.

'What's there to explain? What does it matter?' Duan said.

Their honeymoon was hardly over when the Cultural Revolution began. Duan still remembered the day when the Red Guards stormed the Big Wild Goose Pagoda. It was early one evening in the summer of 1966 and they were about to have supper. Suddenly there was a thunderous noise outside. Before they realized what was happening, a group of Red Guards broke in, shouting, 'Smash the old world, build a brand-new one!' Two of them came into his cell and grabbed the scriptures from his table and threw them on the floor. They ordered him to tread on them to show his support. 'How could I? They were the holy words of the Buddha. I would incur so much wrath, I would be condemned to hell for ever.' He refused.

The Red Guards stamped on the sutras themselves. 'Confess, and we will deal with you leniently; resist, and we will punish you severely. Think carefully. We will come back for you tomorrow.' With that warning, they left the cell.

Outside, some Red Guards were putting up Mao's portrait and posters in large characters, while others were throwing ropes on to the big Buddha and Bodhisattva statues in the shrine hall. The cadres from the Cultural Relics Bureau rushed in to stop them, saying those and the Big Wild Goose Pagoda were not feudal objects but the nation's treasures, from the time of the Monkey King – they had a certificate from the State Council to prove it. The Red Guards were caught by surprise and stood there, not sure what to do. Then one of them started pulling down the silk banners that were hanging from the ceiling. 'These cannot possibly be state treasures,' she said harshly. In a few minutes all the banners were thrown outside, joined by the monastery's precious collection of sutras, many of them Xuanzang's own translations, and other ancient manuscripts. They asked the monks and cadres to come out and stand around the pile, as witnesses to their revolutionary action. Amid mad shouting and clapping, they set the lot on fire. The fire went on all night.

The Big Wild Goose Pagoda survived, but the loss for the whole country was unbelievable. In 1949, there were some two hundred thousand Buddhist monasteries throughout China. One campaign after another accounted for many of them – they were either demolished or turned into schools, factories, houses and museums. By the time the Red Guards finished their work and the Cultural Revolution was over, barely a hundred remained intact. In Beijing, there were, once, more than a hundred monasteries and temples, and now only five belong to the monks. Grandmother was very upset that the three temples in her village were destroyed and the farmers used the stones to build pig-sties and houses. In Tibet, the destruction was almost total. Gone with them was a large part of our history, culture and life – a part we had denounced as antiquated, feudal and backward, a part whose value we did not know until it was gone.

But Duan did not share my sadness and regrets. 'I am so pleased the pagoda has survived,' he said, 'but even that will go one day. Nothing is permanent. When you look at our monastery today, you think it is great. When I first came here, the monastery was run-down and overgrown with weeds; wolves hovered at the gates. It has been repaired a few times since then. And now it looks its best. But in Master Xuanzang's time, this was just the monastery's cemetery, where they buried the ashes of distinguished monks. The monastery itself was a hundred times bigger, if not more, with thousands of rooms, and any number of halls, all connected by streams like in a garden. It could even compete with the imperial palaces in beauty and grandeur. But it is all gone. So what we think of as lasting does not actually last.' He gave me time to take in this very Buddhist view. 'Didn't Chairman Mao say, "Without destruction, there is no construction"? The destruction of the Cultural Revolution gave us Buddhists the opportunity to show our devotion and to accumulate merit for the next life by building new monasteries, bigger and better.' He paused. 'You know, when the Buddha first began promulgating the Dharma two thousand five hundred years ago, he and his disciples simply slept under the trees and begged for alms. We don't even have to have monasteries.'

Did he ever think of resuming monastic life now religion was allowed again? Duan did not hesitate for a moment. 'My wife was very good to take me on in difficult times and has looked after me all these years. The Dharma teaches us to show compassion for all sentient beings. She is getting old and needs me more than ever. How can I leave her? If I have no compassion for her, how can I talk about compassion for anybody else?' He paused, and then added, looking at his wife: 'If she passes away ahead of me, I would like to return to a monastery to spend my remaining days there: that is, if any monastery will take me.' Mrs Duan was all smiles now.

As a Buddhist, Duan attributed his return to secular life to his bad karma. 'I must have left some important task unfinished in my previous life, or obstructed someone un-intentionally,' he said. 'That's why I could only spend half of my life as a monk. You can't escape your karma.'

I find it difficult to accept that Duan was being punished for past sins, that all those people during the Cultural Revolution had done something wrong to deserve their suffering, just as I cannot accept that Grandmother's misfortunes were due to the wrongs of her previous lives. I am still struggling with the idea of karma, a linchpin of Buddhism. For Buddhists, the differences and inequalities in the world can not be explained as simple accidents: they are the working of karma. Why is one born a millionaire, another a pauper? How could Mozart write such heavenly melodies in his teens while others are tone deaf? The Buddha said you reap what you sow: we are the result of our karma, although we can make it better or worse through our own efforts. What I can appreciate is the virtuous effect of believing in it: instead of blaming others and bearing grudges, Duan would always look deeply inside himself and think how he could improve.

They offered me a glass of hot water, with a spoonful of sugar in it – it was all they could afford. I thought about everything he had told me. 'You have had such a hard life,' I said.

'No,' he said. 'I won't say it has been easy. We were very poor when I was small. We lived by begging, and slept at the city gate. I often passed out with the cold; sometimes I woke up with frozen corpses around me. Then my parents died of starvation and my uncle, who could not even feed his own children, left me outside a monastery, and the monks took me in. At least I had food, clothes, a roof over my head. I survived. Life improved after the revolution.'

'But how about everything that happened to the monasteries and the monks? Was that not suffering?'

'We went through many painful things. But the Buddha says suffering is a fact of life. It depends on how we look at it. To me, not to have anything to eat is suffering. I haven't starved since I became a monk, so I can't say I have suffered.'

That night in my hotel room, I could see the pagoda from my window. Mr Duan must be doing his meditation and saying his prayer now, I thought. Before we parted, I had asked him what he prayed for. 'To be a monk again in my next life,' he said. I had meant to ask him about Xuanzang and his teachings and find out what exactly were the doctrines he went to India to find. I did not. But Duan's life had given me something more to think about. Monasteries would be destroyed, but he had a shrine inside himself which was inviolate. In his room, he prayed silently, holding fast to his belief, living by it, unperturbed by all that happened to him. For him, the whole world is a meditation hall, where he put the teaching of the Buddha into ultimate practice. In my eyes, he was a real monk, though a monk without a robe.

I went back to the monastery the next day to have a closer look at it. It was hard to appreciate that what I saw was only the cemetery of the original community. There was still a group of stupas to the right of the pagoda. Originally stupas were built to house the ashes and bones of the Buddha. But gradually over the centuries, they were devoted to lesser and lesser beings, but still of great distinction: the masters who had come closest to enlightenment, the heads of Buddhist sects, the abbots and revered monks of the monasteries. Stupas are supposed not only to commemorate the departed but also to inspire future generations. They are distinguishable by their size but above all by the number of tiers on the spires above the base, with the highest being nine for the Buddha himself. According to my guidebook, Xuanzang's relic stupa was in a separate monastery built specifically for it. The stupas here were all very similar except for one in the shape of a truncated obelisk standing on a lotus flower. The monk's name, Pu Ci, was carved on one side, while the others bore the date of dedication and decorative flowers. It was delicately made. But there were no tiers, suggesting someone of lowly status. And unlike all the others, there was no epitaph giving information about the deceased. I was wondering what this stupa was doing here in this distinguished company when a young monk walked by. I stopped him and asked if he could tell me anything about Pu Ci.

'You don't know about him?' he retorted. Then he seemed to consider something. 'But then, why should you, I suppose? He saved us. Without him, I would not be here today. The Big Wild Goose Pagoda would have been just for you tourists. He was a brave man, a true Buddhist.'

I must have looked as puzzled as I felt, when he launched into an explanation of how the government had decreed in 1982 that any monastery with no monks in residence by the end of the Cultural Revolution would be used for public purposes. 'Pu Ci managed to stay on here, so the Big Wild Goose Pagoda is still a monastery. Without him, it would have been turned into a park or a garden. But he suffered for it.'

If Duan had suffered so much, I could not bear to think what this monk must have gone through.

The young monk said that Pu Ci was the only one who wore his robe throughout the Cultural Revolution. The Red Guards ordered him not to but he simply ignored them. They organized struggle meetings in the shrine hall and made him kneel on the floor and confess his motives for carrying on his 'feudal practices'. He refused to say a word. What was there to say? He had been a monk for so many years and the robe was like his skin. Outraged by his silence, the Red Guards started beating him. Every time they hit him, he uttered the name of Amitabha. They did not know what to do with him. He was locked up to repent but he just meditated all the time. They thought he was mad so eventually they left him alone. I asked how he would have dealt with the blows raining down on him?

'He probably would think of one of the ten attributes of a Bodhisattva. It is called *khanti*, meaning patient endurance of suffering inflicted upon oneself by others and forbearance for their wrongs. There are lots of stories about *khanti* in the scriptures and it is one of the qualities that monks try to cultivate. And he obviously achieved it,' said the young monk humbly.

I remembered one of the old priests at the struggle meetings in my childhood. I could not forget how serene he was. Now I understood what kept him so calm when he was spat on, when he was made to kneel on broken glass. Deep inside, he would have prayed not for the stilling of his pain but for the heart to conquer it. He perhaps would think that the spit was raindrops and they would dry up when the sun came out. Or would he think that the attacks on him might be the result of his bad karma? If so, they were the outcome of his own actions and he should not harbour bitterness towards his attackers. He was in a different world from us, in the midst of pain, yet above it.

I looked at the stupa again, next to the giant Big Wild Goose Pagoda, not even the size of its foundation. Dappled sunshine fell on it through the thick pine trees. I stared at it, thinking of the story I had just heard. I had the sensation that the stupa was expanding, billowing out into a larger dimension, until it was huge. The Big Wild Goose Pagoda embodied Xuanzang's spirit, and the Buddhism he disseminated. It could still be a Buddhist institution carrying on the propagation – because of this ordinary monk. He did not despair perhaps because of a simple belief: if the monks were alive, Buddhism would live on, despite the total destruction of monasteries, statues and scriptures. Xuanzang built the pagoda, Pu Ci preserved it. The spirit they stood for, the faith that sustained them, the spreading of the Dharma they carried out determinedly – the hope of Chinese Buddhism.

But the young monk said there were monks who totally despaired. He showed me a stupa next to Pu Ci's, which looked no different from the half dozen standing there, but with an inscription longer than any of the others. It read as follows:

> Lang Zhao, Secretary of the Xian Buddhist Association, was born in 1893 into a wealthy family in northeastern China, came to Xian and took vows at the age of eighteen; abbot of Wolong Monastery; made donations for the aeroplane that was used to fight against the Americans and supported the Korean people; did farming and built a commune for monks and nuns who lived on their own products and wore their own woven cloth; suffered maltreatment during the Cultural Revolution in 1966 and *took his own life* on August 18 of that year, at the age of seventy-two, after fifty-five years as a monk.

There is something strange about this – it simply is not how a Buddhist master's epitaph usually reads. It seems only to refer to his patriotism, not to his contributions to Buddhism. But what I found even more bewildering is the remark I have italicized near the end: he actually committed suicide – a cardinal sin, a capital offence in Buddhism. Why did he do it?

The first rule of Buddhism is not to kill any living creature, not to take one's own life, and not to help with any killing.

'Rare is birth as a human being. Hard is the life of mortals. Do not let slip this opportunity,' is the advice of the Buddha. I had read that the Vinaya, the Buddhist code of conduct, forbids monks to commit suicide, in any form and for any reason. Those who do forfeit the possibility of a good rebirth, let alone that of entering the Western Paradise. What made Lang Zhao do it?

The young monk explained. Lang Zhao was a very good man. He left home out of compassion for the poor, searching for a way to end suffering. He supported the Party for the same reason – to bring about a better life for millions of Chinese. He raised money for 'Chinese Buddhist' – the fighter plane that Buddhists throughout China had been asked to contribute to the Korean War effort – and he went to the front line to comfort the troops. He tried hard to help the Party realize the Communist ideal of 'paradise on earth'. He was rewarded: he was made the head of the Xian Buddhist Association, the most senior monk in the city.

But for all his efforts, he was one of the first targets of the Red Guards – August 18, 1966, the day he took his life, was when Mao received one million Red Guards on Tiananmen Square, openly showing his support for them. They would be his vanguards for the Cultural Revolution. He met some of them in person afterwards, including a girl called Binbin, meaning 'the polite one'. Mao told her that revolution was not a gentle business and she should change her name to Yaowu, 'with force'. There could not have been a clearer signal for the use of violence. As soon as they heard the message on the radio, the Red Guards in Xian stormed Lang Zhao's monastery, destroying it completely. He felt a great injustice had been done: he had been so loyal to the Party; he had really tried to use Buddhism in helping to build the new China and he had allowed himself to be showcased as an example of a remodelled monk. And in the end, he was repaid for good with evil. He despaired. That very night, he killed himself.

The two monks' stories were grim, but telling. Standing next to each other, their stupas, and lives, invite a comparison. Pu Ci was a simple man, but a true Buddhist monk; Lang Zhao was a master, but in the end shamed himself, however understandably. He was too conscious of his achievements and his sacrifices, too attached to the world and his role in it. He could not bear being reviled after all he had done, by the very people he had tried to support. He was only human. He died, and his monastery with him. Pu Ci just did what he had to do. He raised himself above all his pain and lived; he saved Xuanzang's Big Wild Goose Pagoda and never knew he would be buried and honoured alongside it.

The queue to climb the Big Wild Goose Pagoda was long and those who came down were panting and fanning themselves vigorously, sharing their experiences up there with their friends who were content to admire it from below. They would not bother to stop and examine these little stupas. Perhaps this was why the young monk was happy to spend nearly an hour and a half talking to me. 'The Buddha preached to those who were willing to listen,' he said, when I apologized for taking so much of his time. 'I'm pleased you are so keen on Buddhism. I hope all the visitors will share your interest.'

He had been enormously helpful. I had learned so much from what he told me. It was well past lunchtime and I offered to take him for a meal. He happily agreed, and chose a tiny family restaurant nearby which served nothing but noodles. While we ate, he asked why I was so interested in the stupas. Most people would come, climb the pagoda, have their picture taken and leave. I laughed and told him it was different for me. When he heard that I was going to India, his eyes lit up and he exclaimed, 'Really? Can I come with you? Next year will be Master Xuanzang's fourteen-hundredth anniversary. Won't it be a great thing to do if I could follow in his footsteps too?' But like Xuanzang, he could not get the permission from the government to travel abroad. For a moment, he looked crestfallen, but soon he cheered up. 'You know we are doing something about Master Xuanzang too?' I had heard a little about a Memorial Hall. 'Have you seen the construction behind the pagoda? I'll show you after lunch.'

Against the back wall of the monastery, builders were working away on three huge halls in traditional Chinese style. 'We've always felt ashamed about not doing something special for Master Xuanzang. I am sure you understand why. Now things have changed.' He was getting excited. 'Just imagine. The walls will be decorated with carvings and statues by the best artists and craftsmen in China. The ones at the two ends will show the master's life, his journey to India, his studies in the land of the Buddha, his return to Xian and his translation of the sutras. The middle one will hold the master's statue and on the white marble wall will be carved scenes of the Tushita, the paradise of Maitreya Buddha, the Buddha to Come. This will be the fulfilment of a dream.' He seemed intoxicated by the prospect. 'You will end your journey here, won't you, as the Master did? When you come back, all this will be finished. Then the visitors will learn about the real Xuanzang and all the amazing things he did. No more Monkey King rubbish,' he said with a big smile.

It was near closing time when the young monk finished showing me the site and the monastery. There were very few visitors left. Quiet was descending on the temple and the air

69

was full of the fragrance of flowers and shrubs. Monks walked about briskly on a security round. In the early-evening light, the pagoda looked ever more imposing, austere and majestic. It was extraordinary that it had been standing here for nearly fourteen hundred years. Now I realized its survival was far from being just good fortune.

There were four major persecutions in earlier Chinese history, two before Xuanzang, and two after him in 845 and 955. That in 845 was the most devastating and the most complete. In just one month, almost all the monasteries in the country, some 44,600, were destroyed; the entire Buddhist community, over 260,000 monks and nuns, was forced to return to lay life. It was such a heavy blow, Buddhism was yet to recover from it. The Cultural Revolution effectively demolished what was left. Duan told me a story which showed the low point that had been reached by its end. In the early 1970s, the Chinese government was looking for a rapprochement with Japan. A delegation of over a hundred Japanese monks was invited. They wanted to come to Xian, which they recognized as the fountainhead of their own Buddhism. There was only one problem: where could an equal number of monks be found to meet the visitors? Party officials from the Religious Bureau looked up the records and found where the former monks had been exiled. They combed the countryside – eventually more than a hundred were assembled, many of them now married, disabled or decrepit. And when they had to perform an appropriately grand ceremony, it was soon clear that they had forgotten their sutras and how to chant and play the drums and cymbals. Experts were drafted from Beijing to help rehearse them to an acceptable level. The shaky ensemble managed to perform adequately, and honour was satisfied.

The Big Wild Goose Pagoda has weathered all the storms. Xuanzang was the inspiration. Monks like Pu Ci defended it at whatever cost. If monasteries were destroyed, they would be rebuilt. Even without monasteries, monks like Duan could carry on the faith. Because of people like them, Buddhism has survived in China for almost two thousand years, and will continue to be an important part of Chinese life. I had received a powerful lesson right at the start of my journey: the strength of faith. This was what motivated and sustained Xuanzang. The three monks at the Big Wild Goose Pagoda were his followers. They had already given me an impression of what it was in Buddhism that made them, and Xuanzang, so different, so special. I began to understand what Grandmother had said about monks being the gentlest of men. But they were also the toughest. I began to grasp what our minds could do if we indeed could cultivate them as the Buddha said.

Clack! Clack! There was a sharp, hard sound: a monk walked past us, banging two pieces of wood together. The young monk said it was time for the evening services. Before we said goodbye, he went back to his room and returned with a little book. It had a folded paper in it. 'This has the Heart Sutra translated by Master Xuanzang himself,' he said. 'It is the core of Chinese Buddhism. Whenever Xuanzang was in trouble, he always recited it. Please use it as your guide too. It won't be easy, but keep going. And when you begin to understand this sutra, you will be getting somewhere. I hope you will find the way.'

Late that night, I went back through the city gates, and headed for the station, catching a late-night train for the next stage of my journey, the Jade Gate, the frontier of the Chinese empire in Xuanzang's time. After I had settled down in my hard-sleeper booth, I took out the monk's little book. I opened the folded paper first and found myself face to face with Xuan-zang: young, energetic and purposeful, his eyes firmly on the road ahead and his backpack full of scriptures – it was a rubbing of Xuanzang's portrait from a stele in the Big Wild Goose Pagoda. But his gifts felt heavy in my hands. Perhaps I should not just make the journey for myself. I should try to help bring the real Xuanzang back for my fellow-Chinese, just as the abbot and monks of the Big Wild Goose Pagoda are doing. It would be like restoring a part of our heritage.

THREE

Fiction and Reality

IT WAS AUGUST 627. The great Western Gate of Chang'an closed at nightfall. On the drum tower, the watchman was ready to strike the hour. The streets were emptying. Traders in the Western Market were putting up their shutters and seductive attendants were waiting outside taverns to lure them in. Among the throng of people leaving the capital were Xuanzang and another monk, clad in long robes. They had all their belongings wrapped in cloths slung over their shoulders. They walked briskly, with their heads down, trying to avoid the gaze of the officials, who were checking travellers' passes at random.

Once on the road, Xuanzang took a last look back at Chang'an in the twilight. He was excited; his dream of going to the land of the Buddha was beginning to come true. He had failed to get permission to travel and was leaving in defiance of the emperor's edict, but that could not dampen his spirits. He felt free. How he wished he could fly like a bird to India. But he would have to make his way laboriously, on foot or on horseback, along all the thousands of miles lying ahead.

As the train pulled out of Xian station in the middle of the night, I was excited too. This was the start of my journey in his footsteps. I could have flown, but I liked the pace of the train – I could not walk as he did but at least I would see what he saw. The rhythmical rattling of the wheels sounded a bit like footsteps, though the train did in one hour what took him two days or so. Still, 1,400 years apart, we were on the same highway, the famous Silk Road.

Xuanzang would have known the Silk Road well. It acquired the name in the late nineteenth century, long after its demise, from the German scholar Ferdinand von Richthofen, but its history usually begins with the mission of Zhang Qian in 139 BC, almost seven hundred years before Xuanzang. Zhang, an official in the Chinese court of the Han dynasty, was assigned to seek an alliance in Central Asia to fight against the foremost threat to China, the marauding Huns. He was captured and imprisoned by the enemy, but he never forgot his mission, and managed to escape after thirteen years in captivity. His report and the tale of his adventures inspired the emperor. Before long, watchtowers were built and manned along the way within the Chinese empire. Sogdian merchants began braving the arduous journey to China regularly, trading the most treasured and valuable commodity: silk.

The ancient world, the Romans in particular, could not get enough silk, alluring to the eye and delicate to the touch. They spent colossal sums on it – it was half of their imports. The Emperor Tiberius was so worried that he tried to ban people from wearing it – the Romans would have nothing of that. But they would not have minded paying less for the fabric, which was said to cost as much as gold by the time it travelled the whole length of the Silk Road. Agents were sent out, trying to reach directly the distant land that they called *Sere*, from which came *sericus*, silken, but they never made it. Although the Chinese were willing to sell silk to the barbarians, they did not want to relinquish the secret of how it was made. Pliny, the Roman historian, wrote: 'The Seres are famous for the wool of their forests. They remove the down from leaves with the help of water and weave it into silk.' As late as the mid-sixth century A D, the Romans believed his account.

The Silk Road was not a single road but many, stretching from Chang'an, across the Taklamakan Desert, over the Pamir Mountains, through the grasslands of Central Asia, into Persia and then to the Mediterranean, with spurs into the northern Eurasian steppes and India. Over 5,000 miles long, it traversed some of the most inhospitable terrain, and linked up some of the greatest empires in the ancient world: Rome, Persia, India and China. This was where Xuanzang's journey would lie.

When the day broke and the sun came into my compartment, I saw ranges of mountains, brown and dusty, with terraced fields stepping up them. Walnut and persimmon trees, laden with their fruit, stood here and there in clusters, sheltering old brick houses, their chimneys smoking as people cooked the morning meal. When we left the villages behind, the farmers walking on the windy mountain paths made me think of the Silk Road again.

The Silk Road no longer exists, and most Chinese have forgotten it, although every one of us is familiar with silk. Even I had raised silkworms as pets. One winter, Grandmother came back from a visit to her village and brought us apples, peanuts, chestnuts and a small bag of strange, fluffy white balls – silk cocoons. She said if we looked after them very carefully, putting them in a clean place not too hot, not too cold, and making sure insects would not bite them, we would have butterflies and then silkworms when the spring came.

I put my cocoons in a shoe box next to my pillow and examined them every day. They looked dry and dead. How could butterflies ever come out of them? Grandmother said not to worry, they were only sleeping and would wake up soon. I waited as eagerly as I did for the Chinese New Year. One day when I came back from school, the cocoons were open and there were some white moths. I was fascinated but disappointed; they were quite ugly, not at all pretty like butterflies. Grandmother said I should just wait. And then very soon the moths dropped tiny white blobs on the bottom of the shoe box and a few days later some ant-like creatures appeared. Before long they began to crawl, tiny caterpillars, shedding their skins like snakes. It seemed an extraordinary process, and it was magical to see the beginning of their life.

Every day I ran back as soon as school was over to check them. Grandmother said they liked mulberry leaves best but our city had so few mulberry trees, we had to make do with cabbage leaves. My sisters and I had a competition among us to see who had the fattest and whitest silkworms. But the most fascinating part was when they secreted a shiny thread, which seemed just to go on and on. We asked Grandmother what the thread was for. She said it was silk, and it made the most wonderful material. We did not believe her. Then she opened the wardrobe and pulled out a bright red quilted jacket which I had never seen anyone wearing. 'This was what your mother wore when she got married,' she said happily. 'This is made of silk. You feel it.' It was so smooth and shiny, like my hair. It was hard to imagine such beautiful cloth could have come from those insects in my shoe box.

Looking back, it is equally hard to imagine that the thread from the silkworms could have been the source of so much wealth and beauty, and changed history. Today the Silk Road has declined, but something else, something more enduring, still touches our lives. For over a millennium, religions, technology, philosophy, culture and art were transmitted along its branches. It was through this highway that four of China's greatest contributions spread westward – paper-making, printing, gunpowder and the compass – and it was along the same road, in the other direction, that Buddhism came to China. The seeds of ideas travelled across the barriers of mountains, deserts and languages. Some took root; others died; some flourished and spread extensively. What each traveller carried was small, but wave succeeded wave; and in the process, all the peoples along the Silk Road enjoyed the fruits of the diffusion.

The Silk Road was possible because there were strings of oases to supply the caravans. One of the biggest oases in the region west of the Yellow River was Liangzhou, the capital of several short-lived dynasties set up by nomads as well as the Chinese. It was very popular with the merchants, who had long used it as their base from which to make forays into the rest of China. Mostly they prospered. But things could go wrong. In the early fourth century A D, a merchant based in Liangzhou sent a letter home to Samarkand, reporting that many of his fellow-merchants had died of starvation because of a peasant revolt and war in China, and claiming that he himself was on the verge of death too. 'Sirs, if I were to write to you everything about how China has fared, it would be beyond grief.' He asked his business partners to look after a large sum of money he had left with them, to invest it on behalf of his motherless son, and to give his son a wife when he grew up.

But for all the dangers the lure of the Silk Road and its high profits was irresistible. When Xuanzang arrived in Liangzhou from Chang'an in 627, after travelling over seven hundred miles in one month, he found a bustling city of over 200,000 people, many of them foreign merchants who took up five of the seven wards within the walled city. He was pleased to see monks from as far as India, Central Asia and the Western Regions, in monasteries, temples and caves in and outside Liangzhou. He decided to spend some time there and find out from them, and from the merchants, about their countries and the border crossing.

The local people were delighted to have a master from the capital, and they pleaded with Xuanzang to preach the Dharma. Although he was worried about being exposed as an unauthorized traveller, he could not refuse. Impressed with his clear and eloquent preaching, they showered him with gold, silver and horses to show their appreciation. He kept one horse and some money for his journey ahead and gave the rest to the monastery where he was staying. But as he had feared, his popularity brought him unwanted attention. Warned of his intention of going to India, the Governor of Liangzhou sent for him and ordered him to return to the capital. 'The emperor has just come to the throne and the borders are yet to be secured. No one is allowed to go beyond here,' the governor reiterated the imperial edict. That night, Xuanzang slipped out of Liangzhou, secretly guided by two disciples of a senior monk who had listened to his preaching and sympathized with his ambition.

My train arrived in Liangzhou, or Wuwei as it is called today, the next afternoon, fifteen hours after leaving Xian. The loudspeakers in the compartment were blaring out a potted history of this ancient, glorious city, and its emblem, the bronze Flying Horse, which is about the only thing that ordinary Chinese know about Wuwei. A few peddlers were trying to shove a replica through the train windows. It originates in one of our most famous archaeological discoveries, a pit with eighty of the magnificent steeds: they are shown taking prancing steps on powerful long legs, with defiant expressions and flared nostrils.

In real life they were renowned for their stamina and agility, far superior to China's short, stocky steppe ponies. They were the ideal mount for Chinese cavalry defending against the nomadic tribes, who could not be stopped by the Great Wall. They were so important, they were worthy of a lengthy comment from Si Maqian, the most famous Chinese historian, in his *Record of History*.

> The Son of Heaven greatly loved the horses of Kokand [today's Ferghana valley, shared by Kyrgyzstan, Uzbekistan and Turkmenistan], and embassies set out one after the other on the road to that country. The largest of them comprised several hundred men; the smallest fewer than a hundred ... When they were refused, the Son of Heaven sent a great quantity of silver and a horse made of solid gold in exchange for the horses. The king accepted the presents but refused to part with his horses – he reckoned that he was out of reach of the Chinese army. The ambassador was murdered. So the emperor sent 60,000 men ... and a commissariat well stocked with supplies besides cross-bows and other arms ... Only half the army survived the journey and laid siege to Kokand in 102 BC. After 40 days, they succeeded, and were offered 30 superior or heavenly horses and 3,000 of lower quality. Less than half these survived the return journey but sufficient to provide for judicious breeding under the imperial eye.

I decided not to stop in Wuwei. It is no longer the cosmopolitan city of old, whose music was enjoyed by emperors and commoners alike, whose wine was relished by the rich and powerful in Chang'an, whose inhabitants drank from silver ewers decorated with figures from Greek mythology, and whose remoteness and exotic blend of peoples and cultures fired the imagination of any number of poets. Like many cities in western China, it has languished into a long slumber, and all its ancient past has been erased. The station was just a low building and a dusty platform with a semi-abandoned air. When the train moved off, it sounded a soft peep, instead of the usual strident whistle, as if not to wake anyone in the sleepy town.

I got off at Liuyuan, the Willow Station, in the early morning. It was in the middle of the desert without a tree in sight. I could not understand why the station was here nor how it came by its name. Perhaps it was wishful thinking, taking its inspiration from a Chinese saying: 'Drop one sprig of willow on the ground and a whole forest will come up.'

At least my taxi-driver was happy after sleeping at the station overnight in the hope of a fare. I told him I wanted to go to the Jade Gate, and I was about to explain to him where it was. He cut me off: 'No problem. It's so famous. All the tourists want to go there.' Off we went, into the desert that seemed one endless dusty grey world. Surrounded by a void, it was hard to imagine that we were on what was once a thriving commercial thoroughfare. At least it was a good road.

In less than an hour we were in the district of Anxi, or Guazhou as Xuanzang knew it. This was the oasis he came to after Liangzhou. Here he found himself in serious trouble. His horse died suddenly; the two novices who accompanied him became frightened: one left him and the other was sent back to his master for his own good. Then orders reached Guazhou to arrest him and send him back to the capital. The local governor was a pious Buddhist and after hearing the monk's story, he tore up the warrant and urged Xuanzang to leave as

82

quickly as possible. But Xuanzang did not know the way through the desert and he could not find anyone who dared to challenge the imperial edict and take him past the Jade Gate and the five watchtowers beyond it, the last frontier posts. Finally, after a month's wait, the monks in the monastery where he stayed found Pantuo, a Sogdian merchant, who was willing to be his guide.

We drove through Anxi. It was a quiet town, small and orderly, with few buildings higher than three storeys. The wide featureless streets were empty of cars and bicycles. A scattering of people could be seen walking slowly along its pavements, or lingering to speak to each other before the few shopfronts. There was none of the life of the Silk Road I imagined from my reading. And this was not the actual town where Xuanzang was beleaguered – that is now a ruin out in the desert. I told the driver not to stop and go straight to the Jade Gate.

The gate was the frontier in Xuanzang's time. For the Chinese, it marked the divide between the 'centre of the world' and the 'periphery', the 'civilized' and the 'barbarians'. Over the centuries our poets had poured out their fears of the unknown world, their yearnings for home, their sadness at saying goodbye to friends who ventured further west to conquer the barbarians, and their pity for the royal princesses who were given to the barbarian chieftains as brides and as the price of peace. The poems are beautiful, sad, evocative and haunting, and they live in our memories and imaginations, even today, more than a thousand years later. 'The crescent moon, hung in the void, is all that can be seen in this wild desert, where the dew crystallizes on the polished steel of swords and breastplates. Many a day will pass before the men return. Do not sigh, young women, for you would have to sigh too long.'

Xuanzang shared none of these sentiments. The world beyond the Jade Gate was one of knowledge, learning and wisdom. The earliest Buddhist missionaries came from there, bringing copies of the scriptures and votive images. Then they devoted the rest of their lives to translating the scriptures into Chinese – he and all Chinese Buddhists had been reading their translations for centuries; they had changed Chinese life and culture fundamentally. He could not wait to see this world for himself.

We had been driving nearly an hour and I was worried. The gate should have been very near Anxi. Where was he taking me? 'Are you sure we're going to the right place?'

'Don't worry, Miss. We'll be there very soon.' He turned and gave me a friendly smile, as if to reassure me.

Half an hour later, I caught sight of the Jade Gate from a long distance away. I was greatly relieved. I could see its tower, standing like a vast ruined chimney in the middle of nowhere. My heart began to beat faster as I came near. Once Xuanzang passed it, he would have left China behind. We drove right up to the site. There were railings surrounding it, and at the entrance, a man in a blue Mao suit was sitting in the sun. Behind him was a big sign: 'Ruins of the Jade Gate, Han Dynasty.' I almost exploded. This was the wrong gate, already seven hundred years old and abandoned by Xuanzang's time. 'Where is the Tang dynasty gate?' I asked the watchman.

'It's near Anxi,' he said.

I rounded on the driver. 'What have you brought me here for?'

'You want to see the Jade Gate. Does it matter if it is a Han or Tang dynasty one? Anyway, everybody comes here.'

I tried to calm myself. It was really my fault; I should have explained and made it clear. At least my mistake had cost me only a few pounds for the unnecessary ride. I put it down to experience. I would have to be more careful – this was only the first stop from Xian and I had gone wrong already. But it was odd that the people of the Tang dynasty chose the same name for the new gate; they must have loved it so much.

Having come all this way, I thought I should at least take a look; it would have been similar to the right one. This gate was a fortified military post in the Great Wall, with a courtyard and quarters for soldiers. When I looked left and right, I could see, for miles in a straight line, low ledges of rubble, even neat piles of reeds and desert-willow branches for making repairs, now covered in sand. It was all that was left of the Great Wall here, reduced by time and nature. Once the threat to China had shifted from the nomads in the west to those in the north near Beijing, there was no incentive to maintain it. But in the Han dynasty, this place was crowded with travellers. 'Messengers come and go every season and month, foreign traders and merchants knock on the gates of the Great Wall every day,' say the Han Annals of History. The soldiers checked their passes, and kept bonfires ready to send smoke signals for reinforcements if danger threatened.

I entered the watchtower through a doorway as wide as my arms could stretch. Inside, it was spacious, big enough for a platoon to exercise in. I could see clear up to the sky; the roof had long since collapsed. Through the gaping holes in the thick mud-and-lath walls, I looked out across the desert, shimmering in the heat haze, stretching to the horizon. It was a similar forbidding prospect that faced Xuanzang, and he did not even have a road to follow across it.

The driver felt bad. 'I can take you to where they think the Tang gate was, but why are you interested?' I explained to him as I ought to have done sooner that I was following

Xuanzang's route. 'You should have said. Anyway, let's go back. There is really nothing left of the gate, but I think we should go to the watchtower. There's a little museum there. I won't charge you extra.'

We went back the way we had come, and he brought me to another ruin which archaeologists believe was the first watchtower outside the Jade Gate, now just huge piles of mud and straw. This was where Xuanzang faced the next danger on his journey. You could see why – apart from a large hut next to it, which turned out to be the museum, there was nothing within miles. Any traveller here would be totally exposed. Half of the museum is devoted to the Communist Long Marchers who passed through here in 1936. But the other end has paintings on the walls showing Xuanzang crossing the desert. Colourful as they are, the pictures hardly capture the real drama.

Xuanzang had already had a close shave before he even reached the first watchtower, at his bivouac with his guide Pantuo. They had skirted the Jade Gate in the middle of the night, by crossing a river four miles away, with a raft made of tree branches and reeds. Then Pantuo suggested they rest for a few hours before tackling the five watchtowers beyond. He seemed a perfect guide; he knew the terrain, the habits of the soldiers, where and when they might be able to slip by unnoticed. Xuanzang was relieved, said a short prayer, and fell asleep in no time. But before long he was woken by a noise; he opened his eyes and saw Pantuo creeping towards him, drawing his sword, then hesitating and returning to his sleeping-mat.

Once up at the crack of dawn, Pantuo pleaded with Xuanzang not to proceed. 'This track is long and fraught with danger. There is neither water nor grass except near the watchtowers. We can only reach them at night. And if dis-covered, we are dead men! Please, let's go back.' Xuanzang refused. Finally Pantuo told the truth: he regretted his decision to break the law and now was worried about being caught; he must leave. His strange behaviour last night now made sense: if Pantuo had killed him in the midst of the desert, nobody would have known. But either from superstitious fear or from a last remnant of piety, he changed his mind. He asked Xuan-zang to promise not to mention his name if he was caught by the frontier guards. Then he turned back, leaving Xuanzang an old horse that had made the journey many times – it knew the way, Pantuo said.

And so, abandoned and alone, Xuanzang pressed slowly and painfully on through the Gobi Desert, unsure of his direc-tion and guided only by heaps of bones and piles of camel-dung. The frontier poet Cen Sen left us a description of what Xuanzang had to go through: 'Travellers lost their way in the endless yellow sand. Looking up, they saw nothing but clouds. This was not only the end of earth but also of heaven. Alas, they had to go further west after Anxi.' Through exhaustion, and the heat, Xuanzang saw what appeared to be hundreds of armed troops coming towards him. 'On one side were camels and richly caparisoned horses; on the other, gleaming lances and shining standards. Soon there appeared fresh figures, and at every moment the shifting spectacle underwent a thousand transformations. But as soon as one drew near, all vanished.' Xuanzang believed himself to be in the presence of the army of Mara, the demon in Buddhist mythology who had attempted to distract the Buddha while he was in deep meditation to achieve enlightenment. But it was only a mirage.

A more immediate danger was this watchtower, the first of the five he had to pass. He waited until nightfall and found the little spring that Pantuo had told him about. It is still there today, clear and cool, surrounding the watchtower's ruins. He went down to drink at it and wash his hands. Then, as he was filling his water bag, he heard the whistle of an arrow, which nearly hit him in the knee. A second later, another arrow followed. Knowing he was discovered, he shouted with all his might: 'I am a monk from the capital. Do not shoot at me!'

Xuanzang was brought before the captain, who was a lay Buddhist. On hearing the monk's plan, he too told him to turn back. The road was dangerous and he did not think the pilgrim would be able to reach India at all. Xuanzang was grateful for his concern but told him that he was so troubled with doubts, he just had to go. 'You, a benevolent man, instead of encouraging me, urge me to abandon my efforts. This cannot be called an act of compassion,' he said to the captain, and then added: 'You can detain me if you want to, but Xuanzang will not take a single step in the direction of China!'

Impressed by Xuanzang's determination and fearlessness, the officer decided to help the pilgrim. Xuanzang stayed with him for the night and began his journey with a good supply of food, water and fodder for his horse. He was given an introduction for the fourth watchtower, but was warned against the fifth because the officer there had no sympathy for Buddhism. Instead, he should head for the Wild Horse Spring sixty miles to the west of it, and from there all paths would be clear. But with no experience of travelling in the desert, Xuanzang soon got lost. To add to his grief, his water bag slipped from his hand as he lifted it to drink. In an instant, his whole supply of water vanished into the sand. In total confusion and despair, he turned back and started retracing his footprints. But after a few miles he stopped. He remembered his vow: 'Never take one step back towards China before reaching India.'

I had to keep going westwards too. I could resume my train journey from the Willow Station, and asked the driver to take me back there. When I looked out of the train window I saw nothing apart from the cloudless blue sky, a few lonely white aspens along the railway line, and a vast expanse of sand and gravel, grey, featureless; craggy mountains hemmed a distant horizon, topped with snow, but they looked impossibly aloof. Crossing the Gobi Desert even on a modern train is forbidding. I found it incredible that Xuanzang had journeyed through it alone, with no guide but his own shadow and his faith. I talked to the young man opposite me and told him about Xuanzang's adventure in the Gobi.

'I thought the emperor had all sorts of arrangements made for him. It says so in *The Monkey King*.'

'That is fiction,' I said.

'I know the monkey is a fictional creation. But Xuanzang must have had a lot of protection and companions. You aren't telling me he did it all on his own.' He shook his head vehemently. 'You remember what happened to the famous scientist who disappeared in the desert in the 1980s? He even had satellite communication. But he never came back. Such a waste of a life.'

Xuanzang almost suffered the same fate. For four days he was lost in the Gobi, without a single drop of water. The burning heat and the punishing winds brought him to the verge of collapse. On the fifth day he fell on the sand, unable to take a single step further. His horse fell too. All he had strength for was to mutter a few prayers. He desperately turned to Guanyin: 'In venturing on this journey, I do not seek riches, worldly profit or fame; my heart longs to find the true Law. Your heart, O Bodhisattva, forever yearns to deliver all creatures from misery. I am in such danger. Can you not hear my prayers?'

This was the worst moment in his entire journey. He was young, only twenty-seven, and had never faced the real dangers of life and death. He was determined and thought he was prepared, but he had not expected so much hardship so soon, before even leaving China. The emperor and nature itself had joined forces to put an end to his journey almost before it had begun. He was alone; he was lost; and he was dying. He remembered a sutra with the story of Guanyin saving a merchant who had been shipwrecked in the open sea for seven days. But his favourite Bodhisattva seemed to be ignoring his plea for help, although he prayed all the time to her. Was she really up there somewhere? If so, why would she not come to rescue him? The vast desert looked ready to swallow him up; death could be hours or minutes away. He would become just another pile of bones in the sand.

After praying to Guanyin, Xuanzang began to recite the Heart Sutra. He had learned it many years before from a sick man he had tended. It is the shortest sutra in the Buddhist canon but is regarded as the essence of Chinese Buddhism. He was told to recite it when he was in danger and when everything else had failed. Now he needed it more than ever. When he approached the end, these were the words he would have spoken to himself: 'The world is ultimately empty. The wisdom of the Bodhisattva is such that he has no illusions in his mind, hence, no fear.'

The Buddha taught that having no illusions means seeing things as they really are, which in turn means recognizing the impermanence of everything. The Buddha often told his disciples that life is only a single breath. It is momentary, changing every second, and in one continuum with death. And for a Buddhist death is not an end, just a point between this world and the next. One will be reborn – though in what form depends on one's karma. Xuanzang could hope that he would still be able to carry on his mission in his next life.

So he calmed himself. His panic was behind him, and he could think about what to do next. He picked himself up, and pulled hard on the horse's reins. To his amazement, the old roan staggered up and set off. They struggled for nearly four miles when suddenly the horse turned in a different direction, and no matter how hard Xuanzang tried, he could not make it change its path. He let himself be guided by the creature's instinct. Before long he saw green grass a little way off, and a shining pool, bright as a mirror. He was saved. Old horses indeed know the way.

In the Gobi, Xuanzang had passed the ultimate test. In this contest between nature and will, he triumphed over his anxiety, fear and despair. It had nearly cost him his life, but it gave him confidence. From then on, he felt there was nothing he could not face. I could hardly believe the story, and when I told it to the young man sitting opposite me, he could not believe it either. He thought I was pulling the wool over his eyes, or telling him an episode from the story of *The Monkey King*.

From the Wild Horse Spring, Xuanzang and his horse drank long and deep. Then they followed the beaten track. After two days he was out of the Gobi, and outside China. He was now in the Western Region, a vast territory between the Jade Gate and the Pamir Mountains, consisting mainly of the Takla-makan Desert, the second biggest in the world, with a string of independent oasis city-states along its edge, all depending on the Silk Road for their survival and wealth. Xuanzang would have known the history of the region well. China took it in the first century BC after the Silk Road was opened, but lost it to various nomadic peoples of the Eurasian steppes. At the point at which Xuanzang arrived, the Turks were the overlords, but the Chinese wanted it back.

Today the area is called the Xinjiang Uighur Autonomous Region. The Uighurs were a nomadic tribe of Turkic origin, who migrated from the Eurasian steppes to the Taklamakan in the ninth century AD, not long after Xuanzang passed through the region. It was the Uighurs who have left us some of the most splendid Buddhist art, Nestorian Christian arte-facts, and rare Manichaean documents and paintings. Eventually they took to Islam with the same zeal as they had embraced other religions of the Silk Road. Highly mobile with their versatile and speedy horses, they were one of the biggest threats to China on its northern and northwestern borders. But unlike many other powerful nomadic peoples, the Uighurs never managed to rule China. In the eighteenth century, after the longest military campaign in Chinese history, the region finally became part of the empire again.

Turfan is one of the biggest oases and cities in Xinjiang, situated on the eastern edge of the Taklamakan. A guide from a travel agency would meet me at the station. 'How will I recognize you?' I asked him on the phone after I had told him what I wanted to see in Turfan. 'I'm fat, like a laughing Buddha outside a temple. People call me Fat Ma.' The description was accurate. At the exit of my compartment, I spotted him immediately. He was dressed in a t-shirt and wiping sweat from his face. We looked at each other and smiled.

'You need some rest in the hotel?' he asked, taking my rucksack from me. 'You said you're interested in history and what Xuanzang did in Turfan. You're in for a big treat. Anyway you can make your mind up later, we are still fifty miles from the city.' While we walked to his car I mentioned the oddness of the location of the station, both here and in Anxi. 'Perhaps they could only build straight lines in those days,' he laughed, and then added more seriously: 'We did so many crazy things back then. I wouldn't be surprised if the decision where to put the stations was completely random.'

In five minutes his battered Beijing jeep was out of the station and driving at 100 kph on a tar road as soft as melting butter. It was late summer but Fat Ma was panting more than the old engine. I was a bit worried. 'You should have seen me a few weeks ago. It was over fifty degrees every day. I hardly dared to move. Do you know how officials conducted their business in the old days?' I shook my head. 'They read their papers in the bath-tub soaking in ice-cold water.' But the extreme weather here is not due to global warming. The city is right in the centre of a depression – in fact, it is the second lowest spot on earth, after the Dead Sea. Fat Ma told me Turfan means 'lowland' in the Uighur language. It has been called the Oasis of Fire.

I told him I did not need a rest – he was so entertaining I wouldn't be able to fall asleep anyway. So he suggested we head for the ruins of Gaochang city. 'Your monk really had a hell of a time there,' he said. We were back in the middle of the desert. There were no trees, no farms, not a speck of green anywhere. Perhaps if you are brought up there you learn to spot small details and it seems infinitely variegated. But to the unaccustomed eye it is sad in its monotony, a faceless plain of unrelieved sameness. Surrounded by a void, it was hard to imagine that we were on what was once a thriving commercial thoroughfare, or that this poem, written in the seventh century, actually described what Xuanzang would have seen on his journey through the area:

A good day to start on a long journey,
Wagon after wagon passes through.
The camels-bells never stop,
They are carrying the white chain (silk) to Anxi*.

After driving for twenty miles in the desert, my eyes caught some trees in the distance. 'The oasis,' I nearly shouted, pointing to a spot of green on the horizon. 'Don't get too excited,' Fat Ma said, 'It's still quite a way off.'

We drove for another ten miles. Then I saw poplar trees and suddenly – fields of melons; plantations of vines inside and outside courtyards, spreading on to the walls; children playing by the road, carts loaded with cotton. I had not travelled in the blazing sun for days on end like the old caravans, nor did I experience any danger, but I was overwhelmed by the sudden fertility of the oasis – the renewal of life and succour for the traveller in the midst of the desert. I could only imagine how Xuanzang would have felt when he stepped from the sterility of his Gobi trek into the luxuriance of Gaochang.

The remains of Gaochang city are very grand, fitting for one of the oldest and wealthiest Silk Road kingdoms. For centuries, it was the second major oasis outside China, the starting point for the grassland Silk Road, and an obligatory stop for travellers. The mud walls that surrounded it, now broken in places, were more than ten metres high and five kilometres long. We entered from the western gate – quite a small one, but it opened up a broad, impressive view of the

* Anxi here refers to the Western Region.

city within. The fallen houses and lonely pillars made it look even bigger. Under the blue sky, clouds flew past as if speeded up by a special-effects camera. As far as the eye could see, rugged walls stood erect after more than a thousand years. It was hard to believe that something built of mud could last so long. Straight ahead of us in the centre of the city was a tall, impressive terrace built of baked red clay bricks, the remaining foundations alone more than fifteen metres high. 'We think this is King Qu Wentai's royal palace,' Fat Ma said. I felt my pulse quicken. This was it – the place where Xuanzang had one of his most dramatic experiences on his journey.

The King of Gaochang was a fervent Buddhist and so his capital was a city of temples: Buddhist, Zoroastrian, Manichaean, with one for every hundred inhabitants. There were thousands of monks in the kingdom, but the king felt the country lacked a great master. He was inspired when he heard the praises that caravan traders heaped on Xuanzang after they had listened to his preaching in Liangzhou. It reminded him of the wonderful monasteries and profound masters he had encountered in the Chinese capital: he had gone there to pay tribute to the Chinese court three years earlier. A close relationship with his powerful neighbour was vital for the survival of his small kingdom. He was also very impressed with the way the Chinese conducted themselves – on his return, he ordered all his people to adopt the hairstyles of the gentlemen and ladies in Chang'an. Now he could have an erudite Chinese master from the very centre of learning to enlighten him and his people. How exciting it would be! The Chinese have a saying: 'Something you could only meet but not seek.' He felt this was his chance. He sent his envoys to meet Xuanzang. They abducted him to Gaochang, despite his plans to travel by a different route.

It was here, in this very palace, that the king paced about when he heard the Chinese master would be arriving that night. He forgot to eat, or sleep. At midnight, the guards announced Xuanzang's arrival and he proceeded by torchlight to meet him. The king was so excited that despite Xuanzang's fatigue, he insisted on talking to him all night and for the next ten days, for one purpose alone: to ask him to stay on as the master for his people.

Xuanzang thanked the king profusely for the invitation, but he could not accept it. He must go to India to find out what was missing from the teachings in China, he explained. But the king was unyielding: 'It would be easier to shift the mountains of Pamir than to make me change my mind.'

Seeing how keen the king was to keep the Chinese master, his ministers also put their minds to it and came up with an ingenious idea. Xuanzang was young and single; so was the princess royal. She was beautiful, pious, cultivated, and very fond of Chinese culture and dress. Surely Xuanzang could not refuse such a wonderful bride. When the king broached the subject with his sister, she was only too happy to oblige. She had listened to the clear, deep and profound preaching by the handsome Chinese master. She had nothing but admiration for him; and to spend the rest of her life with such an enlightened man would indeed be *yuan*, her destiny.

But Xuanzang explained to the king that he regarded it as *his* destiny to fulfil his mission to bring back the sacred sutras that were needed in China and circulate them to his fellow-countrymen. Surely the king would not stand in the way of his destiny?

But the king – typically for kings – was unused to his decrees being questioned, not to mention defied. He grew angrier with Xuanzang's obstinacy until at last he issued an ultimatum: 'I am determined to retain you by force, or else to have you escorted back to your own country. I invite you to think the matter over; it is best to accept my offer.'

Without hesitation, Xuanzang replied: 'The king will only be able to keep my bones; he has no power over my spirit nor my will!'

To make the king let him go, Xuanzang began a fast. For three days, he meditated and refused to take food or water. On the fourth day, he was getting weak and had trouble breathing. The king was shocked. He had seen many monks come and go through his kingdom, but never one like Xuanzang – so learned, spiritual and determined, and so fearless, ready even to sacrifice his life for the faith. A true Buddhist, a living example of the enlightened mind. As the *Dhammapada*, the Sayings of the Buddha, described:

> From attachment springs grief,
> From attachment springs fear,
> For him who is totally free
> There is no grief, and where is fear?

The king begged Xuanzang to eat. He would let him continue his journey; perhaps the master could contemplate stopping in Gaochang on his way back from India. Xuanzang had already decided to do that: he was deeply moved by the king's piety and devotion to the Buddha, and the sincerity of his wish for a better understanding of the Dharma. While he was taking some food, the king looked at him, weakened and exhausted by his hunger strike and months of travelling in secret and getting lost in the desert. He recognized the greatness of this young man but wondered whether he could achieve his purpose penniless and alone. In a remarkable reversal, he decided to help the young Chinese monk. He asked Xuanzang to preach for a month, while preparations were being made for his journey.

Fat Ma was melting in the midday sun. He suggested we have lunch in a restaurant outside the gate where we parked the car. It was an oasis in itself; everywhere you looked there was green: pots with fragrant-leaved plants dotted over the floor, an overhead trellis spilling grapevines and casting a welcome weave of shadows on the ground. The grapes hung low enough for you to reach up and pick them. Water gushed in runnels at your feet, circling the place. After the dust, the heat and the ruins, I felt I could breathe again. We ordered a real Silk Road meal: noodles from China, Turkish kebabs and nans from India. After a couple of cold beers, Fat Ma revived, joking and calling for the car-radiator to be filled with water. We were doing just what Xuanzang and all Silk Road travellers would do when they arrived in Gaochang: refuelling with shade, water and food.

Here merchants and travellers from as far as Syria and southern India would check into one of many caravanserais inside the city. After a wash and a meal, they would inspect their pack animals to see if they needed to change them for healthy, rested ones, or simply to trade in one type of animal for another more suitable for the next stage of the journey – Bactrian camels were the favourite for this stretch of the Silk Road: they could sniff out subterranean springs and predict sandstorms; if they bunched together and buried their mouths in the sand, you knew one was coming. In the bustling bazaars the travellers would sell their goods, buy local specialities and stock up on food and supplies. If they had completed a profit-able deal, they could go into one of the many taverns. Gorgeous women from Kucha, the next oasis, and even from as far away as Samarkand, entertained them with whirlwind dances and melodious songs, as they filled their glasses with the delicious Gaochang wine made from 'mare's teat' grapes.

Gaochang, like all oasis kingdoms on the Silk Road, depended on levies from the caravans passing through. On entering the city gate, everyone was asked to show their passes issued in their country of origin. Then the merchants would be charged on the spot by their animal loads and then again when they sold their goods in the bazaars. A camel could carry an average of three hundred pounds, and a horse or a donkey half of that. Caravans could be as small as a dozen travellers or as big as several thousands – the bigger, the safer because the merchants could afford to pay for protection. An annual customs report of Gaochang from Xuanzang's time recorded buoyant trade in large quantities: a man selling five hundred and seventy-two pounds of spices, another eighty pounds of raw silk and a third eight pounds of silver. The list goes on, giving us the most direct evidence of how the oasis kingdoms like Gaochang earned their income. The wealth of Gaochang was such that when China conquered it in the first century B C, its annual revenues could finance the defence and running costs of the entire Western Region.

After lunch we set out for Bezeklik. 'The locals call it "the place with paintings",' Fat Ma said. It is one of the biggest Buddhist cave complexes in the Western Region, dating from the fifth century to the thirteenth century when Islam became the dominant religion in the area. Originally built by monks for meditating in a quiet valley, it soon became a famous centre of worship for lay followers, and the travellers of the Silk Road, who would pray for a safe journey by making offerings to the images of the Buddhas and Bodhisattvas.

Xuanzang did not mention it in his record but Fat Ma was absolutely certain that he visited it. 'It was just over twenty kilometres from Gaochang city,' he said, 'and it would have taken only an hour or two on horseback. The king was so keen to impress Xuanzang, I'm sure he would grab any opportunity to persuade the monk to stay. Judging from the pictures of the murals, it must have been a splendid place.'

I also had seen pictures of the Bezeklik murals and they looked spectacular. Larger than life-size, they were painted in meticulous detail and exuberant colours and seemed as if they had been finished yesterday. Kings and queens, princes and princesses, Indian monks, Persian and Roman traders stood piously in their best costumes on the side walls, facing the altar where the image of the Buddha would be. Their names were written by their heads: they were the donors who had paid for the caves and the splendid paintings. Those murals were mostly painted after Xuanzang's time, but a Tang dynasty record of Gaochang gives us a vivid account of Bezeklik, which it called Ningrong Cave Monastery. This is undoubtedly the Bezeklik Xuanzang would have seen. 'Everywhere you look, there are mountains. Long, open corridors connect the monastery and the caves, with a clear stream running rapidly down below. Tall trees, morning mist and clouds make them invisible at first sight. This monastery has been known for a long time.'

We reached the valley quickly. The mountain is stark, barren and bald. I could hear the sound of water gushing at the bottom of the gully although I could not see it. We were picking our way over a rocky road more suitable for goats than cars when suddenly it opened up to a wide space where half a dozen cars were parked. I rushed to get out; Fat Ma made no move.

'I think I'll wait for you here,' he said. 'The thing with Bezeklik is: if you don't see it, you will regret it; after you've seen it, you'll regret it even more. Go and find out for yourself.'

The caves were indeed a terrible letdown, even with Fat Ma's warning. Gone were the fantastic murals, the pictures of which I so loved. The majority of the fifty-odd caves were barred over, like a zoo without animals; the 'good' ones were virtually bare, just here and there a faint trace of a mural, a featureless Buddha, or a broken flower petal. All I could see clearly were the chisel marks made by the German explorer Albert von Le Coq and his colleagues as they divested the caves of their treasures to take them back to Europe.

In the nineteenth and early twentieth century Bezeklik and other treasures of Xinjiang became the target of frenzied international exploration. This was the age of adventure. As one scholar put it, 'No heroes stood taller in the Victorian pantheon than explorers. These explorers were the dashing film stars of the imperial era. Tinting unknown lands on a nation's map became the embodiment of cultural virility. Plants, animals, falls, rivers, and even entire mountain ranges were named for these peerless travellers. Museums and galleries vied to display their collections. Readers never seemed to have enough books about these far-flung places.'

In Xinjiang, it all started as part of a broader geo-political rivalry between the British in India and Russia's ambitions to the east. But no big power wanted to be left out of the glory, so for almost half a century, adventurers and explorers – Russian, British, Swedish, German, French, Japanese and American – raced against each other to unearth the antiquities of a lost and immensely rich civilization, buried under the sands of the Taklamakan Desert and untouched for more than a millennium. The chase, often with Xuanzang's record as their guide, was all the more intense because of the Greco-Roman origins of many of the treasures – almost as if that made them theirs to despoil. And they were not disappointed. Their finds, measured in tons and thousands of camel loads, have filled major museums around the world and reveal the glorious past of Buddhist history.

The Germans carved out Turfan, Karashar, Kucha and Tumshuq, the major oases on the northern route of the Silk Road, as their sphere of influence. Their man was Albert von Le Coq, who spoke several oriental languages and worked for the Berlin Ethnographic Museum. He and his assistant spent two years from 1904 to 1906 combing through all the ancient sites of Turfan, which were mostly ruins or buried by sand. They heard about Bezeklik from a shepherd and found the caves filled to the ceiling with sand. They were overcome by the murals once they removed the sand: 'If we could secure these pictures,' Le Coq wrote in *Buried Treasures of Chinese Turkestan*, the record of his explorations, 'the success of the expedition was assured.' With a hammer, a chisel, a knife and a fox-tail saw, he and his assistant managed to remove all the best-preserved murals of Bezeklik, which filled 103 huge trunks, each weighing well over a hundred kilograms. After twenty months of travelling they arrived safely in Berlin, where they occupied an entire room of the museum. 'This is one of the few temples whose sum-total of paintings has been brought to Berlin,' he wrote with a great deal of satisfaction. Moreover, he thought he was doing the Chinese a favour by his crude archaeological theft. 'It cannot be too often emphasized that it is solely due to European archaeologists that any of the Buddhist treasures of Turkestan have been saved.' He would never have suspected the Berlin Ethnographic Museum would be the graveyard for these precious objects. After surviving for more than 1,500 years in the desert, most of the murals were reduced to ashes in the bombing of Berlin in 1945. Only photographs remain.

I was in and out of the caves in twenty minutes. I was not the only unhappy visitor. A woman in high-heeled shoes and a long black velvet dress was blaming her partner loudly: 'I'm baking hot. It's all your fault. I told you we should have gone to the bazaar . . .' When I got back to the car, I was complaining to Fat Ma about the destruction by the barbarians.

'It wasn't just the Germans,' he said, 'a friend of mine did his bit too.'

'What? Your friends helped the Germans?'

'No, it is a different story.'

There were still a few murals in some of the caves a decade ago. His friend and five other amateur archaeologists were told to clean them with soap and water. After the grime and mud were washed away, his friend saw a lovely face of the Buddha. He worked very hard for several days to clean the rest of the murals, Fat Ma explained, his voice falling almost to a whisper, as if he were afraid he would be overheard. But in a few days the cleaned murals began to crack and disintegrate; in no time they were gone. The cleaning had washed away the glue that held the pigments together. What had stood for so long and survived various depredations was finally destroyed by the ignorance of good intentions.

It was a sad story, and it matched my disappointment with the caves. Fat Ma tried to cheer me up. 'Come on, lighten up. You're going to see something really interesting. Promise.'

Barely two hundred yards from the caves, by the side of the narrow road, stood a grinning monkey, bright yellow and made of clay, and a pantheon of other characters from the novel – the gluttonous piggy, the novice, a red demon, a crab, a fox and of course the venerable Xuanzang on his white horse. They were crudely made and painted in day-glo colours. I had not noticed them before because I was looking for the water I could hear but not see. There was a terracotta dome in the background and on top of it the Islamic symbol of the crescent moon, presumably to appeal to the local Muslim population as well as tourists. The backdrop of the whole site was the red rock of the Flaming Mountain. 'This theme park is for visitors so they can relive the myths of *The Monkey King*,' said Fat Ma enviously, no doubt regretting that he had not come up with this enterprising idea. Two young men seemed to be enjoying themselves: for 30 pence each, they put their faces through cardboard versions of the Monkey King and Xuanzang, and then had their photos taken. For a pound, they could be the monkey, putting on a mask and a bright yellow martial-arts costume, with a walking stick for his cudgel. If the pilgrim himself took their fancy, they could put on a monk's robe and get up on a real white horse.

I stood surveying the scene, a little shocked that the government had given permission for a theme park to be built so close to a grade-one listed ancient site. Turfan is not exactly crowded – it is as big as Ireland – and most of it is desert. They could have built this garish entertainment anywhere. But Fat Ma said, 'I would have chosen this spot too. It's near the famous site, many people come this way. And after the disappointing caves, why not have some fun?'

'They have the Flaming Mountain,' I said.

'That's where we are going next,' he replied.

In *The Monkey King*, the Flaming Mountain bars Xuanzang's way: for hundreds of miles around it everything is on fire and nothing can grow. To cross it, he has to borrow the magic fan from the princess of the Iron Fan. Waved once, the fan puts out fire; twice, it raises a wind; and the third time, it brings on rain and makes everything flourish. The local people have to sacrifice a child every year to appease the evil princess and borrow her fan for planting and watering their crops. Naturally the princess will not lend it to the monk. So the monkey uses his magic and turns himself into a tiny insect, gets into her stomach and makes trouble there. She is forced to give him a fan, but it is a fake one which shoots up flames almost engulfing the sky. He then pretends to be her husband and takes the fan from their marital bed, but without the right spell. A whirlwind blows him ten thousand miles away like a fallen leaf. He is lucky the third time, with the help of a host of celestial spirits. He puts out the fire and returns the fan to the princess, who now promises to use it for everyone's good. The monkey gathers their packs, saddles the white horse for Xuanzang, and they cross the Flaming Mountain without flames.

The real Xuanzang could not have avoided the Flaming Mountain when he was in Gaochang. It was the most striking feature of this oasis kingdom and it was right on the Silk Road. Just as Fat Ma and I were discussing it, I saw spiky rocks on the horizon. They grew taller, rising inexorably. They almost seemed to throb with their curious red as we drove nearer. I had read about the Flaming Mountain so many times and seen many pictures of it, but still I was amazed at its grandeur. The steep sides are criss-crossed with deep gullies of dark red stone; the mountain-tops make hectic zigzags against the blue sky. Under the blazing sun, it really does seem ready to burst into flames. It made me realize why it was the perfect backdrop for one of the most dramatic episodes in *The Monkey King*, firing the author's imagination, mine and that of everyone who has read the novel throughout the centuries.

I decided to have my photo taken with the Flaming Mountain in the background. I could not return empty-handed from the land of my childhood dream that had been burning in my head for the past thirty years. But Fat Ma said no. I thought he did not want to get out of the jeep in the scorching sun, so we drove on. After another fifteen minutes, we left the main road, cruising on the gravel towards the foot of the mountain. Suddenly we screeched to a stop. 'Photo time now!' he declared proudly. 'I have searched the whole mountain from end to end: this is the ideal spot.' I thought it was very considerate of him to do it just for me but it turned out to be a more serious business matter. In Turfan as in the rest of China in the reform era, everything is about money. Fat Ma said they were having a Flaming Mountain fever right now – half a million people had visited Turfan the year before. 'We should put a billboard on the road, saying "Ideal Photo Spot for the Flaming Mountain",' he said excitedly. 'We will have a guard and charge fifty pence per photo. We will make a fortune.' He seemed to be intoxicated by his dream of riches – or maybe it was just the heat.

Before I read Xuanzang's biography the only thing I knew of him in Turfan was the Flaming Mountain story – and this is still true for most Chinese. I had no idea that it was here in Turfan that the real Xuanzang, by his courage and determination, gave his pilgrimage a solid chance of success. He arrived here penniless, with a warrant over his head, far from certain that he could survive the journey. Now he could carry on with every hope of fulfilling his dream. The king of Gaochang provided him with everything he would need: clothes to suit all weathers, one hundred ounces of gold and three piles of silver pieces, and five hundred rolls of satin and taffeta as donations to major monasteries. He was also given thirty horses, twenty-four servants and five monks to look after him as far as India and back. But most important of all, the king wrote state letters to be presented to the twenty-four different kingdoms along the way. In particular, he asked the Great Khan of the Western Turks, who controlled the whole of Central Asia at the time, to protect the Chinese monk. Xuanzang wrote these words that expressed all the elegance of his mind and his depth of feeling:

> For all these favours, I feel ashamed of myself and do not know how to express my gratitude. Even the overflow of the Jiaohe River does not compare with your kindness, and your favour is weightier than the Pamir Mountains. Now I have no more worries for my journey ... If I succeed in my purpose, to what shall I owe my achievements? To nothing but the king's favour.

The contrast between fiction and reality could not be greater.

The Monkey King has hidden the real Xuanzang, but the fiction has an important role to play. Life for most people in China had always been oppressive. They were subjugated by hardship and tyranny and *The Monkey King* was cathartic, not just as a rich and colourful fantasy world, but as the story of a maverick spirit who symbolized what we could only dream of: rebellion. It was sheer magic. The thrill of reading it for the first time is still with me.

But it had another significance: it carried any number of Buddhist messages. I remember Grandmother trying to explain some of them to me. She said although the monkey could fly up to Heaven and dive into hell, slay dragons and subdue demons, he could also be arrogant, jealous, angry, greedy, selfish and harmful. That was why Guanyin gave him another name, *Wukong*, meaning 'Understanding Emptiness'. Guanyin hoped the monkey would come to appreciate the limits of his power and the vanity of life. We even had a saying: 'Mighty the monkey may be, but even with his 180,000-league jump, he can never escape from the palm of the Buddha.' The monk, on the other hand, was kind, loving, selfless and compassionate. He had the Way – that was the secret of his power over the mighty monkey whom he kept under control simply by reciting the Heart Sutra. It did not make sense to me at the time. Now I can see what Grandmother meant. In fact, the last sentences of *The Monkey King*, which I had not taken in before, make it very clear: 'I dedicate this work to the glory of Buddha's Pure Land. May it repay the kindness of patron and preceptor, may it mitigate the sufferings of the lost and damned. May all who read it or hear it read find their hearts turned towards Truth, and in the end be born again in the Realms of Utter Bliss.'

There was one more thing I wanted to see in Turfan: the archaeological museum. Before I visited it the next morning, I took a walk around the old part of the city. It was pleasant, still full of traditional courtyards, each under its canopy of vine-hung trellises. The inhabitants sat under the vines, enjoying the shade, and the cool of the damp earth that they frequently spray with water. There is a central bazaar, with Uighur women in their bright printed dresses and old men in their skull caps tending the stalls. They sell a huge variety of fruits, fresh as well as dried. Visitors stock up with them, not because they will not be able to buy more on their journeys but because the fruits are so sweet – the result of all the sun and the pure oasis water.

The new part of Turfan, unlike most Chinese cities, is

spacious and clean, with wide streets planted with trees. The museum is located in a quiet corner. The collection here testifies to the vast wealth accumulated by a Silk Road oasis kingdom over two thousand years. It is a goldmine: silk brocades, figurines of foreign merchants, the travel documents they carried, murals, scroll paintings and Buddhist scriptures, even desiccated bread and cakes – many from Xuanzang's time. There is also a segment of Xuanzang's *Record of the Western Regions*, believed by scholars to have been a gift from his disciples to the descendants of King Qu Wentai.

A rich hoard, but perhaps the shortage of funds makes it impossible for them to do a proper job about the exhibits. The rooms are dark and gloomy and the dusty display cases look like antiques themselves. The exhibits progress chronologically: on the ground floor from the neolithic age, to stone, bronze, primitive, feudal societies, and a collection of blackened mummies on the first floor.

The mummies are behind glass. In any museum in Europe, they would be a sensation. But the room is humid and hot, and they have mostly darkened as if they came from Africa. But they are in fact Caucasian, as you can see from one woman's hair, a golden, straw colour. She is from a people believed by many scholars to be the earliest residents of the Taklamakan Desert, going back to 2000 BC. But why and how they came here, to one of the most inhospitable places on earth, nobody is sure. Fat Ma told me there was one mummy of a man who had actually met Xuanzang, but it had been shipped to Urumqi, the capital city of the region, some eight hundred miles away. This was General Zhangxiong. He had been a magnificent man, almost six feet tall and barrel-chested as befits a great warrior. The stele in his tomb said that he was the commander-in-chief of King Qu Wentai's army. He would have been ordered by the king to go and listen to the pilgrim's teaching; also the king had insisted that his entire court come with him to say goodbye to Xuanzang. They rode with him for several miles. General Zhangxiong died in 633, six years after Xuanzang's departure from Gaochang.

While I was looking at the precious objects behind the dusty glass, I could not help thinking that if Xuanzang had his proper place in history as a great national hero, his experience here in Turfan would have made him the focal point in the museum. They could re-create the rich culture of a lost oasis kingdom on the Silk Road and weave in the story of Xuanzang's dramatic experience here. It could be as absorbing as the theme park: it might even surprise the visitors and give them something really valuable, and true, to remember. Instead we seem to value him less today than the king did. As Hui Li tells us: 'On the day of departure, the king and the monks, the ministers and commoners – everyone came out to see the Master off. The king embraced him with tears, while the monks and laymen all felt sad. Their cries resounded in the desert sky.'

FOUR

Exile and Exotica

TURFAN STATION is a lonely point in the silence of the desert. It looks more like a place to be stranded than somewhere you could leave from. The sun had set, and the cool of twilight replaced the day's burning heat. This was the most pleasant time for the Silk Road merchants to travel, but not the safest. My train was standing there; I thought I was late and scrambled on to it. From inside, I saw the silhouettes of a number of armed policemen.

The train was for Korla; from there it would be another four hours by car to Kucha, where Xuanzang stayed for over two months. Before I had time to warm up my seat, the ticket collector came to check our identity cards and passports, asking where I got on and where I would disembark. A transport policeman burst in ten minutes later and demanded to see our documents again. He stared at me for some time and then made a comparison with my passport photograph.

'Are you looking for criminals on the run?' I joked with him.

'What criminals? It's my job,' he said gravely. Before he left he turned to me: 'Please look after your belongings carefully. If you have a lock, please lock your luggage to the legs of the beds or the table. If not, please put everything under your pillow.'

I thanked him. It was strange that he made so much fuss, but it was better to be safe.

I looked at the Uighur couple sitting opposite me. The man threw up his arms, shrugged his shoulders, and returned to his conversation in Uighur, which I did not understand. I felt like an intruder and decided to leave them alone until bedtime. I walked along the corridor, from one carriage to another, till I could go no further. The door was locked and a dark blue curtain was drawn over the glass of the next carriage door. A Chinese man was smoking in the corridor and I asked him if there were some VIPs in there – the security arrangements seemed unnecessarily tight for mere mortals. He laughed: 'You don't live in Xinjiang, do you? You are sharing this ride with criminals on their way to labour camp. When you got on the train didn't you notice the windows in some of the carriages had their curtains drawn?'

Xuanzang could have done with more security for this leg of his journey. He no longer needed to worry about being dis-covered – he was in the Western Region, outside Tang territory and beyond the control of the emperor. King Qu Wentai had equipped him as a royal envoy, opening all doors for him. But bandits, the biggest threat to the Silk Road caravans, lurked around every corner. Shortly after leaving Gaochang, Xuan-zang and his men were stopped by a group of robbers, who were fortunately content with just a share of their supplies. But the scores of foreign merchants in his company were not so lucky: they set out in the middle of the night to cover more ground and when he caught up with them in the morning, he saw their bodies scattered, the sand underneath soaked with blood, their riches gone. They had travelled barely three miles. Hui Li says that Xuanzang was 'deeply affected' by the incident, and made sure they stayed off the road at night after that.

Xinjiang has more robbers and criminals today – but they are behind bars. When China finally brought the region under control in the eighteenth century, it immediately became the most important place of exile. Too many executions would reduce the legitimacy of the emperor; after all, he was supposed to rule with the mandate of Heaven. Banishment demonstrated benevolence and provided the new frontier with manpower. Furthest from the capital, and shielded on three sides by impassable mountains and a huge, hostile desert, Xinjiang was ideal for the purpose. It was where serious offenders from all over the country were sent – political dissidents, disgraced officials and scholars, rebels of all religious sects and murderers. It was China's Siberia. We used it like the British who transported their prisoners to Australia.

The Communist government inherited much of the practice of its dynastic predecessors. Each political campaign – and there were quite a few – created a wave of prisoners, many of whom ended in labour camps in Xinjiang. Periodic crackdowns on crime, together with a regular stream of serious offenders, added to their numbers. In the old days, criminals were treated like slaves. No matter how hard they worked, they could never redeem themselves. They were not allowed to leave Xinjiang even after they finished their sentences, and their descendants made up a large proportion of the ethnic Chinese population in the region. Banished officials were dealt with more leniently: no one was sure whether the emperor might not one day realize the wisdom of their criticisms and call them back. Writing about exile has long been a genre in Chinese literature, and thrillers involving the police and escaped convicts from Xinjiang are a new source of entertainment in movies and television dramas. But it was something much closer to home that I had always associated with Xinjiang – my aunt.

My aunt, Father's sister, came to Xinjiang in 1952. She had seen pictures of it at a government recruiting fair in her village. She said it looked like heaven on earth: under the crystal blue sky, cows and sheep roamed on the endless grasslands; water from the melting snows irrigated fertile land; grapes and melons were as sweet as the handsome Uighur boys and girls. She was also promised a place in a factory. My paternal grandfather was horrified and pleaded with her not to go: 'No one in their right mind would want to go there. That's where they send prisoners.' But she would not listen to his pleas. She did not want to stay in the village all her life; Xinjiang was her ticket to freedom and a passport to the world. One night she left secretly, without telling her parents.

My earliest thought of my aunt was the belief that she lived somewhere beyond the moon. It came from a repeated threat from my parents whenever I misbehaved: 'If you are naughty again, we will send you to join your aunt. You will never see us any more!' When I learned to write, I was encouraged to correspond with her and her family. I was told not to mention our life – it would make them homesick. I simply reiterated how much we missed them and always ended the letter by saying 'we hope to see you some day'. I soon began to realize that day was far away. Mother said the journey would take seven days by train and another day by bus. Neither family could afford the fares but I never stopped repeating my hope until at last my aunt, uncle and their four children came to see us in 1980, after saving up for years. My father and I visited them in 1982. For the rest of the time, letters kept us close.

We also had an annual ritual. Every Chinese New Year, our family would have a group photo taken with all of us grinning madly. We would put it in a parcel with sweets, peanuts, a long letter, a small sum of money, and sometimes a luxury like a radio. My mother still performs it after forty years: 'It is our way of saying we have not abandoned her.'

Before I began my journey, my mother prepared another package, with the most recent photograph of the family, a letter, and a bottle of whisky for my uncle. I felt divided about seeing my aunt, who now lived in Korla. I could not wait to spend some time with her and the family after all these years. But I also dreaded the waves of emotion that my coming would evoke. Aunt and Uncle were retired now, and could think of nothing but their desire to come back home. As the Chinese say, falling leaves return to their roots. It would all pour out. And they would be worried about where I was going and want to come with me. I decided, hard though it was, to wait till I came back from Kucha before I called them.

I did have someone else to look up in Korla; a professor of Islamic studies in Beijing had recommended him to me as a guide and interpreter. The Chinese have this saying: 'Rely on your parents when you are at home; rely on friends when you are travelling.' Xuanzang used a different system: he had the monasteries. Wherever there was a Buddhist monastery – and there were plenty on the Silk Road in his day – he would find food, lodging and the information he needed.

Salim was waiting for me at the station early next morning, ready with his overnight backpack. He held up my name on a piece of paper – I appreciated his giving up the whole day for me. 'Please don't mention it,' he said in a friendly way. 'I have always wanted to see those wonderful caves in Kucha myself. Now you are giving me the opportunity. I can also practise my English.' Salim was a schoolteacher. I could not tell his age: he had dark hair and a short beard, and a somewhat resigned look, but he spoke warmly.

A Uighur driver was waiting for us at the taxi rank. Salim gave him directions in Uighur and in no time I found myself in the centre of a brand-new city, with wide boulevards, grand government buildings and smart high-rise apartment blocks. It was not what I had expected: it was like a prosperous metropolis on the coast, modern and full of promise, not a city in the desert, thousands of miles from the sea. There was no characteristic Islamic architecture in sight, nor many Uighurs.

We were driving slowly on a narrow tarmac road in the country, our taxi jostling with large flocks of sheep, donkey carts driven by old men, and trucks with heavy loads. Tall poplars shaded the road; the fields on both sides were green with orchards. We were back on the Silk Road, the route Xuanzang would have travelled on to Kucha. I was curious to know what Salim thought of Xuanzang.

'After you told me what you were doing, I bought a copy of your monk's book and glanced through it. I want to be a proper guide, you know.

'I think Xuanzang was first and foremost a Han Chinese, and then a Buddhist monk.' He looked at me to make his point. 'Although he was a great master, he did not treat people as equals. If you read his descriptions carefully, they were not exactly flattering about us nomads, especially those who were not Buddhists. He described them as violent, greedy and vulgar-looking. Anyway his book was as much military information as a pilgrim's account.

'Let's take Kucha for example. Xuanzang said the country was very big, in fact the biggest oasis in the Western Region,

with mild weather all year round. The soil was good for growing millet and wheat, rice, pears, peaches and apricots. It was
rich in gold, copper, iron and lead. Monks did not need this
information. It was for the Chinese army. In fact, it says in
the preface that the book was written at the request of the
emperor.'

That was an interesting take on Xuanzang, one I had never
heard before. Salim had done his homework very thoroughly.
Emperor Taizong, the very emperor who forbade Xuanzang
to leave, did ask him on his return to write down in detail
what he had seen and heard of the countries he travelled
through. The result was the *Record of the Western Regions*,
mostly about Buddhism but with many passages of no obvious
interest to pilgrims. I had not thought about it that way, but
I could see Salim's point: the information could be very useful
for imperial expansion, which was exactly what the emperor
had in mind.

Still, what impressed Xuanzang about Kucha, or Qiuzi as
it was called then, was its flourishing Buddhist community.
He tells us there were over one hundred monasteries, with
five thousand monks who were all very diligent in their studies.
A large number of them turned out to greet him. They put
up tents outside the city, with Buddhist statues in them. They
played their drums and cymbals and chanted as he approached,
and gave him flowers to offer to the Buddhas. It took him
until sunset to go around all the tents, receiving the monks'
homage. He must have regretted missing the biggest celebra-
tion of the year at the autumnal equinox. The monks told
him how they decorated their statues with silk and precious
stones and paraded them on carriages through the city, drawing thousands of people to watch. They assembled with monks
from all over the country outside the Western Gate in front

of two giant images of the Buddha, ninety feet high. They stayed there for several weeks and the king and all the people came out to fast, and to listen to great masters preaching. Xuanzang would no doubt want to consult the masters himself.

My first sight of Kucha was a single long empty street lined with shopfronts that seemed to be clones of each other: they were all decorated with shiny white tiles reflecting the glaring desert sun, hardly enticing for customers. There was not a single tree in sight. The Uighurs always planted trees anywhere they moved into. But this was a settlement for the Han Chinese, with everything copied from China proper, no thought given to local culture.

My heart sank. 'Sadly all the towns and cities in Xinjiang are like this, as if they had been built to the same plan,' Salim said, observing the disappointment on my face. 'Xuanzang would not have recognized this place. It used to be rich, fertile and independent. Now it is full of criminals, nuclear waste and Han Chinese migrant workers. Even when I was small, I remember I could pick wild fruit in the city. An open water conduit ran in front of our house directly from the mountains. Now the water is drying up; the desert is swallowing the oases; and I haven't heard birds singing for a long time – there is so little forest left. It's nature telling us there are too many people here.'

The relations between the Chinese and the Uighurs were quite different in Xuanzang's time. The Uighurs were much feared, admired and needed by the Chinese. Their constant threat to the Chinese apart, they actually came to our rescue when our capital, Chang'an, was sacked by the Tibetans in the eighth century. But perhaps they may still regret, even to this day, their decision to supply China with the means for their own defeat. The Chinese had realized the significance of horses since the first century BC. Their paramount importance was stated very clearly in the *Tang Annals*, the record of the Tang dynasty: 'Horses are the military preparedness of the state; if Heaven takes them away, the state will totter to a fall.' In exchange for horses, the Chinese court was obliged to humble itself in many ways, not least by giving large quantities of silk as gifts. For a dowry of fifty thousand horses, a royal princess could be married off to a Turkic prince.

But it was the Uighurs who controlled the horse trade. They regularly brought herds of thousands of ponies to the Chinese frontier and charged an exorbitant forty bolts of silk for a pony worth only one bolt. One year they sent a special agent with ten thousand horses for sale, many decrepit and old. Their price was more than the annual income of the government from taxes. The emperor thought long and hard, and finally took six thousand of them. He tolerated this unequal trade and referred to it in the euphemism of 'Uighur tributes to the court', but it was really their way of paying back the Uighurs for their assistance against the Tibetans, and, more importantly, buying time for their own military preparations. Steadily the cavalry of the Tang dynasty was built up from a few thousand horses to over one million, crucial for the expansion of the Tang empire, and for keeping the nomadic marauders at bay.

Throughout our conversation, Salim was speaking slowly and forcefully from the front seat, occasionally turning to me to get his points across. His profile was that of a typical Uighur man: thick eyebrows, big eyes in deep sockets, straight nose, with a haughty expression. Uighur men were much admired in Xuanzang's time by Chinese women; the women rode about the streets of Chang'an wearing Turkish caps and men's riding clothes and boots. A Tang emperor had to pass an edict forbidding the Uighurs in Chang'an to 'lure' Chinese women into becoming their wives or concubines. I told Salim that. He did not find it amusing. 'Very few Uighur men would dare to do it today, even with no emperor to disapprove. They would be ostracized by their own people.'

How about his coming on this trip with me?

'Oh, there are plenty of unemployed Uighur men looking for jobs,' Salim said seriously. 'They would think I am your guide, interpreter or even bodyguard. I can tell you that not many Chinese women dare to travel on their own in Xinjiang today. It is not safe.'

Then he asked for my guidebook. 'Let's see what it says about Kucha. "Population: thirty thousand", perhaps a third of what it was in Xuanzang's time, three-quarters being Uighurs. "Religion: Islam", with three big mosques in the old town, but six Buddhist sites. "Climate: mild with no rain", the same as in the Tang dynasty, but I think it is getting worse. "Local specialities: Kucha women and music", inherited from at least your monk's days, if not earlier.' I laughed – he was copying the way Xuanzang described Kucha in the *Record*. 'Don't worry. We will find Xuanzang's Kucha,' Salim said confidently, 'on the walls of the Kizil Caves.'

'I hope so,' I said, but I was not so sure now.

After finding a hotel for the night and eating a quick lunch in its restaurant, we headed off for the Kizil Caves, an hour's drive away. The car stopped at the edge of a welcoming stretch of green oasis. From there a rough path wound through bushes and trees, towards the mountain. At its foot a cluster of poplars shades the Kizil Research Institute. Beyond it, the caves, dozens of them, hang from the huge, rugged rock face. Kizil means red in the Uighur language, and in the midday sun it was almost glowing. Xuanzang did not mention the caves – we do not even know what they were called back then. But he must have seen them. This is the oldest Buddhist cave site in China, and in his time, the biggest in the Western Region. They date from the third to the ninth century, and the peak of activity was in the sixth and seventh centuries, just when he was in Kucha. Hui Li tells us he spent some time visiting the sights in and out of the capital.

But what would have moved him most about Kucha was that it was the birthplace of his great hero and his inspiration, Kumarajiva. Xuanzang had learned Buddhism from Kumarajiva's translations of the sutras, as many monks in China still do, alongside his own. Born to an Indian father and the royal princess of Kucha, Kumarajiva went at the age of seven to Kashmir, the centre of learning of his time, to study Sanskrit and Buddhism. After he returned to Kucha his reputation became such that when a Chinese army attacked in 385 AD, the order was to bring him back to China alive. The Chinese emperor admired him so much that he surrounded Kumarajiva with beautiful and intelligent women so they could produce his heirs. He spent the rest of his life in Liangzhou and then in Chang'an, translating the sutras into Chinese, with the help of the hundreds of monks assigned to him. He did more than anyone else before Xuanzang to propagate the teachings of the Buddha in China. Before he died, he told his disciples: 'Accept my work but do not take my life as an ideal. The lotus grows from the mud. Love the lotus but not the mud.'

Near the entrance to the institute stood a bronze statue of Kumarajiva, in the posture of Rodin's *Thinker*. While I was pondering his extraordinary life and how he inspired Xuanzang, Salim was buying our entry tickets. He returned with a young man called Jia who would be our guide. After a very brief exchange and an offer of cigarettes, Salim discovered they had both studied at Xinjiang University. He asked Jia to show us the caves with the best frescoes from Xuanzang's time. 'The best are in Berlin,' he told us apologetically. 'The Germans spent a lot of time in Kucha from 1902 to 1914 and took the best murals away.' The chief perpetrator, Albert von Le Coq, was more than happy with his spoils in Kucha. In *The Buried Treasures of Chinese Turkestan*, he wrote: 'Everywhere we found fresh, untouched temples, full of the most interesting and artistically perfect paintings. The daily recurring surprises gave us such pleasure that we could smile at all life's annoyances.'

'But I will do my best,' Jia said. He told us to follow him up a flight of stairs and then a steep hill. We stopped in front of Cave 205. It was dark inside and I could hardly see a thing. After our eyes adjusted to the darkness, we found ourselves staring at a blank wall.

'What is this about?' Salim asked.

'You might have seen this photo already.' Jia took out a booklet from his pocket and a torch, which he shone on the cover. 'This mural used to be right here, in this cave. The German stole it,' Jia said. The photograph showed a royal couple in the company of a monk. They are extravagantly dressed in gold and green robes. The woman has an ornate head-dress and the man what seems like a halo around his head. They have dark hair and round faces, with cheerful and benign expressions, looking to their left, with their heads slightly lowered. She is holding out the palm of her hand, more in pleasure than in blessing. 'We think they were the king and queen of Kucha from Xuanzang's era. Look at them. Don't you think they could be greeting a distinguished guest from afar, like your pilgrim himself?'

Xuanzang said that the king and queen turned out with the

country's monks to greet him and organized a welcoming banquet in the palace the next day. He felt honoured, but he did not think highly of his host. He tells us that the king was weak, a mere puppet of his powerful ministers, who realized that the Chinese empire was getting more powerful by the day and that it would be wise to keep their easterly neighbour happy. They wanted to find out more about the new Emperor Taizong from the Chinese monk. The last time the Chinese army took Kucha, they needed 20,000 camels and 10,000 horses to take the loot home. After meeting Xuanzang, the king sent a tribute of excellent horses to the Chinese court, hoping to placate the Chinese.

At the banquet, the king and queen must have entertained their important guest with the music for which Kucha was renowned along the Silk Road, from Chang'an to Samarkand. For centuries, thousands of Kuchean musicians and dancers dominated musical life at the Chinese court, introducing their melodies and exotic instruments: the lute, the harp and the long-necked drum. We even have the names of the tunes that might have been played to Xuanzang: 'South India', 'Music of Kucha', and 'Watching the Moon in Brahman Land'.

But was music not more appropriate for royalty than for a monk? The Kucheans did not think so. They worshipped the Buddha with music and dance, the means of expression they knew best. The Buddha said music softens people's hearts and puts them in a more receptive mood for the Dharma. No other people of the Silk Road elevated music to such prominence in their worship. Jia told us that the majority of the Kizil Caves had apsaras, heavenly beings, playing musical instruments while the Buddha was preaching or meditating. He showed us a particularly beautiful one on the rear ceiling of Cave 69. The apsara is soaring through the air, playing a lute. His torso is bare and his legs are covered with a swirling sarong. A green scarf, twined around his neck and arms, floats with him as though he is flying fast but effortlessly through the air. He is the very symbol of grace.

Looking up at these heavenly creatures, I thought of the object that to me expresses most vividly the ancient Kucheans' love of music: a reliquary box which I had seen in the National Museum in Tokyo. On the lid are four angels with wings, ready to take off; on the side musicians are playing all sorts of instruments: a harp, a drum, a flute, a horn and a lute, while other masked figures are dancing energetically. Only the Kucheans and their monks loved music so much that they wanted it to accompany them to their next life. No wonder Xuanzang singled out the Kucheans for their musical talents, of all the peoples he travelled among.

When we came out of Cave 69, Salim was humming. He seemed happier than in the morning. 'I've heard so much about Kizil. I don't know why I didn't come here earlier. They are amazing,' he enthused. 'You know the people of Kucha today are still the best singers and dancers. Their voices are beautiful like larks singing; their whirlwind dances make you feel dizzy just watching them. Every Uighur can sing and dance at the drop of a hat, but no one does it as well as the men and women of Kucha. It must be in their genes.'

I was glad Salim was enjoying Kizil as much as I was, even though many caves were stripped of their beautiful murals or spattered with mud thrown by devout Muslims long ago. What were preserved best were animals, which we found in almost every cave we had visited: swans, geese, tigers, elephants, lions, monkeys, dogs, bears, pigeons and many more creatures. Jia said Xuanzang would not have seen so many animals in any other cave site. It was unique to Kizil because the Kucheans followed Hinayana Buddhism, as Xuanzang noted in his *Record*.

A Kuchean monk sought individual salvation through his own efforts, as people still do in Burma, Sri Lanka and Thailand; his ideal was an Arhat, which means a worthy or passionless being. For him, the Buddha and an Arhat were human and if he followed their example, he could hope for enlightenment. It is difficult – many people find it impossible – but it is not beyond reach, if not in this life, perhaps in future lives. The Buddha said he became enlightened in this world because he had been preparing for it in his many previous lives, even when he was incarnate as an animal. The animal stories that tell of the Buddha's previous lives are called the Jatakas. They are really moral tales – many taken from Indian folklore – of generosity, discipline, renunciation, wisdom, perseverance, forbearance, truthfulness, determination, loving-kindness and equanimity: the ten transcendental virtues of an enlightened being. The animals on the walls of the Kizil Caves are not just beautiful images; they are objects of contemplation for monks who tried to cultivate those qualities, and of instruction for lay followers who could not read.

Xuanzang was very familiar with the Jataka stories – his *Record* is full of them. But unlike a Kuchean monk, he was a Mahayana Buddhist. For him, the Buddha and the Bodhisattvas are both human and divine, which was why he prayed fervently to the Bodhisattva Guanyin for help when he was in danger. He believed in universal salvation through the Bodhisattvas, the enlightened ones whose mission is to help others achieve enlightenment, because it is too difficult for many to achieve on their own. The Buddha is selfless, Xuanzang would have argued, and Buddhists cannot be concerned only with their own salvation and neglect the suffering masses. How can the enlightened beings not help those who are still groping in the dark? When he set out on his journey, he did not think merely of his own spiritual quest, otherwise he would not have needed to bring back all the sutras from India and devote the rest of his life to translating them into Chinese. The Bodhisattva is the Chinese Buddhist ideal; it was what Xuanzang strove for.

Despite his compassion and tolerance, Xuanzang had little patience for his fellow-Kuchean monks. He told them he was going to India to study the Mahayana texts, such as the *Yogasastra*. Mokshagupta, the most revered monk of Kucha, gave the Chinese master a piece of his mind on the Mahayana doctrine: 'What is the use of inquiring into these books which contain only erroneous opinions? These are works which the true disciples of the Buddha do not study.'

Xuanzang could not believe what he was hearing. 'The *Yogasastra*,' he cried, 'is the revelation of the Buddha Maitreya, and to call such a book heretical, do you not fear to be hurled into a bottomless abyss?' For once, Xuanzang lost his temper. The Buddha said there were 84,000 ways to learn his teaching, depending on the individual, but Xuanzang could not tolerate this Kuchean dissenter.

I know very little about Hinayana Buddhism, or Theravada as it is commonly known. It is not often mentioned in China, and when you do hear about it, it invariably has a pejorative meaning – as indicated by its name, the Smaller Vehicle, whereas Mahayana means the Greater Vehicle. I wanted to find out more about it. But Salim was not interested in doctrinal differences. He said I could read about them later on; he wanted to see more of the real people like the king and queen. 'Perhaps people who would even have met your monk or heard his preaching.'

We climbed up and down the hill, and many flights of stairs, and found ourselves face to face with a few gallant knights and elegant ladies. They were the portraits of those who paid for the caves to be carved out and painted. I was fascinated by the ladies. How splendid and harmonious the colours of their costumes were. The harsh desert wind and the ageing of thirteen hundred years had scarcely toned them down. Tight blue bodices with gilt borders, milky white jackets fitted tightly to the waist with large triangular lapels, soft olive-green tunics, long, billowing blue skirts striped with yellow trimmings. No wonder the women of Xuanzang's time followed their Kuchean sisters with acute attention: they were the vision of beauty whose tastes dictated the fashions of the day. Jia had been smitten with them, too. 'If they could step down from the wall, I would marry one of them right now,' he laughed. As a second best, he had a jacket made for his girlfriend exactly in the Kuchean fashion. 'She is so elegant and sexy in it. All her friends ask her where she bought it. Perhaps I should start a business,' he said proudly.

But Salim was more interested in the Kuchean men. He was particularly struck by a well-preserved portrait of a man standing with legs apart, balancing himself on the tips of his toes, and wearing a long coat drawn in at the waist by a metal belt from which his swords hang. His face is a perfect oval, with a long, straight nose and arched eyebrows; his hair is parted into two neat locks in the middle of the forehead, while the rest is brushed back to the nape of the neck and tied with a ribbon. He could have been a knight from medieval Europe – suitably humble, sincere and serene, holding a lamp as an offering to the Buddha.

'This is just the sort of man who would have come to hear Xuanzang preaching,' Jia said. 'He was a rich and fervent believer so he could afford to pay for a cave like this as a shrine hall for his family. They would pray or perform ceremonies here on big occasions.'

Salim walked up to the wall and stared long and hard at the face, as if pondering how to start a conversation. Then he turned around, positioned himself next to the portrait, with his legs apart just like the Kuchean knight.

'Don't we look alike?' he asked.

I had to confess that they looked like brothers, tall, and with big eyes and straight noses.

'Not really,' Jia said without hesitation. 'Look at his hair. It is red. Yours is black.'

'I could dye my hair red. Many people do nowadays,' Salim said. 'Hey, it is over a thousand years ago. Naturally some things change.'

'They spoke Tocharian, an Indo-European language; you speak Turkish,' he reminded Salim.

'Our ancestors spoke Tocharian, then Turkish. Now I can speak Chinese. Perhaps my children and grandchildren will only speak Chinese. Things change with time but I am still a Uighur.'

'Come on.' Jia was getting slightly impatient. 'You're different peoples. As we say, a bull cannot fuck a mare even if they are in love. Anyway, we came to Xinjiang long before you Uighurs did. How could these people be your ancestors?' He was indignant.

'Why not? You Chinese stuck to yourselves as you do now and these people married us, the newcomers.' Salim was equally adamant. He turned to me. 'Do you know the Loulan Beauty?'

It was discovered in 1980 in Loulan, an ancient oasis kingdom on the southern edge of the Taklamakan, now totally buried by sand. She really was a beauty, with big eyes and auburn hair underneath a hat decorated with a single feather. She has on a cape and a pair of leather boots, as if she is just about to embark on a hunting trip.

'The newspapers called her the "mother of our nation" and many people wrote songs about her,' Salim said. 'What did Xuanzang say about the Kucheans?'

'Xuanzang didn't write about their ethnic origins,' I said. Salim looked disappointed. Xuanzang probably thought it unimportant. The Western Region was so cosmopolitan: Kucha was a melting-pot where civilizations converged. Just as the Kucheans welcomed weary travellers from the desert, they embraced their ideas, cultures and faiths. Xuanzang would have met people of many nationalities, speaking different languages and practising many faiths. Now we are all too conscious of national identity, especially in Xinjiang, where there are tensions between the Uighurs and the Han Chinese. Still, I had been shocked by the mummies in Turfan Museum, and in Urumqi, including the Loulan Beauty, whom I had seen on an earlier visit. I could not believe for a moment they were discovered on Chinese territory: tall, blond or red-haired, some wearing woven fabrics that looked like Scottish tartans. I had always thought only nomads, the Huns, the Uighurs and the Han Chinese had occupied this harsh area.

Archaeologists and linguists, foreign and Chinese, have confirmed the mummies' Caucasian identity using the most comprehensive methods – skull and textile analysis, comparative studies of their languages and burial cultures, blood sampling, genetic fingerprinting and DNA. In fact, the greatest appeal of the Kuchean frescoes for Albert von Le Coq and other Western explorers was their European looks. It was as if they had come upon their own forebears from a long-lost time.

René Grousset, the great French orientalist, went so far as to claim that 'no spectacle in history is more moving when we reflect that we have here, before our very eyes, the last representatives of that Indo-European population of the Gobi, so curiously like us in race and aspect.'

Why did these Caucasians leave their homes and live in this inhospitable place? We are not sure how they disappeared in the tenth century either. The Kucheans in the murals are believed to be their descendants, speaking a common language, Tocharian. But Salim's ancestors did not arrive on the scene until the ninth century A D. Salim was perhaps right about the Uighurs absorbing the earlier inhabitants of the Taklamakan – I had seen quite a few of his fellow-people with golden hair and blue eyes. But the truth is that these elegant Kuchean knights and ladies, who impressed Xuanzang so much with their love of Buddhism, music and the good life, are an enigma.

Salim remained pensive on the way to Kumutura, the other famous but much less visited grotto twenty-five kilometres away. 'You're not still thinking of your white ancestors?' I prodded him gently.

He stubbed his cigarette out and threw it out of the window. 'I suppose it was a story I wanted to believe,' he said with a wry smile. I could understand. We would all like to choose our ancestors; but for him it was really important, part of a self-identity that suited the Uighurs' assertion of their difference within China. 'Let's forget the whole thing for now,' Salim said.

We parked our car next to the road, on the bank of the Weigan River. There was a dam and a reservoir there, with a building for the control works. A Han Chinese man emerged from it and we asked him the way. 'Why bother?' he said.

'There is nothing to see. You know, we even had to shut down the reservoir just for those empty caves. It's so stupid.'

Early Muslim converts, foreign explorers, the river and the reservoir – all have done irrevocable damage to the frescoes. Most of the hundred and ten caves are empty except for some figures on the ceilings. A caretaker, a stout old Uighur man, was busy moving sand out of the caves with a spade and a broom. 'It is not half as bad as flooding,' he said wearily, pointing his broom to a watermark almost a metre high. 'If they don't control the water from the dam, it will finish off all the pictures. It may be too late already.' We waited till he finished sweeping and then asked him if he could take us to the caves up in the mountains. 'You mean those rich guys who live in Cave 22?' he joked. 'I'm afraid it's not safe. The ceiling has been propped up with makeshift scaffolding.'

I had been looking forward to seeing this cave more than any other; the fresco on the ceiling of the cave is the jewel of Buddhist art in Kucha. Its reproductions are in every book on the subject. Thirteen Bodhisattvas stand in a circle on the petals of a giant lotus flower. The crowned Bodhisattvas are relaxed, with their upper bodies bare of clothes but richly adorned with rosaries, tassels, jewels and bracelets. I can never forget their little moustaches, like the Chinese character for 'eight', their dreamy, half-closed eyes and expressions of reflective contentment. The Kizil Caves have strong Indian influences: Bodhisattvas who look like Indian princes, and dancers who could have come straight from Indian temple carvings. But nothing could surpass this cave in its authenticity. It looks as if it was created by Indian craftsmen for a rich Indian patron who might have intended it for his family or for monks to pray and meditate in. If Xuanzang saw it, it would have filled him with yearning for India.

I was really disappointed not to see the cave. That evening Salim kindly took me to the old town to make a better end to my day. It was only a street away from the new part of Kucha, but it was as different as the lute from the drum, as Salim said. Here, houses were built of mud bricks, the same colour as the desert. The trees were drooping under a thick layer of dust. We passed a market where the last few stalls open were dispensing their remaining slices of melon, wilted vegetables and fly-infested slabs of mutton. Old men in white caps and long padded coats stood idly in clusters in the evening light. There was no traffic, except for one or two donkey carts and a few bicycles. It was a somnolent place whose best days were long past. But as we neared the night-stall area, we passed a courtyard and heard the sounds of music and shouting coming from inside.

'It's a wedding!' Salim said, a smile spreading on his face. 'Let's join them. You want to see the music-making talent of the Kucheans, don't you?'

'Is it OK?'

'Of course it's OK. We are a very hospitable people. You're with me.'

We entered an old courtyard big enough to hold several stately trees and still leave a lot of room. As usual in a Uighur dwelling, there was a trellis stretching from the rooftops to the trees, supporting fat bunches of grapes. Underneath this green canopy was a square, and around it carpets were spread where people sat, the bridal couple in the middle, women with children running about, men drinking and carousing, and great trays of nan bread, plates of mutton, melons, sweets and dried fruits. There was music playing, and dancers came on to the square. We were invited to come forward and join them. Salim made no effort to explain who I was, the only Han

Chinese in the crowd. People stared at first, but then they smiled, piled loads of food in front of me, and gestured for me to eat and enjoy.

The dance was soon in full swing, and the music rose in crescendo. The dancers wore long voluminous red dresses with black embroidered vests. As the speed of the drum and zither picked up, they twirled faster and faster; their skirts flew out and so, in an accompanying parabola, did the plaited hair under their small caps. I worried they were going to hurt their ankles – they were dancing on swept earth in high-heels. But on they went. The Kizil painters must have seen dancing like this: not just the instruments, which looked very similar to the ones depicted in the caves, but the swirling movements and poses of the dancers. And the man who played the zither had a face just like those in the murals, chubby, compact and handsome. It was as if the musicians on the walls of Kizil had stepped off into the wedding party. Salim was chatting with the men, laughing and gulping down bottles of beer.

For me, the day was closing with an extraordinary contrast: the Western Region as Xuanzang records it and the Kucha I had seen, and the Xinjiang I had grown up thinking of as the land of desolation and exile. I had not expected to find so rich a civilization bearing the influences of so many cultures. The caves were full of sensual apsaras, like those on the walls of Indian temples, dancing alluringly and trying in vain to seduce the Buddha. Knights on horseback in the armour of Sassanid Persia fought over the relics of the Buddha. Birds perching on tree branches, as you see in many Chinese paintings, decorated the borders of the frescoes. In one cave the Greek sun god and moon goddess hovered over us from the ceiling: Apollo sitting on a chariot with his legs crossed, his body circled by a huge white halo and his cloak billowing in the wind; and opposite him galloping away, Artemis, on a chariot, shrouded by a dark halo, symbolizing the night. The portraits of the donors, so vivid, so whole, so individual – they look out at us, silent witnesses of a lost civilization, unable to tell us how they left their homes and came to this harsh environment to make a sort of paradise here – a place of generous respect for different people and their values. A paradise we have lost.

We returned to Korla the next day. It was time to call on my aunt. I had last seen her almost twenty years earlier. When I rang her the evening before from Kucha, she recognized my voice instantly, and burst into tears. I asked her where she was living and said I would be there by midday tomorrow. There was a long silence: perhaps she thought I was playing a trick on her. Now I rang again and fifteen minutes later I saw my aunt and uncle and their two daughters waiting on the roadside in front of their building. I got out of the car. There was no hug. They simply grabbed my hands, my shoulders and my head, patting me all over. They stared at me long and hard, as if I had just landed from space. 'I thought I would never see you again before I died,' my aunt said, crying.

Then they saw the taxi with Salim waiting in it. 'Is that who brought you here?' my aunt asked.

'Yes,' I said, 'we've been visiting the Kizil Caves. I'll introduce him to you.'

My aunt hurried to dry her tears; Salim got out of the car and she shook his hand. She invited him in for a drink, but he declined, and turned to me: 'This is a rare moment for you. Enjoy it. Give me a call before you leave town.'

Once Salim was out of sight, they all started off: 'Where did you meet him? Don't you know it's dangerous here?'

'Come on,' I said, 'take it easy. He was highly recommended

by a friend. He's clever and very thoughtful. Don't you think he's handsome? I quite fancy him.'

'I don't think that's funny,' my cousin said seriously. 'People would say you've gone to the dogs.'

My aunt and uncle are retired and living with my cousin. On the main wall of their sitting room hang three rows of pictures. My grandparents sit regally on top; below them are family reunion photos, and then group photos of each family. My cousin pointed to a little girl like a Japanese doll in one photo. I could hardly recognize myself.

'We miss you and your parents so much.' My aunt broke down as soon as she started speaking. 'How I regret coming here,' she wailed. 'My mother went mad because of my stupidity. I have ruined my own life, and my children's and grandchildren's. What a fool I was!' My cousins looked embarrassed and went out to prepare dinner.

After leaving her village in 1952, my aunt travelled by train, truck and cart for three months, and finally arrived at a vast, desolate plane in the middle of nowhere. There was nothing in sight except for the horizon in the distance, no trees, no animals, no houses. She started screaming and refused to get down from the truck. 'Where is the factory I have been promised?' she shouted angrily, desperately. When the soldiers escorting the truck said she had to build the factory, she fainted.

They had to start from scratch, to reclaim land from the desert, just as the imperial army used to do in the old days to produce enough food for themselves and to guard the frontier. They dug holes in the ground to sleep in and for the first year, they ate nothing but wild plants. They worked day and night to get the first crops planted. Even today, my aunt feels restless on nights with a clear moon: that had meant working through the night. My aunt cried her way through the first year, especially after she heard that her mother had gone mad and drowned in a river. They could not escape because they needed official letters to buy train tickets. Caught without them, they would be sent to prison or returned to the construction farm, where even more severe punishment awaited them.

Having grown up in a village, my aunt was able to deal with the material hardship and the tough regime. What she was not prepared for was the mental agony. She and one million other young girls were recruited as brides for the People's Liberation Army who had marched here two years earlier. She was under enormous pressure to marry quickly. 'Marriage is not a personal matter,' she was told in the endless political sessions. 'It is a political task that concerns the stability of our frontier and the motherland.' The men like my uncle had been waiting for so long and when they set eyes on the young girls, desire and frustration were written all over their faces. 'I felt happy to see even a hen,' my uncle joked. But he had to wait. The senior officers, often old or already married, took their pick first – they usually chose the pretty ones. When it was finally his turn, he had to be content with 'ugly ducklings' like my aunt, small, dark and almost emaciated. 'She looked so alone and vulnerable. I felt I had to protect her,' my uncle recalled. Every Friday he would give my aunt something to eat, the most precious token of love saved from his weekly ration. He was a country boy and pursued her in the only way he knew – through food. After three years' courtship, they married, almost the last couple in the regiment. By then, quite a few of the better-looking women who were picked up first had had nervous breakdowns, overcome by disillusion and the strain of the ill-matched marriages that were thrust on them. 'My poor looks saved me,' my aunt said.

My cousin came out of the kitchen and told my aunt to cheer up and stop complaining. 'You made your bed; now lie in it,' she said gently but firmly. They had prepared a huge feast, with a dozen courses of fish, duck, lamb, even prawns flown in from the coast. I felt bad but it was no use stopping them. 'What do I save money for?' my aunt asked. 'I save money to go and see you and your family. Now you are here, we should celebrate.' I knew how much my being here meant to her. Family ties are of the utmost importance for the Chinese. Before Buddhism spread to China, we built temples for our ancestors, not for the gods. Chinese society still revolves very much around the family. My grandparents are dead, our family is my aunt's link with her past. She clings to it tightly, as if her life would have no meaning once she let go.

'Come on, eat, eat,' my aunt urged me, putting a mountain of food in my bowl. 'I probably won't see you again. I don't think I will live for another twenty years. This may be our last meal together. So you must eat.'

Tears were pouring down her face and into her bowl. I tried to comfort her, mumbling something about phones and planes making it easier than ever to talk and to see each other. I knew I was missing the point. Her dream is to leave Xinjiang, and to return to somewhere near home or what she could call home, anywhere that was not Xinjiang. I remembered my father tried many times to help her leave and did not succeed. It was almost impossible. The Construction and Production Corporation, with over three million people, is the backbone of Chinese rule in Xinjiang. Its real importance, as my guidebook says, is 'the unique role it plays in safeguarding the harmony of all nationalities in Xinjiang, the stability of society and the unity of the motherland'. Now they are retired and nobody would take them in, and their children were not sure they could find jobs elsewhere. They were stuck here.

When my aunt calmed down, she asked me what I was doing here. I showed her my book on the Kizil murals. 'Who are these foreign devils?' she asked, pointing at the red-haired Kuchean knights on the cover of the book.

I quickly explained to her what I saw in the caves.

'Why did they come here? I suppose this was a nicer place in those days, or they wouldn't have come,' she said.

My uncle remembered the good old days. 'It was better when we first got here. At least the locals were friendly. In the market, I could watch the women with their amazing plaits and exotic looks.'

The situation deteriorated in the late 1980s, when the Central Asian Republics became independent and Islamic resurgence turned into a big wave. The ripples came over to Xinjiang. 'Now if you go to the market, you can't even bargain with the Uighurs. They think it means you don't trust them,' my aunt said.

In the two days I was with them, we remembered the times the two families met; I answered their questions about all my relatives and we talked about my father's death. But the pain of their life in Xinjiang, the regret for having come here in the first place, and the erosion of their early idealism – these realities dominated our conversation. I felt very sad. They have been in Xinjiang for fifty years but in an emotional sense they did not live here. It was a life of exile, but also self-exile: the Construction and Production Corporation consisted entirely of Han Chinese, who were totally isolated from the local population. After all this time, they still did not speak a word of the Uighur language. The Uighurs were like some barbarian tribe outside their fortress, a fortress they have built themselves. They live in an impossible dream of returning home, and their longing has become a poison, filling them with loneliness, fear and resentment.

If my aunt had only had to contend with earning a living and making a good life for her family, she might have been happy. But she and all her generation lived through endless campaigns, which put before them ever new goals of improvement, purging ideological impurities, identifying new enemies and demanding new sacrifices. They lived in perpetual agitation and fear. It was like a prison cell where the light was never switched off. Now suddenly it was dark, and there was nothing there. They felt lost and abandoned.

I could hardly bear to say goodbye, thinking I might never be with my aunt again. She came with the family to see me off at the long-distance bus station. She was in tears once more, clinging to me and trying to hold me back. I felt something was tearing me apart. As the bus pulled out, she rushed forward on her unsteady feet to catch a last glimpse of me. I watched her becoming smaller and smaller, desperately waving.

I sat back in my seat and watched the city go by, and then abruptly we were back in the desert, mile after mile of grey sand and pebbles, nothing else except for telegraph poles. It was extraordinary to think that my aunt and uncle and the people in their regiment reclaimed hundreds of thousands of acres of land from the desert, turning them into oases, with little more than their hands and their will to survive. Communism is about changing the material conditions. Mao said we can change heaven, we can change earth, we can even change nature – in fact there was nothing we could not change; that the settlers in Xinjiang have done. Yet they could not change what is in their mind, their attitude and their outlook.

I could not help comparing Aunt with Grandmother. There was someone whose life was full of pain, and for most of it she had nothing. Yet I never heard her grumble; and whatever dreadful things we said to her, she remained loving and kind, all the time she was with us, forever optimistic. Grandmother could have been consumed by her suffering and spent her life complaining and hoping that others would help her. Instead she mastered her pain, as if she said to herself, 'You cannot change your life, you have to change how you look at it.' This is what Buddhism teaches. A monk once told me the story of two girls who loved the same policeman. One said, 'He must love me, he always waves me on.' The other said, 'He must love me, he always holds me up so he can look at me a little longer.' If you want to, you can see things in a good light.

I thought of how Grandmother always tried to make me think positively. I had to wear glasses when I was young. I hated them – they made me look bookish, at a time when books were out. The other children taunted me with the usual 'four-eyes'. The moment I left the house I would take them off. When Father found out, he slapped me. 'We've spent all this money on you. Your glasses are more than your mother's monthly salary.'

Grandmother took a different tack. She said, 'Didn't you say your head teacher wears glasses? It's a sign of intelligence. They suit you. You're a very clever girl. Look at me, I never learned to read and write. I can't even tell the characters for men and women outside the toilet. Don't end up like me. Study hard, a skill is never a burden.'

In those days the more you studied, the more reactionary you were considered to be; young people like my elder sister were sent to the countryside instead of university. I do not know where Grandmother got the idea that studying would be good for me. Perhaps from the old operas she watched, where penniless young men came out number one in the imperial exams and married the emperors' daughters. Grandmother proved right. When the Cultural Revolution ended in 1976, universities began to recruit again. I was fortunate to have gone to Beijing University, and then Oxford – a world apart from Handan, the small city where I grew up. Grandmother was so pleased for me. 'A phoenix has come out of a hen's nest,' she told anybody who cared to listen.

Aunt is so tough, so brave, so strong. Hardship meant nothing to her – she survived so much of it. But she is consumed with self-recrimination and regret, and they have almost overwhelmed her. If only she could have seen her experience differently. Perhaps mind is reality, as the Buddha said: with one thought, we can be in heaven, with another, in hell.

FIVE

Land of
Heavenly Mountains

IT WAS EARLY IN 628, and Xuanzang was beleaguered in Kucha. The wind howled and storms raged over the desert, hurling up the snow from the ground. It was deep winter and the thriving Silk Road was brought to a standstill. Looking out from his monastery, Xuanzang could see the Heavenly Mountains, whose passes were closed. His heart was on fire. He had been on the road for almost six months and had barely made a dent in the journey, considering how long it was. He felt he could not afford to wait any longer.

He went to the caravanserais near the city gates daily, hoping to find some new arrivals with the latest travel information. But it was the same stranded merchants who greeted him. He tried to persuade them to leave at once but they said they would wait; more haste, less speed. It was expensive to keep so many people and animals supplied, but their job was to deliver their valuable goods and guarantee everyone's safety.

After two months' waiting, Xuanzang finally decided to climb the Heavenly Mountains in the deep winter, against everyone's warning. The King of Kucha begged him to stay until it was safe. 'What fear can I now have in facing the passage of the ice-bound glaciers? My only anxiety is that I should be too late to pay my reverence at the spot where stands the tree of wisdom,' Xuanzang replied.

Soon they were climbing towards the Bedal Pass. Hui Li gives us a vivid account of its dangers: 'Since the creation of the world, snow has accumulated here and has turned into blocks of ice which melt neither in spring nor in summer. They roll away in boundless sheets of hard, gleaming white, losing themselves in the clouds. Looking at them one is blinded by their brightness. The path is strewn with cliffs and pinnacles of ice, some of them as much as one hundred feet high, others two or three dozen feet wide. The latter cannot be crossed without great difficulty nor the former climbed without peril.'

It was a terrible passage. Even wrapped in the heavy folds of their furs they could not keep warm; the men were freezing, huddled together shivering. If they stopped, the wind and snow made it impossible to sleep or to cook. The horses wore felt on their hooves but they were frightened and skidded on the ice. For seven days, the party struggled on with hardly any sleep or food. They grew weaker by the day, and kept falling over. The King of Gaochang's men had never been exposed to such cold. Xuanzang himself was soon suffering from some disease that would give him pain for the rest of his life.

'Frequently violent dragons' – as he called avalanches – 'impede travellers with the damage they inflict. Those who go on this road should not wear red garments nor carry hollow gourds or shout loudly. The least forgetfulness of these precautions entails certain misfortune. A violent wind suddenly rises with storms of flying sand and gravel; those who encounter them, sinking through exhaustion, are almost sure to die.' Xuanzang would have made sure no one in the group broke the prohibitions, and the danger made him appreciate the warning of the merchants in Kucha. But it was too late. The avalanche he described struck, and killed fourteen men and many more oxen and horses, destroying most of his supplies – the worst calamity he suffered on his entire journey.

Xuanzang was fearless. Obstacles made him redouble his exertions; danger increased his courage. Ordinary men would become disheartened – the enlightened look straight towards their goal, and do not stop until it is achieved. This is *viriya*, or effort, one of the ten perfections of the Bodhisattvas. But this tragedy brought home to him that his rashness would jeopardize his entire journey. He needed a little caution, more willingness to listen, more careful planning. The lesson was a powerful one; it stayed with him and he never made the same mistake again.

I wanted to go through the pass, following Xuanzang. But the Bedal Pass today is jointly operated by the Chinese and Kyrgyz governments. The Chinese have built their half of the road up to the pass, only two hours from the foot of the mountains on a brand-new tarmac road, but the Kyrgyz have not started work on the way down. I had to take a plane from Urumqi to Bishkek, the capital of Kyrgyzstan, and retrace Xuanzang's footsteps from the foot of the Heavenly Mountains on the other side.

Urumqi is a sprawling city, whose only distinction is to be further from the sea than any other city in the world. What struck me about it were posters everywhere exhorting everyone to safeguard the motherland, to resist the separatists who want to split it. In the Xinjiang Airline office the counter selling tickets to Bishkek had no customers. It was a nice change from the usual scrum. I was offered a one-third discount, and departed on an almost empty plane.

We were soon over the Heavenly Mountains. The plane was

flying very low. The sky was a brilliant blue with only a sprinkling of clouds; the peaks below, wave after wave of them, craggy and snow-clad, stretched as far as the horizon. Looking down, I could see right into the depths of the ravines, cut between them like surgical incisions. Xuanzang survived the avalanche but he was uncertain what would be waiting for him when he descended.

He was now in the territory of the arch-enemy of Tang China, the empire of the Turks. One of the numerous nomadic peoples on the Eurasian steppes, the Turks established, in the short space of barely fifty years, one of the biggest empires in the world at the time, controlling the vast territory between Persia and China, stretching to Afghanistan in the south, and to the north Lake Baykal in today's Russia. The oases in the Western Region such as Gaochang and Kucha all pledged allegiance to the Turks. But their ambitions were not yet fully realized. They looked east to China, and dreamed of taking it with all its ancient civilization and wealth. It would be six hundred years before Ghengis Khan fulfilled their dream.

Xuanzang would have known how dangerous the Turks were. The year before his departure, in 626, more than one million Eastern Turks flung themselves in a bold raid across the Mongolian plateau, and advanced on Chang'an, demanding tributes and threatening to sack the capital. Taizong personally went into battle and drove them away. In order to avoid any recurrence of the Turkish threat, Taizong was advised to restore or to strengthen the Great Wall. Smiling, he said, 'What need is there to strengthen the frontiers?' He would remove the threat once and for all. He used the tactic of divide and conquer: he would first take on the Eastern Turks, who lived on the Mongolian steppes; for that he would need to pacify the Western Turks, who controlled the territory to the west of China. The Western Turks knew the game the Chinese emperor was playing and watched in apprehension, no doubt thinking of their own next move. Taizong's strategy worked and in barely two years he wiped out the Eastern Turks, and the same fate fell on their brothers in the west two decades later, their vast empire subsumed into that of the Chinese. Xuanzang was travelling at the moment of greatest uncertainty during this deadly manoeuvring.

I touched down in Bishkek. Xuanzang would have passed through when it was only pastures and sheep. It was a pleasant place, built by the Russians in 1878; you could see tall mountain peaks in the distance, and trees were everywhere, turning to autumn gold, sheltering wide boulevards, blocks of villas and office buildings. There were not many people about, just some old ladies picking up acorns, and a few women elegantly dressed, as if they had just come back from Milan. A strange somnolence draped itself over the town, as if by decree. After the noise and crowds of Chinese cities, I took it as a welcome respite.

After checking in to my huge room in a gloomy, empty hotel, I rang John, a British economist working for the Kyrgyz government. He was one of hundreds of foreign experts drafted in to try to galvanize the Kyrgyz economy. But this was not international altruism: President Akayev is the only non-Communist head of state in the Central Asian republics, committed to economic reform, free elections and a degree of press and religious freedom. The West was keen for him to survive, as an example of the triumph of democracy in a region still very much controlled by Communism, and struggling with rising Islamic fundamentalism at the same time.

John told me his office was on the main square, opposite the State Museum and next to the Parliament building, two solid masses of socialist-realist construction on a grand scale. I had no trouble finding it – Bishkek was like a Chinese city without the crowds, with landmarks from the Communist era dominating the cityscape. I even felt at home.

'How nice it is to have a visitor.' He extended his long arms to greet me, and gave me a big hug, even though he had never met me before.

'I like it here,' I said. 'It's like a bargain version of Switzerland.'

'It is, you're right. Although not that many people would agree with you right now.'

'Why?' I asked.

He looked at me quizzically. 'Haven't you heard what's going on?'

I had been travelling inside China for nearly three months, mostly in small towns and remote areas, with little access to international news except on Chinese television and in newspapers. Their coverage of the world was minimal and highly selective, to say the least. I did read about the summit in Bishkek on August 24–25 where the presidents of Kyrgyzstan, Kazakhstan, Tajikistan, Russia and China met, as they had done every year since 1996, and 'discussed closer cooperation in regional development and in fighting terrorism, religious extremism and separatist movements'.

'You don't know about the IMU, the Islamic Movement of Uzbekistan? Their militants kidnapped fourteen people and held two villages in August.' John spoke calmly. He did not want to frighten me.

'Where did it happen, who are the hostages?' I asked. I had heard nothing about this.

'In southern Kyrgyzstan. The hostages included four Japanese geologists working for a mining company, villagers, government officials, soldiers. They even took a Kyrgyz general who went to look for the Japanese.' John laughed awkwardly. 'They kidnapped the Japanese on the twenty-third of August, the day before the opening of the summit in Bishkek. You can imagine the chaos.'

'What happened to the hostages?'

'Uzbekistan sent planes to bomb the villages held by the IMU. They killed a dozen villagers. The Kyrgyz government is frantically negotiating behind the scenes for the release of the hostages but they can't agree to the conditions put forward by the IMU. So, stalemate.' John shrugged.

'What do the IMU want?'

'Lots of money, of course,' John said. 'They've also demanded the release of fifty thousand Muslims from Uzbek prisons, and a couple of other things.'

'Why is this all happening in Kyrgyzstan, not Uzbekistan?' I was puzzled.

'Kyrgyzstan is easier to get in and out of. The Uzbek government has a much tighter grip on its country, just like the old Soviet days,' he explained. 'So here you are, right where the action is. But I don't think you should worry.' John tried to reassure me. 'In fact, it is the safest time. The Kyrgyz and Uzbek governments are closing in on the hostage-takers, with a bit of help from the Russian and Japanese secret services. It will be winter soon. The drama will have to end somehow, otherwise the IMU cannot get back to their base in the mountains, on the Afghan border.'

Before I came on the trip I had read that apart from Kyrgyzstan, all the republics of Central Asia see the revival of Islam as a threat, as dangerous as democracy, to be contained at all costs. Immediately after its independence, Tajikistan was torn apart by a civil war fought between the old Communist government and the popular Islamic Renaissance Party. Tens of thousands of Tajiks died; whole villages were emptied as people fled the country to Afghanistan and Iran. After five years of guerrilla war there was a fragile peace, a coalition of Communists and Muslims. But in Uzbekistan, President Karamov refuses to accommodate the growing popularity of Islam. Police question anyone with beards and women can be arrested for wearing the veil. Muslims can pray only in mosques approved by the Party and madrassahs are closed down regularly. It is as bad as the Soviet times when people had to hide the Koran inside Communist textbook covers. All this suppression only helps to ferment Islamic fundamentalism, which is why the IMU declared a jihad against President Karamov.

What John did not tell me, as I discovered much later, was that the IMU also included Xinjiang in its jihad. Perhaps he did not know, or he did not want me to worry too much. There are half a million Uighurs living in Central Asia – fifty thousand in Kyrgyzstan alone – and quite a few of them are fighting for the IMU. They want to establish an independent Eastern Turkestan Islamic Republic in Xinjiang. The Chinese government is stepping up its own crackdown there; at the same time it has provided technical and military assistance to Kyrgyzstan and Uzbekistan, in return for their help in keeping a grip on the Uighurs in their countries. Both have obliged; Uighur publications and offices were shut down; Uighurs critical of Chinese policies were arrested; border control was tighter than ever before, to prevent the export of arms or funds to Xinjiang. But it is a difficult task. A few months after I left, Uighur militants held a Chinese businessman in Bishkek for a ransom of 100,000 dollars, killed his nephew and burned down the Chinese market in the city. When a senior Chinese government official came from Urumqi to investigate the case, he was killed too.

I had dinner with John and his wife that evening, and we discussed my visit. He said he would give his interpreter a few days off to keep me company. 'You will have to pay her – this is Kyrgyzstan,' he said. Back in the hotel, I went to my room and tried to sleep, but I was awake for quite a while. There was a drunken brawl on the street; a car honked; footsteps in the corridor outside my room gave me a little fright. What if some Uighurs burst in and took me hostage? I began to realize why this beautiful city was so quiet; there were few tourists, and the streets were so empty when I arrived. I was a walking target, and there were not many others. Had I been careless? The hostage crisis had been going on for almost two months, and I knew nothing of it. I had no idea Uighur fundamentalists were fighting their holy war outside China. There was trouble in Xinjiang, even bombing, but it was mainly against organizations like the police, and high-profile Uighurs working for the government. I had never heard of their kidnapping ordinary Chinese, but perhaps they were learning from the IMU. Did I have too much faith in the Chinese government's ability to keep everything under control? The situation in Xinjiang was even more serious than I had realized. No wonder Salim said no Chinese woman would travel in Xinjiang alone, and my aunt and her family felt so hostile and fearful.

The severity of the situation dawned on me. Xuanzang's mission was more important than his life. He was truly fearless, and nothing would stop him until death came along. Even then, he could vow to continue the journey in his next life. I cannot say my journey was more important than life, and I did not have to complete it in a hurry. But strangely, I was not worried about death, not because I am brave, nor because

I do not value life. But I would not know anything at the other end of the dark tunnel. So what is there to worry about? The more I thought of it, what really worried me was pain, the pain of torture. I still remembered watching revolutionary films which showed Communists being tortured by Japanese soldiers or the old government secret police, their bodies covered with blood, their faces seared with burns, an iron rod heating up on the fire. Of course they never gave in, never betrayed the Party. I always came out of the cinema sweating like a pig and scared to death. I dared not tell anyone but I knew I would be a traitor under torture. How the Communists dealt with it, or the monks in the Cultural Revolution, I still cannot grasp. Physical pain is physical pain, whether you think it is inflicted unjustly, your own fault, or down to your bad karma. When we were asked to write reports on what we had learned from the films and how we would cope, I pretended I was brave and said I would rather kill myself for the revolution than be caught by the enemy. I could only hope I was never put to the test.

The longer I thought about it, the less I seemed to have the option of going back. The current problem in Xinjiang and the whole of Central Asia was not going to go away; it might worsen before it improved. I had to give Afghanistan a miss because of the war there, and I was still trying to get my Uzbek visa. Kyrgyzstan was the only Central Asian country Xuanzang visited that I knew I could get to. I could not simply walk out now; I had to persevere, not give up at the first hurdle. I just had to be extra careful, make as thorough preparations as I could, go nowhere on my own – and concentrate on two crucial places: Karakul, the biggest town in Eastern Kyrgyzstan, at the foot of the Heavenly Mountains where Xuanzang would have rested after his close shave with death; and Ak-beshim, one hour's drive from Bishkek near Tokmak, where Xuanzang met the Yagabhu Khan, the man who would ensure the monk's safe journey through his empire. I still had a long way to go. No doubt there would be more headaches to contend with.

The interpreter, Guljan, came to my hotel in the morning. She was a short, quiet and attentive woman in her mid-thirties. She was happy to come with me – she had never been to Karakul, a famous holiday resort. We caught a bus there along the northern shore of Lake Issyk-Kul. The bus was very much like a Chinese one, battered and dirty, filled with bent old men and women, and a dusty goat. It took its time, rumbling along at a leisurely thirty miles an hour, and stopping frequently to let passengers on and off. I worried that we would not be able to reach our destination before dark. But I was too tired from the endless scenarios I had imagined in the night. I fell into a deep slumber.

Karakul is a well-kept little town at the far end of the lake; I woke up as the bus reached it. The sun was going down. A flaming red ball that seemed as if it was going to melt the white peaks of the mountains soaked the lake in a rosy light; even the geese on the water looked more like flamingos. The spire of the Russian Orthodox church was caught in this intense evening glow, and so was the upswept roof of what appeared to be a Chinese pagoda.

This was the landscape, dotted with a few yurts and their nomadic dwellers, that would have greeted Xuanzang after his struggles on the mountain. It remained unchanged until the mid-nineteenth century when the Russians set up a military post here and began to map the peaks and valleys that separated their empire from the Chinese. Karakul means 'black wrist' in the local language, presumably referring to the hands of the early Russian settlers. But it is most closely associated with another Russian, the famous explorer N. M. Przhevalsky. The town was renamed Przhevalsk after he died here preparing his fifth expedition to China, which would have taken him through the same pass Xuanzang took more than a thousand years earlier. For all Przhevalsky's extraordinary achievements in mapping many uncharted territories, including the sources of the Yellow River and the Yangzi River, Xuanzang would not have appreciated the Russian's undisguised hatred of his beloved country: 'The Chinese here is a Jew plus a Muscovite pickpocket, both squared. But the lamentable thing is to see Europeans being polite to this rabble.' He might even have lost his calm, as he did in Kucha, if he had heard Przhevalsky denouncing Buddhism as 'a religion that sapped vitality and hindered progress'. The Kyrgyz people hated him just as much. As soon as the Soviet Union collapsed, they demanded to restore the town to its old name.

But what was the Chinese pagoda doing here? Could there be descendants of the people Xuanzang described in his *Record*? He says he passed an isolated village where 'there are three hundred households, all Chinese. They are captives of the Turks and have decided to settle down and live together in this place. Their clothes are similar to the Turks' but their language and their moral beliefs are Chinese.'

I received an answer soon enough from Galina, a warm, energetic woman in her forties who ran the hostel where we stayed the night. 'Oh, that is called the Dongan Pagoda,' she told me, intrigued with her first-ever Chinese customer.

'But who were the Dongans?' I asked.

'They are Chinese, just like you,' she said, looking puzzled, as if I should know my countrymen living here. 'There are hundreds of thousands of them in Kyrgyzstan. You can go to the market tomorrow. They sell everything we use. We would starve to death without them.'

Over dinner, Galina and her husband asked me what I would like to see and do in Karakul. Most people used it as a base for mountaineering and trekking. I had not found it easy to explain to people what I was doing – most Chinese thought I was slightly mad. But foreigners presented a different kind of problem. A Chinese monk, who went to India in the seventh century, looking for what he thought was the true Buddhism? There were so many things to explain, I did not know where to start. As I was struggling to come up with something simple and comprehensible, Galina pressed her palms together like a monk and said, 'You are following Xuan-zang.' Before I could express surprise she had put down her fork, excused herself and run out. In a minute she was back with a big map. Her husband stood up, pushed the plates aside, and helped her spread the map on the table. I could not believe my eyes. In the lower right-hand corner was Xuan-zang, like the portrait in my rubbing from the Big Wild Goose Pagoda. 'He is a great hero for us,' Galina said. 'You know he kept such a detailed record of our country. And so accurate! We are very grateful to him. He was a truly remarkable man. He almost lost his life here, on the Heavenly Mountains. That's why we honour him by putting him on this map.' With a big smile, Galina folded up the map and handed it to me. 'Please keep this as a souvenir.'

I was literally speechless. I was in an unassuming guesthouse in a tourist town in Kyrgyzstan, among non-Chinese and non-Buddhists, and my hosts were displaying more interest in Xuanzang than I had encountered in my homeland. They not only knew of Xuanzang, he was on the map of their country.

I felt shamed, yet also elated. Over the last few months of my journey, I had realized just how little my fellow-countrymen knew about Xuanzang. I had begun to wonder what I would be able to find out about him outside China, except for visiting ruins and talking to academics. And here he was, a local hero. I began to forget the dangers, and to be more confident about my journey. I was already finding out things about Xuanzang at this early stage. And how much more I would be able to discover when I reached India.

Galina asked me what I wanted to see in Kyrgyzstan. 'You should go up the Heavenly Mountains,' she said. 'You can experience what your monk went through.' I could do it on foot, by horse, or in a Russian military truck. It took three days to get to the top. 'Not much faster than Xuanzang.' She looked at me. 'He took seven days up and down the mountains in deep winter.' Galina was standing up again, this time to get some photos she had taken of the path.

Looking at her pictures of the snow-covered mountain, the travellers with their rucksacks, and the packhorses that carried the tents and cooking gear, I could almost visualize Xuanzang among them. Things really had not changed much; Galina's snapshots reminded me of the pictures of nineteenth- and twentieth-century travellers like Aurel Stein and Albert von Le Coq. They both talked about the difficulty of crossing the mountains. Von Le Coq and his men came across heaps of bones and mummified bodies on their route. On the roadside there were piles of stones, the graves of men who died and were fortunate enough to be buried by their companions. If a caravan was overtaken by a snowstorm, the German explorer tells us, 'The loads of the fallen animals are all put together in orderly fashion in as sheltered a spot as can be found near the scene of disaster. Later on they are fetched away, and the caravan code of honour most strictly forbids any interference with these stores belonging to other people. We ourselves often pass such heaps of property.' To prevent snow blindness, they cut the tails off yaks and horses, and put them underneath their hats to cover their faces. The other danger for the Germans was mountain sickness, which he said only attacked strangers to the mountains. It was lethal, causing severe headaches, nausea and the swelling of hands and feet, and then death within twenty-four hours.

I asked Galina what food they took with them when they climbed. 'It's different now, with lots of convenience food. But in the Silk Road days, they had a lot of dried meat, dried fruits and nans. If they happened to kill a wild boar or an antelope, they could roast it whole, or cut the meat up and package it in the animals' stomachs. You left them in the ashes of your bonfire. The next morning you would have a delicious stew. Of course, Xuanzang would not have touched it. But there are wild mushrooms, walnuts, pistachios, juniper berries, apple trees in the ancient forests – lots of nutritious things, good for medicine too. All the caravan leaders knew their life-saving properties. But a real feast for a caravan when they had done a big deal was to get hold of a partridge, a pheasant, a ram, a wild boar and a horse. Some say a camel as well but I doubt it: they are so important. Very expensive too. Anyway, I would leave it out. You put the animals inside each other and roast them till they are done. It would make a great banquet.'

I was tempted by the idea of going up the mountain. It was not like the other overland route between China and Kyrgyzstan, where you simply drove through customs. This was actually the real adventure, as Xuanzang had done it. I asked Galina how it was organized. 'We should have three or four groups now, coming along the Silk Road from Kashgar in Xinjiang, but they have all cancelled. This hostage crisis has really affected us, and the whole town. We live on the tourism of the Silk Road, just as our ancestors did on its trade. After drug trafficking, tourism is the biggest foreign currency earner, but it's not happening this year. I have had only half a dozen backpackers like you. Normally we would have twenty times more around now,' Galina said ruefully. 'The good thing is,' she added, 'you have our fullest attention.' Alas, though, I could not do the climb. I had to go with a group. As with the old caravans, you needed security in numbers, especially now.

After breakfast next morning, Galina took me to see Lake Issyk-kul, which I had only glimpsed the evening before. As we drove along the shore I could see the white summits of the Heavenly Mountains filling the horizon, and below them a green expanse of forest and pasture, hemmed by fertile fields alongside the road. By the lake birches, poplars and apple trees rustled in the mild breeze, and beyond them stretched the water, a rippling, dark, cerulean blue. Xuanzang must have been relieved to reach here and find some repose after his escape from the avalanche, although he must have arrived on a much windier day: 'This lake is about 500 kilometres in circuit, extensive from east to west, and narrow from north to south. It is surrounded by mountains on all sides; a great number of rivers flow into it. The colour of the water is a bluish-black and it tastes salty and bitter. Its vast waves spread out in immense sheets, and they swell and heave violently.' The sense of brooding threat Xuanzang so vividly describes seemed unimaginable now, with the lake under a calm blue sky. He observed it with his usual accuracy. He called it Hot Sea, as the Chinese still do, and said it never freezes because it is so deep. He added what the local people probably told him:

'Dragons and fish live in it and occasionally some monsters rise to the surface. Although the lake is abundant with fish, nobody dares catch them. Even travellers passing by stop to pray for their safety and fortune.'

I thought the myths he relates had vanished: I saw women by the roadside selling fresh and smoked salmon and trout. 'We look all the same to you, don't we – just as we think all Chinese are alike,' Galina read my mind. 'But those women are Russian. We don't fish in the lake. In fact, the Kyrgyz did not eat fish until the nineteen-seventies. Even today many old people refuse to touch it. They think it will bring them bad luck. The first time my mother ate fish, a bone stuck in her throat. She thought she was being punished by the monster in the lake.' Galina laughed. She told me that the old people never swam in the lake either. They were worried it would disturb the monster sleeping at the bottom. To the Kyrgyz, Issyk-kul is sacred, to be worshipped and prayed to. In the spring, people living around the lake make their ritual offerings for rain and a good harvest.

'That's what is so amazing about Xuanzang,' Galina exclaimed. 'He came here thirteen hundred years ago and wrote down what he saw and heard. Today, people still believe it. Nobody was like him. OK, Marco Polo found a ram and called it Marco Polo's sheep, Przhevalsky named a wild horse after himself, but Xuanzang left us invaluable information. Ecologists are very pleased to have his description from so long ago. They can see how the lake has changed over the centuries.'

That afternoon we went to the market. For a moment I was not sure where I was. There were rows of stalls selling the exact same things I would find in China: pickled vegetables, spring onions, coriander, Chinese leaves, bean curd, jeans, sweaters, children's clothes, and utensils. The women behind the stalls looked just like me; they wore the same dress as peasant women in northern China, bold floral patterns in bright red, green, yellow and pink. I smiled at them and they smiled back. Then they started talking animatedly in an incomprehensible dialect.

'Where are they from?' I asked them through Guljan.

'Shanxi in northern China, also Gansu,' several women said at once.

'When did they come here?'

'More than a hundred years ago,' they said loudly in chorus. Meanwhile more women were joining us. We chatted a bit longer, but Galina was worried the gathering crowd would disrupt the market. She suggested we go to the mosque to find out more.

The mosque was closed. Galina thought for a moment. 'I've got an idea,' she said. 'The women in the market all come from the big Dongan village fifteen kilometres away. There must be lots of old folk there.' Her husband had visited it once and he could take us. He agreed immediately. He was a charming man, not very talkative – he hardly put in a word at dinner the night before – but full of information whenever I asked him anything – except about the Dongans. 'They keep very much to themselves and have nothing to do with us, except for selling us stuff.'

There was hardly a soul in the village, apart from a group of children playing in the street. Guljan asked them where their parents were. 'In the fields,' they replied. They were looking at me with a mixture of curiosity and excitement, pulling at my bag and my shirt and gabbling at me in their language, thinking I would understand. Guljan had to explain to them in Kyrgyz that I came from Beijing, to which they replied that their great-great-grandfathers came from Shanxi. We asked them if they could show us their homes. Now they were all pulling me – I chose the nearest one.

As in a northern Chinese village, all the houses had wooden latticed doors with carved lintels above them, and old trees on either side. In the courtyard there were heaps of onions, potatoes and tomatoes, and farm tools. The main room was dominated by a huge *kang*, the baked-earth bed that was heated up by the kitchen stove during cooking. There were photographs on the walls, wedding pictures and family portraits, with every woman wearing the brightly coloured, elaborate traditional Chinese dress that we put on for ceremonials. The quilts, the calendar, the chairs, the teapot and cups, even the food left over on the table – everything was Chinese.

In the village mosque, we found a young man, Hamid Yusupov, who was training to be an imam. He was born in the village and grew up there. He greeted me warmly, shaking both my hands. We still had to communicate through Guljan: he could not understand my Mandarin, nor I his Shanxi dialect. The story he told was shocking. Most Chinese Muslims lived in the northwest of China. We call them 'Hui Hui', the people who must go back to where they came from. In 1862, Hamid explained, they started a rebellion that lasted fifteen years and almost brought down the Chinese empire. The Muslims' grievance was an old one: oppression by the Han Chinese. 'Allah says hell is where all evils are but this world is worse than hell,' one Muslim rebel groaned at the time.

The imperial army put down the rebellion after a protracted campaign: whole villages were massacred, and their farms and forests burned. Those who survived the reprisals were uprooted from their homes and resettled in wild, isolated places to prevent them for making trouble again, but not too isolated, so the government could keep an eye on them. In Gansu Province, two million Muslims, 60 per cent of the population, were killed; in Shanxi, where Hamid's great-grandparents came from, they were almost wiped out. The remaining rebels and their families were pushed right to the border of China and Russia. Facing the daunting peaks of the Heavenly Mountains, and the pursuing Chinese army, they decided to cross over into what was then Russia.

Most of them succumbed to the deep snow and freezing cold. Hamid's great-grandfather lost most members of his family: his mother, with her bound feet, could not keep up the pace and he had to abandon her halfway up the mountain; his two young sons kept themselves warm at night by sleeping under the belly of a cow but he found them frozen to death one morning. Only six thousand out of fifty thousand people survived, and very few of them were women. 'But we have not been exterminated,' Hamid said proudly. 'Allah knows how much we wanted to live, to carry on our faith, to seek a new homeland where we can live in peace, dignity and justice.' His village was where the first group of survivors came to, in January 1878, when they struggled down the northern slope of the mountains, beaten, cold, hungry, but defiant.

Today the Dongans have grown into a community of 100,000, dispersed in pockets in Kyrgyzstan, Kazakhstan and Uzbekistan. They are still expanding: their women have an average of seven children.

'We have to preserve our people and culture,' Hamid said.

I told him the Dongans seemed to me more Chinese than the people in China.

'We marry among ourselves and try to keep our traditions intact. Otherwise who are we? We would be like plants without roots, shadows without substance. Besides, our great-grandfathers would have sacrificed for nothing if we lost what they treasured. But we would never have left if we had not been forced to. We love our country and still feel attached to it.'

I know something of how he felt. However long I stay in the West, I will never lose my attachment to China. Living in England has given me so much freedom, so much opportunity to explore myself and discover what I am capable of. I remember the first time I told my mother that I wanted to make documentary films; she just laughed, and said 'You?' – as if this was some wild fantasy that might possibly be realized if I had a beautiful face or married somebody powerful in the right position. In China we believe our circumstances tell us what we can do. 'Toads should not dream of turning into swans.'

All the same I will always feel Chinese in my bones. More than anything else, the ease of shared assumptions and values, the power of the language and the culture, and the pride in our long civilization, tell me who I am. And that is not going to change. All the pain my family went through in this century, in the company of most Chinese, does not affect that. On the contrary, it reinforces my sense of where I belong. I write and speak English all day long, but I dream in Chinese.

After two most memorable days, Galina and her husband put me and Guljan on the bus back to Bishkek. I wished I had been able to stay longer and learn more; they had been so warm and helpful. Guljan said it was because they had nomadic blood in their veins. 'That's what makes them friendly and welcoming to strangers.'

As our bus toiled along the lake, I noticed the hosts of Muslim tombs that crowd up to the edge of the road, the grandest of them surmounted by arches with little towers on either side, topped by domes or crescent moons. Inside the arch is a black-and-white photo of the deceased, looking out at the water. With the mountains behind them and the beautiful lake in front, they need no other paradise. It is here. I had to ask Guljan, though, why with so much space they do not build the tombs further back.

'They are nomadic people too. They live on their own with their herds most of the time. It is very lonely. So in their next life they want to be with others, enjoying the company of cars, horses, tourist groups, holidaymakers. It makes up for the silence of their lives.'

Did their nomadic life make them less religious than the other Central Asian peoples?

'I guess we Kyrgyz are not very religious really,' Guljan said. 'We worship nature more than anything else – the sun, the moon, the rain, the earth. Anyway the nomads cannot come down from the mountains and go to the mosque every Friday, can they?'

I had heard from John that young Kyrgyz were also joining the IMU. 'They are paid to fight the jihad,' Guljan said, much to my surprise, 'quite a handsome salary too, by our standards, ten or fifteen dollars a day. How can they make a living otherwise? Nothing is working in this country. Eighty per cent of young people are unemployed. They are desperate. They will do anything for money.' Guljan told me that poverty forced over four thousand Kyrgyz women to work as prostitutes abroad, some of them in China – they earned more foreign currency than tourism, second only to drug trafficking.

It was a sad, if familiar, story: many parts of China had yet to overcome the backlog of inefficiency left by the socialist economy. So the calm of Bishkek, which I had found so charming, was not a blessing, but a sign of stagnation. Still, I really liked it. After my return from Karakul in the late afternoon, I went to the Pubovy Park in the city, a haven of trees and sculptures, with ancient stone statues, simple and organic, next to gigantic busts of heroic socialist workers and abstract modern works, even a giant statue of the head of the Soviet secret police. In front of the grand State Opera House, a few magicians were entertaining a group of children, producing pigeons from nowhere and making their hats disappear in the air. Their young audience was completely absorbed; a Silk Road tradition was still alive.

Xuanzang would have had magicians, storytellers, fire-eaters and acrobats in the caravans he travelled with, who were mostly from today's Central Asia. A ceramic figure of the Tang dynasty has a whole group of them on camel-back, on a platform – the best camels were said to be able to run with a cup of water on their noses, and not spill a drop. Each night performers took turns telling stories and doing their acts. Xuanzang would have made his own contribution by preaching. Monks could also be useful when the caravans went through customs – they did not have to pay tax, and sometimes they would carry goods for the merchants, which they said were for religious purposes. I am sure Xuanzang never stooped to this.

Apart from its acrobats, musicians and dancers, Kyrgyzstan fires the imagination of the Chinese for another reason. Akbeshim is called Suiye in Chinese. Here Xuanzang had one of the most important encounters on his entire journey, with the powerful Khan of the Western Turks. Here once lay the frontier of the Chinese empire at its biggest and most powerful during the Tang dynasty. I had to go there.

John's driver, Dima, came to pick me up with Guljan. John

had also sought out Valentina, an archaeologist in her early fifties from the State Slavonic University working on pre-Islamic history, a rare speciality in Kyrgyzstan. If the shock of discovery on my arrival had left its shadow on my mind, I forgot all about it in the company of these three wonderful characters. Dima was a young Russian of heavy build and few words, who exuded an impressive but slightly dangerous authority. While Guljan was her usual quiet self, Valentina was a redhead, a bundle of energy, warmth and knowledge. She was so excited at meeting someone interested in what she did, she never stopped talking. She could not wait for Guljan to translate for me, and seemed to think we could talk to each other despite the language barrier. Occasionally she slowed down, when I was completely lost and turned to Guljan in desperation. After Valentina had spoken for ten minutes, ending with a sigh, Guljan could only sum up in one sentence. 'Most of my colleagues are working on the Muslim period, as if nothing existed before.'

Valentina had been with Japanese archaeologists on digs in Ak-beshim. It was a flourishing Silk Road town when Xuanzang arrived; his was the earliest record of it. Not long after, it became a garrison for the Chinese army when Taizong's son defeated the Western Turks and took over their empire. It took us an hour to get there. To a casual eye, it looks like baked earth, as if farmers have been digging out mud to make bricks. There were remains of soldiers' quarters, monastic cells, a palace – but it was not much to look at. After one glance Dima decided to wait for us in the jeep. 'Why are you wasting your time here?' he said to me. 'If you really want to see something of the Silk Road, you should go to Samarkand or Bukhara. The bazaars are so colourful, and the mosques are spectacular.'

But Valentina knew its value; to her it was a mine of information. She surveyed her kingdom of ruins with pride, and spoke to me excitedly. 'This was a junction of the routes across the Taklamakan and over the Heavenly Mountains, and the grassland routes to the north. Our excavations were very much based on Xuanzang's information. He says the town was about three and a half kilometres in circumference, which turned out to be very close to what we found. Xuanzang also says that merchants from surrounding countries congregated and lived here. They supplied the caravans with horses and camels, trading their leather, fur and livestock for luxury goods from the east and west.' Then she opened her bulky bag and took out half a dozen pictures. The first one showed a pile of Chinese coins, round with a square hole in the middle. 'We found so many of these here. Everyone must have used them. I think they would have been as popular as US dollars today. It was the profit from the Silk Road. That was one of the main reasons the Turks were prepared to fight you Chinese at any cost. Do you remember Xuanzang's first impression of the Khan?'

Hui Li has given us an amazingly detailed and colourful account of Xuanzang's meeting with the Khan. What struck Xuanzang first was the Khan's beautiful horses and the silk which was everywhere. The Khan 'wears a coat of green satin, and his hair is loose, pulled back from his forehead with a silk band some ten feet long which drapes down his back. On his left and right stand two hundred officers, all clothed in splendid costumes of brocade silk. Outside are the troops mounted on camels or horses, dressed in fur and fine woollen cloth, carrying long lances, banners and straight bows; the line stretches so far that the eye cannot tell where it ends.'

To maximize their revenue from the Silk Road, the Turks even sought direct trade with the Romans, who, they knew, had an insatiable appetite for silk. In the eastern Roman empire, rulers, aristocrats, merchants – everybody of importance wanted to dress themselves in silk robes; Christian churches abandoned their earlier ascetic traditions in favour of decorating their altars with elaborate silk banners and cloaking their bishops in silk. Valentina told me that it was through the Western Turks that the Romans heard more about the *Sere* land. 'In this vast country,' the Romans were told, 'there are no temples, no prostitutes, no adulterous women, no robbers, no murderers, no victims of murder.' The Chinese were no better informed about the Romans. As late as the fifth century, the Chinese court chronicler wrote: 'In general, the inhabitants are tall and well-built. Some of them resemble the people of the Middle Kingdom and for that we call the country Greater China.' It was in the interests of all the peoples of the Silk Road, in particular the Persians who controlled the silk trade, to keep China and Rome from direct contact. It was not until Marco Polo that the mysteries shrouding China began to disperse.

The Khan received Xuanzang in his tent, which was decorated with golden flowers whose brilliance dazzled the eye. Inside, his officials, all dressed in embroidered silk, sat on mats in two long rows in front of him, while armed guards stood behind him. Xuanzang was given an iron chair with a cushion to sit on. Then the envoys from Gaochang presented their credentials and the state letter to the Khan. He opened the letter immediately. 'The Chinese master is my younger brother,' it read. 'He wishes to go to India to search for the teaching of the Buddha. I wish the Khan will treat him with kindness just as he would treat me.'

After he finished reading the letter, the Khan ordered wine to be brought in and music to be played. 'He drank with the envoys,' Hui Li tells us. 'The guests grew more and more lively, and then challenged one another to drink, clashing their cups together, filling and emptying them in turn. While this was going on, there sounded the crashing chords of barbarian music. Although they were half-savage airs, they charmed the ear and rejoiced the mind and the heart.' In a little while food was served. Xuanzang was given a special 'pure' meal of grape juice, rice cakes, milk, sugar, honey and raisins, while the rest wolfed down boiled flanks of mutton and veal.

In the lively atmosphere of the banquet Xuanzang could at last relax. He was now welcomed by the man the Chinese both feared and admired. 'He was valiant, prudent and excelled in warfare, both in attack and in defence,' say the Tang Annals. 'He had hegemony over the West. Never before had the barbarians been so powerful.' This was the man who would give Xuanzang protection for the rest of his outward journey.

'But Xuanzang was not exactly very flattering about the Khan, was he? Given the help he was going to get,' Valentina said. She was right. This was what he said: 'Although he was only a barbarian sovereign, living under a tent of felt, one could not look at him without a mingled feeling of admiration and respect' – exactly what Salim had complained about. Of course Xuanzang wrote the book for the emperor – he could not praise his enemy. But he did share the Chinese bias against the barbarians, which extended to practically any non-Chinese – the Middle Kingdom mentality of superiority. For a long time I was not aware that we were in fact under 'barbarian' rule during half of our history. We always felt this way; if they adopted our dress, language and mores, this was our victory – we had turned them into Chinese – it was further proof of their inferiority.

Much to Xuanzang's surprise, when the wining and dining

were over the Khan asked him to 'enhance the occasion' by telling them something about Buddhism, of which they knew very little. Looking at the mutton and veal left on their plates, Xuanzang preached a subtle sermon about the need for love of all living creatures and the religious life that led to final deliverance. He would have then talked about the Buddhist concepts of good government. The wise ruler put his people first, and ran his country with benevolence and compassion. And perhaps he would have added a Chinese simile: the ruler and the ruled were like a boat on water; the water could carry the boat, but could also overturn it. Everything depended on the ruler being fair and just.

Whether or not the Khan liked what he heard, he was keen that this erudite young Chinese should tell him more about Emperor Taizong, his chief rival. He begged Xuanzang to stay. 'You must not go to India. It is such a hot country that the temperature is the same in winter as in summer. I fear your face might melt there. The inhabitants are black and the majority are naked, with no respect for convention. They do not merit a visit from you.'

When Xuanzang made clear his firm intention of continuing on his way, the Khan relented. He selected a young officer who could speak Chinese to go with him, and wrote letters of introduction to his vassal states, all as requested by the king of Gaochang, whose sister had married his son. As a parting gift, the Khan presented Xuanzang with a ceremonial robe made of red satin, and fifty pieces of silk. All these proved invaluable: after his disaster in the Heavenly Mountains, Xuanzang was now guaranteed a safe journey all the way to India by the most powerful ruler in Central Asia. He must have felt very fortunate, and relieved. This was the last kindly act of the Khan, who was to die soon after in a coup.

Xuanzang might have kindled the Khan's interest in Buddhism, but it was the Chinese settlers who made Suiye a flourishing Buddhist town on the Silk Road. Valentina fished out yet another photograph, a rubbing from a stele, which they discovered in 1982 and was now in her library. 'See, Xuanzang's idea of propagating the Dharma to the Khan and his people was realized. This was an inscription by Du Huaibao, the Governor of Suiye,' she said, pointing to each of the characters in the photo. The governor said that he erected the foundations for a statue of the Buddha and two Bodhisattvas, for the purpose of protecting the emperor, all of the people in the empire, and obtaining a better life for his dead parents in another world. But Buddhism was not to last. China lost out to the Arabs, who conquered the whole region in the middle of the eighth century and spread their faith, which persists till this day. But the memory of an empire extending this far is with us Chinese still, always associated with the name of Suiye, and its most illustrious son, Li Bai.

Li Bai is arguably the best poet in Chinese history. With his bold, uncontrollable imagination and big nomad heart, his love of Chinese fine culture, his bitterness at his talent not being appreciated enough for him to secure a mandarin post, he poured out his feelings, one hundred years after Xuanzang, and left us some of our most brilliant poems. They are loved by literati and ordinary people, old and young. 'The moonlight through the window, I thought it was frost on the floor. I looked up at the moon, then lowered my head, remembering my home town.' I often remembered these lines when I was away from home. I tried to tell Valentina about the poem, but I did not get very far. To my surprise and pleasure, she completed the verse for me. 'I love Li Bai. What imagination that man had,' she said. Then she produced a line from another poem: '"The path to Sichuan was hard, harder than climbing up to Heaven." For Xuanzang, climbing over the Heavenly Mountains might have been equally difficult. But he did it. I'm sure you'll make it too.' She was so thoughtful, and so knowledgeable; she had really brought Suiye to life for me.

I wish I had been given a protector like the Khan to help me visit Bamiyan and Samarkand. It was said the giant Bamiyan Buddhas were built during the Khan's time. But now there was a civil war and Afghanistan was off-limits. Samarkand is the quintessential Silk Road city, and the golden peach that the King of Samarkand sent to the Chinese court symbolized to Tang China all that was exotic. When Xuanzang came to Samarkand, he was very impressed at the variety of foreign treasures he found there. As he records, the inhabitants, the Sogdians, were the best merchants. Every caravan had a Sogdian as its leader; Sogdian was the language of the Silk Road. The Tang Annals made them even more vivid: 'Mothers give their infants sugar to eat and put paste on the palms of their hands in the hope that when they grow, they will talk sweetly and that precious objects will stick to their hands. These people are skilful merchants; when a boy reaches the age of five he is put to studying books; when he begins to understand them, he is sent to study commerce. They excel at commerce and love profit; from the time a man is twenty he goes to neighbouring kingdoms; wherever one can make money, they have gone.'

But they never forgot their home. With the riches they made abroad, including from China, they built huge mansions that were almost like palaces, and decorated them with scenes of life from distant lands, including Chinese orchestras and Chinese men and women: Xuanzang could have seen them in Panjikent, a prosperous Sogdian town outside Samarkand. In Afrasiab, the old town of Samarkand, there is a mural showing a Chinese emperor hunting with court ladies, illustrating the might and splendour of the Chinese empire, which briefly protected the small kingdom. All these were painted around the time Xuanzang passed through. I really wanted to go there.

On returning to Bishkek, I tried one last time to get an Uzbek visa. The answer was the same as in London and Beijing: No. Even the tone of rejection was the same. A man asked me in a low, rumbling voice, with a hint of menace, what I wanted – exactly how I imagined KGB agents had once sounded. I said I needed a visa.

'What for? What is your agenda? Why now?'

I told him about my journey.

'Are you part of a government delegation?'

I said no.

'Then we can't give you a visa.' He put the phone down.

I dialled the number again.

He picked it up: 'Don't try again. You can't go to Uzbekistan.'

And that was that.

SIX

Imagining the Buddha

X	UANZANG'S JOURNEY through the heartland of Central Asia was long and hazardous. 'The roads were more dangerous and harder to travel than among the ice mountains or in the desert,' he says. 'Thick clouds and flying snow never ceased for a moment, and at the worst places the snow piled up for scores of feet.' It must have reminded him of his perilous encounters in the Taklamakan and over the Heavenly Mountains. He had learned his lesson: he was travelling carefully, stopping constantly to check his direction. But the whole world was one big white sheet. As he dreaded, he and his men were lost again. While they were struggling to find the way, a group of hunters appeared and guided them back to the road.

Xuanzang arrived in Peshawar in the autumn of 628, a year after he had been on the road. This was the moment he had been waiting for with great anticipation. Peshawar, the capital of ancient Kingdom of Gandhara, was the second holy land of Buddhism, where many Mahayana sutras originated. The Buddhist canon was full of stories about the previous lives of the Buddha that had unfolded in this kingdom: where he had washed his robe, where he had left his alms bowl, where he had subdued the dragon that was terrorizing people, where he appeared in the Indus River as a fish for the starving, where he had fed himself to a hungry tigress and her cubs, and where his relics were buried. Xuanzang had been reading them since he was a child, reminding himself constantly of the sacrifices that the Buddha had made. Now he was going to see where they had happened. Peshawar had another significance for him: it was home to Asanga and Vasubandhu, two of the greatest Buddhist philosophers, and of his own Yogacara school. They had motivated Xuanzang to undertake his journey in the first place. At last he had a chance to receive instructions at the monastery of the Yogacara masters. He would be able to clarify the doubts that had been wearing him down.

But he was shocked by what he found. The White Huns, a nomadic Turk-Mongol people of the Eurasian steppes, had completely destroyed Peshawar when they passed through it on their way to conquer India two centuries before. 'There is no king and the country is governed from the neighbouring country,' he writes sadly. 'Towns and villages are almost empty, and abandoned. About a thousand families live in one corner of the capital ... They are timid and gentle and they love literature. Most of them are heretics and very few believe in the Dharma.'

I flew to Peshawar via Islamabad, in December 1999. My arrival was as unpromising as Xuanzang's. I had been told to write my name on a piece of paper and hold it up for a driver to identify me. I never took it out of my pocket. Towered over by two ranks of Pashtun men on either side of the arrival gate, tall, bearded and overbearing, some with machine-guns slung over their shoulders, I shrivelled to jelly. Their faces were as cold and blank as stone, betraying nothing, but their deep eyes were sharp as knives, ready to dissect you if you dared to meet their stares. I had put on a shalwar-kameez, a long dress with trousers. But going native was no defence against their intense scrutiny – wearing a burkha might not have been a bad idea. All I could do was to focus my mind and my eyes firmly on the ground, while walking faster and faster, almost bursting into a sprint. I found myself a quiet corner behind the public telephone booth. I did not know how the driver was going to find me but I simply did not want to go back there. After what seemed to be ages, the crowds dispersed, until there was only one man standing there, anxiously looking around while talking into his mobile. That was the driver.

After his initial shock, Xuanzang settled down in one of a few monasteries that still had monks in them; it was overgrown with weeds. The very monastery where he had dreamt of studying was all but abandoned, although it still retained traces of its former glory, with long open corridors, dark spacious halls in building after building. He saw the plaque outside a room where Vasubandhu used to live, but when he enquired about Yogacara from the few monks there, they knew nothing about it. He must go on to India to continue his quest. But first, he wanted to pay his homage to the numerous sacred places associated with the Buddha in Gandhara. Travelling from one place to another, he recorded the details of the stories linked with them, and how people still worshipped there. Largely due to the precision of this information, Alfred Foucher, the great French Sanskrit scholar and archaeologist of India and Pakistan, was able to identify the most celebrated Buddhist monuments in Peshawar and the surrounding areas.

Of Peshawar's rich Buddhist past, only some sites which Foucher located are still in evidence. But I had enough to see. My host Peter, whom I had met only once before through a mutual friend, took me to his cosy home in the quiet university area, and over dinner with his wife we discussed my plans. I told them of my experience at the airport. Peter apologized for not coming to meet me in person. He had been in Peshawar a few years, working for the United Nations. He said the place was becoming increasingly fundamentalist. Only a few days before he had seen a Pashtun waving his gun at a young woman who was not wearing a burkha. I could go around town on my own if I wanted, he said, but he did not think it a good idea. Happily, a Pashtun bodyguard had turned up who was bored – his employer had gone back to England on holiday. He would be happy to shepherd me around. After the experience at the airport, I certainly felt I could do with his presence, both for assurance and for protection.

Keewar came to pick me up in the morning. He was shorter than the Pashtuns at the arrival gate, but stocky, strong and grave, and his face was inscrutable. He had on a grey kurta pajama under a blue fleece jacket, and a pair of sunglasses. I asked him if I could bring my camera and take pictures. 'Why not?' He looked at me blankly from behind his dark glasses. 'We shoot people dead in the street, no reason why you cannot take their pictures.' I was surely in the land of the Pashtuns. I looked at him again. I was glad he did not carry a gun. That would be too much. He laughed and asked me if I wanted to see one. Like a conjuror, he slid a hand-gun out from under his fleece jacket. 'Is it real?' I asked. 'Feel it,' he said. I had never held a gun before. It was cold, hard-edged, repellent. 'This is Peshawar. Every man, young or old, has a gun. You need one just to survive, preferably more than one,' he said matter-of-factly. 'There's an arms bazaar on the outskirts of Peshawar. You can buy anything you want, bandoliers, Kalashnikovs, anti-aircraft guns, even rocket-launchers. Do you want to see it? It is on the way to the Khyber Pass.' I said I would think about it.

I wanted to go to the Khyber Pass, the frontier post of Pakistan with Afghanistan. Xuanzang came through it to Peshawar. I was keen to trace it, even if backwards, to see what the place was like. First I had to get special permission from the tribal authorities. From the outskirts of Peshawar all the way to the hills of the Afghan border was the Pashtun homeland. The area was in effect out of the control of the Pakistani government – a practice inherited from the British; the Pashtuns had their own laws administered by the tribal council. In a spacious courtyard in downtown Peshawar, for a few dollars, the authorities issued me a pass, and a Pashtun frontier guard, armed with a machine-gun and a belt of bullets around his waist. He would conduct me and Keewar to the Khyber Pass and back. With him in the front seat and Keewar next to me, I never felt so safe in my life. Xuanzang had soldiers from the Khan of the Western Turks to protect him. Now I had mine, and off we went in our Morris taxi.

We did drop in at the Darra arms bazaar, just over the border of the tribal areas. From a distance, it looks like a normal bazaar, a street lined with endless shops. But as we came closer, the strange reality dawned. No fruit, vegetables or household goods, just weapons and ammunition. Heavy gear like rocket-launchers was left outside the shops; inside, over the counters, in glass cupboards, and hanging on the walls, was a range of guns, shells and bullets which I had only ever seen in films. I did not know what most of them were, and I walked as though I was on egg-shells, worried I might set something off. But Keewar and the frontier guard were like boys in a toy shop, wanting to try everything. They slung American automatics over their shoulders as I would try a handbag.

'But do people actually use the weapons?' I asked the two

of them, who were going in and out of the shops, comparing prices.

'Why not?' the guard replied in surprise.

'But on whom?'

'On your enemies, on your relatives, even on your friends if they cross your path,' Keewar said, his eyes now fixed on a Lee-Enfield. 'Isn't it a beauty? They make them here.' And then he turned to me. 'That is how the Pashtuns settle their disputes and blood feuds, with guns.'

'What about the tribal council? I thought their job was to keep law and order.'

'They try, but people don't have to listen to them, especially if the clan is big, with lots of men. In the end only your guns can protect you.'

My mind still full of guns and bullets, we reached Landi Khotal, the summit of the Khyber Pass, near lunchtime. Our guard whispered something in Keewar's ear and then disappeared, leaving us to a dozen soldiers who were checking a long queue of trucks filled to the brim with Afghans. This was called the gateway into Asia, and standing here I understood what that meant. The steep mountains on both sides converge here, and have left a space barely wide enough for two trucks. As the Chinese say, 'If a man stands here, ten thousand men will not be able to take it.' Xuanzang would have been thoroughly checked, as were the passengers on the trucks today. Little seemed to have changed in this barren land. This narrow pass was the only way into India before the sea routes opened. The fabled riches of India – precious jewels scattered on the ground like dust, and fields so fertile that crops would grow on their own – were an irresistible lure. Throughout the centuries, the Khyber Pass has seen invaders of all kinds with their minds set on conquering the Indian subcontinent –

Greeks, Persians, the Kushans, Huns, Turks, Arabs, Mughals and the British. Each bringing destruction, as Xuanzang had experienced so painfully, but each also bequeathing their culture and their men and women to settle here. The Pashtuns, of Iranian descent, were among the last to arrive in the fifteenth century.

I wanted to walk down the pass – the border is barely a mile away, but the soldiers waved me away with their rifles. Reluctantly I turned back. In the distance, I could see the roads and villages inside Afghanistan on this cloudless, warm day. Keewar said if he got a lift, he could be home for dinner with his wife and three children, whom he had not seen for a long time. They lived in a village not far from Kabul. He did not bring them over because they would have to stay in a refugee camp until he had saved enough money to rent a house. I asked him why he had not gone to visit them.

He shook his head. 'The Taliban are really crazy. If I walked in the street like this, I would be fined on the spot, or even locked up,' Keewar said, touching his beard, 'because this is way too short by their standards. You know every man has to wear a beard, up to the required length; every woman has to wear a burkha. I could not listen to music or read books, or hang pictures in my house. My kids cannot fly kites or play in the park. How can people live like that? They are fanatics.'

The Taliban, or 'Students', were mainly Pashtuns. They made themselves known to the world when they took Kabul in 1996. Before that, they were just one of the warring factions in the fighting in Afghanistan after the Soviets' humiliating defeat. At first people were impressed by their toughness and efficiency; they were even welcomed by many Afghans for bringing order to the country and eliminating corruption. But soon their religious fanaticism shocked the world. Intent on establishing the purest possible Islamic state, they pursued the most extreme form of Islam, including all its harsh punishments, amputating thieves' hands and stoning adulterous wives; as became well known, they were particularly oppressive towards women, forbidding them to work or visit doctors, hospitals or schools, virtually confining them like prisoners to their homes.

I found them horrifying, as did most people. They seemed to be returning Afghanistan to the Dark Ages. But Xuanzang would have found their fanaticism true to form. 'These people are remarkable, among their neighbours, for the strength of their faith,' he says of the locals. 'From worshipping Buddha, the Dharma and the Sangha, the three jewels of Buddhism, down to the worshipping of local spirits in their hundreds, they have the utmost devotion of heart and sincerity.' Xuanzang's observation, remarkable for its continuing relevance, came from his personal experience, as well as his historical knowledge. According to legend the first disciples of the Buddha were two merchants from today's Afghanistan. They met the Buddha just after his enlightenment and offered him wheatcakes and honey; in return, the Buddha taught them what he had just realized. Xuanzang says they were so impressed, they asked for something to remember him by. The Buddha gave them a lock of his hair. When they returned to their country, they built a stupa in the way that the Buddha had taught them and put the hair in it. This, Xuanzang tells us, was the first stupa in the world. He even saw it when he travelled through the country.

For over a thousand years, Buddhism flourished in Afghanistan. The giant Buddhas of Bamiyan, the tallest in the world, were witness to the piety that Xuanzang records. Not content with worshipping the Buddha in their own homeland, the

Buddhists in Afghanistan played an important role in promulgating Buddhism along the Silk Road. The Chinese canon records the names of seventeen distinguished monks from the Kabul valley who, risking their lives, arrived in a strange land with sacks full of scriptures, and devoted themselves to translating them into Chinese. Only the Indians did more to spread Buddhism in China. Xuanzang was trained on their translations and when he passed through the country, there were still tens of thousands of monks. Their knowledge and earnestness affected him so deeply that he spent four months studying with them, in particular the doctrines of Theravada Buddhism, which he felt he should know more about, after his experience in Kucha.

Xuanzang was moved by the teachings – and something more. He found Afghanistan full of places that were made sacred to the Buddha in the Mahayana sutras. He was particularly joyful when he visited the town of Hadda, whose shrines he tells us held the Buddha's skull bone, his eyes, robe and staff. Xuanzang donated a large share of the King of Gaochang's gifts to the shrines. The guardian priest then told the pilgrim that he could tell his fortune for his journey by making an impression from the skull bone, with incense powder wrapped in silk. He simply could not resist the idea. He had been on the road for a year, a very difficult year, and he was now on the edge of the holy land. He wanted to be assured that his journey ahead would be successful. On his piece of silk was an impression of the Bodhi Tree, the tree of enlightenment. Xuanzang was overjoyed when the priest told him, 'That is a rare omen; it signifies that you will surely realize Bodhi.'

A casket made for the Buddha's relics is still with us, bearing the inscription 'For the Lord's relics, in honour of all Buddhas'.

It contained a small round reliquary of pure gold, with images of a standing Buddha flanked by Brahma and Indra, the Indian gods who became part of the Buddhist pantheon, and two Bodhisattvas. It is a prized possession of the British Museum. The explorer Charles Masson discovered it in the 1830s in a ruined stupa at Bimaran west of Jalalabad – a few miles from Hadda. His beautiful drawings of the stupas, monasteries and caves that littered the plains of the Kabul valley and Jalalabad give us some reminder of the great riches of the Buddhist past of Afghanistan that Xuanzang saw. Until fifteen years ago, the Hadda museum housed some of the most beautiful Graeco-Roman friezes: the heavenly god who looked exactly like Hercules, a Buddha like Zeus, and a classical temple dedicated to the Buddha. The whole museum was reduced to ashes in the Afghan civil war.

Keewar said Jalalabad was a stronghold of the Taliban. He pointed it out in the distance. 'I never knew it had such a rich history.' He turned to me. 'I thought it was just another shanty town. But if the Taliban have their way, we will not have any history left. Since they took control of Bamiyan, their soldiers have turned the cells behind the Buddhas into barracks and storage rooms for ammunition. Then they blew off the head and shoulders of the small Buddha and fired rockets at the big Buddha's groin. They even threatened to destroy them.'

So it was out of the question for me to see them? Even if I went in dressed in a burkha?

He turned around and looked at me as if I was mad. 'Do you really want to end your journey there?' he said, shaking his head. 'Taliban won't let you near the statues. You can't go, it's too dangerous. I wouldn't dare to myself.'

Another time, I said to myself.

Keewar suggested we go and find our guard. We came to

a house not far from the pass, a group of old men sitting outside, drinking *khawa*, a clear, sweet Chinese green tea. Inside it was dark, with only a ray of sunshine slanting through the window, glistening in the dusty air. Our guard was nodding off in a druggy haze in the corner. I wondered if he was capable of fighting back if his fellow-Pashtuns attacked us. But this is the home of the drug trade. Keewar said every drug was available here. The men who served us food would sell us hashish, opium and heroin. 'Most of the drugs in Britain come from here. That's what keeps the warlords going in Afghanistan.' From the look of our guard, it also gave the Pashtuns themselves one of the few comforts in their harsh and violent world.

We arrived back in Peshawar in the early afternoon, and returned our guard safely to the tribal authorities. From there it was only a short distance to the Peshawar Museum. It holds a superlative collection of Buddhist statues, some of which Xuanzang may have seen in their original stupas and monasteries.

Keewar was not interested. 'We Muslims don't go in for idols, you know,' he said.

'I need you to protect me,' I joked.

'Don't worry. It's absolutely safe there. That's one place you won't need me,' he said seriously. He dropped me in front of an elegant Victorian colonial building, with oriental turrets on the roof.

I went inside, and the noise of the streets gave way to a profound silence. There was no one there. The main hall is quite grand, its two floors surrounding a central atrium, from which you walk under stone Islamic arches into the galleries on either side, filled with Buddhist statues, reliefs and stucco heads collected from monasteries all over the Peshawar valley.

It was so quiet: the only sound was my own footsteps on the marble floor. I looked around. Some Buddhas and Bodhisattvas stood against the pillars of the hall, larger than life-size, looking down benignly at me. Others were in deep meditation. There were rows of busts and heads, some brightly painted, with expressions of sadness and serenity. The longer I gazed at them, the more I felt as though I was in a monastery.

Would Xuanzang have found anything unusual about the statues – the curly hair tied in a knot on the crown of the Buddha or Bodhisattva, the robes they wear over one shoulder or both, with flowing folds cascading down to the ankles, the sandals on their feet? On the panels and reliefs depicting the life of the Buddha, there are buildings with Corinthian columns, trefoil arches and triangular pediments. I remembered being puzzled by the Buddha's curly hair in Chinese temples and asked a monk about it.

'The Buddha is an Indian,' he said indignantly, as if I had asked something foolish.

'But the Indians have straight hair like us,' I said.

'What are you implying?' He raised his voice. 'Do you mean the Buddha was a Westerner?'

'Of course not,' I said, 'but his curly hair is rather unusual.'

'They always make it like that,' the monk explained patiently. 'You haven't seen many so you are surprised easily.' He used a Chinese idiom to bring his point home.

But the curls did belong to Westerners, or the Greeks, to be more precise, as I discovered to my surprise. The making of these images of the Buddha is one of the most extraordinary stories of cultural fusion on the Silk Road. The Buddha forbade the worship of his image. 'Follow my teaching, not me,' he told his disciples repeatedly. For several hundred years, his followers adhered to the advice, worshipping the Bodhi Tree under which he became enlightened, his footprint, or a stupa. They also felt that nothing could express the sublime state of enlightenment. As the Sutra Nipata, a text of the Pali canon, says, 'He who (like the sun) has gone to rest is comparable to nothing whatsoever. The notions through which his essence might be expressed are simply not to be found. All ideas are nothing; all modes of speech are, with respect to him, unavailing.'

Xuanzang would have seen these Greek-influenced statues in many places he visited, and possibly he saw the particularly fine ones in Gandhara, without knowing they could have been among the earliest images of the Buddha to be produced. If anything, he looked for a divine origin. He records this story. After his enlightenment, the Buddha spent some months in Tushita, the paradise of the Maitreya Buddha, preaching the Dharma to his mother who had been reborn there. An Indian king who revered him was worried that he might not return, and wanted to have at least his image. By magical means, a Bodhisattva sent an artist up there to memorize the Buddha's features and come back and carve a figure of him in sandalwood. When the Buddha did return the statue rose to welcome him. This was supposed to be the first Buddhist statue in the world. Xuanzang was so impressed, he had a replica made of it and brought it back to China.

The truth was that sculptors working in the Greek tradition represented the Buddha in human form some five hundred years after his death. The Greeks first came to the area with Alexander the Great. Having conquered the entire classical world and brought the Persian empire under his control, he made his way through Afghanistan. Once past the valley of Peshawar, meeting with little resistance, he was poised on the edge of India. But his men were unimpressed: they were worn out and homesick after eight years of continuous fighting. They had had enough and wanted to go home. Facing a potential mutiny, Alexander had no choice but to turn back, leaving a series of Greek garrisons behind to guard his conquests. He died on the return journey in Babylon in 323 BC, and his empire fell apart. But one of his generals, Seleucus Nicator, came back to take hold of parts of India in 305, eventually giving them all back except Bactria in the northern Afghanistan of today. The Bactrian Greeks, in turn, were eventually pushed southwards, but Greek influence persisted in the region for a long time, as we know from coins and sculptural reliefs.

One of the most famous converts in the history of Buddhism was the Indo-Greek King Menander of Bactria of the second century BC, or Milinder as he is known in Buddhist scriptures. Learned and wise, the king was fascinated by the teachings of the Buddha, but he had many questions, and doubts. If lay people like him, living at home and enjoying the sensual pleasures of the world, could achieve enlightenment, what was the use of monks inflicting austerity on themselves for the same goal? Why did the sutras say if the faithful worshipped the remains of the Buddha, they would go to paradise, while the Buddha told his disciples not to worship them? Why was there no self in Buddhism? What was the nature of nirvana, the highest goal and the final liberation for Buddhists? These are some of *King Milinder's Questions*, a classic Buddhist text, with which Xuanzang would have been very familiar. The questions are like the FAQs on the Web; they cover the kinds of difficulties many people have with Buddhism, especially when it is completely new to them. That is why it is a very popular text. It responds to doubts I have myself.

Nasagena, the great Indian master, made the most subtle,

difficult and transient concepts easy to understand by using metaphors and similes. Deeply embedded in the Greek philosophical tradition of reason and logic, King Milinder found the notion of nirvana difficult to grasp, as many people still do. He thought it could not exist.

'Is there, great King, something called "wind"?' Nagasena asked him.

'Yes, there is such a thing.'

'Please, will Your Majesty show me the wind, its colour and shape, and whether it is thin or thick, long or short.'

'One cannot describe the wind like that. For the wind does not lend itself to being grasped with hands, or to being touched. But nevertheless there is such a thing as "wind".'

'Just so, Your Majesty, there is nirvana, but one cannot point to nirvana, either by its colour or its shape.'

We do not know why images of the Buddha appear round about the first century AD. Someone may have asked the same question a Chinese Buddhist was to ask later, when he inscribed this on the bottom of a Buddha figure: 'The highest truth is without image. Yet if there were no image the truth could not manifest itself. The highest principle is without words. Yet if there were no words how could the principle be known?' An image could not attain the ultimate truth, but it could help the faithful meditate on the truth, lead them by its very beauty to the verge of the absolute, and enable them more easily to transcend the bounds of worldly phenomena.

Some argue that the very first Buddhist images came from Mathura in northern India. Precisely how the very different Gandhara style, as it is called, percolated into the local sculpture is uncertain; it was just part of a prolonged cultural exchange between Asia and the Graeco-Roman world. But not long after the Mathura images were created, Buddhists in

Gandhara – conceivably descended from Greek settlers in the region – wanted images of the Buddha of their own, and perhaps based them on icons they knew, statues of the Greek gods. The artists dressed the Buddha in a toga and Athenian sandals; they also followed the Greek tradition of giving him becoming curly locks rather than depicting him as a bald-headed monk. But they did not forget that he had been an Indian prince, so he was given perfect almond-shaped eyes and a finely trimmed moustache, and his earlobes were lengthened, a reminder of the heavy jewels that he used to wear. The Gandhara Buddhas are unmistakably Indian in conception and Greek in execution.

What these artists achieved was to come as close as humanly possible to an image of an enlightened being. Whether standing with their hands raised in the symbolic gesture of protection or seated on a lotus throne in deep meditation, the best statues of the Buddha in the Peshawar Museum have an air of calm, tranquillity and spirituality. Their eyes open or half-closed, they seem detached, faraway, withdrawn into the realm of emptiness by deep meditation. Buddhists immediately took to them. From the Buddhist images of Afghanistan to the Buddhist caves in the oases of Chinese Central Asia, from the murals and statues in the heartland of China to the temples of Korea and Japan, the Buddhas and Bodhisattvas of Gandhara might have been startling at first, as they were to me when I saw them in Kucha, but they soon took over the Buddhist imagination. Now it is hard to think of Buddhism without them: carved out of giant rocks on main trade routes, as the focal point of temples, on altar tables in private homes, and hanging from pendants worn by men and women, they have become the universal emblem of Buddhism.

I stayed in the museum until closing-time, almost in a

trance, moved both by the sculptures and the thought that Xuanzang may have looked on them himself. But eventually I had to come down to earth, or almost: the evening that lay ahead was slightly unreal too. Peter and his wife took me to the club near their house. It was a bungalow with a huge and beautifully kept garden. The air was cool, there were women wearing beautiful pashmina shawls and men in smart jackets. The tablecloths were beautifully starched, the wine glasses sparkled under the chandeliers, the napkins were folded into impeccable peacock's-tails, as were the ends of the waiters' turbans. The food was quintessentially English, lamb and mint sauce, custard tart. You could not believe you were in one of the world's most strife-torn regions.

The day was one of the strangest of my life – the morning full of guns, drugs and tales of violence, the afternoon a meditation surrounded by ethereal Buddhist presences, the evening a piece of post-colonial theatre. I could not fit these together, except by thinking that Xuanzang went through something comparable: he witnessed the destruction of the White Huns, but saw the greatest Gandharan Buddhas, and met strange foreigners who populated the land, descendants of the Greeks, Kushans, Persians and Turks. It is a volatile place, forever being trampled on. The Pashtuns had learned to survive, and perhaps need a faith as forceful as Islam. The miracle was that Buddhism once flowered so finely here, and that so many beautiful monuments to it were still here to be seen.

Over dinner Peter confirmed what I had expected: it really was impossible for me to go into Afghanistan. The Taliban were not only being uncooperative, they were harassing UN staff on the ground. He had heard that a Taliban general had physically beaten up a UN official who would not agree to his terms. Nobody was sure what they were going to do next;

they seemed to be a law unto themselves. The UN was thinking of pulling all its people out. The Taliban were mad, Peter said, they would not listen to anyone. He tried to cheer me up – the everyday life depicted on the Gandharan reliefs, the feel of a Silk Road city as Xuanzang would have known it, could still be found in the old Peshawar.

The next day Keewar and I took a taxi to the old town. Keewar decided not to take his gun. 'You're a beautiful woman, no threat to anyone. Just put the scarf of your shalwar-kameez over your head. That's enough protection.' He laughed. As we drove along, one thing struck me forcibly – there were hardly any women to be seen, and the few who walked by the road-side were swathed in blue from head to foot, invisible. I had just come through Xinjiang and Kyrgyzstan, where women mingled freely with men everywhere I went, and I never felt out of place. I had intended to ask Keewar about this the day before.

'It must be awful having to wear the burkha,' I said, thinking also of his wife in Afghanistan.

'Every woman has to under the Taliban if she doesn't want trouble.' After a long pause, he added: 'Given how things are, perhaps it is better for her to hide behind a burkha, or to be a prisoner inside the house.'

I asked him what he meant by that.

'You don't know the Taliban,' said Keewar. 'They've been fighting non-stop for many years. Most of the time they're stuck in the mountains and never see a woman. They're all charged up, but have no relief. So when they take a place the soldiers go on a rampage of raping, from young girls to old women, anything that has breasts. I think the urge is still there. It is best for women to keep out of their sight.

'Is it true the Chinese women used to have their feet bound?'

he came back at me. 'Why? That sounds worse than wearing the burkha, don't you think?'

Keewar was right in a way. Foot-binding was the worst kind of male domination. Men thought it made women look sexier. But it also crippled them and stopped them running away, although they still had to do all the hard work. But at least we put a stop to it ages ago. That was one of the best things Communism did for us: making sure women could all go to school, get jobs and choose their own husbands.

'You've done pretty well, haven't you?' He looked me in the eyes. 'I mean, travelling around on your own like this. Is your husband happy?'

'He isn't happy,' I said, 'but he wouldn't stop me doing what I want to do.' Keewar stared at me, perplexed by the freedom I enjoyed, which would be unthinkable for an Afghan wife.

We passed several mosques and I told Keewar that it was a real pity that women were not allowed in. 'I think you'd be too distracting for the men. So we'd better keep you away,' he said jokingly, and then became serious. 'I don't know why women are considered to be unclean.'

I told Keewar Buddhism has restrictions on women too – a nun, however senior she is, has to walk behind the youngest monk in Buddhist ceremonies, but at least in Buddhism women have the same potential for enlightenment as men. Women like my grandmother are the backbone of the faith. They look after the family altar in the house; they go to the temples; they say prayers and make offerings – I cannot imagine Buddhism without women. The favourite Bodhisattva in China is Guanyin, a woman.

'That was also what our people believed over a thousand years ago. Very interesting,' Keewar said with a thoughtful look. 'But here we are – time to find what you are looking for.'

We had reached the centre of old Peshawar. Fittingly for a Silk Road town, it is called the Storytellers' Bazaar. Here the caravans that Xuanzang travelled with would have camped and exchanged information about their commodities and journeys ahead, and then been entertained by storytellers. Xuanzang would have stayed in a monastery, although he must have wandered in the bazaar and collected the history and legends of the Kingdom of Gandhara, some of which found their way into his *Record*. More than a thousand years later, after all the wars and destruction that have taken place in this region, there is nothing to be found that he could have seen. But the bazaar is still, as in the old days, the centre of the town's life.

A wide avenue, it was thronged with cars, carts, men and children. Instead of storytellers, loudspeakers were playing Qawali music. Narrow lanes spiralled away from the bazaar, up steep steps and around corners into a maze of stalls specializing in vegetables, fruits, spices, clothes, hardware, grains, money-lending, jewellery, anything you can think of. Some alleys were so constricted you could not even walk two abreast. I would have been scared to go down them alone: there were so many hidden doorways into which someone could snatch you and you would never be seen again. But with Keewar there I felt safe. I could not help noticing that the sandals on people's feet and the jewellery displayed in the windows of the silversmiths were almost the same as those worn by the Bodhisattvas in the museum. The bright blue eyes of men and children that met my gaze reminded me of the former Greek settlers. I really did feel I had gone back in time to the old days of the Silk Road, when Xuanzang came here.

The bazaars at that time were probably even busier, for the

Romans had an insatiable appetite for Indian spices and the Indians were as fascinated by Chinese silk as the Romans, not only to make beautiful garments but also to adorn their stupas and shrines. And there were other treasures. In the third century BC the great Indian ruler Asoka built a road linking the heart of the Gangetic plain with the northwest of his empire. This made Peshawar one of the richest cities along the highways of the Silk Road. Wealth flowed into the pockets of the merchants of Gandhara, and their coffers paid for the innumerable monasteries that Xuanzang records.

One place in the bazaar that I was particularly interested in was the grain market, where the guidebook says a pipal tree had once been. Xuanzang tells us this was an important pilgrimage site in Peshawar at the time – where the Buddha sat, and where he told Ananda, his favourite disciple, that four hundred years after his death, there would be a king by the name of Kanishka who would worship the Dharma, and build a stupa near the pipal tree to hold his relics. It did not seem to matter that the Buddha never came to Peshawar, nor that this forecast of Kanishka's conversion to Buddhism was perhaps added to the sutras much later. Xuanzang believed, as all Buddhists do, that the Buddha had gone through numerous previous lives, many of which he spent in the Kingdom of Gandhara, for his final enlightenment. Kanishka would have been a very familiar figure to Xuanzang. His people, the Kushans, were descended from the Yuechi, a nomadic tribe, who originally lived beyond the Great Wall, and were driven out of their homes by the Chinese; they migrated westward, and finally set up an empire of their own, stretching from the oases in the Taklamakan Desert to the northern Gangetic plains of India, with its winter capital in Peshawar. Although worshipping Persian deities, the Kushans also embraced Buddhism, in particular under King Kanishka, the greatest of the Kushan rulers, and his successor, in the second century A D. The many richly endowed stupas and monasteries that Xuanzang saw in Peshawar and nearby came from this time, as did the sublime images of the Buddha and Bodhisattvas first created in the Kushan empire. There were even coins bearing the image of the Buddha on one side and Kanishka himself on the reverse.

At the time of Xuanzang's visit, the stupa that legend says Kanishka built to hold the Buddha's relics was destroyed by a fire. The locals told him it was the third time that this giant stupa of almost 150 feet had caught fire, and that 'after the seventh time, Buddhism would disappear'. Buddhism did indeed disappear from Gandhara, and the stupa was destroyed in the tenth century and its remains were buried under a mound of earth until Xuanzang's record led the British archaeologist Alexander Cunningham to identify it in the nineteenth century.

The pipal tree lasted much longer – till the nineteenth century; it was referred to by the great Mughal emperors Babur and Akbar. A friendly-looking shopkeeper invited us to sit with him among his sacks of corn, maize, flour and two dozen different kinds of lentils, green, yellow, brown and black, and we joined him for a cup of *khawa*. I asked him if he knew about the tree.

'Many Japanese visitors come to look for the tree,' he said. 'What is so special about it?'

I told him that the Buddha once sat under it.

'So?' He looked at me, expectantly.

'So they want to come and pay homage.'

'Are you a Buddhist?' he asked.

I said I was very interested in Buddhism.

'Are you interested in Buddhist statues?' he said in a quieter voice.

'I saw some beautiful ones in Peshawar Museum yesterday.'

'Sometimes you people try to buy one.' He seemed to think I was a rich Japanese.

'Is that possible?'

'It can be arranged. There are people dealing in this sort of thing. Are you interested?' he asked as casually as he could.

I had heard antique-smuggling was rife in Peshawar. The Kabul Museum was hit so many times: the roof had fallen in and the façade had been demolished by rockets. Its collection, one of the most precious in the world, over 100,000 pieces, had been plundered since the withdrawal of the Soviet armies in 1992. Among the best were the magnificent Begram treasures, which included exquisitely carved ivory panels from India, Roman bronzes, and the finest of all, a glass vase representing one of the seven wonders of the ancient world – the famous lighthouse at Alexandria. People said it was easy to acquire valuable antiques here, and I decided to try for myself. I asked the shopkeeper what he had.

'Anything you want,' he said confidently. 'Statues, stucco heads, coins, jewellery.'

'Could I take them out of the country?' I asked.

'No problem. We will help you.'

'Can I have a look at a small Gandhara head and some coins?'

'Just wait.'

He disappeared. I asked Keewar what he knew about antique-smuggling. 'It's a big business here. Everyone is involved – farmers, tribesmen, politicians, parliament members, customs officials. It is as well organized as drug trafficking, and perhaps even more profitable.'

The man reappeared half an hour later, with a little sack. We retreated into the back of his shop. Slowly from his sack emerged handfuls of copper coins, whose dates or authenticity I could not determine. But of the beautiful stucco head of a Bodhisattva, there was no denying the antiquity. The expression on the face was so otherworldly. I doubted whether anyone who did not truly understand the message of the Buddha could copy it so perfectly. It was like some of the best pieces in the Peshawar Museum. Its price was thirty thousand pounds. I could not afford it, but he said there were plenty of eager buyers. From the maze-like bazaars of Peshawar, the treasures of Afghanistan and Pakistan, piece by piece, will wriggle their way to private owners, dealers and museums in the Far East and the West, until there will be nothing left inside the country. Thank God, I remember thinking, they could not smuggle the giant Buddhas of Bamiyan.

As everyone now knows, the worst was yet to come. On 26 February 2001, a year after I had tried in vain to enter Afghanistan, Mullah Mohammed Omar issued this decree:

> In view of the Fatwa of prominent Afghan scholars and the verdict of the Afghan Supreme Court, it has been decided to break down all statues/idols present in different parts of the country. This is because these idols have been gods of the infidels, who worshipped them, and these are respected even now and perhaps may be turned into gods again. The real god is only Allah, and all other false gods should be removed.

The destruction started with the Buddhas of Bamiyan. 'The statues had been left over from our ancestors as a wrong heritage,' the international community was told and its pleas, protests and requests to purchase them were completely ignored. As the world watched helplessly, tanks and anti-aircraft rocket-launchers fired round after round at the Buddhas, knocking off the heads, the legs and the heavy folds of their robes. But the statues which had been standing there for over a millennium, and had withstood the onslaught of Genghis Khan's army, would not surrender.

I thought of Xuanzang often during those fateful weeks of destruction. He had stood right there, just after they were built. He received a warm reception on reaching the Kingdom of Bamiyan. The king came out to meet him in person and invited him to the palace. He was, Xuanzang says, so devout that he frequently assembled his people and the monks in the country to give away all his possessions, only to have them bartered back by his ministers and officers. On meeting Xuanzang, the monks were surprised, Hui Li tells us, 'that there should be such a great master in a country as distant as China. With great courtesy they accompanied him to all the holy places.' This is how Xuanzang describes the bigger of the statues: 'To the northeast of the royal city there is a mountain, on whose slope there stands a stone figure of the Buddha, erect, 145 or 150 feet in height. Its golden hues sparkle on every side, and its precious ornaments dazzle the eyes by their brightness.'

Disturbed by how long it had taken to destroy them, Mohammed Omar instructed that a hundred cows be slaughtered around the country 'to atone for the delay in the demolition of the statues'. To speed up their action, soldiers climbed up and down the tunnels behind the giant statues and filled them with dynamite. Then the final moment came. The Taliban filmed the whole act of destruction, and put it on video, showing it around the world, as yet another gesture of their defiance. I watched it on the Internet at home in disbelief, as a huge explosion shook the ground amid cheers and cries of delight, 'God is great,' and 'Whatever God wills'. Then a cloud of dust and smoke filled the air and the valley, shrouding the entire mountain. When the dust settled and the smoke cleared, where the two Buddhas had stood was nothing but two gaping holes. On the ground lay two huge piles of rubble that were once the Buddhas of Bamiyan. Then the Taliban soldiers scrambled up into the empty spaces, waving and shouting in triumph. They looked as small as scorpions but just as deadly. Their commander who oversaw the destruction later announced to the world: 'First, we destroyed the small statue. It was a woman. Then we blew up her husband.'

The two colossal Buddhas were gone. So too were most of the sculptures that had survived in the Kabul Museum. The Taliban soldiers burst in there and for three days smashed with hammers and axes what was left of the thousands of statues. The last one to go was the finest piece in the museum's collection, the second-century limestone statue of King Kanishka, the great patron of Buddhism. They laughed while they hacked it to pieces, until it was reduced to yet another pile of rubble. Every trace of Buddhism, every image was to be erased from Afghanistan. Their ancestors had built the biggest statues of the Buddha that the world has ever seen to prove the strength of their faith; now they proved themselves to Allah by destroying them.

In the end, the Taliban achieved something they never intended. The weeks of shelling and the final destruction of the statues focused the whole world's attention on Afghanistan's rich Buddhist past, the history of these stone sculptures, and, as Xuanzang described, the fervour of the local people's devotion which led them to create them. Afghanistan was known for war, strife, starvation and fanaticism. Now its hidden history was revealed. When the statues were standing there, they were ignored, their existence unknown to most people. Now they are gone, they have perhaps acquired a lasting place, more beautiful and more revered, in people's hearts. From this brutal act something invaluable was born: an understanding of Buddhism has spread where it had not reached before. Out of death comes rebirth – this was a Buddhist message after all.

SEVEN

Light from the Moon

I NEVER KNEW where our name for India came from, or even what it really meant, until I read Xuanzang's *Record*. It was called *Tianzhu* before, and he explains how he chose the new Chinese characters, *Yindu*, which we still use today. The word sounds like 'Hindu', but it means 'the moon'. He said the land of the Buddha, with its innumerable wise men and sages, was like the moon, shining in the darkness of human existence.

His reverence for India was profound, and now as he was about to set foot in the holy land after a year of travel, he must have been elated. He had dreamed of this moment from his boyhood. The monastery in Luoyang he entered when he was thirteen was not far from the White Horse Monastery, the very first in China, which featured in an important legend that he would inevitably have known. One night in 65 AD, the Chinese emperor saw a golden man in a dream and he told his courtiers. They said it must be the Buddha, whose teachings were reputed to save all beings from suffering. Promptly he dispatched envoys abroad to find out more about the saint. A year later, they brought back two Indian monks, Dharmaraksa and Kasyapa Matanga, who arrived with a white horse laden with sacred texts and images. This was supposed to be how Buddhism came to China.

Over the next five hundred years, thousands of Indian monks went across the Himalayas or navigated the Indian Ocean and South China Sea. They set about translating the vast canon of the Buddha's teaching. Xuanzang learned about Buddhism from their work – until he himself undertook it, there was no translation by a Chinese. But the more the Chinese learned from their Indian teachers, the more determined they were to seek the source of this knowledge and clear the doubts in their minds, as Xuanzang wanted to do. They were also keen to see the land of the Buddha for themselves. From the fourth century AD, Chinese monks began pilgrimages in tens, or even hundreds. Few people know about them – most left no record and many died on the way, but it was one of the largest missionary movements in the first millennium. One of the earliest and most renowned pilgrims was Fa Xian, who left China in 399 at the age of sixty-five and returned fifteen years later. He wrote *Record of the Buddhist Countries*, the first Chinese account of India that has come down to us, though a brief one. This book left such a deep impression on Xuanzang, he decided that 'the duty of a great monk is to follow in their steps'. Now he was here.

I was as excited as Xuanzang about going to India, but I knew much less about the country than he did. I learned in school that India and China fought a brief war in 1962 over a disputed border in the Himalayas – before I was born; India started it by taking Chinese territory. Chairman Mao wanted to teach a lesson to Nehru, that running dog of imperialism, blackguard of feudalism, rentier of the bourgeoisie. The Chinese army marched down from the Himalayas, meeting hardly any resistance. But China declared a unilateral ceasefire, gave back all the territory it had taken and held on to that we regarded as ours, and withdrew its forces. After that all was quiet on our western frontier, and we forgot about India.

Then suddenly Indian movies hit our cinemas in the late 1970s. The tuneful songs, romantic storylines, handsome actors and beautiful actresses captured our hearts. My favourite, and everyone else's, was *The Wanderer*, a sentimental, tear-jerking black-and-white film. I saw it a dozen times and invariably came home with puffy red eyes. But this influx ended as suddenly and mysteriously as it began, leaving me and tens of millions of Chinese heartbroken. Nobody asked why there were no more Indian movies: you took what you were given – a fact of Chinese life. From then on anything else we learned about India, which was not much, came from television. Twice a year, perhaps, when some disaster struck India, we were shown the same images of the poor: stick-thin, wearing rags and looking as if they were ready to drop dead any minute. The message was clear: China was marching on, leaving India far behind, trapped in its feudalism and the turbulence of democracy.

That was why when my mother was helping me pack for the journey, she stuffed my suitcase with instant Chinese noodles and medicine. 'Do you really have to go there?' she pleaded with me. 'It is so poor, so dirty. You will get sick; the food is horrible, you will starve.' She was shocked by a series of live reports from India, shown on a major Chinese channel recently. They portrayed India as the dirtiest, poorest and most chaotic country in the world: Iran was paradise by comparison and even Iraq was more desirable with its wide roads and clean restaurants. The Indians were not just backward; they were the tragedy of mankind.

I wanted to see India for myself.

*　　*　　*

I flew to Delhi from Lahore in late January 2000. The security at the airport was exhaustingly thorough, an indication of the tension between Pakistan and its neighbour. But I was feeling very happy. At last, I was on my way to India. On the plane I began a conversation with the woman sitting next to me, a fabric designer. She was wearing a beautiful scarf, gauzy and soft, with subtle, almost elusive pale colours. I loved it and asked if it was one of her designs. 'Yes, but you have such fine silk in China,' she enthused. 'You know what the Indian word for silk is? Chinamshuka, which means "Chinese cloth". We got it from you.' Then she went on to tell me other things that India received from us and gratefully acknowledged. They are identified with the prefix *china* or *chini*, which means 'of China', such as *china badam*, Chinese nut or peanut, *chinarajaputra*, Chinese prince or pear, *chinakapu*, camphor, *chinaja*, steel, *chinavanga*, lead. 'And of course, *chini*!' she said in a singing voice, pointing to the sachet of white sugar on my tea tray.

The links between China and India are well illustrated by the sugar story. Indians were the first people in the world to make brown sugar from sugarcane, as they still do today. Merchants and pilgrims carried it along the Silk Road to China just when Xuanzang was coming to India. But by the time it had completed the three-thousand-mile journey, it was as hard as stone. For want of a better name, the Chinese called it 'stone honey'. Emperor Taizong enjoyed this exotic delicacy very much and sent a special envoy to India to learn the secrets of making it. But he did not like its colour – it reminded him of dirt. He asked his courtiers if they could do something about it. The emperor's wish was their command. In no time, they came up with a sugar as white as snow, fit for imperial consumption. Indian merchants took it back to their country and that was *chini*.

It was early afternoon when I landed in Delhi, and slightly chilly, with hazy sunshine. I got into a battered black-and-yellow taxi. The air was grey and heavily polluted; the road was crowded with cars, buses, trucks, motor scooters and bicycles weaving crazily in and out of each other's path. It might sound odd for me to complain about crowding, but somehow our streets seemed more orderly. Still, being here filled me with happiness and expectation. Coming to India was what Xuanzang dreamed of; it was my first encounter with this other vast country, and a civilization as ancient as ours. Would I find much of what he saw? Was his a name to conjure with, as my Oxford friend suggested? Was Buddhism a thing of the past? Would the land of the Buddha be a spiritual experience for me, as it was for him? All that lay ahead.

My host, Prem, was waiting for me at his house, welcoming me with a big hug and a broad smile. He was an old friend of my husband's and we had already met briefly in London. We sat down in his drawing-room and I felt immediately at home. There was a big Japanese screen on the wall, pale gold with a black pagoda among mountains, and a pair of lamps made from blue-and-white Chinese pots. Prem was a great admirer of all things Chinese, and of course Xuanzang. 'We know all about your monk from school. We call him Hiuen-Tsang. He is our hero,' Prem said. I was keen to hear what he knew about Xuanzang but I thought first I should ask him what he was writing for his newspaper column. 'Oh, let's not talk about that. It's too depressing.' He threw up his hands. 'India is in such a mess. Unlike the Chinese economic reform, ours is not getting us anywhere. The infrastructure sucks. Industry is growing at a snail's pace. Very little foreign money comes in and nobody cares about the poor. I know there is corruption in your country but at least those who take the bribes do the job for you. Here they take the money and do nothing.' He sat down suddenly in a glum heap. Prem was a flurry of contradictions: a moody, highly intelligent man burdened by the early death of his wife, he seemed to relish making an inventory of his country's shortcomings.

Prem still vividly remembered his visit to China in 1990. 'It is so impressive what China has done,' he said, enthusiasm reigniting in his eyes. 'Nobody is starving. People seem cheerful and hard-working – and everything they make, they make better and cheaper. God, you are such disciplined people. No wonder you are so far ahead of us.' He told me he was writing a book comparing the Chinese and Indian economic reforms. 'There is so much we could learn from you. Sometimes I even think a little authoritarianism would do India no harm. We need a strong government to get us out of this mess. It is hopeless. I want to go and live in China.' He launched his hands into the air again in exasperation, but they fell back to land inertly in his lap.

I reminded him that he was lucky – his Chinese colleagues would be envious of the freedom he enjoyed. Prem's expression became serious. He was well aware of restrictions on the press in China, but I had the feeling he had conveniently forgotten this in his desire to find a model, such was his frustration with his own country. 'I suppose you're right. We have a constitution that respects the individual, even if it's not always observed. I can say what I like, I can criticize the government as I see fit and they can't send me to a labour camp.' He smiled.

Did he not resent the Chinese, especially after India's humiliating defeat in 1962?

'Of course, how can we forget? The war came as a total shock. Nehru loved China – its history, its people, its determination to change its fate.' I knew of Nehru's fondness for China. Reading his autobiography, I copied out this quote, which rather touched me. 'My mind was filled with the days of long ago when pilgrims and travellers crossed the oceans and mountains between India and China in search of the rich cultural inheritance which each country possessed. I saw myself in the long line of those pilgrims journeying to the Heaven of my desire.'

'Nehru was so keen to continue his friendship,' Prem said. 'He put China at the centre of India's foreign policy and brought the Indian people to share his admiration. We had been chanting "Hindi, Chini, Bhai Bhai! – Indians and Chinese are brothers!" And all of a sudden, you declared war on us.'

Whether it was China that started the war, as Prem said, or India, as I was taught in school, it was incredible that the two countries abandoned their friendship of almost two millennia and went to war over some disputed territory, the barren Himalayan Mountains along the McMahon Line, drawn arbitrarily on a map by a British officer. Perhaps we will understand its real cause one day. But China lost its closest ally, and Nehru was shattered by the defeat, personally and politically. Nothing in his long career, Prem said, had hurt and grieved him more. 'It finished him off,' Prem remembered. 'What was left of his vigour was gone, and he became another person.' He died in 1964, barely two years after the war, a painful reminder of his despair. Prem gave a rueful smile. 'All this would have made Xuanzang so sad. He really loved India.'

'If anything, I think he had almost too much affection for India, as if once he had set foot in this holy land, everything was holy. You can tell from his glowing account,' I said.

The love Xuanzang had for India is clear from the *Record*, which is so detailed, so specific and so sympathetic, not just in its treatment of Buddhist monasteries and sacred sites, but about everything in India. He wanted his fellow-countrymen, and posterity, to benefit from the knowledge he had acquired, and to appreciate the greatness of the country. He wrote of the towns and cities, how they all had gates and high walls, but tortuous and narrow lanes and streets. He discussed how the country was run by wise kings, and found it 'remarkable for its rectitude', with people upright, honourable, considerate and polite. He noticed how important education was, how learned men were respected by the king and the common people alike. Their study of the classics reminded him of his own in China, except they were much broader here, covering arts, astronomy, medicine, morality, as well as religious training. He could go into great detail, much of it still familiar today: 'Their clothing is not cut or fashioned. The men wind their garments round their middle, then gather them under the armpits, and let them fall down across the body, hanging to the right. The robes of the women fall down to the ground . . . They use flowers for decorating their hair, and wear gem-decked caps; they ornament themselves with bracelets and necklaces . . . They are very particular in their personal cleanliness, and allow no remissness in this particular. All wash themselves before eating; afterwards they cleanse their teeth with a willow stick and wash their hands and mouth.' And he was not above recording small points of etiquette in among a botanical list: 'It is difficult to name all their plants, so I only give those most esteemed by the people. Dates, chestnuts, the persimmon, they do not have. But pomegranates and oranges are grown everywhere. Onions and garlic are little grown and few people eat them – if anyone uses them for food, they are expelled beyond the walls of the town.'

I had not realized just how important Xuanzang's

information in the *Record* was to the Indians until recently. And I wanted to find out more about it. I had received a fax from Ajay Shankar, the Director General of the Archaeological Survey of India, or ASI as the Indians call it. Of all the people I had contacted before my trip, I was most keen to meet him: the sites I wanted to visit and the people I wished to talk to were all under his jurisdiction. I had written to him about my plans and received an immediate and most welcoming reply, giving the names and telephone numbers of the key people who could be of help to me. I rang one of those mentioned on the fax, Dr Agrawal, an archaeologist who had led many ASI excavations on Buddhist sites and currently its Director of Monuments. When I explained to him who I was, there was a long silence. For a moment, I thought the line had been cut off. 'I have some bad news for you, Madam,' he said slowly. 'Mr Shankar was killed in a car crash last night. If you switch on the television, it is on the news.'

I rushed to turn on the television. After a few items in the news bulletin on Doordarshan, the Indian government channel, a picture appeared in the top right-hand corner of the screen behind the newsreader, the face of a bespectacled middle-aged man with a benign expression. This was the man who had been so kind, and he was gone. The suddenness of his death was brutal: my father's did not shock me as much, perhaps because it was after a long illness. As the Buddha reminded his disciples, life is only a breath of air, and it can end at any moment. I remembered reading about a Zen master who meditated in front of a poster with the Chinese character for death written on it. What a way to live, I said to myself. But the line between life and death is so thin; the monk was only dwelling on the impermanence of things.

Still feeling the sadness of Ajay Shankar's death, I went

straight to the ASI. It was on Janpath, an imposing avenue that runs through the middle of New Delhi, from Parliament to Connaught Circus, the commercial centre. It is leafy and spacious, almost empty, with grand government buildings and smart hotels – it reminded me of Tiananmen Square and the Avenue of Eternal Peace in the heart of Beijing. I had no problem finding the place – stone carvings and statues welcome you at the entrance. The compound was eerily quiet and in a tiny room right at the back, I found Dr Agrawal. As soon as I sat down, he pulled from under a pile of papers and pamphlets on his desk his copy of Shankar's fax to me. 'This is our late Director General's will. So how can I help you?'

I told him I was following in Xuanzang's footsteps and would like to visit some major Buddhist sites and monuments mentioned in the *Record*. He smiled with his eyes and his voice became more cheerful. 'You could say Xuanzang is my guide and his *Record* my holy book. You cannot imagine how important he is for us.' He suggested we go to the National Museum next door. It had a fantastic collection of Buddhist statues, some of which Xuanzang would have seen. 'You could say he even helped us get them here,' he said emphatically.

The sun came through the glass of the corridor on the ground floor, casting a gentle light on the beautiful and imposing statues of Shiva, of Ganesh and of Vishnu, carved in polished granite, limestone, red sandstone. Together they form a superb parade of sculptural styles. I was particularly fascinated by the *Yakshis*, the fertility spirits, with their exaggerated female charms – thrusting breasts, hour-glass waists, strong and full hips and smouldering looks. I could not help admiring the sensuality and vitality, the love and beauty, the passion and joy they express – something we never see in Chinese art. The halls devoted to Buddhist statues, sculptures and paintings on the ground and first floors had an ambience of serenity and peace, a contrast to the force and energy that permeated the Hindu statuary. The Buddhas and Bodhisattvas were smaller too, as if to tell people that they were only human, not gods. I did not have to crane my neck to see them; I could look them in the eyes and feel not overpowered, but assured by their compassionate gaze.

Looking at the Buddhas and the Bodhisattvas, beautifully displayed and softly lit, it was hard for me to imagine that until 150 years ago, both the Indians and people in the West had little idea who the Buddha was. 'Whether Buddha was a sage or a hero,' wrote Francis Wilford in the early nineteenth century, 'the founder of a colony or a whole colony personified, whether . . . black or fair, he was assuredly either an Egyptian or an Ethiopian.' Even as late as 1942, the *Encyclopaedia Britannica* began its entry on Buddhism by defining the Buddha as 'one of the two appearances of Vishnu'. This ignorance beggars belief, given that Buddhism is older than Christianity and Islam, that it reigned supreme for more than a thousand years in India, that the whole of Asia embraced it, that Genghis Khan, one of the most powerful rulers in his tory, adopted it throughout his empire, that Marco Polo and Franciscan missionaries to Japan, China and Tibet all encountered it, and reported their findings to a curious West. So here were two utterly extraordinary stories: one, the virtually complete disappearance of the knowledge of the Buddha from the land of his birth – as if the identity of Christ had been forgotten in Palestine, or the Chinese did not know who Confucius was; the other, the equally remarkable recovery of this past by the British and the Indians, with the help of records kept by two Chinese monks in the first millennium.

I was hoping that Agrawal would enlighten me about both stories.

'We owe Xuanzang a lot. So much of our history would have been lost without him,' Dr Agrawal said as we sat down in the courtyard café of the museum. 'Open any book on early India, he is there. But more than anything else, he brought Buddhism back to life for us.' Over the next two hours, he went on to tell me the most astonishing story of the rediscovery of Buddhism in India: an account I later filled out with my own reading.

Dr Agrawal made me realize just how different the Indians and the Chinese were – and that was why Xuanzang was so important for India. 'People tend to talk about the differences between East and West. But China and India seem to be humanity's polar opposites.' The Indians are philosophical, spiritual and transcendental, while the Chinese are practical, materialistic and down-to-earth. For the Chinese, the world we live in is all there is. Confucius told us that 'to dedicate oneself seriously to the duties towards men, to honour spirits and gods but to stay away from them. That can be called wisdom.' For Hindus, religion dominates life. Their ultimate goal is *moksha* – the final liberation from this mundane and ephemeral world into blissful eternity. And they have a staggering 330 million gods and goddesses to help them achieve it. So it must be puzzling to a Hindu that Confucius, who has guided the Chinese for two and a half thousand years, was merely an itinerant scholar with no divine aura.

Another striking difference between the two peoples is in their attitudes to history. 'You Chinese are the best record-keepers in the world, and Xuanzang was very much in the tradition,' Agrawal told me. It is true that we take history very seriously. Keeping meticulous chronicles is an important and rewarding task and it serves a political, rather than intellectual, purpose. Since Confucius's time, scholars have carefully recorded every year of our history in minute detail – the long or short reigns of every single emperor and their bizarre sexual habits, the periodic upheavals of peasant revolts, and the voluminous output of the poets and writers. All in the hope that the emperors and the Mandarins would avoid the mistakes and repeat the successes of the past. History is a mirror, reflecting yesterday and projecting tomorrow.

Xuanzang was no exception. He was born into a scholarly family and he learned the Confucian classics and traditional values from his father at a very young age. Hui Li, his biographer, told a story to illustrate the point. One day Xuanzang's father was reading aloud to him a passage from *The Ode on Filial Piety*. Suddenly the eight-year-old boy stood up. His father was surprised and asked him why. He replied that the wise in the old days stood while receiving instruction from their teachers. 'Surely Xuanzang dares not sit at ease while listening to Father?' Even after he became a Buddhist monk, he never forgot what his father had taught him, including a reverence for history, and the Chinese tradition of record-keeping.

'For us Hindus, this life is only transitory,' Dr Agrawal said, slowly sipping his Darjeeling tea. 'So what is history and historical knowledge but a kind of unnecessary baggage? The *Puranas*, the Hindu sacred texts, have a few names of kings and royal families, but they are shrouded in divine and mythological clouds, not very useful clues for archaeologists. The Buddha was an Indian, and possibly the greatest man ever born here, but we had no historical record of him. When Xuanzang came here Buddhism was already in decline. In the eleventh century, the Afghan invaders dealt the final blow. Jungles swallowed all the thousands of Buddhist monuments, and mosques or Hindu temples were built on their foundations. The Buddha was all but forgotten in the land of his birth. But Xuanzang's *Record* tells us everything.'

The rediscovery of the Buddha began with a small group of British colonial officers who had fallen in love with India, in particular, Alexander Cunningham, the first Director General of the ASI. Back in 1834, Cunningham, a twenty-year-old lieutenant in the Royal Engineers, had recently arrived in India from Scotland and was stationed in Benares. Outside the city and across the Ganges was Sarnath, a quiet retreat from the crowded Hindu holy city. Here, among ancient trees and overgrown grasses, was an imposing 145-feet-high domed edifice with superbly crafted sculptural ornaments on its surface. What was it for? Why was it so beautifully made? Why was it here? Cunningham was curious. The general belief in Benares was that it held the ashes of the 'consort of some former rajah or prince'. He asked several Brahmin priests, the acknowledged guardians of India's ancient traditions. They were not helpful at all – they had even refused to teach the English sahibs their sacred language, Sanskrit. His repeated enquiries with them gained him no answers.

He decided to do a little exploration. He received some financial help from the Asiatic Society in Calcutta, an organization whose only requirement for membership was 'love of knowledge'. Being an engineer himself, Cunningham built scaffolding as high as the dome and sank a five-foot-diameter shaft from the top all the way down to the foundation. After fourteen months of labour and an expenditure of more than five hundred rupees, he found nothing but a stone with an inscription he could not read. In a nearby mound, he found sixty exquisite statues, although he had no idea what they were either. He was bitterly disappointed. He sent a copy of the inscription to the Asiatic Society and packed off twenty of the best-preserved statues to Calcutta. 'The remaining statues, upwards of forty in number,' he recorded in his diary, 'together with most of the other carved stones that I had collected, and which I left lying on the ground, were afterwards carted away by the late Mr Davidson and thrown into the Barna river under the bridge to check the cutting away of the bed between the arches.'

His colleagues in the Asiatic Society were not certain either. The inscriptions were deciphered as a standard confession of faith in the Buddha. By now they knew from their field officers in Burma, Thailand and Sri Lanka that the Buddha, despite his depiction with curly hair, straight nose and thick fleshy lips, was not 'an African Negro' from Ethiopia or Egypt, and Buddhism did not originate in Africa, as they had previously thought. Nor was he an incarnation of Vishnu as the Brahmin priests assured them. He was a real man born somewhere in northern India. The Buddhist scriptures in Sri Lanka even specified where the Buddha was born and died but they could not be identified with any place in India. They did, however, make clear that Bodh Gaya and Sarnath were the most important.

Much else was made plain by the publication in English of the eyewitness accounts of two Chinese monks, Fa Xian's *Record of Buddhist Countries* in the 1840s and Xuanzang's *Record of the Western Regions* in the 1850s. Copies of both books had always existed in China and now they were 'discovered' by European orientalists, and were translated for the first time into French and then English. Between the two of them, they had mapped out the whole of Buddhist India, spanning over a thousand years, with all the main sites, their locations, their importance, their histories and the details of monasteries and the monks who inhabited them. When Cunningham wrote about the impact of their records, he expressed what many must have felt: 'It is almost impossible to exaggerate the importance of these travels; before, all attempts to fathom the mysteries of Buddhist antiquities were but mere conjecture.' The magnificent monument that he had explored in Sarnath was a stupa marking the sacred spot of the Buddha's first sermon after his enlightenment.

Reading these accounts was like a sudden flash of light for Cunningham. He immediately conceived an ambitious plan: to use the Chinese monks' records as his guide and throw light on more than a thousand years of the history of Buddhist India. The idea filled him with exhilaration, but the British rulers of India wanted to hear nothing of the past of their inferior dependency. As Macaulay infamously declared: 'It is, I believe, no exaggeration to say that all the historical information that has been collected to form all the books written in the Sanskrit language is less valuable than what may be found in the most paltry abridgements used at preparatory schools in England.' Surely such a culture was not worth exploring. So although Cunningham had devoted every minute he could spare from his military duties to studying the Chinese records and the material remains of ancient India, he had to wait almost thirty years before the wind began to change. In 1861, now aged forty-seven and retired from the army with the rank of major-general, Cunningham finally landed the job he had been dreaming of: he would head the new Archaeological Survey of India, a grandiose name for him and his two assistants. He was ecstatic.

Cunningham chose to follow Xuanzang's footsteps. The

Record was invaluable, with accurate information about directions, distances and major signposts, and even described the layout of all the major monuments. So with a modest caravan and his assistants, Cunningham took to the field. For the next twenty-five years, he retraced Xuanzang's tracks up and down the country, inspecting and excavating all the major sites that the Chinese monks had described. In *India Discovered*, John Keay paints a vivid picture of how Cunningham pursued this mission in the autumn of his life:

> One can imagine the little caravan descending on some forgotten group of temples. The tents are up as the old General emerges, stooping, from a sculpture-encrusted porch. His tweeds reek with the sickly smell of bat dung; but a quick 'tub' and he is back to work, recording the day's discoveries on a shaky camp table. As the sun dips behind the trees and the parakeets go screeching home to roost, the lamp is lit, and the General, issuing instructions for an early start in the morning, retires to bed with a dog-eared copy of Xuanzang.

The darkness that shrouded Buddhist India receded with each of Cunningham's excavations – Bodh Gaya in Bihar, where the Buddha became enlightened; Sravasti, where he spent most of his life teaching; Kushinagar, where he died; Rajgir, where the Buddha had his first royal patronage; Mathura, home to the Mathura school of sculpture that had created the first and some of the finest Buddhist images. Where he left off, others stepped in, also following Xuanzang's account – Patna, the centre of Indian polity and the home to King Asoka, arguably the greatest king in Indian history and a patron of Buddhism, and finally Lumbini, now in Nepal, where the Buddha was born. Although Cunningham's methods were, by modern archaeological standards, basic or even crude, he mapped out the India that Xuanzang saw, forgotten by Indians themselves. He brought Buddhism back to life. And he knew he owed it all to his two Chinese guides, and Xuanzang in particular: 'It is impossible to exaggerate the importance of Xuanzang. He was the light in the darkness of mediaeval India.'

It was getting late and the museum was closing. We stepped out into Delhi's gentle winter-evening light; it came filtering through the big trees on Janpath, with the slight chill that marked the fading of the day's sunshine. In this first of many conversations with Dr Agrawal I felt great empathy for him – Xuanzang brought us closer. His admiration for the Chinese monk was infectious. 'We can never thank Xuanzang enough,' he said to me, as we stood outside the museum. 'Of all Chinese, past and present, he is the only one to have penetrated India, mind, body and soul. You can almost say he is one of us, except he is more than one of us – he brought with him another world, which greatly enriched us.'

We said goodbye, and I walked slowly for a while down the wide avenue. I hardly noticed the cars and the people going by – my head was full of all the things I had learned. I had no idea Xuanzang was so important to India and that they still think so highly of him 1,300 years later, so much more than we do ourselves. They could not have hoped for a better ambassador for their civilization. There is no doubt the Chinese and the Indians are very different; but as Xuanzang had shown, and as Rabindranath Tagore, the Indian poet and Nobel Prize winner, told his Chinese audience in 1924: 'Let what seems a barrier become a path, and let us unite, not in spite of our differences, but through them. For differences can never be wiped away, and life would be so much poorer without them. Let all human races keep their own personalities, and yet come together, not in a uniformity that is dead, but in a unity that is living.'

I began to feel that everything was starting to fit together, and I was reaching a deeper appreciation of what my coming here could mean. I understood Xuanzang much better, and saw how he could be a bridge between the past and the present, and between China and India. I was ready to follow him in the land of the Buddha.

The state of Bihar would be the most important stage of my Indian journey – it is where the Buddha became enlightened, where he spent most of his life teaching, and where he died. The word 'Bihar' actually comes from *vihara*, 'Buddhist monastery'. Xuanzang devoted nine of his thirteen years in India to Bihar, where he sought the true meaning of the Buddha's teachings and paid homage to the Enlightened One. I would go there as a kind of pilgrim to see Xuanzang's inspiration made real for me.

Prem, a Bihari himself, tried to dissuade me from going: 'Bihar is no longer the holy land Xuanzang saw. You have no idea what it's like today. Ask my servants – they all come from there. There're no schools in the villages, no electricity, no roads. Men don't have jobs, children starve, women are gang-raped. We Indians call it "the hole in the heart of India". Do you know nearly fifty thousand people were murdered in Bihar in the last six years? Perhaps we should let China have it for a while and see what your people can do,' he joked.

'How did Bihar get into this state?' I asked.

'It is caste,' Prem said. 'Bihar played a very important role in our Independence movement. I guess the Brahmin

229

landlords got the credit for it and they dominated Bihar politics and the Congress Party for a long time. But they never did anything for the lower castes, and eventually those people rose up and elected their own leaders. The new men might have done a lot of good for the confidence of their followers but they didn't run the state properly. Slowly everything fell apart.'

Was that not true of the rest of the country?

'Bihar has the largest number of big landlords in the country. It also has the highest population of people without land in the country. You put the two together, you have a recipe for strife.' He looked resigned.

'Buddhist pilgrims still go there,' I said.

'They are very brave,' he said. 'But I wouldn't advise it. There was a piece in the *Indian Express* last week. I will go and get it for you.' He went to his study and when he returned showed me this: 'A busload of Japanese pilgrims and Buddhist monks were robbed at gunpoint in Bihar. Most of their possessions were taken, and two people were badly injured. The government advises people to stay away from the area until a safer time.'

'You must know about the state elections in Bihar too?' Prem asked, handing me another paper, with the headline: 'Two shot dead by police when trying to capture the election booth. Fourteen dead in clashes. Seven hundred people arrested on the first polling day.' But I cheered myself up when my eyes caught this line: 'An election supervisor locked himself up in his room and refused to attend to his duty because of the violence.' He was a brave man.

'And you still want to go?' Prem stood there, holding the papers, looking at me askance.

I had no choice.

*   *   *

Late that morning I flew to Patna, Bihar's capital and the gateway to the heart of the Buddha's land. The airport was true to form. Built just a few years ago, the toilets in the arrival hall had never opened. When I approached them, an attendant said, 'You must go and do it outside.' I had arrived. I was glad that something was working: the driver arranged by Prem's travel agency was waiting for me, a small, dark and very alert young man called Yogendra. There was only one slight problem: Yogendra spoke only a little English, and he was to take me on my Buddhist tour. I had so many questions, but he would not be the one to answer them.

The drive from the airport into town was a shock. The roads filled up with traffic, buses and motor rickshaws coughing out black smoke, an occasional cow munching in the middle of the thoroughfare. They had built flyovers to ease the congestion, but they did not do much for the traffic – they were too narrow and some of them were already crumbling away. Instead they provided shelter for new settler colonies, more hovels for the huge numbers trying to scratch a living in the city. Mini-vans with loudspeakers, election banners and jubilant supporters tried to blast their way through the solid traffic jam, but nobody was getting anywhere. While we were stationary, I noticed Yogendra checking the handles on his door and the back door several times.

'Is Patna as dangerous as people say?' I asked him.

A long pause and then came his measured reply. 'You want to know?' He watched my reaction through the rear mirror. I nodded. 'Things not good here. Even in daytime, with policeman watching, men hold guns to you at traffic lights, tell you get out, drive off in your car. It happens often. I see with my own eyes.'

'What happens to the owner?'

'If you know police and pay money, they get your car back. They are like this.' He clasped his hands together.

Xuanzang had troubles with thugs too. Patna is on the south bank of the Ganges, and it was on this famous river that he had one of his most dangerous encounters. He was crossing it in a ferry with hundreds of passengers when they were ambushed by ten boatloads of pirates. The passengers were so frightened, several jumped overboard and were drowned. All the rest were ordered to strip off their clothes on the bank. The pirates worshipped Durga, the river goddess, and they thought the handsome Chinese priest would make a pleasing sacrifice. Xuanzang pleaded with them: 'I have come here from a long way off to pay my respects to the Bodhi Tree, and to acquire the sacred books and the Law of the Buddha. If this poor and defiled body of mine really is all right for your sacrifice, I will not grudge it to you. But I have not yet done what I came for, and if you kill me, it may do you more harm than good.'

The pirates would not listen to him. They built a terrace from tree branches and mud and led Xuanzang on to it. Knowing that he would not be spared, Xuanzang asked them to give him a little time so that he could pray. He later told Hui Li the thoughts that went through his mind. This time, he faced death with total calm. 'He meditated hard and concentrated his thoughts on the Maitreya Buddha in the Tushita Heaven. He prayed to be reborn there so that he would have an opportunity to learn the Yogacara Sutra, which he had not fully understood. Afterwards, he hoped to come to this world again and propagate the Dharma for the benefit of all beings. He concentrated so intensely that he went into a trance, where he saw in his mind's eye the Maitreya Buddha. At that moment he felt so happy, both mentally and physically, that he forgot completely that he was on the makeshift altar, and would be offered at any moment to the river goddess.'

But suddenly a gale blew up, churning the Ganges with giant waves and overturning boats. The pirates were taken by surprise and asked their passengers who the priest might be. They replied that he was a great master from China and that the storm was a sign that the river goddess had been offended. Watching the gale becoming fiercer and the Ganges more turbulent, the pirates hurriedly went up to the altar to release Xuanzang. As they touched him, he opened his eyes and asked: 'Is it time now for me to die?' They gave back his robes and asked for his forgiveness.

When he arrived in Patna, he was shocked to find a city totally destroyed by the invasion of the White Huns in the sixth century and then a massive flood. 'Nothing but the old foundations of the royal palaces remain,' he tells us, 'and of several hundred monasteries, only two or three have survived.' Still he spent seven days in this wasted and desolate place. Whatever the destruction, he would have looked on everything he saw with visionary intensity. This was where the Buddha crossed the Ganges to spread his message, and where so many eminent masters had taught and congregated to write down the entire Buddhist canon. This was where India's greatest king, Asoka, had renounced violence, embraced Buddhism, and taken the Dharma throughout his empire, the most expansive in Indian history.

Patna was Asoka's capital in the third century BC, as it had been his father's and grandfather's. The Greek ambassador to his grandfather's court described Patna as a large and fine city, with an unbelievably beautiful palace and very efficient bureaucrats who controlled the empire with a vast network of spies. Xuanzang stood on the ruined foundations of the royal palace and looked north towards the Ganges. Just by the palace there used to be the prison where Asoka practised his reign of terror before his conversion to Buddhism.

According to Asoka's own inscription, his change of heart came after one particularly brutal campaign in eastern India, where his troops killed more than 100,000 people, with many times that number dying from wounds and famine afterwards. Asoka was haunted by the deaths and the suffering inflicted by his men. He was filled with remorse and became a pious Buddhist, giving up hunting and becoming a vegetarian. He sent his son and daughter to Sri Lanka to spread the Dharma. He went on pilgrimages himself and was reputed to have built 84,000 stupas in the important sites associated with the Buddha's life. He constructed vast networks of roads in his empire, lining them with banyan trees, and providing wells, mango groves and rest-houses at regular intervals. 'I have done these things in order that my people might conform to Dharma,' he proclaimed. To reinforce his message, Asoka appointed officers of Dharma to inscribe royal edicts on rocks or pillars throughout the empire, instructing people how to live a virtuous life. Xuanzang recorded several of Asoka's edicts, including this famous one:

This inscription of Dharma has been engraved so that any sons or great-grandsons that I may have should not think of new conquests, and in whatever victories they may gain should be satisfied with patience and light punishment. They should only consider conquest by Dharma to be a true conquest, and delight in Dharma should be their whole delight, for this is of value in both this world and the next.

This remarkable man's life came to an extraordinary end. Xuanzang visited the Kukkutarama Monastery in the south-eastern corner of the city and left us this story about the impermanence of everything. Asoka had built the monastery for a thousand monks and paid for its upkeep. In his last days, he wanted to donate all his belongings to the institution, but the ministers who were taking over from him did not comply. One day, as he was eating a mango, he held the fruit in his hand and asked his attendant: 'Who now is the lord of India?'

'Only Your Majesty,' came the answer.

'Not so!' Asoka sighed. 'I am no longer lord; for I have only this half-fruit to call my own. Alas! The wealth and honour of the world are as difficult to keep as it is to preserve the light of a lamp in the wind.' He asked the attendant to take the half-fruit and offer it to the monks, telling them, 'I pray you receive this very last offering. Pity the poverty of the offering, and grant that it may increase the seeds of my religious merit.'

Nothing much remains of Patna's glorious past. I asked Yogendra to drive straight to the Patna Museum on Buddha Marg. Its prized possession is the Relic Casket containing the Buddha's bones, excavated in the ruins of one of the Asoka stupas in Vaisali, sixty kilometres from Patna across the Ganges. Xuanzang had worshipped at this very stupa, which marked the spot where the Buddha announced his impending departure from the world. Xuanzang was so affected, he even had an image of the Buddha made there. But there was another item in the museum that I very much hoped to pay my homage to – Xuanzang's own skull bones. It was a great honour to Xuanzang, to be placed under the same roof as the Buddha. They were given as a token of friendship by the Dalai Lama on behalf of the Chinese government in 1957. The guidebook warns that it might take some time to locate anything in the museum – there are more than 50,000 rare and precious arte-facts and statues, and a few unusual objects, the sort of thing that seems to be regarded with awe by Indian villagers: the guidebook notes a stuffed goat with three ears and eight legs. Insects and rats have been steadily devouring the exhibits and most of them have no labels.

The museum was closed. It was supposed to be open from 10.30 a.m. to 4.30 p.m. Now it was only 3 p.m. An extended lunch break? A Hindu festival, a public holiday, or the election? Yogendra was not surprised. 'They are worried. Election is dangerous. People go mad and do big damage.'

I was really disappointed not to see Xuanzang's relics. They were intended to celebrate millennia of friendship with India. The Chinese had chosen something of Xuanzang's to sym-bolize the depth of our intertwined histories, and knew the relics would be all the more prized in India because they would be worshipped, like the bones of a saint. I felt I would be close to the actual remains of the man I had followed all this way, at the centre point of his journey. But it was not to be. Like Duan at the Big Wild Goose Pagoda, I had to content myself with walking by the building; but I did not share Duan's composure.

Yogendra suggested that I check in to my hotel. 'Nothing to see in Patna, nothing old, nothing new. Dead city,' he said. I was taken to my scruffy but friendly hotel on the edge of the city. Its only virtue was that it was easy to leave from there – clearly I had no incentive to stay. Before he went off, Yogendra warned me not to go out. He would come and pick me up at six the next morning. While I was showing the receptionist my passport, I noticed half a dozen soldiers standing in the lobby with their rifles. 'It is our normal security staff,' she said. 'We want to make our guests feel safe.'

I had time to think about where I was. Apart from Xuan-zang's relics, Patna was known to me for only one thing, which gave it an insidious link to China. Historians might know about it but most Indians do not. Xuanzang would not have dreamed that the fountainhead of Buddhism could be the home of a great evil that almost destroyed China: in the late eighteenth and nineteenth centuries, the British East India Company, and then the British Crown, controlled the pro-duction of opium, and its processing and distribution, from Patna. The Mughals had introduced the crop to India in the sixteenth century. Production started on a small scale, in-tended for private and medicinal use. Then the Dutch took it from here to the southern coast of China as a possible com-modity to sell. When the British forced the Dutch out of India, they took over and greatly expanded the opium trade to balance their huge deficit with China, caused by the importing of tea.

The British loved Chinese tea, not only the leisured classes but also the workers. A historian even claimed, 'Without tea filled with sugar, the poor diet of the factory workers could not have kept them going during the Industrial Revolution.' In the first decade of the nineteenth century, Britain imported nearly 300 million pounds of tea. Lancashire woollens were shipped to China but could find no takers. The deficit climbed steadily and became a heavy drain on the British economy. They brought tea plants from China in 1832 and tried them in Assam. This proved a huge success, as if tea were native to the Indian soil. Tea plantations mushroomed and spread throughout the subcontinent. Most of the crop, and the best, was for export to London. Even that could not satisfy the British demand. At the same time, the Indians were also acquiring a taste for this almost medicinal drink, practically an addiction.

Then the British came up with the solution: opium. Cash advances were offered for cultivation in Bihar but very few farmers accepted them. Poppies were harder to grow than grain and the price was low. The agents and collectors working for the Opium Department of the Bengal government – more than five hundred of them – complained: 'Without coercive measures, it is almost impossible to prevail upon them to raise poppy production.' Coercion they did not hesitate to use; even during years of famine poppy farmers were not allowed to switch to growing grain or vegetables. So a steady supply of opium was channelled through Patna to China, averaging 25,000 chests a year, with each chest weighing 149 pounds. On the eve of the first Opium War in 1839, profit from opium for British India was nearly ten million pounds a year.

The British were fully aware of the effects of the drug: they prohibited its use among their own people, both in the UK and in India. But they justified the trade by saying the use of opium was not a curse, but a comfort and a benefit to the hard-working Chinese. The Chinese were not strong enough to resist it – but who is? No country today is immune – and China was almost destroyed. Young people tried it and loved it; court eunuchs could not live without it; bureaucrats were so addicted they turned into smugglers; magistrates were too doped to appear in court; hallucinated troops went into battle and were defeated without firing a shot; even Buddhist monasteries became opium dens for the rich and powerful.

The rest of the world probably does not appreciate what a trauma this was for China. For two thousand years we had believed we were the centre of the world, the Middle Kingdom. Our pride in ourselves as a great nation was blown to pieces in our first major encounter with the West, the Opium War of 1839–42. The gunboats and technology of the new world, employed in an evil cause, were too strong for the old world. We have been licking our wounds ever since. Even today, we are still reacting against the psychological damage inflicted on us a hundred and fifty years ago. With my head full of these painful thoughts, I dozed off.

When I woke up the next morning and saw the day's newspapers, I was worried. On the front page of one of them was a picture of policemen standing over dead bodies; the headline was 'Police shoot dead six men in riots in Nalanda District'. When Yogendra came to pick me up, I showed it to him. Nalanda was where we were heading for that day, sixty miles from Patna. I asked him how he felt about driving me there. 'Buddhists, brave people. I have family to feed,' was all he said.

On the way we passed quite a few trucks carrying soldiers. A quarter of a million Indian troops were mobilized to supervise the elections in Bihar and the neighbouring state. The special Rapid Action Force was given strict orders to 'shoot troublemakers on sight'. From the newspaper reports, Nalanda seemed to be a troubled area, so it was reassuring to see forces being moved there. The road to Nalanda, however, was less than ideal. Although it was part of National Highways 30 and 31, it was disfigured by potholes so big they looked as if they had just been blown out by landmines. We bumped along and my head kept hitting the roof. It would have been more comfortable travelling as Xuanzang did, on a wooden bullock-cart, or on an elephant. So these were the Bihar roads I had heard so much about. Apparently Bihar's Chief Minister Laloo Yadav flew everywhere by helicopter, and he did not think his people needed roads. Not so long ago, a group of farmers met him on his campaign trail and fell at his feet, begging for a road to their village. 'But whatever for?' he chortled in disbelief,

'Where are your cars that you need roads? I thought you are electing me to bring you honour, not for something as trivial as roads!'

On the verge, large numbers of very young children were playing dangerously, darting on and off the road like kittens. They were very thin, with no shoes and hardly any clothes. Their mothers were clearing up empty courtyards near the road, far from the village proper. Some old women sat slumped in the shade of banyan trees, staring into space. Men were rarely seen. Yogendra said they had gone to the cities to look for work; they had no land. Many of them used to catch rats in the fields to eat, but they did not even have rats any more: fertilizer had finished them off; there was nothing going for them. The only activity I noticed was around a few brick kilns, though the huts were all made from poles, sugarcane leaves and plastic sheets. They looked so fragile, it would be a miracle if they could survive the monsoon. 'You're right, Ms.' Yogendra shook his head in the Indian way which actually meant he agreed with you. 'Monsoon destroys them. Children die too from cholera. In winter people die from cold. Very bad here. Trouble never stops.'

The glimpse of life in Bihar I was seeing reminded me of something familiar that I couldn't quite identify. I turned my thoughts to Xuanzang. When he travelled through Bihar, it was covered with thick forests of banyans, sals, rose-apple and mango. There were also bel trees and ashok, sacred to the Hindu god Shiva, and pipal, so much venerated that its wood could not be cut for fuel. Birds and animals abounded. Falcons, partridges, sparrows and many more, elephants and tigers. People who lived by the forest surrounded their houses with bamboos and thorn bushes, and built them on stilts to keep the animals out.

Hui Li says Xuanzang had no fear of wild animals. He must have been inspired by the Buddha who spent six years meditating in the forest before his enlightenment. 'Surrounded by lions and tigers, by panthers and buffaloes, by antelopes and stags and boar, I dwelt in the forest,' says the Buddha. 'No creature was terrified of me, and neither was I afraid of any creature. The power of loving kindness was my support.' Buddhist lore is full of monks following the Buddha's example, living in the woods; murals in temples and caves paint them in the company of tigers, each looking as if they knew the other was totally harmless. In Bihar today, wild elephants and tigers have been hunted to extinction, and ancient forests have been cleared. But the brutal reality of today's Bihar was every bit as frightening as wild animals would be to me, and personal safety could not be taken for granted. Our test was patience and endurance. The true believer must be patient, and fearless too.

After driving barely twenty miles we reached a complete gridlock. The queue stretched as far as I could see. The lorry-drivers must be used to it; they were making good use of their time. Some were crawling on the ground, inspecting their overburdened axles; others were sleeping, chatting, playing games or bringing out their paraffin stoves to prepare a meal. We managed to get to the front after three hours, driving on the wrong side of the road, swerving on to the narrow shoulder or finding a gap just big enough in the queue when we were about to collide with an oncoming car. The cause of the jam? A truck had broken down in the middle of a narrow bridge. There was no shortage of help, but the truck was giving the drivers a long and thorough test of their mechanical skills. After waiting for another two hours in the heat, dust and blaring Bollywood music, Yogendra manoeuvred skilfully to the front of the queue. The drivers tackling the broken truck all stood aside to make space. Our Ambassador just scraped through the narrow gap between the truck and the rail of the bridge. Everyone cheered and waved at us, and I gave Yogendra warm applause.

We did not get to Nalanda until lunchtime, taking six hours to cover sixty miles. Yogendra was in a very good mood all the same, gesticulating and talking rapidly, but I had difficulty making out what he meant. He kept mentioning the name of Lord Krishna, a favourite god of the Hindus, and in particular of the Yadavs, Yogendra's own caste. But what did Krishna have to do with Nalanda? I did not understand. I asked him to wait till we had found our lodgings, a Chinese monastery. Nalanda had no hotels – there was not much to the place, just the village and a few monasteries built by various countries. The Chinese monastery was built in the 1930s and was now maintained by monks from Thailand, Burma and Tibet. I asked the Thai monk in the office to help me understand Yogendra's excitement. The answer was a complete surprise. Yogendra had been trying to tell me this was a great capital in the Indian epic *Mahabharata* and Lord Krishna had graced this place with his presence many times because his father-in-law lived here. I looked at the Thai monk for confirmation but he shook his head uncertainly. Perhaps Krishna had been here, but that was definitely not why Xuanzang came here.

Xuanzang recorded that Nalanda was the very centre of learning and the biggest monastery in mediaeval India, drawing monks from China, Korea, Mongolia, Tibet and Central Asia. Originally it was a mango grove, and five hundred merchants bought it for the Buddha. After the Buddha's death, the king of the country built Nalanda, which means 'insatiable in giving', in memory of the Enlightened Being. The king's descendants continued their devotion for six generations, each adding their own temples of worship. Some of India's greatest Buddhist masters, such as Nagarjuna, Asanga and Vasubandhu, had studied here. Santarakshita went to Tibet from Nalanda to spread Buddhism. Sariputra, the foremost disciple of the Buddha, was buried here.

When Xuanzang arrived in Nalanda, a grand welcoming ceremony awaited him. Since setting foot in India in the winter of 628, he had been seeking out great teachers in one remote monastery after another, spending long periods learning from them and taking part in their debates. He stayed over a year in Kashmir alone, mastering Sanskrit, and some new sutras. Soon monks throughout India heard that the Chinese master was making his way through all the major monasteries in the country and the sacred sites. So when they learned that he was coming to Nalanda, two hundred monks and over a thousand lay devotees walked miles to greet him, carrying banners, umbrellas, flowers and incense. They brought him to the monastery, where all the monks assembled to receive him formally into their community.

Then came the great moment for Xuanzang, the one he had been waiting for. After the welcoming ceremony, twenty monks took him to see the Venerable Shilabhadra, the master of Nalanda, the most eminent monk in India, and the patriarch of the Yogacara School. This was the very man he had heard so much about, whose temple he had visited in Patna, and under whom he hoped to study to clear all his doubts. Xuanzang was on his knees, with his head bowed to the ground. He kissed Shilabhadra's feet. When Shilabhadra heard that Xuanzang had come all the way from China to learn Yogacara, he cried. Xuanzang was too shocked to ask why but he had an answer soon enough from the master's nephew. Shilabhadra suffered from rheumatism and each time he relapsed, he was in a lot of pain. The illness had troubled him for more than twenty years and three years earlier it had become so severe that he wished to end his life by fasting.

One night he had a dream in which he saw the Bodhisattva of Wisdom. The Bodhisattva said to him, 'As we saw that you intend to abandon your body without any good purpose, we have come to give you some advice. You should act according to our words to propagate the Dharma and preach the Yogacara Sutra and the other books to people who have not yet heard about them. You will then gradually recover from your illness and you need not worry about it. A Chinese monk who wishes to learn the great Dharma will come to study from you. You may wait to teach him.' He saw in Xuanzang the realization of his dream.

Xuanzang knew he had finally found the intellectual and spiritual home he had been searching for. He tells us admission to Nalanda was competitive: a few questions by the monks at the gate sent most aspirants home; those who got a foot inside the door were grilled by the masters, who would reject four out of five. The 10,000 monks who were finally admitted were the *crème de la crème*. In them he found a true match for his curiosity and appetite for learning. 'They are very distinguished and there are many hundreds whose fame has spread far and wide,' he writes with pride. 'From morning till night they engage in discussion; the old and the young help one another. Those who have no command of the Tripitaka, the Buddhist canon, are not respected. They are obliged to hide themselves for shame.'

The majestic ruins of Nalanda are ten minutes' walk from the Chinese monastery. They spread over fourteen acres, with block after block of monks' cells, five temples and eleven monasteries laid out in a long rectangle. I could understand why Cunningham thought it was a royal palace when he first saw the mound covering them. Xuanzang's *Record* revealed the truth, and it was confirmed by the excavation of a seal of red clay bearing the stamped inscription: 'Venerable Community of Monks of the Great Vihara of Honoured Nalanda'. You would have some idea of the magnificence of the place today if you imagined four or five of the largest Oxford colleges placed side by side, and then destroyed as if by an earthquake. There is an eerie silence, no monks scurrying about, no chanting, no gongs sounding – just a few visitors lost in the immensity of its spaces. It was rightly called Mahavihara, the Great Monastery.

Walking on top of the blocks, some two or three storeys high and set in quadrangular courts, I wondered which cell could be Xuanzang's. His description of the view from his cell sounds like a paradise on earth. 'The richly adorned towers and the fairy-like turrets like pointed hilltops are congregated together. The observatories seem to be lost in the vapours of the morning, and the upper rooms tower above the clouds. From the windows one may see how the winds and the clouds change shapes, and above the soaring eaves the conjunctions of the sun and moon.' In the early morning, he would get up to the sound of a gong and then take a bath in one of the ponds with a hundred, sometimes a thousand other monks. He meditated and prayed in his cell instead of going to the five temples because they were not big enough to hold all the monks. In the evening, children and servants carrying incense, lamps and flowers would appear in the courtyard outside his cell, and the presiding monk would chant sutras and hymns.

I also found what the guidebook described as a lecture-hall. Nothing remained of 'the pearl-red pillars carved and ornamented, the richly adorned balustrades, and the roofs covered with tiles that reflect the light in a thousand shades'. But it was in the lecture-halls like this one that Xuanzang mastered Sanskrit and grammar – his mission was to translate the vast canon from Sanskrit into Chinese. He believed that 'the one who is skilled in Sanskrit may write his compositions without any ambiguity and may express himself in a most elegant manner'. His precise translations, his meticulous *Record* and the eloquent phrasing of his correspondence – all were proof of his love and command of this ancient language. He also acquired profound knowledge of Indian philosophy, logic, medicine, mathematics and astronomy. As to the sutras and doctrines of all the different Mahayana and Theravada schools, he went through each several times until he completely comprehended them.

It was also in one of the lecture-halls that he conducted public debates with erudite Hindus who claimed to have a superior faith. He told one Hindu ascetic in the audience, whose body was smeared all over with ashes, that he looked like 'a cat that has slept in the stove'. Another whose skin was all cracked and chafed from exposure reminded him of 'a withered tree by the brook side'. 'How can you Hindus regard these things as proofs of wisdom?' he asked. 'Are they not evidence of madness and folly?' One particularly confident Brahmin hung up a notice of forty-four propositions, declaring that he would be willing to forfeit his head if anyone could refute even one of his arguments. Xuanzang took up the challenge. According to Hui Li, he refuted all of them one by one. He, of course, did not ask the defeated Brahmin to 'forfeit his head'. Instead he insisted that the two of them engage in long conversations so that he became thoroughly familiar with the arguments of his opponents. The Brahmin was completely won over and when he left, he spread Xuanzang's good name wherever he went.

Xuanzang had many great teachers. One of them was a lay recluse called Jayasena who lived in the hills near Nalanda, and repeatedly refused offers of grand titles from the king. He said he had quite enough on his hands as it was and could not do a rajah's job as well. He happily gave two years of his life to teaching Xuanzang everything he knew. But of all his mentors, Xuanzang felt most honoured to be taught by Shilabhadra, the incomparable metaphysician, who explained the Yogacara Sutra to him three times. He clarified the confusions in his Chinese disciple's mind about Yogacara, cut through the myriad arguments of all the different schools, made clear the most abstruse points, and revealed to him new insights about the essence of the Buddha's teachings. Xuanzang's gratitude to his master was clear from this passage: 'Despite my mediocrity, I was improved by his noble company. He led the exhausted traveller to spiritual treasure, and opened up new vistas for those who had lost their bearings. He was at the same time a vast ocean, a lofty mountain and a pillar of the edifice at the Gate of Buddhism.'

Xuanzang had finally removed the doubts about the Yoga-cara Sutra that had wearied him so much, but I still could not come to grips with it – nothing exists except in the mind. How can that be? What about the Dharma or the very idea that everything in the world is the creation of the mind? Is it illusory too? If so, what is the point of understanding it since nothing is real? Why did Xuanzang risk his life to make sense of it? What is its importance in the scheme of Mahayana Buddhism? I remembered asking a monk about them in the Big Wild Goose Pagoda. He told me he could not understand Yogacara at all. Then he said, 'If the Buddha came back to the world, perhaps he would say, "Hey monks, did I really say all these things? They are so profound, I can't even understand them myself."' I suppose for him and his fellow-monks, and most Buddhists, it is enough to try to live by the teachings of the Buddha, to pray to the Bodhisattvas for help to end their pain and suffering, not only in this life but the next one as well, and finally gain a place in the eternal bliss of the Western Paradise.

But in Xuanzang's view, a Buddhist should penetrate the nature of things. Without that knowledge, our mind will be polluted by ignorance, which is the root cause of our suffering. If a doctor does not know the real cause of a disease, he will not cure the patient. If we are ignorant of the ultimate character of reality, we will continue to live in illusion and suffer. So understanding things as they really are is essential to Buddhism.

I thought I might find some monks in the New Nalanda Mahavihara to answer my questions. It sounded the perfect place for my enquiries. According to the brochure I had picked up in the monastery, the New Mahavihara is a residential centre of education of international importance on the lines of the ancient Vihara. It aimed to spread the Dharma and Indian culture as it once had done so successfully: 'Even at present, the very name of Nalanda is a living source of inspiration and people are anxious to see Nalanda restored to its pristine glory.'

It was in an idyllic spot, facing the ancient ruins across the Nalanda River, but a little less imposing than the brochure had led me to expect. It was a two-storey white bungalow, which would fit in one rectangular court of the old Nalanda. In the entrance hall I found two men chatting desultorily, one sitting behind a bare desk, the other leaning against a windowsill. A young monk in a maroon robe was standing close by, listening quietly. They seemed startled to see a visitor. I raised my hands palm to palm and muttered *namaste* in the traditional Indian greeting. The monk reciprocated and introduced me first to the man at the desk, Dr Singh, head of Ancient Indian and Asian Studies, and then to his colleague Dr Mishra, the head of the Department of Philosophy. He himself was called Nayaka, and came from Burma. Dr Singh asked how they could help me. I showed him the brochure, saying I was interested to find out more about their teaching.

He laughed, passing the brochure to Dr Mishra without even a glance: 'If I were you, I wouldn't believe a word of it. How many teaching staff does it say we have?'

'Twelve,' replied his colleague.

'The other ten must be djinns because we are the only teachers here.' Seeing the puzzlement on my face, Dr Singh slowed down. 'Djinns are spirits, invisible to mere mortals. Wouldn't it be wonderful if they could teach Chinese, Tibetan and Sanskrit, or the other languages? It would certainly do some good to the 120 monks we have here. They are attracted by the fame of the old Nalanda and have come from Sri Lanka, Thailand, Tibet, Japan and Burma. But we are wasting their time.' Dr Singh gave Nayaka a gentle, almost paternal glance, when he finished his barrage. Then he asked for tea for all of us.

Slowly I began to understand Dr Singh's anger and frustration. It was very much a Bihari problem, a perfect illustration of how the state is run. By decree of the Bihar government, the Chairman of their Board of Management is His Excellency, the Governor of Bihar. No decisions, big or small, could be reached without the chairman's approval. But His Excellency had been so busy that for the past eighteen months he could not attend any of the board meetings. As a result, the lion's share of the academic budget had to be returned to the central government, unspent for two years in a row. 'The money could have solved all our problems – staff shortage, broken computer, rundown building and scholarships for monks from the really poor countries like Burma. Yet nothing is done. Such is the madness.' He threw up his hands.

I really was keen to talk to Dr Mishra about Yogacara, the school of Buddhism that Xuanzang embraced and studied under Silabadhra, here in Nalanda. But he said it was not his speciality – as I was later to discover, few people feel they understand it completely. It appealed to Xuanzang because of his desire to understand the very nature of experience and reality. He was to write a whole book about it and establish a Chinese school of Yogacara, or *Faxiang*, when he returned to China. Yogacara has a complete theory of what we can know and what exists, and it describes three levels of our knowledge. One is our ordinary everyday perception of the material world, with subjects and objects, people and rocks and rivers – but this is illusory. As the Diamond Sutra says:

> This fleeting world is like
> A star at dawn, a bubble in a stream,
> A flash of lightning in a summer cloud,
> A flickering lamp, a phantom and a dream.

There are different versions of this illusory world in Yogacara; in some, the things we see and feel are there but are imperma-nent; in the most extreme version, which Xuanzang espoused himself, the material world does not exist. All we have is the second level of knowledge, an ever-changing flow of feelings, sensations, volitions, consciousness – though Yogacara gives a complicated explanation of how we can have shared experiences, as if there was a real world out there.

This second level of knowledge, our experience, really does exist. If it did not, there would be nothing at all. In fact Yogacara came into being in the midst of fierce philosophical debates in India in the fourth century A D, with some claiming that nothing existed at all – Yogacara opposed this 'nothingness' doctrine, but because of its emphasis on the mind, it was known as *Cittamatra*, or 'Mind-only'. And beyond the second level, there is a third, perfected knowledge, achieved by intense meditation – Yogacara means the 'practice of meditation'. This is really the essence of the Buddha's discovery in his enlightenment: it is seeing beyond the misleading world of subjects and objects, people and things, and understanding the true nature of reality. It is the Self in relation to the things of this world which causes the desires and passions that give rise to suffering. The Buddha taught that the Self does not exist as the fixed entity we believe it to be; we have to abandon our attachment to it. Once we train our minds so that we genuinely live this detachment, we achieve liberation – complete equanimity, and release from the torrent of *samsara*, the cycle of birth and rebirth.

I felt really thwarted not to be able to discuss these questions with anyone in Nalanda. There was so much I did not understand. If our experiences exist, surely they have to have a body to exist in? Then how could Xuanzang deny that things like bodies had a real existence? Especially after all the hardships he suffered on his epic journey, his near-death in the desert, his hunger strike, the avalanche. He seemed to me to have had some very real encounters with a very real world. But perhaps I am one of those pragmatic Chinese who find philosophies like Yogacara too abstruse, too complicated. We have always been that way. Certainly Yogacara was not destined to last very long in China even with Xuanzang's advocacy; its decline began barely twenty years after his death. I felt like a child in a maze with this philosophy, this school of Buddhism that Xuanzang gave his life to, and I was sad to be defeated by it. I simply could not get inside his mind.

It was early evening when I said goodbye to Dr Mishra and Dr Singh. They said I must not miss the Xuanzang Memorial Hall and told me how to get there. I walked with Yogendra along the river to a small lake. A path lined with willow trees zigzagged across it on a causeway and then through a young forest. For a minute, I thought I was in a Chinese landscape, searching for a secluded monastery. The sun was warm, the reeds were dancing in the breeze; washer-women were spreading their colourful clothes on the stones; there were children leading goats through the fields, and other women carrying loads of dry sticks on their heads; two fishing boats were bringing in their catch. I wondered if this was the life Xuanzang saw when he took a stroll out of the monastic complex. The surrounding villages had been endowed by successive Indian kings for the upkeep of Nalanda. In Xuanzang's time, two hundred households made daily deliveries of rice, butter and milk to the monastery, and then cooked, washed, cleaned, provided medicine for and waited on its 10,000 monks. Xuanzang had a daily ration of 120 betel leaves for chewing, 20 betel nuts, 20 cardamoms, an ounce of camphor and one and a half pounds of rice. He did not have to collect the ration himself – in recognition of his distinction, he had ten servants looking after him, instead of the usual two, so that he could devote himself exclusively to study and the progress of the mind.

The gate of the compound was locked and Yogendra had

to bang on the door for quite a while before a man opened it. When he saw my face, he knew I was a Chinese. He smiled and led us in. The compound was empty, the size of a football pitch, with half a dozen cows grazing the grass. At the far end of it stood the magnificent Memorial Hall. 'It is just like the temples you see in China,' I exclaimed to Yogendra.

When the keeper unlocked the door, a strong smell of paint hit me. Ladders, barrels and construction materials were piled high to the ceiling, as if the craftsmen had just finished building it. It was actually completed in the late 1950s when India and China were still enjoying their honeymoon. Not long after came the border war of 1962 and the hall remained closed for decades. 'Now our president is going to visit China, and we will have a VIP delegation from China in return,' said the keeper enthusiastically. 'They are going to decorate the hall with wall hangings painted by Chinese and Indian artists. There will be the master himself and the Buddhas and Bodhisattvas. In the centre we will put a sculpture of the master.'

This would be something akin to the Xuanzang Hall at the Big Wild Goose Pagoda. I was quite moved. It was a symbol of India's appreciation of Xuanzang, which I had felt so strongly since I arrived in the country. I had only to mention his name and doors opened, and the Indians talked about him as if he were a national hero. And this was not a recent phenomenon either; a Japanese monk visiting India in the ninth century recorded that in a large number of Buddhist temples, Xuanzang was painted as a demi-god on the walls, mounted on multi-coloured clouds with his hemp shoes and chopsticks, and on every fast day the monks bowed to his image in respect. Xuanzang wanted the Chinese to know about the holy land which he revered, and his *Record* has done more than that: it has recovered a large part of India's past that would otherwise have remained lost. The Indians are grateful to him for that. Xuanzang could never have dreamed, either, that he would have been responsible for resurrecting the historical Buddha in the land of his birth and identifying the most important places in his life. And here, all would be remembered.

Something else was brought home to me here: that there was a lot of admiration for China in India, and Xuanzang was only a part of that. The two ancient civilizations have given each other so much over the centuries. Perhaps we have received more than we have given; as I have learned, Buddhism in particular has fundamentally changed Chinese society, from our rituals of birth and death, the gods the Chinese pray to, the novels we read, the pagodas we admire, the music we hear and the musical instruments we play, the paintings we look at and the language and concepts we use. The effects are everywhere. We cannot open our mouths without using words and concepts from Buddhism. It is no surprise that words like Buddha, Bodhisattva, monk, monastery, pagoda, nirvana and reincarnation came into our language this way. But I never suspected we borrowed from Buddhism concepts such as heaven and hell, gods and ghosts, fate and faith, principle and truth, reality and equality. Nor did I know that our novels really started as stories from the sutras recited by monks in public places to attract followers. The Confucian literature was dry and practical, full of instructions about morality and conduct: it was incapable of producing something as fanciful as *The Monkey King*. The Chinese word for 'novel' is still 'little talk', an earlier Confucian expression of contempt meant to discredit the realm of imagination and so-called triviality. But our mind was freed by the vast pantheon of gods, goddesses, devils and spirits in Mahayana Buddhism and the mythical worlds where anything was possible. Ever since our lives have been enormously enriched by a huge outpouring of novels, one of the glories of our culture – we cannot imagine being without them, but nor do we remember where they came from. This hall would testify to this wonderful exchange from a time when both were enjoying their finest flourishing. Perhaps in this place where Xuanzang had completed his studies one could dream of a future when it will happen again.

Xuanzang had not just learned about Buddhism on his epic journey; he had put it into practice, overcoming the dangers along the way. He had at last mastered the knowledge he had hoped to acquire, and was living by it. His mind was now clear of doubt. A verse from a Buddhist scripture ends with a metaphor that stands for this clarity:

> Self-nature, complete and clear,
> Like the moon in the water.
> The mind in meditation, like the sky,
> Ten thousand miles without a cloud.

EIGHT

Not a Man?

XUANZANG HAD one of his rare lyrical moments when he saw the Nairanjana River, now the Phalgu, in central Bihar, 'with its pure waters, its noble flights of steps, the beauty of its trees and groves, and the pasture-lands and villages which surround it on all sides'. His emotion reveals itself in every line in which he described to us the road between Patna and Bodh Gaya, the very heart of Buddhism, the sacred spot where the Buddha achieved enlightenment.

Travelling on the same route I felt myself that the scenery could almost be what Xuanzang saw. There were very few modern intrusions save the occasional string of telephone poles. By the roadside, mango groves stretched deep into the interior, a mass of gnarly boughs and dark leaves with sunlight glinting through them. Women in bright saris, carrying their babies, led strings of goats through the trees; bullock-carts driven by old men creaked gently by on the edge of the narrow tar road. A man in a white dhoti walked slowly in the shadow of his elephant carrying a small mountain of wood. I had not seen nature and life in such beauty anywhere on this trip; it was like a dream of another world, as if intact from ancient times. The Phalgu stretched as far as I could see. It was the dry season, but the river was in flow, peacefully reflecting the blue sky and white roaming clouds. Some boys were having a serious cricket match on the wide stretch of land near the bank, while small children enjoyed themselves in the muddy puddles. Their homes, small hamlets in the distance, were nestled against a range of low forested hills.

This was the serene landscape where the Buddha decided he would pursue the final struggle for his enlightenment. He had left his luxurious life in the royal palace at Kapilavastu in the foothills of the Himalayas at the age of twenty-nine. His goal was nothing less than to find a way to end human suffering. He had sat at the feet of holy men and yoga masters in the forests of the Gangetic plain, penetrating the mysteries of discovering the True Self. This True Self had nothing to do with our mundane thoughts, our lusts and hatreds. It was eternal and free; we had only to find it, buried somewhere deep in the recesses of our consciousness. The Buddha was told that yoga would train his mind to focus so completely that he would enter into a kind of trance, pure, empty and infinite: he would feel he was in the realms inhabited by the gods. There he would find the True Self, unperturbed by anything. He achieved it – but it was not what he was looking for; once he was out of the trance he still felt envy, greed and passion. Man could not live in a trance all his life.

He abandoned yoga and turned to extreme austerities, which many believed would lead to the suppression of passion and then to liberation. For six years he wandered about almost naked, slept rough in the open in the cold of winter, and took no food for days or drank his own urine. His hair fell out, his eyes grew blurred and sunken, his skin turned black and peeled away, his body shrivelled until he looked more a skeleton than a man. Yet all was in vain. In fact, starvation made him more aware of himself and of his cravings. The bitter realization that he might die without achieving anything forced itself upon him. Was enlightenment an illusion? He might have wondered. But he was not going to give up. He left the cave in the forest, accepted a bowl of porridge from a milkmaid, washed off the filth of six years in the Nairanjana River, and put on an old shawl given to him by a funeral party. Then he headed for a pleasant grove on the riverbank, sat down under a pipal tree, and vowed that he would not leave the spot until he attained supreme knowledge.

The road to Bodh Gaya, wide and smooth, and shaded by tall, leafy ashok trees, was unlike the ones we had been battling on so far. Yogendra was all smiles. 'Best road in Bihar. Japanese built it for Buddha.' 'Buddha Land', 'Pilgrims' Inn', and numerous other guesthouses and hotels stood neatly by the roadside. Frequently a spire or a golden roof in the distance indicated the position of one of a dozen monasteries – Sri Lankan, Thai, Burmese, Bhutanese, Nepalese, Tibetan, Japanese, Chinese – just about every culture with a strong Buddhist tradition was represented. Xuanzang would have found this very familiar; it was in one such monastery that he lodged for seven days when he was in Bodh Gaya.

I checked in at a small hotel on the outskirts of Bodh Gaya that had been recommended by the travel agency for its cleanliness and efficiency. Rajiv, the young man at the desk, was bright, courteous and helpful. Within five minutes I was in my room on the second floor, spacious, clean and cool. When I opened the window, the sun was shining brightly on a landscape of flowers, vegetables, grazing cows and an expanse of empty fields behind the hotel. In the distance, the mist was receding, revealing a calm and peaceful countryside.

This was more like the Bihar I had imagined from reading Xuanzang.

I decided to have an early lunch and then go and spend the rest of the day under the Bodhi Tree. While I was waiting, Rajiv took me outside and pointed to the empty land I had seen from my room. 'You must come back again in five years' time,' he said emphatically, 'we are going to have the biggest statue of the Maitreya Buddha in the world in our back yard. It will be over three hundred feet high.' Was the land all his? I asked. 'No, no.' He gestured. 'The Brahmin families in our village got together and sold forty acres of land to some Buddhists who wanted to build this extraordinary thing. It is going to be in the *Guinness Book of Records*. People will come from all over the world and my hotel will have the best view. This is going to be a goldmine for us. Can you imagine?' He could not conceal his excitement; his eyes gleamed with the prospect of dollars pouring in like the monsoon rains. He should be grateful to the Buddha, I said.

'Yes and no,' he replied hesitantly. 'The Buddha's teaching is not good for our community really. Things used to be fine. The tenants did what they were told. Then they were fed ideas about equality and rights and all those polluting things. Now they don't want to listen. They follow some crazy people who tell them to convert to Buddhism, demand high wages, grab power from us and get rid of caste. They even threaten our lives. Still the government gives them privileges all the time,' he grumbled.

'So what do the Brahmins do?' I asked him.

'We have no choice but to organize our own private armies, what we call the *senas*. The government does nothing for us. We have to protect ourselves. We cannot let them ruin our life,' he said firmly.

'I have heard the police side with the upper castes,' I said.

'That is not true. They have far too much on their plate anyway,' he replied.

'So what do the *senas* do?'

He shrugged. 'Just tit for tat.'

The waiter, a timid young boy, brought my drink of fresh lime soda on a tray, and then stood aside in the corner quietly, waiting for more orders. 'How could he say we are all the same?' Rajiv said slowly, his eyes on the boy. 'There are always high and low in any society. That is why we have castes. How can I be the same as my servants?'

'You think he should be your servant?' I asked, my voice lowered, in case the boy heard.

'Absolutely,' Rajiv replied. 'He is born a low caste. Nothing is going to change that. It is his fate.' What caste was I? 'Oh, you are of high caste. You are my guest. As they say in the West, customers are god,' he said without a trace of irony.

But as a Brahmin, was he really supposed to run a hotel, an occupation traditionally reserved for the Banyas, the trading caste, the ones the Brahmins used to call 'thieves that are not called by the name of thief'? I thought better of asking him. He was brought up to believe he was superior to everyone else. According to Manusmriti, the sacred Law Book of the Hindus, the Brahmins were the first-born, springing from the mouth of the supreme creator, and therefore they were by right the lords of the whole world, entitled to whatever exists in the universe; even when they killed people, they could not be punished by the king, and their conscience was cleared simply by their reciting three times some passages from the Veda, another sacred Hindu book. Of course the Brahmins actually wrote all the sacred books, as they were the sole cus-todians of knowledge, and the mediators between gods and men. What if Rajiv came a peg or two down the order? His servants must stay where they were.

When I was about to set off, Rajiv told me that I should return to the hotel before dark. 'Only a week ago, a woman pilgrim was dragged out of her rickshaw, badly beaten up, and all her things taken.' As if this was not enough, he said two masked gunmen broke into the Burmese Monastery three days ago, locked up the abbot at gunpoint, shot a monk in the leg and got away with all their savings and donations. 'It is all these poor, good-for-nothing people. They beg by day and rob by night. They are such scoundrels.'

I felt uncomfortable listening to more of his justifications, but I was not in a mood to argue, and was glad to head into town. The street was busy; shops on either side sold incense, candles, rosaries, prayer books, Buddha statues in all sizes, samosas, soft drinks, tea and Indian sweets. Painted signs advertised long-distance phone rates; young men grabbed my arm, and informed me I could call Japan. Women seated on the ground tugged at my trousers offering flowers and garlands for sale. Beggar children put their hands on their mouths, asking for change. As I picked my way through the throng I feared the worst – another holy place spoiled by the tourist industry. I turned the corner, past a small Hindu temple on the left, bought my ticket at the grille, took off my shoes and walked through the gate. Suddenly all was calm. I walked along a cool marble path lined with low shrubs and there at the end was the Mahabodhi Temple, tall, majestic, with its pyramidal tower soaring into the sky, crowned with a symbolic stupa at the top and four small shrines at its base. Unlike a Hindu temple with its sensuous figures, it is decorated only with chaste niches in which Buddhas once sat. Apart from the vanished golden statues which had struck Xuanzang as particularly beautiful, and the burnt lime colour in which he said the temple was painted, very little seemed to have changed from what he described.

But then very little is what it seems. A drawing of the Mahabodhi Temple in 1799, made by a British officer working for the East India Company, showed a lonely structure covered from top to bottom with weeds, its remaining statues in the niches strangled by plants, its roof fallen in and its walls cracking. Camels and horses grazed the grounds and a few pilgrims were depicted filtering out of the bare entrance. They were there to worship Lord Vishnu, the Preserver of the Universe, whose feet were carved on a stone in front of the temple. The other object of their devotion was the celebrated Brahma Pipal, which they believed was planted by Brahma, the Lord of Creation. At each spot, the pious Hindu pilgrims performed their devotions, offering flowers, oil, sweets and money. The caption to the drawing says it all: 'East view of the Hindu Temple at Bode Gya'.

In the winter of 1811, another employee of the East India Company, Dr Buchanan – a surgeon, a keen botanist, an amateur antiquarian and a jack of all trades – came to Bodh Gaya, charged by the Governor-General of Bengal to do a detailed survey of the area. He had already sensed from his travels in Burma and Nepal that the Buddha might be a real historical figure, who was born somewhere in northern India in the fifth century BC and had spent many years of his life teaching in Bihar. From the mohant, the leader of the Hindu ascetics who lived at the temple, he learned that two Burmese had recently come here, sent by their king. They said this was a holy place for them – the Buddha had lived here and it was under the same pipal tree the Hindus worshipped as Brahma's tree that the Buddha sat and meditated. But the mohant could not tell him why the Burmese looked on this place as the centre of their world.

The first excavation that Alexander Cunningham undertook after his appointment as Director General of the Archaeological Survey of India was, appropriately enough, in Bodh Gaya. He found Xuanzang's detailed description of the place an immense help. 'He described minutely all the temples and statues which surrounded the celebrated Pipal Tree,' wrote Cunningham in his first report. 'Several of the objects enumerated by the Chinese pilgrim I have been able to identify from their exact correspondence with his description.' The identity of Bodh Gaya was confirmed beyond all doubt as the place where the Buddha became enlightened under the Bodhi Tree. Later Cunningham returned to restore the dilapidated temple originally built by Asoka to its former glory – the Mahabodhi Temple we see today. He painstakingly followed Xuanzang's description of its overall shape, the materials used and its decoration. In his final report on his work, Cunningham made this very clear. Once again, in this most sacred of all Buddhist shrines, everything, down to the smallest detail of the reconstruction, owes its existence to Xuanzang's *Record*. 'This description of the Mahabodhi Temple, as it stood in 637 AD, tallied so closely with the Great Temple as it now stands, that, in my opinion, there can be no reasonable doubt that it is, in spite of all its repairs and alterations, the same building which was described by the Chinese pilgrim.' Right behind the temple is the Bodhi Tree, enthroned on a square platform of stone. The tree, as Xuanzang tells us, 'is the sacred point from which all else in Buddhist faith emanates'. As Buddhism rose and fell in India, the Bodhi Tree had many changes of fortune. It survived the attack, first of all, by King Asoka before he embraced Buddhism. And when he had his change of heart and began to propagate the Dharma in earnest, he sent a cutting of the Bodhi Tree with his son and daughter to Sri Lanka. 'Afterwards it was cut down several times by evil kings,' Xuanzang records. 'At present, it is only fifty feet high. The trunk of the tree is of a yellowish-white colour and the branches and leaves are green and will not wither even in the autumn and winter season.' The guidebook says the current tree was grown in turn from a cutting of the Bodhi Tree in Sri Lanka.

There was a flurry of activities going on under the tree. A big congregation of more than thirty Singapore pilgrims was holding an elaborate prayer service. They had set up an altar ten metres away, draped with yellow silk and piled with flowers, fruit and candles. Wearing the brown robe for lay devotees, and pale blue scarves around their necks embroidered with the name of their group, they sat four to a row, each on a comfortable grey cushion. They chanted joyfully and fast, turning the prayer books on their music stands at breakneck speed, only occasionally looking up to see the sacred tree, or the two video cameras recording them. Closer to the Bodhi Tree a group of Japanese was bowing silently in single file – two of them took out a long banner from a rucksack, holding it proudly over their heads for a group photograph. Then they left quickly to catch their coach. There was no emotion on their faces, no noise of excitement, no exchange of glances of understanding, just a series of gestures. Tibetan monks were doing what they always do: prostrating themselves thousands of times a day; their foreheads were covered with sweat and the cotton gloves they used to push themselves full-length on the ground were worn bare. A young Sri Lankan monk was tying a string of prayer flags to the railing next to the Bodhi Tree. In front of him was a young man with blond curly hair, sitting with his legs crossed, deep in meditation and oblivious of the world around him. But most dramatic were the Burmese: eight young women were having their heads shaved for their ordination; their families watched attentively and then picked up the tresses of long, dark hair from the white marble floor. Occasionally, a gentle breeze came and the shiny, slender heart-shaped leaves of the Bodhi Tree shimmered; a few dropped to the ground and were scooped up by the pilgrims to take home as precious keepsakes.

Coming to Bodh Gaya is the crowning moment of the pilgrims' life. The first feeling must be one of intimacy: this is the place they have long read about – how the Buddha sat down at the foot of this tree to meditate, how he was attacked by Mara, the lord of evil, with arrows, pieces of rock and darts of burning flame, how in vain Mara sent his three daughters to seduce the Buddha. All his tricks failed. After seven days, the Buddha finally achieved enlightenment. When he wondered whether what he had realized was too difficult for people to comprehend, the gods Brahma and Indra begged him to go out and preach it to the world. This is the message the pilgrims have learned and pondered and practised. Now they are actually here, sitting under the world's most revered tree, the primal source of everything they have followed. The teaching was hard to understand at times; the precepts difficult to observe when faced with the problems life threw at them; meditation was too demanding; sometimes they felt what the Buddha realized was not for them, mere mortals. But here, once again, it is all real. The Buddha found his way here, on his own. The Burmese ordinands wanted to start their new life as he had done. But all pilgrims try to communicate with the great teacher in their own way, to intuit for themselves the lesson he taught.

For what the Buddha has given them, the pilgrims feel immensely grateful. The flowers, the banners, the music, the lamps, the ceremonies, the prostrations, all express their gratitude. The Buddha pointed out a different way of life for them, purer, simpler and happier. Now they have found comfort and hope where there was none; they can overcome the craving at the very centre of existence in a materialistic world, the fear of losing everything they hold dear; they can cope with the pain of life and transcend it. They pray that they will persevere just as he did, and hope that they too will reach final awakening.

Although I was still struggling with many tenets of Buddhism, and even more with its practice, I too found it moving to think that everything began here, under this tree – the grand monasteries from India to China along the Silk Road, the little village temple where my grandmother prayed daily, the sublime beauty of Buddhist art and the changes in the lives of so many people, in so many countries, for the past 2,500 years. Looking at the pilgrims performing their devotions, I could begin to appreciate Xuanzang's reaction 1,300 years ago. I even had the sense he was among them, feeling the same excitement, gratitude and reverence, 'scattering flowers, burning incense, playing music as they go from one sacred site to another, paying their homage and making their offerings'.

But when he came to worship at the Bodhi Tree, he broke down. Hui Li tells us that Xuanzang 'cast himself down with his face to the ground in worship and with grief. With tears in his eyes, he said, "I do not know where I was at the time when the Buddha attained enlightenment. I can only have reached this sacred place now. How bad must my karma have been not to have been born in his time?"'

This is the only occasion in his entire eighteen-year journey that he showed his emotions. The fatal avalanche that almost killed his entire company, the vicious bandits who held knives to his head, the beautiful princess whose hand was offered to him, the highest honour given to a Buddhist monk – all were recorded by him in a simple, matter-of-fact manner, with no note of triumph for the things accomplished, obstacles removed and praises showered on him. But in front of the Bodhi Tree, this calm, fearless and indomitable man surrendered to his feelings. Like a wandering child, he felt he had finally come home, he could let go.

How Xuanzang wished he could have heard the Buddha's very words before later generations produced their conflicting commentaries! Although he had cleared many of the doubts in his mind and achieved much of the purpose of his trip, he must have felt he still had a long way to go for the final liberation. The physical exhaustion accumulated during all those years of travel, the decline of Buddhism in India that he had seen exemplified in ruined stupas and monasteries, the anxiety of whether the Dharma would suffer the same fate elsewhere – they could not shake his determination, but they made his quest more difficult.

I stood there in the courtyard. The chanting had stopped; the only sounds were the wind threading itself through the leaves of the Bodhi Tree and the respectful murmur of pilgrims' voices. I had the sudden sensation that I could share a moment of recognition, across time, with this man I would never meet, but whom I had been searching for. In following his footsteps, I had made a point of trying to identify with his feelings, thoughts and reactions, to understand him and his world. Occasionally, he or Hui Li tells me what went on in his mind, as when he was on the altar, ready to be sacrificed to the river goddess by the pirates; I was always grateful for such insights. Sometimes, I had vague ideas of what he would have thought of a particular situation, such as the avalanche in the Heavenly Mountains, but it was perhaps as good as 'scratching an itch through a boot'; I needed a lifetime to grasp fully the serenity and total detachment he embodied. At other times I failed miserably; the pages of miracles in the *Record*, for example, were simply beyond my comprehension, as was Yogacara: we were worlds apart. But here under the Bodhi Tree, halfway through my journey, surrounded by pilgrims and almost overwhelmed by their devotion, reflecting on Xuanzang's outpouring of emotion, I felt I could enter his world – he was human too. His presence, as if in another dimension, inaccessible but none the less real, was chaperoning me, silently.

I had a sudden urge to share my moment of understanding of Xuanzang's experience with some of the pilgrims. After their service was over, I asked a young woman from the Singapore group how she felt about being here. 'If you don't know, I cannot tell you. It's inexpressible,' she said piously. A small group of Indians whom I mistook for Sri Lankans were more forthcoming: 'He is the incarnation of Lord Vishnu. He is kind, loving and very generous. And this place is lovely, very good for a day's outing.' Not what I was expecting. I went back to where I had been standing. I was wondering if the young man in meditation would talk to me when he finished. I had no idea how long it would be but it did not seem to matter. I could be here and watch the world go by. Another hour passed and he stood up. He was more than happy to talk to me. He said his name was Andrew and asked me what the time was. I looked at my watch: it was one thirty in the afternoon. He had been up since five o'clock so he would not mind some food first. 'After all, the Buddha only gained enlightenment after taking a bowl of porridge from a village woman,' he said with good humour. He would come back in twenty minutes.

Back under the Bodhi Tree, Andrew sat down in his meditation position and told me he was on a retreat, his eighth. He was a systems engineer from Wisconsin. He spent ten months every year working and two months in Bodh Gaya. He was searching for the transcendental happiness in Buddhism. 'After all, the pursuit of happiness is written in our constitution, it's our right,' he said seriously, the gentle smile disappearing. 'But are we happy? I would say no. I'm a good example. I know what makes me happy – racing cars, designer clothes, exotic holidays and so on. But the pleasure never lasts and you know, I'm kind of tired of chasing them. When do we have enough and where do we stop? That's what I wonder. What's really happiness? The Buddha was a prince and his father surrounded him with beauty and luxury. But he gave it all up to search for lasting happiness. And he found it here, under this tree.'

'What do you think the Buddha realized here?' I wanted to hear it from someone who was obviously searching diligently.

'I could talk about it till the cows come home,' he said, a slow smile spreading across his face. 'I'm sure you've read a lot about the Dharma. But for me, the key is the "right understanding" of the human condition. The first thing we do when we are born into this world is cry. Even if we are lucky enough to avoid illness, life doesn't always live up to our expectations. We become frustrated, disappointed, feel despair, not to mention anger, greed, jealousy. Sex in my dreams. Life can be pleasant: the Buddha knew that from his years in the palace, but it doesn't last. I don't know, it seems to me that what's behind all suffering, really, is wanting things. The Buddha said our mind was like a monkey in the forest:

it grabs one branch, lets it go, seizes another. We'll never be satisfied.'

He paused to gauge how much I was taking in, or as the Chinese say, to see if he was playing violin to a cow. When he was reassured I was following him he went on. 'Once we have let go of our attachments to ourselves, we can learn kindness and compassion, as the Buddha taught, and not to harm others. If you keep making the effort and stay aware of what you do and how it affects other people, if you keep practising meditation, you can change your life. But even that doesn't mean the end of pain. The Buddha fell sick, grew old and died just like everybody else. By enlightenment, the Buddha showed us how to find inside yourself the strength to live with pain, to transcend it. Suffering is all around you, but you can still find peace of mind.'

This Buddhism based on self-exertion was not the one I learned about in school; nor did it resemble what my grandmother practised. If anything, Chinese Buddhism seemed the exact opposite: it had little to do with individual effort and everything to do with gods and goddesses. The most telling evidence is our written character for the Buddha. I demonstrated it for Andrew on my notebook. It is pronounced Fo, and its left half is the character *ren*, human or a man, its right half means no, or not. Combined, 佛, the Buddha, means 'not-a-man'. If a man is not a mortal man, he must be a god. That is what the Buddha is for the Chinese, an almighty, omnipresent and omniscient god who can answer all your prayers, realize all your dreams, and of course, deliver you to the Western Paradise or any other paradise you want, and grant you the final awakening. The past Buddhas and the countless Buddhas-to-be, the Bodhisattvas, all have the same magical powers, as numerous sutras tell the followers.

In her daily prayers, my grandmother vowed to take refuge in the Buddha, the Dharma and the Sangha. I think she took it very literally, or she simply did what the sutras told her to do: to pray sincerely and make offerings to the best of her capacity, and leave the rest to the Buddhas and the Bodhisattvas. Grandmother's wishes were simple and few, although they changed from time to time. After my brother was born, she stopped praying for a grandson; instead, she asked for the Bodhisattvas to help my sisters and me find good husbands when the time came. But ultimately, she wanted us all to reunite in our next life in the Western Paradise and live happily afterwards. She was sure that her favourite Bodhisattva Guanyin would grant all her wishes. I remembered joking with her: if I had robbed a bank and offered half the money to Guanyin, would I get her protection? Grandmother looked horrified by my question, and then said after a momentary hesitation, 'Yes, of course. The Bodhisattva is for everyone.' That was my impression of Buddhism until a few years ago.

Andrew listened to me carefully, nodding his head now and then. 'That is one interpretation of the Buddha's teaching,' he said when I finished. 'I guess it tries to draw as many people as possible to Buddhism in the first place. Once they learn more about it, they would realize it is good for them and they would not need the extra incentives. That was exactly how the Buddha persuaded Ananda to become his disciple, by promising him five hundred incomparably beautiful wives. But after a while, Ananda discerned the monastic life was his calling and enlightenment his goal. He did not want even one wife, let alone five hundred.'

Andrew followed the Theravada tradition, which regards the Buddha as human; he was born a man and died as a man. 'How can he,' the Buddha once asked, 'by whom we were

274

created, be permanent, constant, eternal, unchanging, and remain so for ever and ever, while we who were created by Brahma are all impermanent, transient, unstable, short-lived, destined to pass away?' Everything is impermanent. How can there be an everlasting god? 'By oneself is one purified; by oneself is one defiled,' the Buddha told his disciples. He had shown the path: he had demonstrated through his own example the latent power of the human mind. Now it was left to his followers to find their own way. Even his own teachings must be jettisoned once they had served their purpose. He compared them to a raft, telling the story of a traveller who had come to a great expanse of water and desperately needed to get across. There was no bridge, no ferry, so he built a raft and rowed himself across the river. But then, the Buddha asked his audience, what should the traveller do with the raft? Should he decide that because it had been so helpful to him, he should load it on to his back and carry it with him wherever he went? Or should he simply moor it and continue his journey? The answer was obvious. 'In just the same way, my teachings are like a raft, to be used to cross the river and not to be held on to.'

I would have loved to talk to Andrew longer. He was so knowledgeable and the Buddhism he practised made a lot of sense to me. For a long time, I had been led to think that what Grandmother believed in was all there was to Buddhism. The gods and goddesses of Mahayana Buddhism were exactly the targets of our ferocious attack on Buddhism at school, and in Communist propaganda. We were never told there was another side to Buddhism, and I never knew the Buddha did not approve of gods at all. But Andrew had to leave. He was studying with a Sri Lankan monk in a nearby monastery, learning how to remove the five poisons of the mind – ego, pride, hatred, ignorance and attachment. 'I still have plenty of them, I can assure you,' he laughed. He meditated in the morning; he took lessons in the afternoon; in the evening, he meditated again and reflected on what he had learnt during the day. He said being in Bodh Gaya helped him a lot because there were many good teachers and seeing these devout pilgrims made him try even harder to reach his goal.

When he stood up, he said he must tell me one more thing. Once upon a time, a monk came to Bodh Gaya and started praying earnestly to the Buddhist statues. Then he thought he saw the Buddha praying to the images too. He was shocked. 'You are the Buddha. Why are you praying to yourself?' The Buddha replied: 'That is my point. Pray to yourself, not to anyone else.' 'That's what I think we should do,' Andrew said. I wished him well and wondered if his homeland would ever be the next new world for Buddhism to flourish in.

Andrew told me to look out for Asoka, a Bodh Gaya guide and a Buddhist. He would be able to tell me a lot about the place and about Buddhism in India. I had turned down one guide at the ticket office when I came in – the ones I had used before simply recited what I already knew from the guide-books, and their accents were so strong, I could understand only half of what they were saying. I prayed it was not Asoka I had refused. Of course, it was: a man in his late forties, of short build, with a childlike cheerful expression. 'Wandering sheep do come back,' he said with a smile. 'Welcome to Bodh Gaya.'

Asoka proudly showed me, one by one, the shrines marking the spots where the Buddha spent the first seven weeks after his enlightenment, every one of which Xuanzang describes in detail in his *Record*: where he gazed at the Bodhi Tree from a distance, where he reflected on what he had achieved; where he meditated again; where he was shielded from a severe storm; where he tested his findings on a few people. Near the entrance was the spot where the Buddha had talked at length with a Brahmin. 'You know what the Buddha told him?' Asoka asked excitedly, and then quickly answered his own question: '"I do not call a man a Brahmin because of his birth. He is indeed arrogant and wealthy. But the poor man, who is free from all attachment, him I call indeed a Brahmin." That's Buddha's greatness: we are all equal. God cannot make one person superior, the other inferior.' He was making his point with both his hands raised, his face agitated. 'Upali, one of the Buddha's chief disciples, was a barber; Sunita, honoured by kings and nobles as an enlightened man, was a scavenger; Amrapali donated a garden where the Buddha spent many rainy retreats in Vaisali, she was a courtesan.'

If he was so emotional about this aspect of Buddhism, I realized, Asoka was probably from a backward caste himself, or a 'dalit', the 'oppressed people' as they call themselves. I was sure an Indian would know at a glance. But to me he looked like everyone else. I had always been struck by how revolutionary the Buddha must have been to call for equality in such a stratified society as India. I asked Asoka to tell me more about it.

'Buddhism was a rejection of Brahminism and caste,' Asoka stated emphatically. 'In the Sangha, everyone is treated as equal, whether you are a Brahmin or a sweeper. It is revolutionary, the first of its kind. It shows the world how a community based on equality can work. Like the Mahabodhi Temple, it opens its doors to everyone, even women – they were fourth-class citizens for a long time in India, and could not go near the temples.' Asoka looked at me and a stream of pilgrims walking past us quietly, and went on. 'The Sangha here does not mean the usual assembly of monks and nuns. It means anyone who embraces Buddhism. The Buddha believed that every one of us has the potential to become a Buddha, through our own efforts, not through our birth.'

Why then did Buddhism disappear in the country of its birth?

Asoka said it was killed by the Brahmins, who stole lots of ideas and practices from Buddhism – the Sangha, the puja, the saffron robe, the Buddhist compassion for all creatures. 'If they even made the Buddha an incarnation of Vishnu, what could they not do? One minute animal sacrifice was the pillar of their belief and the next they were all vegetarians.'

The real reason was more complicated, as I was to discover. But even at its height, Buddhism never completely dominated Indian life, nor was caste eliminated, although the social stratification was less rigid. Xuanzang noticed the caste system wherever he went and his account of the social segregation is still apposite today. 'Butchers, fishermen, dancers, executioners and scavengers, and so on, have their abodes outside the city. And they are seldom seen among men. In coming and going they are bound to keep on the left side of the road till they reach their houses, which are surrounded by low walls . . . They are despised, scorned and universally reprobated.'

If Buddhism had never eradicated caste even when it was at its height, how could it be the answer to Bihar's caste war today? I could not see that the Brahmins would surrender their privileges. That was why they had *senas* to defend what they regarded as their birthright. I told Asoka about my conversation with Rajiv back at the hotel.

Asoka assured me that killings of the dalits happened almost daily in Bihar, and Gaya District was one of the worst places in the state. Of all the *senas* in Bihar, the Savarna Liberation

Army was the most atrocious, and their leader, Ramadhar Singh, is reputed to have said: 'In history my name will be written on the funeral pyres of labourers.' The SLA had masterminded many attacks on villages, killed hundreds of dalits, raped their women, and burned their huts and crops. Their most heinous act was a 'mass rape' campaign in Gaya and the neighbouring district in 1992. In the space of five months, week after week, village after village, a group of their core members raped more than 200 dalit women, aged from six to seventy. They said they wanted to teach them a 'lesson': if they dared to take on the landlords, their women would be humiliated. They calculated that the stigma attached to rape victims was such that the families would be too frightened to challenge them, for the time being at least. They were wrong. The dalits fought back. 'Hardly a year ago, in Gaya, hundreds of dalits stormed a village in the middle of the night,' Asoka said. 'They grabbed thirty-five upper-caste land-lords from their beds, marched them into the fields, and slit their throats with a sickle, one by one. The spiral of killing is still going on.'

But it was not just the *senas*. I heard that the Naxalites, Maoist guerrillas originally from the hills of West Bengal, were also very active in Bihar. They believe armed struggle is the only solution to India's entrenched problems of poverty and inequality. They model themselves on the Chinese Communist Party of old: they arm themselves, go to the most impoverished villages, organize strikes by landless labourers in support of demands for land or better pay; and failing that, they single out the most brutal and oppressive landlords, seize their fields and give them to the dalits, and then publicly humiliate the 'enemies of the people' before executing them. Police and police informers, government officials and *sena* activists are also their targets. Their goal is to bring revolution to India's nearly two hundred million dalits, overthrow the government and build a new People's Republic of India.

'But they are not getting anywhere,' Asoka said. 'They grab land but they cannot hold on to it. They must live in fear, fear of revenge. For every Brahmin killed, ten dalits have paid with their lives. And where will it end? We know from the Buddha that hatred only begets hatred and evil begets evil. That cannot be the way.' He shook his head vehemently.

As a Chinese brought up in the language of class struggle, I find the Indian caste system stupefying. Talking to Asoka about it, I suddenly realized why I found my glimpses of life in Bihar so familiar. It was like the propaganda films of the old China I watched over and over again in my childhood and teens. I can see them clearly: dilapidated straw huts on barren land, howling winds whipping up enormous clouds of dust, farmers in threadbare coats, and their malnourished children clinging to their mothers' apron strings. They were meant to show us what life in China had been like before the Communist revolution. It was a life of destitution, famine and despair. And this was what I was seeing and what I had read about Bihar, fifty years after India's independence and the promise of a new start. I was grateful I was born under the red banner of Communist China.

I thought the Chinese landlords were bad enough. We all learned at school about Zhou Bapi, or Zhou Skin-you-alive, a man of legendary meanness. His labourers had to work from the first cock's crow till dark, so he got up two hours ahead of the cocks and crowed himself in the chicken-run to get them going. All the time, he lived a luxurious life, wearing silk and satin, and eating fish and game. Every semester, my school invited aged peasants to talk about how they used to be exploited by wicked landlords like Zhou Skin-you-alive. We all wept, and shouted with them at the end: 'Never forget the pains of class exploitation! Never forget the tears of class hatred! Long live Chairman Mao! Long live the Communist Party!' Afterwards each of us was given a taste of the old life, a piece of bread made of rice husk and maizeflour, the staple food of the poor. I remembered saying to myself: 'I'd rather die than eat that stuff.' I took a piece home to ask Grandmother whether they really used to eat it. 'Yes,' she said, 'many months of the year.'

I had something to conceal at these meetings. There was a landlord at home, my paternal grandfather. Although he had died long ago, his photo was hanging on our wall. With his long gaunt face, I thought he even looked like Zhou. I asked my father if he had been just as cruel. Father defended him; he said Grandfather had only four acres and did not live a luxurious life. He was kind to his two labourers and he ran a traditional pharmacy in the village and gave people medicines when they could not pay. 'Don't talk about him at school,' he warned me. I would have been in trouble if I repeated what Father said – not that I believed him, so complete was my indoctrination. I saw the harsh treatment for old landlords and their families: humiliation at endless struggle meetings during each political campaign, social stigma, even exile or 're-education' in labour camps. They could never overcome the taint of their class backgrounds. My father and our family escaped a similar fate because he had turned his back on my grandfather by joining the People's Liberation Army at the young age of sixteen and risked his life to liberate the country; innumerable confessions to the Party denouncing his father, even in the front line of the Korean War, also helped. Yet, for all his loyal service, my father was not trusted, never receiving the promotion he deserved. His only consolation was that it could have been a lot worse. Despite all this, however, everything I had learned in school told me: if the landlords suffered, it was their fault; the peasants had had much more of a raw deal.

But on top of their physical and material deprivation, the dalits were treated as if they had no right to exist, to breathe the same air as other people. If I were a dalit I would be very tempted to become a revolutionary. What would I have to lose but an existence so humiliating it can hardly be called life?

I was aware my sentiments were very un-Buddhist, especially since the revolution in China almost pushed the people back into the abyss from which they had been saved, all in the name of the Communist ideal of absolute equality. The peasants, like the rest of the country, were so equal that nobody wanted to work: however hard they laboured, they were paid the same. The whole nation lived on rations for more than thirty years – I still remember how I craved lard; for a long time we were allowed only two ounces of oil a month. And then we suffered one of the worst famines in history, when over thirty million people died of starvation in the early 1960s, most of them in villages. But would the Chinese peasants have preferred no revolution, knowing the pain it would bring? I doubt it.

The ideal of equality is very far from being realized in India, but it has spread widely, wherever Buddhism has taken root. In China, equality began with Buddhism; the very word for it did not exist in our language until the sutras were translated into Chinese. We all have the potential to become the Buddha; we are all equal. It was for this very reason that the emperors, the Sons of Heaven, found Buddhism subversive, but most

Chinese took to it naturally. With temples in almost every village, Buddhist ideas and practices were deeply entrenched in people's lives. They gave them comfort and respect, if not in this life, at least in the next. But many found the world such a painful place that they could not wait to change it. Chinese history is filled with peasant rebellions under Buddhist banners, in particular in the name of the Maitreya Buddha. Ambitious rebel leaders claimed they were the incarnations of Maitreya, who had descended to bring equality, security and certainty to a turbulent, unjust and corrupt society. One could imagine the attraction of such a claim for peasants who were so ruthlessly exploited. Mao's revolution was a continuation of this peasant tradition, but in the name of Communism, with equality as its hallmark.

Revolution does not seem to be the Indian way; at least, not in the Chinese style anyway. The Communist Party of India has never had a real chance of running the country, despite Mao's high hopes. On receiving their congratulations in 1949, he sent this reply: 'I firmly believe that relying on the brave Communist Party of India and the unity and struggle of all Indian patriots, India will certainly not remain long under the yoke of imperialism and its collaborators. Like free China, a free India will one day emerge in the Socialist and People's Democratic family.' It has not happened, and perhaps never will, at least not in the sense of alleviating the oppressions of the caste system and the vast inequalities it promotes. The Naxalites have been ruthlessly put down, but the root cause of their rebellion – inequality and poverty – has yet to be tackled. The Buddha's message was revolutionary 2,500 years ago, and still is today.

My guide Asoka had met strong opposition to his conversion to Buddhism: he was almost disowned by his own family and his caste. But he felt he had found his real calling. He even changed his name because King Asoka did more than anyone in history to spread Buddhism. Now he did not try to convert anyone: that was against Indian law, and 'the Brahmins don't like us to take their servants away'. He only hoped that people would leave Bodh Gaya with something to remember – a statue, a stupa, a story, or a special person they had met. 'It is like planting seeds; one day they will grow into big trees.'

I told Asoka it was the same with the Indian monks who went to spread the Buddha's teachings in China, or with the Chinese monks who came to India in search of the Dharma. Each of them took one seed or cutting at a time, which had later grown into a forest, so deeply rooted in Chinese soil that nothing could destroy it.

Asoka smiled. He was full of admiration for those monks. 'Master Xuanzang, in particular,' he said emphatically. 'He is such an inspiration for me. He had will, wisdom and compassion. Every guidebook they are reading has a section on him.' He pointed to the pilgrims in the compound. 'And what he achieved! I wish he could come back and help us now.'

The sun was setting in a dusty pink sky, casting a warm glow on the whole compound and suffusing it with a pervasive calm. The leaves of the banyan trees, almost black behind the spire of the Mahabodhi Temple, rustled in the faintest of evening breezes. Tiny oil lamps and candles appeared in the niches of the stupas, flickering like stars. It was time for Asoka to say his evening prayer. He asked me to join him: he found Bodh Gaya in the evening even more inspiring than during the day. 'Xuanzang stayed here for seven days and I am sure he must have prayed by day and by night,' he added, as if I needed further encouragement. He went to get some candles. We walked by all the sacred spots again and at each one he lit a candle for me and another for himself; then he prayed and I meditated for a few minutes. Buddha lived and died as a man, a very human figure, but he left behind a powerful message. You could improve yourself. You could rely on your inner resources. You could find your own way. Finally it came home to me: like candles in the night, Buddhism shone light into the darkness of life. Even those without faith, like myself, could not help but be inspired. At last I felt a rare moment of peace in Bihar: for all its poverty and violence, it is the home of the Buddha.

NINE

Nirvana

AFTER HIS ENLIGHTENMENT, the first place the Buddha set out for was Benares. He learned that the five ascetics who had practised austerity with him near the banks of the Nairanjana River now lived in a forest outside the ancient city. They had left him with contempt when he abandoned extreme asceticism. He thought they must still be searching, and he wanted to tell them what he had realized under the Bodhi Tree. They were to become his first disciples.

From these five followers the propagation of Buddhism began. Two hundred years later it reached the far corners of King Asoka's empire, which stretched as far as today's Afghanistan. In another two hundred years it came to China, and eventually pervaded all the countries of Asia, changing them for ever. The countless monasteries, the giant statues, the numerous masters and the fervent piety of kings and commoners that Xuanzang encountered on his journey showed him that Buddhism had struck a chord valuable to all people, and it started here in Benares. For this, the city was given a special place in Buddhism and Buddhist scriptures; so many of the Jatakas of the Buddha's previous lives begin with 'Once upon a time in Benares. . .'.

With his mind full of such inspiring thoughts, Xuanzang reached the city in 632. He was very impressed by it, but also a little taken aback by what he saw. 'The people are gentle and humane, and esteem highly those who are devoted to a studious life. The majority of them believe in the heretical doctrine (of Hinduism), and few follow the Dharma,' he writes sadly. 'In the capital there are twenty Brahmin temples and they are built in elaborate tiers, embellished with a wealth of sculptural decoration, and the parts made of wood are painted in a variety of dazzling colours. They all stand among giant trees surrounded by pools of clear water.'

Xuanzang would have no doubt learned quickly the reason for such a profuse outpouring of devotion by the 'heretics' here. Benares was the most sacred city in India. Lord Shiva, the Destroyer of the Universe, was said to have found this spot on the bank of the Ganges so beautiful that he chose it from all places on earth to be his abode: he called it Anandavana, or the Garden of Bliss. The Ganges was a river of Heaven that Shiva channelled down to the earth through his matted hair, and people believed it to have the power to purify all sins. This trinity of Shiva, the Ganga and the Garden of Bliss convinced the Hindus that dying in Benares was liberation from *samsara*. Benares became a great centre of religion and learning long ago, filled with philosophers, learned men of law, medicine, astrology and music, Hindu sages and holy men, and it boasts of no fewer than twenty thousand Brahmin priests today.

In this stronghold of belief, the Buddha decided to spread his message – if he could gain support and followers here, he surely would do so in the rest of the country. A Jataka story tells how the Buddha converted the people of Benares. As a young prince, he was appalled by the Brahminic rituals of animal sacrifice. This could not be good either for men or gods, he told himself. True religion sanctifies life, not killing; true faith offers peace of mind, not cruelty. He came up with a plan to stop the practice. Each year he made offerings of incense, flowers, sweets and water to an ancient banyan tree. When at last he ascended the throne, he called his ministers and all the prominent men of Benares to the palace, and told them he had made a promise to the banyan tree that if he became king, he would offer a special sacrifice. Everyone agreed and said, 'We must prepare this sacrifice at once. What animals do you wish to kill?' The king replied, 'I promised the great god of the banyan tree that I would sacrifice anyone who destroys life, takes what is not given, misbehaves sexually, speaks falsely, or loses his mind from alcohol. Let my promise be known throughout the kingdom.' And so the people of Benares renounced the practice of animal sacrifice and became renowned for observing the five Buddhist precepts.

The real story of the Buddha's preaching in Benares was equally challenging. At first, the locals might have regarded him as one of the innumerable holy men wandering in the city, promising yet another way to end life's suffering. But after five years, he won the heart of the king and ordinary people alike. Brahmadatta, King of Benares, figures prominently in the early sutras, and is perhaps not an entirely mythical character. Yasa, the son of a rich Benares merchant, had everything he desired but was not happy. He came to talk to the Buddha one day and made up his mind on the spot to leave home and join the Sangha. He was the Buddha's sixth disciple. His parents, fifty of his friends and many of the mercantile class in Benares, and later throughout India, became the Buddha's ardent supporters. The most beautiful courtesan in Benares, who was reputed to earn every day as much as half the city's daily taxes, liked the Buddha's preaching and wanted to be a Buddhist too. When her admirers heard the news, they came out and blocked the road; the Buddha had to send a nun to ordain her in her own house.

And now, more than a thousand years after Xuanzang's visit, Benares still retains the sanctity and vitality he describes. The labyrinth of narrow lanes and buildings piled on top of each other reminded me of Xuanzang's simile, they were like 'the scales on a fish'. There are now more temples devoted to Lord Shiva, more people living in the city and more pilgrims. Xuanzang also described the numerous ascetics in the city. 'Some cut their hair off, others tie their hair in a knot, and go naked, with their bodies covered with ashes. By the practice of austerities they seek to escape from birth and death'. The naked ascetics with matted hair and ash-smeared bodies are still there, oblivious to the faithful who pour through the temples in their thousands.

Nowhere is more congested and noisy than the Golden Temple in the heart of Benares, the holiest of all Shiva shrines. As I neared it, the lane narrowed to hardly more than a metre, and the souvenir shops that crowded it seemed almost to meet over my head. I was barely walking, borne along rather in the press of people and the heady smells of incense and garlands. I could not tell whether the statue of Shiva was as impressive as Xuanzang describes – non-Hindus are not allowed inside. What struck me was the mosque standing behind it, part of the temple site that Xuanzang visited. In the late seventeenth century, the Mughal Emperor Aurangzeb destroyed the old shrine, together with almost all the Hindu temples in Benares, and built two mosques. Now guarded by a watchtower and barbed wire, they sit uneasily on Hindu ground.

What has remained unchanged is that life in Benares converges on the Ganges, as it has done for millennia. Yogendra and I went to the riverfront. It was dawn. The rising sun was reflected in the river and made its rippling surface dance with yellow and orange light. The temples and shrines, ashrams, mosques and pavilions that stretch along the river for over three miles were bathed in a golden glow. The long flights of stone steps called *ghats*, or 'landings', were crowded with pilgrims and locals who could not wait to go into the river.

Yogendra wanted to bathe too. I left him and boarded a boat which took me slowly up and down. An extraordinary panorama of life unfolded against the backdrop of the grand but dilapidated houses, temples and mosques that lined the riverbank. The pilgrims carefully floated flowers and small clay oil-wick lamps on the water, and then immersed themselves. When they reappeared, facing the sun, they scooped up water in their cupped hands; with a murmur of prayer, they poured it back into the river, as an offering to their ancestors and the gods. When the ritual was over, they remained in the river, talking and laughing like children, before they finally filled their brass vessels and waded back to the shore. At Panchaganga Ghat, the most popular *ghat*, with its myriad riverfront shrines, a Brahmin priest was blessing a groom, his bride and their large families. Away from the crowds, a man was brushing his teeth and washermen were beating hotel laundry on stones, splashing it with water clouded by droppings that had just been released by five cows a little way upstream. In the less popular *ghats*, open sewers were pumping into the river the night-soil and waste of the people of Benares, over one million of them, not to mention the pilgrims. At Manikarnika Ghat, the cremation ground, flames were engulfing three funeral pyres while the relatives of the dead watched quietly; more corpses arrived and were left at the water's edge; and lingering on the surface of the water were ashes from bodies cremated earlier, mixed with wilted flower-garlands. This is where Lord Shiva is supposed to whisper the 'prayer of the crossing' into the ears of the dead, and where Lord Vishnu dug a well at the beginning of time. This is the place of creation and destruction, the place of liberation, alive day and night, drawing Hindus from all corners of India.

'It is said in the books of the country that the Ganges is a river of felicity,' Xuanzang wrote. 'Those who bathe in it will be purified of all sins; those who wash their mouths with the water will be saved from calamities; those who drown in it will be reborn in Heaven. So men and women flock to the bank of the river.'

Xuanzang did not believe in the purifying power of the Ganges, and he was not the first sceptic; he told us how Deva Bodhisattva from Sri Lanka showed the Hindus what was wrong with their belief. He walked into the river and started splashing water in a southerly direction. The pilgrims were puzzled and asked him why. He replied, 'My parents live in Sri Lanka and they are thirsty. I very much want the water to reach them.' Everyone laughed at him. 'You are wrong, master. How can you do such a stupid thing? You should use your brain. Your home is a thousand miles away. It is like walking backwards but trying to catch up with the people ahead of you. It cannot be done.' He nodded and said: 'The sins in hell are uncountable, and this water is supposed to purify them all. I am only separated from my family by a few mountains and rivers, why cannot they be saved?' The pilgrims, Xuanzang said, realized the fallacy of their belief and implored Deva Bodhisattva to be their guru.

It is rare, and refreshing, for Xuanzang to question miracles. But I found him somewhat contradictory here. He was so disdainful of Hindus' belief in miracles, while he swallowed so many Buddhist ones himself. In every place he visited on his journey he recorded the local legends and myths. I noticed when I read the *Record* I always skipped the pages covering yet more extraordinary feats performed by the Bodhisattvas, as if I did not want them there. Of course, some stories in his account can be de-mythologized, just as some Christians do with the parable of the loaves and fishes – they say the real miracle was that Jesus encouraged people to share their food, so that everyone was fed. But, as with miracles in general, you just have to accept their veracity or not. Xuanzang obviously believed those of Buddhist origin.

Most Chinese Buddhists accept them too, as did my grand-mother. This is exactly where the Communists went for the kill – if the Buddhas and Bodhisattvas were so powerful, why did they let so many people suffer? When our teacher explained to us that this was all there was to Buddhism, we all agreed that Buddhism was nothing more than superstition. I asked Grandmother once whether her favourite Bodhisattva Guanyin could really deliver all the things she prayed for. 'If you believe enough and do everything right,' she said, 'she can.'

Only after I had started on the journey did I realize that the Buddha himself did not approve of miracles: they were impediments to spiritual progress and the final awakening. He even dismissed Brahma, the supreme Hindu god of creation, by asking: 'If no limits can restrain his wide power, why is his hand so rarely spread to bless? Why are his creatures all condemned to pain? Why does he not give happiness to all?' The story goes that the Buddha once met an ascetic at a river crossing who told him he had achieved such mastery over his physical body that he could now cross the river by walking on the water. The Buddha's disciples wanted him to take up the challenge and perform the same feat. The Buddha said, 'Let us take the ferry.' When they reached the other side he asked the boatman what the fare was. 'One penny,' the boatman replied. The Buddha turned to his disciples. 'That's how much the miracle is worth.'

I watched the dense crowd of people in the river, their heads bobbing on the water. Obviously many Indians still believe in the magical power of the Ganges, just as their ancestors have done for thousands of years. I wanted to ask them, as Xuanzang did, about their beliefs. There was no better person to answer my questions than V. P. Mishra. He is the head priest of Sankat Mochan, one of the principal temples in Benares. He is also a professor of hydraulic engineering at Benares Hindu University, specializing in the environmental problems of the Ganges. I left the boat at Tulsi Ghat and found his house perched at the top of the steps.

Mishra looked fresh and alert, with his thick snow-white hair combed straight back, matching his white dhoti and the spartan white-washed sitting-room where he received me. He had just finished his morning ritual: a dip in the Ganges and praying at his own temple.

I told him why I was in Benares. 'Of course Xuanzang could not miss it,' he said, as if we were talking about a mutual friend. 'What did he say about the Ganga? I bet it was much cleaner in his time.' I told him that Xuanzang described the colour of the water as emerald green, extremely pure. I also mentioned what I had seen on the river earlier. Was he not worried when he was in the Ganges?

'I am aware of the consequences of my actions.' He looked me in the eye. 'But I must do it. I need it to live and I want to do it until the last day of my life. It is the most important part of Hindu life. That's why we have to clean up the Ganga.'

He has devoted the last twenty years to the Clean the Ganga Campaign, working with scientists in America, trying to adopt a new organic sewage treatment system. 'Then our people can be granted the holy water again without the worry of disease,' he said, his face creasing into a broad, optimistic smile.

Mishra's temple was devoted to Hanuman, the monkey god from the epie, Ramayana, whose miracles are every bit as exciting as those of our Monkey King, his 'incarnation' transported along the Silk Road. But for us Chinese, the Monkey King, no matter how powerful, is only a fictional character; for Hindus, Hanuman is an almighty god, and I had seen temples dedicated to him everywhere. My guidebook has this verse from a prayer to him:

You perform tasks only Gods can do,
So what problem of mine can you not set right?
Come quickly and help me,
For who in the world does not know your name is
    Remover of Difficulties?

'But Hanuman seems to be standing by while the Ganges is getting worse and worse. Even priests like you cannot bathe in it safely,' I said to Mishra, not entirely innocently.

'Hanumanji has inspired me to my life's work,' he replied calmly, as if he had encountered such scepticism many times. 'Isn't there an English saying, "God helps those who help themselves?" Hanumanji is not going to take the task out of my hands. I have to do the work. But with his inspiration I will do it; I'll have hundreds and thousands of other people to help me. We will prevail.'

I told Mishra about the Chinese version of Hanuman. Did he believe his Hanuman actually existed, and was not a fictional creation like ours?

'I know he is always with me, protecting me,' he said, pointing to his heart. 'I suppose this is what you call faith. I'm sure your monk had a lot of it.' I guess I would expect that from Xuanzang. But Mishra is a scientist. How did he square faith with science? Like millions of people, I want to believe what reason supports, what science proves.

'As a scientist, I work to solve problems in this world, the world we understand with our minds and our senses,' he explained. 'But there is a spiritual world. I often think of the Ganga as life, with science and faith as its two banks. The banks never meet but the river wouldn't flow without them. Without science we would be back in the dark ages; but without faith life would be poorer. My campaign to clean the Ganga comes from both. They make me the person I am.'

Mishra made me think about faith, that faith which moved him to work to save the Ganges, as it moved Xuanzang to embark on his journey, and Grandmother to overcome the pain in her life. If only I could make the leap of faith myself. There is so much in Buddhism that I am beginning to learn, and that I know would help me, as Grandmother had hoped. But something holds me back. I do not know precisely what it is. It lies ahead of me, to be discovered. Perhaps I need another journey, a journey of a different kind.

From the terrace outside Mishra's house the great concourse of buildings and the thronging crowds of Benares are not visible, only a huge expanse of water, ending in a faint grey horizon of land, pure light above it. Maybe life, like the Ganges, has its other shore.

In the afternoon I crossed the Ganges to the far side, heading for the Deer Park in Sarnath, a complete contrast to the teeming crowds and noise of Benares. This is where the Buddha found the five ascetics and told them what he had realized, and he came here again and again for his retreat during the monsoon season. Xuanzang tells us how the Deer Park was given its name: from another Jataka story. The Buddha in a previous life offered himself as a stag in place of a pregnant deer to the King of Benares' hunting party. The king was so moved he gave up hunting and offered the forest to the deer. The name has lasted all these years.

As usual, Xuanzang noted down the many sites and legends here commemorating moments associated with the Buddha, in particular the giant Dharmarajika stupa erected by King Asoka to mark the spot where the Buddha gave his first sermon. Not far from it stands a later stupa that Cunningham had drilled through in vain before he had Xuanzang's *Record* to guide him. When Xuanzang saw it, it was a lofty monument of over one hundred feet, covered from top to bottom with rare treasures. Today it is reduced mostly to rubble, with little trace of its decorations. Fallen pillars, broken walls and small statues in the niches of the walls are the only remains of a magnificent monastery nearby. Peace permeated the quiet ruins. Three Tibetan monks sat under a leafy tree, their eyes fixed on the ruins, in silent contemplation. Even without its thriving community of 1,500 monks, or its magnificent monastery, here more than anywhere I felt that this was what the Buddha would have wanted, not for us to commemorate him, but to remember his teachings.

Much of what remains is in the splendid museum near the park. The lion capital from Asoka's pillar greets you at the entrance. Xuanzang saw it in its original place: 'The stone is as bright as jade, it is glistening, and sparkles like light,' he says. It still does. Four lions sit on a circlet that is decorated with an elephant, a bull, a horse and the wheel of law, or *chakra*, and below that a lotus, the symbol of purity. The lions point in all four directions, proud and roaring benevolently. The message is clear: the Dharma would spread far and wide. And it did. Rule of righteousness, victory by virtue, and a unified country where all people live in harmony – these are Asoka's legacies; they are also the fundamental beliefs of the founding fathers of the Republic of India, enshrined in the Indian constitution. The *chakra* appears on the Indian national flag, and the lion capital is the national emblem with the motto: 'Satyameva jayate' – 'Truth always triumphs'. Nehru was even quoted as saying 'I cannot be a Buddha. But Asoka, I can try to be.'

Further inside the museum there is one supreme seated Buddha, in front of which I, like everyone else, stopped and stood in humble silence. It is called the 'Buddha Preaching the First Sermon', or 'Turning the Wheel of Law'. It is regarded as the finest of all Buddha statues. Xuanzang was profoundly touched, seeing it in its original setting near the Dharmarajika stupa. Anyone would be. You are drawn first to the head, set against the large and intricately carved circle of its halo. The eyes are almost closed, looking down but somehow at you at the same time. He appears to be smiling but to be elsewhere. As you stand and gaze, you cannot help wishing to contemplate as intently as he does – you are enveloped by his serenity. The rapt features of the face sum up everything the Buddha stands for: selfless compassion, the overcoming of suffering and the achievement of inner peace. Then you take in the lotus and his legs crossed on it, and your eyes move up to his hands, one palm facing outward, the other with a finger pointing to it, symbolizing teaching. Everything is in motion, and everything is still. You know it is stone, but the figure has a luminous softness that is almost alive. Xuanzang loved it so much he had a copy made in sandalwood to take back to China.

I thought often of that heavenly expression on the Buddha's face the next day when we were driving to Kushinagar, the place of the Buddha's death, or nirvana, in the far north of Bihar, near the border with Nepal. It was the longest day's journey of my Indian trip – one hundred and eighty miles in thirteen hours. We started at dawn and reached Kushinagar in the dark. But I was not upset in the least. That image definitely had a calming effect on me.

In Kushinagar, I was staying in the Indian government guest-house, a complex of bungalows, flowering bushes and green lawns. The dining-room was huge, with canteen-like tables, chairs and cutlery. They clearly expected quantities of pilgrims. But only half a dozen people turned up for breakfast, simple fare of lentils, potatoes and rice. I was sitting next to an old Sri Lankan couple: the husband with snow-white hair, white shirt and white dhoti, looking serene, if slightly tired; the wife more robust, asking the waiter to bring hot water to fill their thermos. They had arrived late the night before from Patna after a gruelling journey. It must have been tough for them – even I found it hard going, getting up most days at the crack of dawn, driving on the impossible roads for hours, staying in each place for one or two nights, and then taking to the road again. 'So you can imagine how difficult it must have been for the Buddha two thousand and five hundred years ago. He was old and he was not well,' the husband said in his gentle voice.

With a body he compared to 'a worn-out cart', the Buddha sensed that he would soon pass away, and he wanted to go on a last trip to propagate the Dharma. Outside Kushinagar he took a meal of wild mushrooms, collected from the woods and prepared by Chunda, the local blacksmith. After the first mouthful, the Buddha knew something was wrong and that night he suffered violent pain and dysentery, perhaps food poisoning; but he was more concerned for Chunda – people would say he had poisoned the Buddha. He told Ananda how to console the distraught blacksmith: 'You have done well, Chunda. You gave the Teacher his last meal, and then he died. There is no greater gift.' Then the Buddha proceeded to a forest outside the city where he asked to be placed in a clearing in a grove of sal trees. Here, the Buddha preached his last sermon, the Great Nirvana Sutra. And then, with his head pointing north, his face to the west, he breathed his last breath. He was eighty years old.

Xuanzang tells us how deeply affected the local people were by the Buddha's death. He gave them these words of mourning: 'The Buddha has left us and entered the Great Nirvana. Now we have no refuge to seek and no one to protect us. It is like a poisonous arrow penetrating our body and the fire of sorrow burning us up without remedy. To cross the vast sea of life and death, who will provide us with a boat and with oars? To walk in the shadow of a long night, who will henceforth be our guide and our torch?' It is hard to believe that these plaintive words were not the expression of his own feelings.

We owe something greater to Xuanzang, nothing less than the rediscovery of Kushinagar. Alexander Cunningham recorded how he read Xuanzang's description of the temple that marked the spot where the Buddha died. Within it, Xuanzang said, 'there is a figure of the Buddha. His head is towards the north, and he looks so serene he might be asleep.' Cunningham sent his assistant Archibald Carlleyle here in 1875 to supervise the dig. It was not easy: the whole place was jungle. Cunningham told him to check the descriptions and distances in the *Record* again and again, and they pointed to a mound covered in earth and trees. When these were cleared away, the ruins were found ten feet deep in the ground, complete with the reclining Buddha exactly as Xuanzang had described it. Cunningham's reaction reveals his excitement: 'To the west of the stupa, we found that famous statue of the Buddha's Nirvana, as recorded by the Chinese pilgrim. I have no doubt this is the statue that Xuanzang had seen personally, as there is an inscription on the pedestal . . . of the Gupta period.' Xuanzang has given us back this place, returning it from the graveyard of history, into the light, into recognition, into worship. It really is an astonishing story. If we owed only Kushinagar to Xuanzang it would be remarkable enough. But I could not get over the fact that everywhere I went in Bihar, it was to him that we are indebted for restoring the sacred Buddhist sites. Every day, Xuanzang's significance was growing greater in my mind.

The depiction of the Buddha's nirvana is one of the most popular themes in Buddhist art. I had seen it in almost all the caves and museums along the Silk Road. I remember in particular one mural in Kucha: on the entire back wall of a cave, an elongated body of the Buddha lay in the centre of a forest; around him were a circle of mourners, some looking very sad with tears pouring from their eyes, some clutching their chests and collapsing with grief, others touching the Buddha's feet and saying prayers; the flowers on the ground bent their heads, and the birds on the tree branches stopped chirping. The perfect composition and the vivid expressions, albeit in faded colours, combined to create a masterpiece, not unlike Da Vinci's Last Supper. This was the image I had of Kushinagar.

But it was not what I saw when I stepped out of the house. The road between the guesthouse and the Nirvana Temple was the high street – the only street – of Kushinagar. There were a few shops and restaurants that served pilgrims, but they looked deserted, unusual for Indian towns or villages, which were always full of people milling about. The pilgrims had postponed their trips; the locals were perhaps all huddled somewhere watching their election votes being counted. But I was not the only one to feel let down. Ananda was devastated when he arrived with the Buddha: 'O Lord,' he cried, 'do not go to your Final Rest in this dreary little town, with mud walls, this heathen, jungle outpost, this backwater.' Xuanzang was also disappointed when he saw it: 'The capital of the country is in ruins, and its towns and villages lie wasted and desolate. The walls of the city have collapsed and the streets are deserted and ghostly, with very few inhabitants.'

But the statue of the Nirvana Buddha was enough to compensate for any disappointment. It lies on its side in the centre of the temple, just as Xuanzang saw it, with a huge red ceremonial robe draped over the body. A caretaker was wiping the dust from the statue. He was so gentle and careful, as if he was afraid to wake the Buddha. The expression on the Buddha's face is one of supreme tranquillity and unearthly detachment. You feel he has not a care in this world. This is what the Buddha preached all his life and what the best of Buddhist art so successfully conveys, like the statue in Sarnath. The longer I looked at it, the more I began to understand what Xuanzang and every Buddhist strives for – the ultimate goal of nirvana, a departure, *ni*, from those defilements that are called *vana*.

Nirvana is not paradise, as is popularly supposed. There are two nirvanas, one in this life, the other after death. The Buddha achieved the first one under the Bodhi Tree: he had extinguished the fires of greed, hatred and delusion, and achieved absolute equanimity and compassion for all beings.

But what is the final nirvana, or the greater nirvana as the Buddhists call it? How is it different from the first? If it is liberation from *samsara*, does it mean extinction? If so, why is extinction such a glorious achievement? If it is not Nothingness, where does the liberated being go thereafter? I know Xuanzang would not have asked these questions. The Buddha positively discouraged monks from speculating on the nature of the final nirvana because it was no help for their final emancipation. 'One thing only does the Buddha teach, namely, suffering and the cessation of suffering,' said the Buddha. There was a monk who kept asking about it; the Buddha compared him to a man who was wounded by an arrow but refused to have treatment until he learned who had shot it at him, what village he came from, what caste he belonged to, and what the arrow was made of and how it was decorated. The Buddha told his disciples, 'If anyone says, "I will not follow the holy life under the Blessed One till he answers these questions," he will die with these questions unanswered by the Teacher.'

As I stood there trying to navigate my way through these difficult thoughts, a group of Indians walked quietly into the shrine. There were nearly forty of them. The women's saris had lost their bright colours from years of wear; the men's garments were clean but almost worn through; and the teenage boys and girls with them were neat but quite threadbare too. They had only a small garland, a few flowers and incense sticks, which they placed reverently by the statue's head. Then they knelt down and started chanting a slow, solemn prayer. Their eyes were shut, as if in a trance; their voices were deep and resonant, each word uttered with yearning.

When they finished, I followed them out. I was curious to know who they were and where they were from. There was something different about them. I asked the monk who led their prayers, and the man who made the offering – he seemed to be their leader – told me they were from Maharashtra. 'Are you Baba Ambedkar's followers?' I asked. Suddenly smiles appeared on their faces; they looked at each other, and then me. 'You know Babasaheb too?' they asked animatedly. 'My name is Ramtirath Ambedkar,' said their leader, a tall man in his late forties, who raised both his hands to me, while looking warmly at me with his large round eyes. 'We are all from Maharashtra.'

Maharashtra is home to Ambedkar, or Babasaheb, the Mahars' endearment for him. He is credited with reviving Buddhism in modern India. By all accounts, he was an extraordinary man. He was the first dalit to get degrees from universities in the West, and three at that: in economics, law and politics. His father and grandfather had worked for the British army, which provided education for the children of all its soldiers. It made a tremendous difference to the lives of tens of thousands of dalits. But in the eyes of Hindus, Ambedkar was still a Mahar, traditionally a community of 'inferior village servants', such as watchmen or messengers, people who would run errands and do menial jobs. The Mahars were deemed Untouchable because it was their work to haul away dead cattle, and they ate carrion to save themselves from starving. At one time, they were compelled to go about with brooms tied to the end of their loincloths and earthenware pots hanging from their necks: the brooms were for covering up their footprints and the pots for spitting in.

Ambedkar suffered the humiliation that his caste had to bear from very early in life. The Brahmin teacher in his school refused to teach him or mark his exercise book, telling him there was no point in educating him. Even after he returned from the West and obtained a job with the Maharaja of Baroda, he had to quit after only a few days: nobody in the city would rent him a room; his subordinates treated him like a leper, throwing files and papers on to his desk from a safe, un-polluting distance. His bitter experience and the plight of his people made him determined to challenge the caste system and fight for the rights of the dalits. He asked his own people to abandon the traditional Mahar work of removing animal carcases, to look and act like Hindus of the highest caste and send their children to school. He set up political parties to put pressure on the British government and the Congress Party. He met fierce opposition, from Gandhi in particular, who saw the caste system as divinely ordained, essential to social harmony. 'One born a scavenger must earn his liveli-hood by being a scavenger,' Gandhi said, 'and then do what-ever else he likes. For a scavenger is as worthy of his hire as a lawyer.' Gandhi regarded Untouchability as a perversion of true Hinduism: the solution was a voluntary change of heart by caste Hindus. Ambedkar had no such illusion. He demanded equal constitutional rights for them, and this led to a dramatic clash with Gandhi.

With his undisputed talents, Ambedkar did go on to become Minister of Law in the first government of independent India and was the man behind India's new constitution. But he was bitterly disappointed with the lack of any real progress for his people, let alone a 'change of heart' by caste Hindus. 'I was born a Hindu, which I could not choose, but I will not die a Hindu,' he vowed. He finally decided to embrace Buddhism, a religion that would treat his people with respect, dignity and, above all, equality. On October 14, 1956 more than 400,000 men, women and children answered his call and arrived in Nagpur in central India, all clad in the spotless white shirts and saris prescribed for the occasion by their leader. Some had made it by train, bus and bullock-cart; the majority had simply walked, some of them over huge distances. The mass conversion was a remarkable moment: a great Indian religion, dormant for a thousand years, was reawoken, in an attempt to put an end to unspeakable suffering.

Ramtirath's father was one of those converts. He gave his son a new surname: Ambedkar. 'Babasaheb is our father, our guru, our leader.' Ramtirath remembered what his father often told him. 'God did not make us suffer, it was the Brahmins. If God had intended us to be untouchable, why didn't he make us look like monsters with three arms and four legs? And how could God be so cruel to his own children, forbidding us even to enter his temple to worship him? The Buddha is different: he is not a god. He makes us believe in ourselves. He makes us strong. Nobody has done that for us. Nobody, except the Buddha and Babasaheb.'

They now saw themselves differently; they felt human again. But did the upper castes treat them differently? 'You cannot straighten a dog's tail,' said an old man forcefully, his silver moustache quivering. 'We have to free ourselves from the mental slavery we have grown up with. That's our worst enemy. They cannot go on making us do the dirtiest work, paying us nothing, and taking advantage of our women. We refuse to take their orders unless they treat us properly.' He was rapturously applauded by the women and the younger members of the group.

I was touched by his words. But I felt sad too. I looked at the people around me closely and intensely, particularly the women. They were cleanly dressed, perhaps in their best clothes for the pilgrimage. They were beautiful, with high cheek-bones, large eyes and long slim necks and arms. Some of them wore jewellery and shoes, which were not allowed before. But they still lived in constant danger of rape – although the upper caste men would not touch them otherwise, they had no compunction about raping them. Their families still had to live outside the villages, with no right to visit the same temple or drink water from the same well as the upper castes. Progress has been made through the government's reservation programmes, and their husbands, or even they themselves, might get jobs and their sons and daughters could go to school and even university. But every step forward for the dalits is deeply resented by many caste Hindus. When the reservation quota in education and employment was raised for the lower castes in the early 1990s, students from the upper castes went on hunger strike, some even burned themselves in protest. For most dalits life continues to be a daunting struggle.

Did they not become impatient and want to do something drastic, like the dalits in Bihar?

'No,' Ramtirath said quickly. 'All those years Babasaheb worked for us, he was always against violence. He knew what is best for us.' The older man nodded his agreement. Ambedkar was totally convinced that non-violence and democracy were the only way forward for the dalits. Revolution might be quick, but its results could not last; change had to come from people's minds – that was the only durable solution. As he told the caste Hindus: 'Had my mind been seized with hatred and revenge, I would have brought disaster upon this land.' He loved India, for all its injustices.

The Buddhism which Ambedkar and his people embraced differs profoundly, however, from what other Buddhists believe. They do not accept karma and rebirth, the two fundamental principles of Buddhism. Ambedkar did not want his followers to have any crutches, any false hope. You must fight to improve this life, he believed, not some imaginary future one. Hinduism was based on karma and rebirth too, objectionable for that reason. Under it dalits were expected to perform their prescribed duties with humility and not to pollute the higher castes. The reward might come in some very distant future, after several incarnations; dalits could be reborn in some modestly better state, but not with any likelihood as a Brahmin. They were told extra rewards would come if they died defending Brahmins, cows or women. No wonder Ambedkar totally rejected the doctrine of karma, rebirth and the intervention of divinities on his people's behalf.

But those were exactly what my grandmother believed, I told Ramtirath. He looked puzzled. 'Your Buddhism sounds like Hinduism, with gods doing everything for you,' he said hesitantly. 'What's the point of being a Buddhist then?' He was right – it was the same problem I had wrestled with myself until recently. But what he had to say next surprised me more. Given how hard they were struggling, did he not sometimes wish for the incarnation of Babasaheb to come back and help them? 'No,' he insisted firmly, without the slightest hesitation, 'Babasaheb cannot come back. There is no rebirth, no god. Only we can help ourselves. That is what the Buddha told us. "Be your lamp unto yourselves. Hold fast to the Truth as a lamp. Look not for refuge to anyone but yourself."'

Ramtirath spoke like a Zen Buddhist. He put me in mind of the famous Zen dictum: 'When you meet the Buddha, kill the Buddha.' There is no other Buddha except what is inside you. As the Sixth Patriarch of Zen, Huineng, told his disciples, 'The Dharma is here in the world; enlightenment is not apart from the world; to search for Bodhi apart from the world is like looking for a hare with horns.' But even Zen Buddhists believe in karma and rebirth. I supposed that in a belief system without a supreme creator, karma provides the only sanction: there must be some punishment and reward; otherwise the world would be an unjust place.

Some call Ambedkar and his followers new Buddhists. Others question whether the Ambedkar movement is more motivated by politics than faith, which are increasingly intertwined in modern India. But I have every sympathy with Ramtirath and his people. More than that, with these people, I sensed a fellow-feeling. I felt I could be this kind of Buddhist, inspired by the rationality, the compassion and the self-reliance in the Buddha's teachings. Since the Buddha denied the existence of a permanent entity or an immortal soul, then what is it that transmigrates from this life into the next one? It could not be the genes, which would be the most obvious choice, because one might be reborn as a sheep or a butterfly if one's karma was not good enough for rebirth as a human being. Buddhists say it is the karmic force that is transmitted, which is neither material nor immaterial. There the theory loses me and I am still in the dark, waiting to be illuminated.

They were leaving the shrine. I asked Ramtirath where they were staying. 'Oh,' he said, 'under the sky, under the trees.' They were camping in the forest. I could imagine how hard their life must be – even on their pilgrimage they had nothing to spare – and they must have saved up all their lives for it. I asked if I could take their photo in a group, and have their address. I would have something to remember them by and I would send it to them. They rushed to sit on the steps and spruce themselves up. As I focused on them, I looked at them through the viewfinder for a long time. I could not help admiring them. Most of them were illiterate and Ramtirath, who was the village schoolteacher, taught them from *The Buddha and His Dharma*, which Ambedkar wrote to guide his followers – no monks had visited them. But wresting their own dignity and peace of mind from their circumstances and overcoming so much suffering was a kind of enlightenment. I hope they received the picture. I keep a copy in a frame on my desk.

From the Nirvana Temple, I walked past fields dotted with monasteries to the Rambhar Stupa, which marks the place where the Buddha was cremated. The stupa is now just a large mound of bricks. A lonely Sri Lankan monk stood there with his palms pressed together, lost in thought. It was already in ruins when Xuanzang came here. He would have been saddened both by the death of the Buddha and by this further evidence of the decline of Buddhism in India in one of its most sacred places. But he remembered the Buddha's last words to Ananda, who was inconsolable: 'Do not be sad. Do not despair. Everything that exists is perishable. Take the Dharma as your teacher. Persevere and strive for your salvation.' Xuanzang must have felt the words could have been addressed to him. The Buddha is dead, but the Dharma is with us. The Buddha is the Dharma, the Dharma is the Buddha. The two are the same. Spread the Dharma and the Buddha will live on. More than ever, Xuanzang was determined to propagate the Buddha's teachings, not in the land of its birth, but in China. This was the task that awaited him.

I arrived back at the hotel at dusk and found the old Sri Lankan couple sitting on a bench on the lawn, gazing towards the Nirvana Temple. They looked a little dejected.

'You're looking unwell,' I said to the husband.

'No, I have a little stomach trouble.' He smiled ruefully. 'I shouldn't complain. The Buddha had the same thing in Kushinagar and he died of it. He was like us, just human.'

That night I took a call from the travel agent. He was

concerned. The Bihar election was now reaching its apex of horror. The *Hindustan Times* carried the headline 'Body Counts on Final Day'. The Rapid Action Force shot dead seven people who tried to capture election booths; three policemen died in an ambush; one man lost his life in a bomb explosion, and the leader of one party was stoned to death by supporters of another. Par for the course in Bihar, it seems: the paper did not sound surprised. Every day I said to myself: 'This can't get any worse,' and each time I was wrong. And now it was reaching a dangerous point; the travel agent said whatever the election result, there would be more violence. He advised me to get out of Bihar and skip Lumbini, where the Buddha was born, the last sacred Buddhist place identified in 1907, with the help of Xuanzang's *Record*. He was going to cancel my hotel booking in Lumbini and send me on an early train from Patna to Madras. 'We don't want to lose you,' he said. Regretfully, I followed his advice.

Xuanzang headed for South India in 636, after five years of study in Nalanda. His goal was to visit Ceylon: the home of Theravada Buddhism and many of its greatest masters. On the eastern coast, he passed through Kalinga, modern Orissa: as Xuanzang would have known well, the scene of Asoka's bloody victory which led to his shame and conversion to Buddhism. Xuanzang stayed at a seaport, a particularly lively place where 'merchants depart for distant countries, and foreigners, coming and going, stop on their way.' He was struck by the quantity of rare goods in the city, some of which would have come from as far away as Rome. For ships going out to southeast Asia, rice, indigo, brown sugar and textiles were the more common cargoes. He might have found lodging in one of the five monasteries outside the city, right on the sea, seeing the ships sailing off. He let his thoughts wander off with them, in the warm tropical night, to Ceylon. 'Every night when the sky is clear and cloudless, a thousand kilometres to the south is Ceylon, where the precious diamond placed above the Stupa of the Buddha's Tooth casts a dazzling light that can be seen from afar. The radiance resembles a torch hanging in mid-air.' But he was advised by the monks not to take the sea route, which was very dangerous. He should travel overland to Kanchipuram in South India, and from there he could cross the sea to Ceylon in three days.

The journey to Kanchipuram took Xuanzang more than a year, as he frequently stopped to study with any great master he could find. I was there in one day on the Coromandel Express to Madras, and another two hours by bus. The road was crowded but the countryside still fitted his description: 'The soil is fertile and finely cultivated, and produces abundance of grain. There are also many flowers and fruits.' Through the window I could see lush paddy fields hemmed by palms and every now and then white-washed houses studded with a profusion of pink, red and yellow flowers. The bus entered town along a few ordinary shopping streets, except that above the shops loomed the *gopurams*, the towers, of its great temples. Xuanzang noted that the place was famous for 'precious gems and other articles'. But today the main sale was silk, or *China-mshuka*, the Sanskrit name as I fondly remembered. Kanchipuram silk was known throughout India and there was plenty of it here, in shop after shop and street after street, rolls of it, in every colour you can imagine: pale lime next to cerise, livid purple and gold, like jewels and baubles displayed row on row.

Xuanzang felt very much at home here and stayed for several months. Kanchipuram was the capital of the Dravida kingdom, which boasted over a hundred monasteries and 10,000 monks.

The people were courageous, honest, truthful, and esteemed learning and learned men. But what drew Xuanzang even more to Kanchipuram was the memory of Dharmapala, who was born to a noble family here. He was Shilabhadra's teacher. Xuanzang had studied at the feet of Shilabhadra for five years, received the most profound teaching, and finally understood Yogacara. The wisdom had come down from this man, to whom Yogacara and he owed a great debt. He was particularly influenced by Dharmapala's commentaries on the Yogacara school of thought. On his return to China, he used them as the main source for *The Doctrine of Mere Consciousness*, his synthesis of the major arguments of Yogacara; the work became the key text of this school in China and Japan.

Today Kanchipuram is still a holy city, thronged with pilgrims – but they are Hindu pilgrims. In fact, Kanchipuram is one of the seven holiest cities in India, and its Shankaracharya is regarded by many Hindus as one of their five spiritual leaders. I walked from one temple to another, in a daze at the sheer number of them – over seventy – in this small place, each more grand and beautiful than the last. I was particularly keen to see the Kamakshi Temple and its mandapa, the square shrine in front of the Shiva sanctum. It is sacred to Shankara, the great reformer of Indian religion – local legend says he died here. For me this is a profoundly symbolic place. Xuanzang told us of the ascendance of heretic temples and believers in many towns and cities. He talked about evil kings who cut down the Bodhi Tree, killed monks and destroyed monasteries. But he did not know that the most fatal blow to Buddhism came from Shankara only a hundred years after he left India.

Shankara was born in Kerala in about 700 A D, and became an ascetic in his teens. Like every seeker of the truth he studied in Benares, rapidly showing his brilliance and acquiring a reputation as a philosopher. But knowledge, even personal salvation, was not his final goal. He was unhappy with the numerous sects, each claiming supremacy and creating discord. He felt the Brahmin priests were mainly intent on emphasizing their separateness and safeguarding their privileges, leaving out a large section of society. Something needed to be done to reclaim the ground, moral, doctrinal, ritualistic, as well as social, that had been lost to the Buddhists.

'Who are you? Who am I? From where do I come? Enquire thus and you will realize that the entire world is but a dream, a mere hallucination, born of imagination. With such a realization, you will be freed from the delusions of the world,' Shankara wrote. *Brahman*, the Absolute, is the only reality, which is manifested in Shiva, Vishnu, a Brahmin – it is everywhere and everything. Xuanzang would have found himself almost agreeing with this Hindu philosopher's doctrine of Advaita, oneness or non-duality. Even the Absolute is close to the pure consciousness of Yogacara, except that it is eternal, not as in Buddhism, in a continuous state of flux. Through his commentaries on the classics, the Vedas and Upanishads, Shankara took on Buddhism on its own ground, arguing that all the elements that were the source of its broad appeal could be found in the Hindu holy books.

For fifteen years Shankara travelled all over India, teaching his new creed. He started in villages until he had a considerable following. Then he went into the cities where the Buddhists and Jains were strong. Here the battle for people's minds began. He convinced and converted a great many people by inviting them to challenge him – if they lost, they would become his followers. Observing how important the Sangha was for Buddhists as a centre of learning, propagation and worship, he too set up monasteries which the Hindus call *mathas.* Today they are the holiest places for many Hindus: in the east, in the west, in the south and in the north, and here in Kanchipuram. The five head priests are called Shankaracharyas, Shankara the Teacher, and they are the leaders of the Hindu faith.

The mandapa shrine dedicated to Shankara in the Kamakshi Temple is not so ancient, perhaps three or four hundred years old, but as beautiful as anything I had seen. Its intricate sandstone carving had retained its delicacy and strength, and even the florid sculpture was not overwhelming. Simplicity and harmony permeated the stone and the space around it. A crowd of pilgrims were piling marigold wreaths, sweets, candles and small jars of water in front of it. As I watched, a priest appeared in a saffron robe and smiled absently at me. I asked him if he spoke English and he smiled again, this time with interest. 'My first degree was in English, before I became a priest,' he said. His voice was warm and deep – one of those instantly reassuring voices priests so often have. I asked him if Shankara really died here. 'We think so, although he is also thought to have died in the north, in the Himalayas. But you can say he is everywhere.' He pointed to the pilgrims. 'That was his real contribution,' he said. 'He was not just a great philosopher – he would never have won so many converts with philosophy alone. He had a message for everyone, it was *bhakti*, it was devotion. The Absolute One is in everything and everybody. Celebrating it is celebrating the purest in all of us. As is said in the Upanishads: "It is his Self alone that a man should venerate as his world. From his very Self he will produce whatever he needs."'

I could see how liberating Shankara was. But surely the Brahmins were angry with him?

'His Brahmin opponents called him "a Buddhist in disguise". But he wanted to open the religion to everyone,' the priest said. 'The Brahmins are still spiritual teachers but they don't have a monopoly any more. Everyone has hope. Shankara was the liberator.'

Shankara was indeed responsible for creating a unified Hindu religion, which reduced the appeal of Buddhism as a refuge from Brahmin dominance and caste prejudice, particularly in South India. Buddhism was deeply undermined and never recovered; and the physical destruction wrought by the Afghan invaders four hundred years later completed the process. In the whole of North India there was scarcely a statue that was not defaced by the invaders, scarcely a temple that was not ravaged, with all the monks either killed or fleeing to Nepal or Tibet. Muslim chronicles record that an order went out from the new ruler to find someone capable of reading the books in a monastery library, but no one was found alive. Hinduism survived because Hindu temples were not the be-all and end-all of the religion: Brahmins were the custodians of the sacred texts and knowledge; holy men, sages and sadhus wandered the country; people could perform pujas at home; in time new temples were built again, many on Buddhist sites. But for Buddhism, the Sangha was all-important and when the monks were gone, Buddhism in India was dead.

As I was about to leave the Kamakshi Temple, another group of pilgrims came up to Shankara's shrine. This time they were saying a short prayer, perhaps one of the beautiful hymns Shankara wrote. When I read these hymns, I was struck by how Buddhist they sound: 'We wallow in our ignorance as in mire. Our life on earth, snared in the cycle of birth, old age and death, is but vanity and sorrow. Glory be to those who see this bondage for what it is, cut the knot with the sword of knowledge, and stand firm in their wisdom.' Perhaps

Buddhism was not dead after all. It has lived on and its influence can be felt in all aspects of Indian life, reaching even into the deepest recesses of the Hindu mind. I remember I was puzzled when I read this bold claim in a study of Buddhist culture in India during the seventh and eighth centuries: 'Every Hindu is a Buddhist, in spite of all outward appearances to the contrary.' I began to realize what it meant.

It was sad, however, not to find any trace of that Buddhist past in this once great Buddhist city. I thought of Xuanzang's disappointment here too. He was waiting for ships to sail for Ceylon, but none was leaving for some time. Then one day he discovered why from a group of monks who had just arrived from there. Their king had recently died, and a severe famine was ravaging the country. The best monks had all fled. If he had any questions, he could ask them. He did just that, devoting a whole chapter of his *Record* to Ceylon based on what the monks told him, and then joined them on their pilgrimage to the North.

I knew Ajanta, my next destination, would have everything, unlike Kanchipuram. For some unknown reason, Xuanzang did not visit it. However he described it from what he must have heard from other monks and traders because Ajanta was so famous then and remains so now. 'In the east of the country is a mountain range, ridges succeeding ridges, peaks succeeding peaks, all surmounting steep cliffs of rock. In a deep valley lies a Buddhist monastery, its lofty halls and long chambers quarried in the stone. Tiers of canopied portals and terraces one above another lean back against the rock and face a ravine.'

As is so often the case, I was finding that Xuanzang's is the only historical record. Ajanta was lost for centuries, and was rediscovered only in 1819 by a British soldier hunting a tiger:

he saw it going into a cave, and followed it. From that point on the beauty and grandeur of the caves were revealed, and the world came to know of the greatness of Buddhist art at its height. I had seen photographs of the sculpted temples and reproductions of the murals, but nothing prepared me for the reality. Xuanzang's description of the setting is remarkably accurate, considering that he never visited Ajanta. From close to, the place has the air of a pastoral dream, a horseshoe-shaped valley surrounding a tree-covered hill with a stream winding round it. The sheer scale of the site impressed me even more, cave after cave, temple after temple, mural after mural.

I walked through one of the 'canopied portals' into Cave 26, the only one that Xuanzang described in detail. He says, 'This monastery was built by the A-che-lo of Western India' for monks on their retreat in the rainy season, and an inscription confirms it: 'The monk Achara (A-che-lo) built a cave dwelling for the Buddha out of gratitude'. There was the statue of the Buddha he mentions, though it is a reclining, not an upright one; as the evening light filtered into the cave, it glowed and radiated calm, like the Nirvana statue in Kushinagar. Xuanzang continues, 'The four walls are covered with sculpted scenes of the Buddha performing various good deeds, of the propitious signs when he became enlightened, and of the omens attending his final passing away.'

The carvings are still there – the first caves of Ajanta were hewn in the second century BC, and Cave 26 in the fifth century AD. Not only that, every panel and pillar is finely carved, and a majestic stupa in the centre rises fifty feet from floor to ceiling. When I lifted my head to look up at the ceiling, its enormous vault carved to imitate wooden beams, I asked myself how many decades this took, every inch created with nothing but a hammer and chisel. It is as if the artists wanted to demonstrate their faith by breathing life into the cold stone – as if they could make permanent what the Buddha told them was impermanent.

Xuanzang did not mention this, but Ajanta is even more famous for its murals than for its sculpture. And I understood why when I saw them. The sculpture inspires reverence and awe; it is there to be worshipped. But the murals are rich and exuberant; they embrace you with grace and sensuality. As well as Buddhist messages, they carry all the marks of their era, and provide a panorama of how Indians lived in ancient times. The courtly life is depicted with some extravagance, the royals and aristocrats going about their pleasures with joy and zest, but the whole of society unfolds in front of you, ascetics and priests, towns and countryside, people of every kind, farmers, artisans, entertainers, musicians. It is history alive in pictures, most of which were produced in the fifth and sixth centuries. I felt I was seeing just what Xuanzang saw in his years in India.

The finest of all the caves is Cave 1, where a great seated Buddha in a recess of carved panels faces you as you enter. On either side are the most magnificent of all the murals. I lingered in front of each of them, but I could not help being aware that I was coming to the one where most visitors stop longest: finally I stood before the Bodhisattva with the blue lotus. It is so finely painted, you see at once why it focuses everyone's attention. The longer you contemplate it, the more you are held by the tender sadness, the serene concern, the compassionate gaze. As Basham, the great historian of India, put it: 'The Bodhisattva has shared the sorrows of the world; his gentle eyes have seen countless ages of pain, and his delicately formed lips have spoken words of consolation to

321

countless sufferers. The artist has conveyed its message: the universe is not indifferent to the sorrows and strivings of its creatures.' I only wished Xuanzang *had* been here.

Instead, he went further north and one of the places he recorded with special attention was Malava, the modern Malwa. It had by far the largest number of monks of any place in India in the *Record*, some 20,000, and the most Buddha-like king, who never spoke a harsh word to his people, and even had the drinking water filtered in case small insects were killed. But what impressed Xuanzang in particular was something more secular. 'Their language is elegant and clear. Their learning is wide and profound,' he tells us. Perhaps he heard about Kalidasa, the greatest Sanskrit poet and dramatist, who lived in Malava in the fifth century, and whose plays are still performed today. His amorous verses are loved by Indians, but Xuanzang might have been pleased by this somewhat more decorous couplet:

> I bow to the parents of this universe, Parvati and Shiva;
> like words and their meaning are they entwined.
> I pray that my words and their meaning may shine
> forth through their grace.

Determined to see every corner of the holy land, and keen to learn from any master, however remote his monastery was, Xuanzang pushed on. His pilgrimage took him to the Kathiawar Peninsula on the Arabian Sea and the monasteries along the Indus River in present-day Pakistan before he returned to Nalanda in 639. He had already found the best of teachers there, unsurpassed in the rest of India.

But then one night he had a strange dream: Nalanda was deserted; in the distance, a great fire was consuming all the villages and towns. He woke up disturbed. What could it mean? He thought about his dream for several days, and divined it as an omen telling him to return home. When the monks heard of his decision, they all tried to make him change his mind. He was in the holy land of the Buddha, in the best monastery, in the company of incomparable teachers. Why did he want to go back to China, where 'good people are not respected and the Dharma is despised, which is why the Buddha was not born in that country'? The roads were so dangerous. How could he be sure he would return in one piece? They asked Shilabhadra to persuade him to stay. Hui Li tells us how Xuanzang explained himself to his teacher:

> India is where the Buddha was born and I am very happy here. But my purpose in coming was to study the Great Law and then use my knowledge for the benefit of all living creatures. I have visited and adored the sacred sites of our religion, and heard the profound exposition of all the various schools. My mind has been overjoyed, and my visit here has been of the utmost profit. Now I want to go back and translate the texts I have studied, so that anyone so disposed may have access to what I have learned.

To Shilabhadra, Xuanzang spoke like a true Bodhisattva, and he embodied the very qualities of one – discipline, renunciation, truthfulness, forbearance, determination, wisdom and compassion. How could he stop him from propagating the Dharma?

But Xuanzang was not without worries. The roads were indeed very dangerous, as he knew only too well. But it was just himself before. Now he had collected more than six hundred sutras and seven statues, one four feet high. How could he get them back, and safely, to China? He was not sure. He went to pray to his favourite Bodhisattva Guanyin in a temple near Nalanda. The statue there was supposed to have divine power, and was protected by a high wall. He was told if his offering of garlands were to land on the arms and the neck of the Bodhisattva, he would have his wishes granted. He was beside himself when it did. Now he was ready to go.

Just when he was about to leave, the King of Assam sent a messenger with a request for the Chinese master to visit him. Xuanzang was keen to go home and declined. The messenger came back, saying that if he did not agree the consequences would be severe. Shilabhadra advised him to comply. But he had hardly arrived in Assam when King Harsha demanded he proceed to his capital Kanauj on the banks of the Ganges. The King of Assam protested but he received this reply: 'Send the Chinese master or your head.'

Harsha was no stranger to Xuanzang. He was the most powerful ruler in India at the time, controlling half the subcontinent. His appreciation of Buddhist monks was well described by his court biographer, a contemporary of Xuanzang: 'You and your fellows are the pillars to support the world under its grievous calamities. You are the lamps of religion, softly bright with kindness, and powerful to dispel the darkness of delusion.' Xuanzang had passed through Kanauj earlier, while the king was away touring his empire. As usual, he noted down what he saw and heard, but in somewhat flowery language – no doubt he admired Harsha as a strong patron of Buddhism. 'The king is a man of heroic character and has great administrative abilities. His virtue moves heaven and earth; his righteousness influences men and gods. So he can rule over India. When order has been restored in his domain, people live in peace. Military campaigns have been put to an end; weapons are disused and good deeds encouraged. He orders that no living beings should be killed in his kingdom and his people are not to eat meat. He has built many monasteries at the holy places and each year he entertains all the monks in the country for twenty-one days.'

It turned out that Harsha was not only a great patron of Buddhism but an admirer of China – he had sent an envoy there the year before to establish friendly relations. Now he could find out more about that distant and enigmatic people. When he heard Xuanzang had arrived in the early evening, he could not wait to meet him. He proceeded along the Ganges with several thousand soldiers who carried candles and marched to the beat of two hundred drums. When the drums stopped and the dust settled, Xuanzang saw this majestic man, with a powerful body and moon-like face, and clad in silk and jewels. The stately figure bent down and touched Xuanzang's feet. They had a brief talk and a longer one the next day. Harsha was greatly taken with him, and decided to hold a grand public debate, at which the 'Master from China' would speak first, followed by any Brahmin priests and Theravada monks who might wish to challenge him.

The great assembly opened with a royal procession. A large and finely caparisoned elephant carried a golden Buddha on its back. King Harsha walked on its right and the King of Assam on its left. Xuanzang and Harsha's personal teachers followed. Then came the kings, ministers and distinguished masters from all over India, everyone on elephants, amid chanting monks and musicians beating drums. When they arrived at the assembly point, Xuanzang saw a forest of canopies, palanquins, chariots and elephants that stretched for miles along the Ganges. A thousand monks came from Nalanda alone to applaud him. They were concerned for him, but Xuanzang was undaunted. He had studied every school of Buddhism and the Brahminic texts, all with the best teachers alive. He was ready for the biggest challenge of his journey. 'My studies may have been superficial and my knowledge may be slight,' he said to the monks, 'but you need not worry. If by any chance I get the worst of it, I am merely a monk from China.'

The royal visitors and their ministers, the religious masters and heretics, all crowded into a hall specially built for the debate; many had to sit outside. For the next five days Xuanzang expounded the sutras and the tenets of Mahayana Buddhism: the salvation and enlightenment not just of oneself but of all people. Interruption was forbidden, but when he finished, he expected to be questioned. Not a single opponent dared to come forward. Xuanzang's eloquence, his mastery of all the doctrines of Buddhism and the Brahminic texts, his persuasiveness and the power of his presence were overwhelming. He was beyond challenge.

Harsha was proud, and deeply gratified. He declared Xuanzang the undisputed master, who was then given the title of 'Mahayana Deva' and 'Deva of Liberation', the greatest of all honours for a Buddhist. The king ordered a large elephant to be decorated with tapestries and invited the Master to ride on it and go round the city, announcing his victory. Xuanzang declined. So his robe was placed on the elephant and a crier walked in front of it announcing that the Master from China had been victorious in his debate. Xuanzang must have felt very honoured, although he does not tell us so. Amid praise, the Buddha says, the wise man does not exhibit elation: 'As a solid rock is not shaken by the wind, the wise are not ruffled by praise or blame.' He also respectfully declined Harsha's offer to build him one hundred monasteries throughout his kingdom and put him in charge. In the summer of 641, riding an elephant from Harsha, Xuanzang left the land of the Buddha for his long journey home.

I returned to China from Bombay after Ajanta: beyond there I knew there was very little to see that would recall Xuanzang's journey. I had been travelling for six months, hardly a match for Xuanzang's eighteen years, but challenging in a different way. I could not wait to find out what the last leg of my journey would reveal.

TEN

Battleground of the Faiths

X UANZANG BEGAN his journey home in style, riding on a white elephant, and accompanied by King Harsha's escort. He carried the fruits of his travels, most importantly the scriptures he had set out to find. But soon he ran into dangerous terrain: in the Punjab there were so many bandits that he sent a monk ahead as a scout, to tell them, 'We are monks from a very far country to learn more of the Dharma. All we have with us are some holy books, relics, and statues. You generous men, we ask your help and protection.' But he could do nothing about the turbulent water of the Indus River. His boat nearly sank in the middle of it and a man fell in with fifty of his books of scriptures.

The next challenge was to scale the Hindu Kush and the Pamir Mountains, two of the highest ranges in the world. 'So high was the mountain and so stormy the wind that even birds could not fly over them,' Xuanzang wrote of the Hindu Kush. As to the Pamirs, he must have recalled with some trepidation the avalanche that killed most of his retinue on the way out. The same desolate landscape was waiting for him: no trees, no crops, no human traces, just endless expanses of snow. But this time he was more cautious: he waited in a caravan site in a valley for over a month until the snow stopped. This was the spot where a caravan with thousands of merchants and their animals perished in a blizzard. A monk built this caravan-serai so that merchants and travellers would have somewhere to rest when the weather was really bad.

But where nature was benign, man was not. Just when Xuanzang thought he was safe, a band of robbers attacked him. They swooped in, dozens of them, like a swarm of wasps. His men scattered. The robbers took all the provisions Harsha had given him, and, fortunately, left the sutras and statues, though a number of them were lost on the back of his elephant, which was so frightened it jumped over a precipice into a ravine. Once again, Xuanzang was lucky to escape with his life. He remembered his promise to King Qu Wentai to preach in his kingdom, but he had learned from travelling merchants that Emperor Taizong had taken over Gaochang. So he kept on towards Khotan on the southern route of the Silk Road, an oasis kingdom he had always wanted to visit. It was the spring of 644, two and a half years after he had set off from King Harsha's court.

'The people are polite, honest, gentle and respectful. They love literature and arts and are very good at them. They lead a prosperous and contented life.' This is how the Khotanese struck Xuanzang. But he also appreciated Khotan for some-thing closer to his heart. This was the first country in the Western Region to embrace Buddhism. Xuanzang even tells us how this happened. An arhat came from Kashmir to prom-ulgate the Buddha's teachings and the King of Khotan said to him: 'Let the great saint show himself. Having seen his appear-ance I will believe in him, build a monastery for monks, and advance his cause.' An image of the Buddha duly appeared. Xuanzang reported that the Buddha was supposed to have come and blessed the kingdom in person. This is perhaps more a legend than reality, but it is true that Kashmiri monks were the first to take Buddhism eastwards in the first century BC. The kings of Khotan had been great patrons of Buddhism ever since, encouraging the people to live by the Dharma, and building monasteries of great beauty and grandeur. It was to Khotan that the earliest Chinese pilgrims travelled in search of the sutras, and masters to expound them. They left glowing accounts of the people and their faith, and a wonderful collection of stories called *The Sutra of the Sage and the Fool*, which Xuanzang must have read, and which Chinese monks still study. Now an equally flourishing Buddhist kingdom awaited him, with more than one hundred monasteries and five thousand monks.

Xuanzang could not have found a more welcoming country in which to stay. Khotan was China's closest ally in the Western Region. When the Chinese were about to conquer the region in the first century BC, the King of Khotan decided to throw his weight behind them. He sent the crown prince to the Chinese capital as a token of his trust and goodwill; he helped to persuade other principalities of the Taklamakan to surrender to Chinese rule; when some refused, he lent 25,000 of his men to the Chinese general to wipe them out. But later the imperial commissar became suspicious of Khotan's unreserved loyalty and cut off the head of the king in a coup, only to see the Khotanese and the whole region rise up and rebel. Then the Kushans and the Turks took control. Now with China unified and becoming strong again under Emperor Taizong, the King of Khotan could not help but worry for his country. He sent Taizong a jade belt; he also dispatched his son to join the emperor's imperial guard, all in the hope that his small oasis kingdom would be left out of the clutches of the new Chinese empire.

So when the King of Khotan heard a distinguished Chinese master was coming, he could not have been more hospitable. He went in person to the border and had a tent set up there. After he was satisfied with all the preparations, he made his sons and ministers wait on the spot and he returned to the capital to receive the Chinese pilgrim formally into his kingdom three days later. Xuanzang was greeted by a jubilant crowd beating drums, burning incense and throwing flowers on the ground he touched.

Thirteen hundred years later, my reception was not so warm. I knew things were not good down south. I had heard in Korla that some Uighurs who wanted an independent 'Islamic Republic of Eastern Turkestan' had been discovered in their secret hideout in the Khotan prefecture and in the shoot-out that followed, several of them and a couple of policemen were killed. A state of emergency was declared throughout the whole region.

It was not the first time that the Chinese government had to deal with the Uighurs' desire to break away. China's last dynasty, the Qing, brought Xinjiang under its control again in the eighteenth-century. But we have not had an easy time with the Uighurs ever since: there has been an uprising every decade or so and a major upheaval every thirty years. Each one was devastating and added to the mistrust and hostility on either side. But the most shattering of all was the rebellion in the 1860s and 1870s, just after the Opium War, when the Chinese emperor often wondered if he should simply wash his hands of his troublesome frontier region. He did not have the courage to do so; he would have been condemned for losing the territory that his forebears had fought so hard to acquire – an unforgivable sin. Eventually, his general, Zuo Zongtang, regained Xinjiang for him, but not without earning himself the nickname 'Zuo the Butcher'. It was said that he told his soldiers to bring back the heads of all the Muslims they killed, but there were so many, the troops could not carry them and they brought back the ears instead, in sacks. The campaign was so long – fifteen years – that the young willows the general had planted on his way out were all thick trees when he came back. The Uighurs rebelled again and again, though rarely after 1949, until the collapse of the former Soviet Union and the rise of the pan-Islamic movement in Central Asia. And here I was, right in the thick of it.

Strangely I felt there could not have been a safer time for a Han Chinese to visit Khotan: surely it would be foolish for anyone to cause trouble when the whole army was on the alert. So I found myself in the oasis city late one evening. The streets were wide, lined with brand-new buildings, all decorated with white tiles as in any other Chinese city. There were people everywhere, moving slowly but purposefully. Conspicuous by their uniforms were the vast numbers of police. What was happening? I asked the young Uighur man next to me on the coach. He looked at me with surprise: 'Tomorrow will be your National Day. I think they are going to celebrate it with fireworks tonight.' I had lost track of time. The next day would be the first of October and it would be the fiftieth anniversary of the founding of the People's Republic of China. I read in the newspaper that all government institutions would have to organize festivities to mark this important occasion. Before we boarded the coach, the drivers at the depot were singing a revolutionary song from the 1950s, called 'No Communist Party, no new China'. It praised the Communist Party for having led China from darkness into light, from poverty to riches. I remembered thinking how strange it was that they were churning out this old stuff. It never occurred to me they were rehearsing for the big day.

I checked into a small hotel and called Yang Weijiang, a friend of Fat Ma, the travel agent in Turfan whom I had come to know well. She was not at home. I had a quick meal in the hotel restaurant and then went into the streets. I followed the crowd and soon came to a square in the centre of the city; it was packed but the mood was curiously sombre. As I looked round, I began to see why: wherever there was a cluster of people, there were men with walkie-talkies. They must be policemen; and I could only assume there were more of them less easily identified. The fireworks were late but nobody seemed to mind, as if they knew it was a difficult decision for the municipal government: the crowd was an obvious target for the separatists and an explosion would cause not only great damage but also huge embarrassment; if the authorities decided to cancel the festivities, they would be seen as caving in to pressure. It was a tricky situation. As I was pondering whether to leave or not, I heard a big explosion some distance away. I jumped, thinking it might be a bomb. Then I saw this beautiful cloud of colours in the sky turning into a rain of falling comets. The fireworks had finally begun. But there were no joyful shouts, only audible groans of relief. And then with each fireball shooting into the darkness of the night, first my heart thumped in fear and then I relaxed a little. The tension of a nightmare scenario of carnage gnawed away any sense of joy and fun. After a while, I went back to the hotel.

Xuanzang had a worrying problem in Khotan too. This was the last stage of his journey, only three months' travel to Dunhuang, on the old Chinese frontier. He was buoyed up by the prospect of coming home. He had been travelling for eighteen years. He had kept to his purpose and declined all

336

the honours and positions that might have delayed him in achieving his ultimate goal of bringing what he thought was the true Buddhism back to China. There is a Chinese saying, 'The returning heart is like the flight of an arrow'. He was impatient to be back – but the arrow had to stop in mid-air.

He had originally left China in secret, violating Emperor Taizong's prohibition against travelling abroad – a grave offence for which he could be put to death. How would he be treated when he returned? Would the emperor forgive him? He was not sure. Furthermore he had come a long way in understanding not only the Dharma but also the importance of propagating it. He knew he must secure the emperor's endorsement for the translation of the scriptures he had brought back from India. The purpose of his pilgrimage was to find the truth for himself, but also to reveal it to followers in China. How many scriptures could he translate on his own even if he devoted the rest of his life to them? How many copies could he distribute? And how many people could benefit from the fruits of his journey? As Daoan, one of China's great monks, said two centuries earlier: 'Without imperial support, the Dharma will not flourish.'

With much uncertainty, and with even more at stake, Xuanzang wrote a letter to Taizong. He used his characteristic charm, his brilliant, persuasive skill and his astute sense of judgement to please, flatter and impress. It is worth quoting at length because it shows how this great mind worked to achieve its goal. The letter began with references to the great sages in Chinese history, the guardians of our morals and ethics. If the ancient kings and emperors supported the learned, how much more should a great man like Taizong. After confessing how he had left against the emperor's command, Xuanzang continued:

I have accomplished a journey of more than fifty thousand li. Yet despite the thousand differences of customs and manners I have witnessed, the myriads of dangers I have encountered, by the goodness of heaven I have returned without accident, and now offer my homage with a body unimpaired, and a mind satisfied with the accomplishment of my vow ... I have seen things not seen before and heard sacred words not heard before; I have witnessed spiritual prodigies exceeding all the wonders of Nature, have borne testimony to the highest qualities of our august Emperor and won for him the high esteem and praise of the people.

Xuanzang sent the letter with his trusted servant, and while he was waiting for a reply, he taught the King of Khotan and the monks about Yogacara and other sutras he had learned in India. He would also have spent some time visiting various places in the country because his record of Khotan was very detailed, perhaps second only to his account of the holy land of the Buddha. Reading Xuanzang, I often wondered why he recorded the things he did, apart from what was important to him as a Buddhist. Sometimes they seemed quite random; sometimes they seemed to be dictated by the emperor's desire for information. But in Khotan I realized what his purpose was. He observed what really mattered to the people here, their faith and their very survival in this fragile oasis on the edge of the Taklamakan Desert. Nothing more and nothing less.

I wanted to experience as much as possible of what Xuanzang saw and recorded: first, the Buddhist ruins which figured so prominently in his description. Here I had another guide besides Xuanzang, the British explorer Aurel Stein. Born of Hungarian parents in 1862, Stein from a very early age was fascinated by campaigns and travels in far-flung places. His hero was Alexander the Great, his guide and patron saint Xuanzang, his bible *Record of the Western Regions*, and his first expedition Khotan. In four explorations into western China spanning thirty years between 1900 and 1930 he retraced Xuanzang's footsteps in the desert and excavated many sites described in the *Record*. What he found were some of the most extraordinary antiquities discovered in the twentieth century: rich hoards of documents in Kharoshthi, an ancient Indian script, buried in rubbish dumps; classical murals of winged angels painted by a Roman artist named Titus in a ruined monastery; countless stucco heads of Buddhas and Bodhisattvas in the Gandharan style; and most stunning of all, over ten thousand manuscripts from the Dunhuang Buddhist caves. Stein was hailed by some as 'the greatest explorer of Asia since Marco Polo' and was knighted by the British government for his contribution to the understanding of Central Asia. His secret weapon was Xuanzang. As he said proudly, 'My well-known attachment to the memory of Xuanzang . . . had been helpful in securing me a sympathetic hearing both among the learned and the simple.'

I called Yang the next morning about my plan in Khotan. She apologized for not having come to see me the night before: 'You couldn't have come at a worse time. The government has put us on a twenty-four-hour rota. Everyone was on duty last night. We are in a war situation.'

She had more bad news for me: Fat Ma had asked her to find me a Land Rover to go into the desert, but due to the state of emergency, all vehicles were on standby and their use had to be given the go-ahead by the mayor's office. She could not get any car, let alone a Land Rover. She would continue her search. She asked me what I would like to do in the meantime. Without hesitation, I said the bazaar, which I had heard was one of the most colourful in Xinjiang. There was a long silence. 'Why don't you rest for the morning? I can take you there during my lunch-break. It is not safe for you to go there on your own, especially now,' said Yang gently. I could hear the concern in her voice, but she was busy and I could not sit in the hotel and venture out only when she could accompany me. I told her I would be very careful. 'Don't buy anything. Don't bargain with them. Don't linger,' was her parting warning.

The Khotan bazaar did not show itself immediately. You knew something was coming because the streets were full of people, carts and bicycles almost in gridlock. As you got closer, you began to hear the voices of stallholders crying their wares, rising to a great din once you were actually there. It was all in the open. A pall of sand and dust hung in the air and covered everything with a thin film. The huge bazaar was divided into hundreds of sections in a myriad of lanes, selling everything you could imagine.

In a street leading from the eastern side of the bazaar was the market that sold the most prized commodity of Khotan – jade. It was everywhere, on stalls, on tables, on the ground, and being passed from hand to hand, in dazzling variety. It was all unworked, smoothed by water and picked up every September when the snows melt from the beds of the Karakash and the Yurungkash, the Black and White Jade Rivers. The locals used to believe that jade was feminine, so women would be better at finding it. Now the job was left to men, who seemed to have found plenty. There were huge brown rocks, smaller dark green stones with a glossy lustre, and the finest ones, tiny, translucent and milky-white, called Lamb's-Tail-

Fat. I felt like a child in a sweet shop, spoilt with choices. I wanted to touch, caress and hold every piece to my skin, like a man with a woman. It was clear why jade, especially the white varieties, represents female beauty to the Chinese: smooth, glowing and sensuous.

Xuanzang of course tells us that Khotan was known for its jade, which the Chinese treasure more than gold. We have a saying, the best jade is worth more than scores of cities. The First Emperor sacked Handan, where I grew up, and killed 400,000 people, because he had been refused a famous jade disc. We have been besotted by this precious stone since the early Neolithic age. For a long time it was worshipped as a repository of divine power and used to honour the deities. But it was not reserved only for gods. Emperors loved to sleep on jade pillows which supposedly gave them wonderful dreams; aristocrats were buried in suits made of jade; officials wore girdles of jade plaques as tokens of their rank and prestige – the emblem of their office was a seal made of jade; Buddhists carved statues of the Buddha in jade to show their piety. In classical Chinese literature, we read poems and lyrics in praise of its toughness and fine texture: they symbolize the Confucian virtues of the upright man and his humanity and benevolence.

If jade had all these symbolic meanings, I also loved the silk market of Khotan. This was the first Silk Road town where I actually saw silk, in all its forms, being sold. Men squatted on the ground selling delicate cocoons in baskets; bundles of yarn hung on clothes-lines; eye-catching fabrics of bright colours and geometric patterns were spread out on carpets; young women tried out silk dresses in the latest fashion. Perhaps this could be what Xuanzang would have seen, a busty oasis kingdom prospering from the vast number of merchants of the Silk Road, all with a keen eye for its fabled commodity.

The Khotanese actually made silk, as well as trading it. Xuan-zang soon found out how they acquired the secret of making it – a Chinese monopoly for a long time – and told us this enchanting story.

The King of Khotan was a very clever man. He saw how popular silk was with merchants, and he wanted it for his country. But his easterly neighbour refused to pass on the secret. So he decided to ask, with a valuable dowry and humble words, for the hand of the princess of the silk kingdom. His request was granted. He told his envoy who was to fetch the princess to give her this message: 'Khotan has no mulberry trees or silkworms. Your Highness should bring the seeds for both so that you will be able to make the gorgeous clothes that you are used to wearing.' China had always kept the making of silk a secret, for good reason. Knowing she was forbidden to take the seeds out of the country, the princess hid them in her headgear. When the wedding party crossed the border, the guards searched everywhere except her head-dress. The princess planted the mulberry seeds in a nunnery and raised silkworms on the leaves. Xuanzang even saw tree-trunks which he said were the original mulberry trees. When Stein excavated the ruins of a monastery in Khotan, he found a painting on wood. An elegant lady with dark hair stands in the middle, with an elaborate head-dress and a basketful of cocoons in front of her. On either side is a female attendant, one pointing her finger at the lady's head while the other is busy at a weaving machine. It is the perfect illustration to Xuanzang's story.

From Khotan cocoons were taken further west, beyond the Pamir Mountains, across the Oxus River of Central Asia, and finally reached the Mediterranean. It was said that a Zoroast-rian monk hollowed out his staff and hid the cocoons inside it and then presented them to the court of Byzantium in the sixth century AD. Whether it was a monk or a merchant, it is fairly certain that it was from Khotan that the secret of silk-making came to the West, where the myth that silk grew on trees was laid to rest at last.

I bought a handful of cocoons. I also wanted to buy a piece of Khotan silk, just as a memento. A pile of fabric in front of a very old Uighur woman drew my attention. It was different from the others, very thick, more like brocade than cloth, and the design was simple, even modern, with black and white squares like a chessboard. I asked her where it came from.

'My families, relatives and people in my village make them,' she said proudly, and then added, 'all by hand, feeding the silkworms, spinning the cocoons and weaving.'

Where did they do it? I asked.

'In a village with lots of mulberry trees,' she said.

How long had they been making it?

'I can't remember.' She hesitated. 'Our mulberry trees are very old, hundreds of years old. We must have been making silk back then.'

I bought one piece of her fabric, and took down the address of her village.

I met Yang for lunch in a Chinese restaurant. She was in her early forties, the same age as Fat Ma, who was at college with her. She looked older than her age, not because of the wrinkles on her forehead but her worried expression, like my mother's, but she was very warm when she spoke. She asked how I enjoyed the bazaar, and I showed her my purchase.

'You can get it anywhere. Look here, it isn't even good quality,' she said, pointing to a white thread in the black

343

square, the imperfection of all hand-made cloth, which many thought added to its charm.

'But it's special for me,' I said, and then told her Xuanzang's story.

'Oh.' She paused. 'I never understood why we have so many silk factories here.' She was almost speaking to herself now.

I asked if the factories made silk as beautiful as the chess-board silk. She shook her head: like state enterprises every-where, they were on the verge of collapse. 'Even I prefer the silk made elsewhere. It's better quality.' Yang pulled the corner of her collar out from her jacket to show me. 'And much cheaper.'

Yang was happy to come with me to the family silk cooperative during her lunch-break, if we could find a taxi. There seemed so few of them around and I had not been lucky in the morning. I was relieved when after twenty minutes a battered old car pulled up in front of us. It was not a comfort-able ride; the driver, a Uighur in his late twenties, started complaining as soon as we got into the car, with good reason. A week ago the government had pulled nearly all the taxis out of service for fear that the drivers would use them to help troublemakers get away. Today was his first work in a week, and he was not compensated for the loss of earnings. 'Is there such a crazy logic in the world?' he almost yelled at us. He was only partially appeased when we told him we would double the fare on the meter if he would wait and bring us back.

When we told him where we wanted to go, there was another tirade of indignation. It took me quite a while to understand it. In order to preserve Khotan's silk industry, the government required a tax of twenty grams of baby silkworms from each villager. It did not sound very much, but the price they offered was so low that farmers could not be bothered with it, although this was not the only problem. Silkworms were very delicate creatures: constant feeding day and night, clean habitat in semi-darkness, moderate temperatures, everything had to be just right, as I knew from my own days of keeping them as pets. The season in Khotan is May and August. August happened to be the harvest time for the much more profitable melons and other fruit. The villagers simply did not want to spend a month taking care of the silkworms. It made no sense to them either, especially now all the silk factories were bankrupt. But if they failed to hand in their specified quota, they would be fined. Looking at the seemingly endless mulberry trees on the roadside, I felt sad. They were once the 'money trees', providing eight feeds a day for as many silkworms as the Khotanese could manage, day after day, year after year, and century after century. For the nine months Xuanzang was here, he must have seen women busy picking the tender leaves for the silkworms, heard the non-stop sound of the shuttles on the wooden handlooms, and watched the hustle and bustle of animals being loaded with silk and heading off as far as India and Byzantium. But there was no sign of any activity in the forest of mulberry trees today. The leaves drooped under a thick layer of dust and looked as if they had not been picked for a long time. On some of the trees near the road hung big banners: 'Down with the Separatists! Strengthen the unity of the motherland. Stability is the cardinal principle!'

Policemen and Uighur militias with guns slung over their shoulders stood in the middle of the road, waving us to stop. They stared at the driver long and hard and checked his papers thoroughly before they allowed us to continue. After many check-points, the taxi screeched to a halt again, this time in front of a big sign for the silk cooperative. Through the gate we came immediately upon skeins of multi-coloured silk thread that the workers were drawing into patterns, ready for the weavers. Beyond them were three rooms where old Uighur men and women were weaving on wooden handlooms. There was hardly any light, just a low-voltage yellow bulb making a feeble attempt to dispel the gloom. The looms were utterly primitive, looking as if they had been there for centuries. The weavers were old, like the woman in the bazaar, perhaps in their seventies or eighties. And dust covered almost everything, except for the bright silk that rolled out from the looms. Through a broken side window I found myself staring at a giant cauldron in the back yard where two women fished cocoons out of boiling water and passed them over a big spinning wheel four feet across. Their faces were pink with the heat and their blouses were soaked with sweat.

This must be how they used to make silk long ago. I said as much to Yang excitedly, my camera clicking away. 'I am not sure the wealth of the Silk Road or of Khotan was really made in this primitive way,' she argued. But it was. Ancient documents discovered in Khotan reveal that two families in one district handed in as much as forty-two metres of silk in tax in one day – Khotan had tens of thousands of households! Court papers exist recording the debts owed to silk weavers. 'There are no Chinese merchants coming here,' one document reads, 'so we could not investigate the silk debt. We have to wait for their arrival and conduct more investigations. If there is any dispute, we will settle it in the royal court.' Although producing in great quantity, the Khotanese could not compete with the Chinese for the quality of the silk: as Buddhists they refused to boil the cocoons before they were hatched. The thread was too short and the silk was coarse, but also cheaper, taking not a small portion of the silk trade. When they finally perfected their skill, they even sent their brocade as tribute to the Chinese emperor. At the turn of the last century, Khotan produced over 55,000 kilograms of cocoons, half of which were exported to Russia and Britain. The manager of the cooperative, a young Uighur in his thirties, told us there are still over two million mulberry trees in Khotan today.

I asked him how they could survive when all the silk factories in Khotan were closing down. 'It's in the family,' he said, looking around his workshop. 'We've been doing it for a long time. When I was small, I used to help my grandmother feed the silkworms, thinking I would like to play with them all my life. Now I'm doing just that with the help of customers like you.' Tourists cannot make up for the merchants of old, but it would be sad if after so many centuries this ancient craft were to disappear.

On the way back, Yang asked me why Xuanzang recorded silk-making in Khotan. 'Monks aren't even allowed to wear silk,' she said.

I was wondering about it too. Did he think the emperor would want to know how this close ally acquired its wealth? Or was it part of Xuanzang's practical concern for his faith: if the people were prosperous and content, the country would be stable, monasteries would be supported, and Buddhism would flourish.

'He sounds more human than the one in *The Monkey King*,' Yang said. He definitely was.

I dropped Yang at her office. I decided to go to buy some stamps for letters home. The place looked deserted. Above the high counter of the post office were olive-green bars that went up to the ceiling. On the bars was a wanted poster for a dozen members of the separatist movement. They were all in their twenties, but looked much older with their heavy moustaches.

Some had a red tick against their names, which meant they had given themselves up. The poster appealed to the families of the rest to report them to the police or give their whereabouts. It ended with this warning: 'Give up and you will be given a chance; resist and you will come to a bad end.'

I had plenty of time to imagine what the bad end would be before a middle-aged Uighur woman appeared from behind a door, rubbing her eyes, not quite awake from her siesta. I said I wanted to buy twenty stamps for postcards. She pulled out a sheet and then asked me: 'Which nationalities do you like?' I thought it very strange. Then I saw they were the commemorative stamps for the fiftieth anniversary, with the fifty-six officially recognized ethnic groups in China all celebrating it. I said I did not mind. 'I will leave out whichever nationalities you dislike,' she said in a matter-of-fact way. I decided to take them all and get out quickly. When she gave me the change, she said with a smile: 'It is very cheap to buy all nationalities. Don't you think so?'

I almost fled. Outside under the bright sunshine, I calmed down, unfolded the big sheet and had a closer look at the stamps. They were indeed very beautiful, each one showing a different nationality, wearing their national costumes and demonstrating their best-known activity – singing, dancing or playing a musical instrument. It reminded me of a popular Chinese song: 'Fifty-six nationalities are like fifty-six flowers; fifty-six nationalities are one family.' It is easy to put them all in one song and on one set of stamps; but to make them into one big, happy family will need more effort.

I told Yang about the incident when I went over to her house for dinner that evening. 'That's why I didn't want you to go to the bazaar on your own this morning,' she said warily. 'I hardly go there at all. It's a pity. It's such a lively place.' She was standing over the kitchen sink, preparing our meal, her shoulders stooped. She was alone – her husband had gone to Shanghai for a trade fair and her daughter was with Yang's parents in Urumqi.

I asked her why things were so bad in Khotan.

'This is different from Turfan. Turfan has a lot of Han Chinese and oil workers. Here we're a minority and I guess we feel threatened.' She was heating up half a dozen dishes she had prepared.

I told her that I had heard that the armed police in Khotan had put on a parade for three days to show they would crush anyone who dared to make trouble.

Yang nodded. 'My male colleagues even have to hand in their exercise weights and clubs. The government thinks they could be used as weapons in a confrontation.'

Were we not overreacting?

She paused. 'You know since the shoot-out and the murders, all of us in the government have been going to villages, telling people not to follow the separatists. You know what they said to me? "We don't want much. Can we have our own head of village instead of a Han Chinese who is too young to grow a beard? Can you treat us equally and let us grow what we think makes money on our own land?"'

Just like the taxi-driver complaining about the silkworm quota?

She nodded, and continued. 'You're following Xuanzang. I don't know if you're a Buddhist. I have trouble understanding Buddhism. I think we have trouble understanding Islam too. You know the saying: "You are not fish, how can you know the fish's pleasure?" Our education, our beliefs and our lives have nothing to do with religion. Religion is a bad word, synonymous with superstition, backwardness, feudalism. The

Uighurs are devout Muslims. That's part of our problem. My parents have given their lives to Xinjiang – my name is Weijiang, "Defending Xinjiang". It's sad things have not turned out the way they hoped.'

I apologized again for putting her to so much trouble. 'Don't be silly,' she said, putting yet another mountain of food in my bowl. 'It's rare for us to have a visitor. No Han Chinese wants to come here. I'm only sorry I can't spend more time with you, or find you a proper car.' She had managed, however, to find an old jeep that was not earmarked for the emergency. 'Perhaps it isn't suitable for the desert, but that's the best we can do,' she said resignedly. But she had persuaded a colleague to come with me. 'He knows all about the desert and your monk too. You're in safe hands.' She had put so much thought and effort into my visit and I thanked her again. 'You're Fat Ma's friend so you are my friend. Don't we say, one more friend, one more option.'

Next morning I got up early – Yang said we should leave before it became too hot. But by eleven o'clock there was still no sign of the elusive vehicle or the guide. I called her on her mobile and it rang for three minutes before she answered. Then she mumbled into the phone, clearly only half-awake. She had been called out, not long after I left, for a training exercise, hunting for a canister of mock explosives hidden somewhere in her work unit. 'It took us so long to find it. If it had been a real one, you'd be talking to a ghost now,' she grumbled. The good thing was that she had been given the morning off and she would be able to accompany us. She said she would come straight away.

Finally she arrived in a decrepit Beijing jeep with a driver and her colleague, a big Uighur man in his fifties. I had visions of spending the whole day getting stuck in the desert, running out of water, and losing the way when the sun began to set, as Xuanzang did when he crossed the desert for the first time. But there was no choice. Heaven knew when the emergency would end. Off we went, shuddering jerkily along for fifty kilometres before we came to the desert road. Then the jeep began to groan and stop and start until it was completely stuck in the sand with the wheels spinning wildly. Yang's colleague, Yashkar, suggested that we walk the last five kilometres to the stupa, while the driver went to get help at the nearest village, six kilometres back. We were barely in the desert!

As we set out on foot for the stupa, I was first struck by the beauty of the desert, the sand sculpted into dunes and steep curving hills, and the valleys rising and falling between them. It was all minimal, bare and elemental. But as we went further in, my aesthetic pleasure was overwhelmed by the heat and the threatening void. What Xuanzang had faced was suddenly brought home to me. The dunes stretched out, wave after wave, to left and right, ahead of me and behind, and as far as I could see, a trackless immensity. It was awe-inspiring, terrifying. An inexpressible fear gripped me and I stopped. Yang turned round and asked me if I was too hot. I blurted out my anxiety: how did we know which way to go? Yashkar picked up some sand and showed me the coarse, heavy grains. 'This is the deposit from the bed of the White Jade River,' he said, and then pointed towards the white tree-stumps and the tamarisks that dotted the landscape here and there. 'I think they once grew near the river. In the desert, the road follows the river, and the monasteries were never far from the road. This used to be an oasis when Xuanzang came here. You will see, such a splendid thing could not have been built way out in the desert. But over the centuries, the White Jade River changed its course. Without water, the oasis turned into desert.'

Yashkar worked on the problems of desertification in Khotan. He had visited most of the ruins in the region, trying to figure out why people had abandoned their homes, sometimes even entire towns. It could be the decline of caravans on a particular route; it could be wars or epidemics. But mostly it was to do with water, or the lack of it. 'Water is the lifeblood of the oasis and irrigation the arteries,' Yashkar said. 'Without the two, we are as good as dead.' Then he told me he had Xuanzang's *Record* on his shelf, and he referred to it constantly. 'You can't believe how poignant his stories are. If you look at what he said about Khotan, environment was very much on his mind.'

Yashkar was right: Xuanzang begins his account of the ancient Khotan by saying 'the greater part of the country is nothing but sand and gravel and the irrigated land is very limited'. He tells us the capital was carefully chosen by a holy man to make sure it was surrounded by water. It was remarkable. You would think that as a monk passing through the country, his mind would be on holy things. But he noticed the problem, one that Khotan still faces today. Environment was very much a Buddhist concern. According to Buddhism, everything is interdependent: to destroy our habitats is to damage ourselves. The Pure Land, the final destination that my grandmother and many Chinese Buddhists dream of, is described as clean, peaceful, harmonious, graceful and majestic: it is ideal for cultivating a pure mind. It is a goal that Buddhists want to realize here on earth too. Xuanzang could not help but be impressed how Buddhist Khotan was struggling to maintain its fragile balance in one of the most inhospitable environments on earth. Of the many stories he recorded in Khotan, I particularly like the one about the minister who sacrificed himself to get the White Jade River flowing again.

The White Jade River, which supplied Khotan with jade and irrigation water, dried up one day. The king went to a Buddhist temple to consult the monks, who told him to prepare a ritual ceremony on the riverbank. The king obliged. As he was performing the ritual, the river goddess appeared. 'My husband has just died,' she declared, 'and I am lonely. If I can have one of your ministers as my companion, the river will be filled with water again.' She cast her glance at one of the king's ministers who was tall, handsome and with a noble appearance. He came up to the king and said: 'I have been holding this important position for a long time but never really contributed very much to the country. Now is my chance. To save the people, why worry about losing a minister? I am here to serve them. So please do not hesitate, Your Majesty. My only wish is for you to build a stupa and to pray for my good karma.' When the stupa was built, the minister mounted a white horse, bade farewell to the king, and disappeared into the river. The White Jade River started flowing again. Xuanzang even visited the stupa and was sad that it had fallen into disrepair.

Yang burst into laughter when she heard the story. 'Find me one official like that today and I'll give you a million dollars,' she said to Yashkar. Just then, Yashkar cried out: 'Rawak, the Mansion. We've found it!' I looked up. Then I saw it too, at the edge of the horizon. A long stick of tamarisk bent by the desert wind stands on top of a stupa of the classic Indian type, a square base with a round dome. As we walked towards it, it grew bigger one minute and disappeared the next, as if it were just a mirage. When we climbed the last dune, we saw it without a shadow of doubt.

The mud-brick stupa with steps leading to its top is still intact. Surrounding it are the high walls of a quadrangle enclosing the court; they have fallen in here and there, and in places sand has already engulfed them. I told Yashkar that it looked very much like the picture Stein took after his excavation. Yashkar laughed. 'If we come back in again in a few months, this will be half buried by sand. The site is on the government's conservation list. They have people clearing the sand and looking after it. There're huge statues just underneath the surface. The treasure hunters can't wait to get their hands on them.'

In Xuanzang's time treasure hunters were already probing into the buried cities and monasteries. He tells how a rain of sand and earth engulfed one entire city – the Buddhist message was that the inhabitants did not take the advice of an arhat who prophesied its doom, and even humiliated him. Later people heard about the treasures buried there and went to look for them, but a furious wind sprang up, dark clouds gathered, and the treasure hunters disappeared. This fable lived on. When Stein and other twentieth-century adventurers set off for the desert, that was exactly what the local people told them: don't go! The ghosts of the dead are guarding the treasures. You will become a ghost too.

Stein excavated for nine days in Rawak in 1902. After removing mountains of sand he found eighty-one Bodhisattva statues on the southwest and southeast walls of the courtyard. They were colossal images, richly decorated with elaborate drapery and intricately carved strings of jewels on the breast and arms, all in the Gandharan style. On some of them he found remains of gold leaf patches, reminding him of a quaint custom recorded by Xuanzang about miracle-working Buddhist statues: 'Those who have any disease, according to the part affected, cover the corresponding place on the statue with gold leaf, and forthwith they are healed. People who address prayers to it with a sincere heart mostly obtain their wishes.'

Much to Stein's regret, he could not remove the statues without destroying them. So he had to content himself with photographing them, recording their exact positions, and burying them again in the sand. 'It was a melancholy duty to perform,' he wrote, 'strangely reminding me of a true burial, and it almost cost me an effort to watch the images I had brought to light vanishing again, one after the other, under the pall of sand which had hidden them for so many centuries.' But when he returned five years later on his second expedition, he found that all the heads of the statues had been smashed by treasure hunters in the belief that they could find valuables inside. Then more tomb robbers came. Yashkar said there were still a few statues left, barely half a metre under the sand, but for how long?

I stood in the midday sun, my legs sinking in the sand up to the knees, as if I was drowning in a dream. It was remarkable that Rawak is still here one thousand five hundred years after Xuanzang's visit, having withstood the onslaught of time, nature and human destruction. But it is also a poignant reminder of just how far the oasis has receded, as he had feared. In the battle between nature and man, nature seemed to be winning.

The sand of a thousand years buried the stupa. Though it was not nature alone, but the Muslim crusaders who wiped out Buddhist Khotan. Nowhere did the battle of faiths leave a clearer mark than on the Gosringa Mountain, or the Kohmari Mazar as it is called today.

We decided to visit it on our way back to Khotan. This is how Xuanzang describes it: 'There are two peaks to this mountain, and around these peaks, on each side, is an undulating line of hills. In one of the valleys is a monastery, with a statue of the Buddha which emits rays of glory from time to time. This is the place where the Buddha formerly delivered a concise digest of the Dharma to heavenly beings, and where he prophesied a kingdom would be founded and the principles of the Dharma would spread.' According to the Tibetan Gosringa-Vyakarana Sutra, the Buddha even asked some of the heavenly beings to stay on here to protect Khotan. The mountain was an important centre of pilgrimage for Buddhists; the Lotus Sutra says it is one of the twenty-five most sacred places of Buddhism.

We left the jeep at the foot of the mountain and started a long and steep climb. It was totally barren, without a single tree or blade of grass. I was not sure it was like this when Xuanzang came up here: Buddhist monasteries were normally surrounded by trees and water. We were passed by a Uighur family, who were walking briskly. Yashkar said they were pilgrims going to make offerings to Maheb Khwoja, one of the direct descendants of Mohammed the Prophet.

'He led the crusade to conquer Khotan?' I asked.

'He was the man.' Yashkar nodded.

More than halfway up the mountain, near the edge of a cliff, we came to the cave where Xuanzang says 'an arhat is plunged in ecstasy and awaiting the coming of the Maitreya Buddha'. He tells us he did not see the arhat because giant fallen rocks had blocked the entrance to the cavern. The king had sent his soldiers to remove them but swarms of poisonous wasps had thwarted their attempts.

The cave was open now and reachable by a ladder. The path leading to it was lined by ramshackle huts for pilgrims to stay in, and next to them stood two rows of fencing divided into cubicles. Yashkar said he had to clean himself before entering the cave, just as he would do before going to the mosque. He excused himself and disappeared into one of them. When he reappeared a few minutes later, he led the way up the ladder, through the narrow gap, and we found ourselves in a black hole. There was little light inside, and the cave was empty; the walls were covered with soot. Yashkar explained that the locals believed that the soot was from the smoke that suffocated Maheb Khwoja when he was hiding here – his enemies set fire to the whole mountain, which explained why it was barren. Could Xuanzang have imagined that a Buddhist master and an Islamic martyr would share the same shrine?

The crusade against Khotan in the tenth century was one of the longest and bloodiest wars waged by the Arabs. They first captured Kashgar, the westernmost oasis of the Taklamakan Desert. From there they launched repeated attacks on Khotan. Yashkar said there is a local record with a vivid description of the 'holy war'. 'They laid siege to the cities and sent in messengers, asking the inhabitants to surrender: "We are the descendants of the Prophet and we are part of the 140,000 crusaders fighting to spread Islam. We are here to convert you all. You must surrender. If you do not, we will kill you, keep your children as slaves and raze your place to the ground." The reply was: "We will never betray the religion of our ancestors."'

The King of Khotan did everything he could to ensure the survival of his kingdom. Huge portraits of the Buddha were commissioned, special ceremonies were performed in monasteries throughout the country, and his people prayed day and night – all to evoke the protection of the kingdom as told in the sutras. But he did not just leave things in the hands of the gods. He sought an alliance with local rulers in Dunhuang in Western China. He also sent his own children to the Chinese capital to plead for help. The letters that the princes sent to their father from Dunhuang revealed just how desperate they were. They were beleaguered in Dunhuang: bandits had taken away their luggage, their supplies, their tributes and letters of state to the Chinese emperor. They begged the king to allow them to stay in Dunhuang longer, but in vain. They were told to carry on regardless, with no further delay. In one letter, the princes were in despair: 'How can the Chinese emperor reward us even if we turn up in the capital? We are like beggars. There is a war and many people have died in the next town. If you indeed order us to proceed, you will be forcing us to walk into the fires of hell and we will not come out alive.' It was not clear whether the king had insisted on his children risking their lives, but he was looking death in the face, for himself and his country. He had no choice but to pay the ultimate price, as a father and as a king.

As a pious Buddhist, the king must have questioned whether he ought to fight in the last resort. Not to kill is the first precept of Buddhism, and non-violence its hallmark. Buddhist scriptures are full of stories about kings and princes who will not fight wars even to defend their kingdoms. The King of Benares once opened the gate of his capital to invaders. 'Do not fight just so I may remain king,' he told his people. 'If we destroy the lives of others we also destroy our own peace of mind. Let them have the kingdom if they want it so badly. I do not wish to fight.'

Even for selfish reasons, Buddhists should not fight – it brings bad karma and impedes their liberation. A village head-man once asked the Buddha where he would go if he died in battle defending his people. 'You will be reborn in the hell called the realm of those slain in battles.' The Buddha said the man's mind was already seized by the thought: 'May my enemies be struck down, slaughtered or annihilated. May they not exist!' There could not be a holy war in the name of the Buddha. Buddhists have never waged a war to propagate their faith, or persecuted believers of other religions. Asoka sent people to spread the Dharma armed with sutras, not guns; the message was peace and compassion.

But the King of Khotan decided to defend his kingdom at all costs; after all in the sutras, even the Bodhisattvas killed devils to protect the faithful. But he had to fight alone against the tidal waves of crusaders. The Chinese never came to his rescue – China was in a deep turmoil of its own: peasant rebellions, attacks by nomads in the north, and the crowning of a new emperor. In the end, after almost half a century of lonely resistance, Khotan fell to the crusaders, who could not conceal their joy at conquering this stronghold of Buddhism, even though they had suffered terrible losses – in Khotan today, there are more tombs for Islamic 'martyrs' than in any other place in Central Asia, a reminder of the protracted battles of the faiths. The *Dictionary of the Turkic Language*, edited by the Islamic scholar Muhammad Kashgar in the eleventh century, collected this verse:

> Like river torrents,
> We flooded their cities;
> We destroyed their monasteries,
> And shat on the statues of the Buddha.

Some monasteries were turned into mosques; but most were burnt to the ground, leaving blackened walls and charred beams still visible today. The gold and precious gems that decorated numerous Buddhist statues in the monasteries became the spoils of the crusaders. Monks who dared resist the sword of Islam with their bare fists were killed or buried alive; others fled up the ancient paths into the Karakoram

Mountains and found refuge in Tibet – today, the most complete and systematic source of the history of Khotan in the first millennium is in Tibetan. The destruction was complete: a thousand years of Buddhist civilization were gone, and with them the language, the culture and the very people of Caucasian and Indo-Iranian origins. It was true: the Khotan I was visiting was not what Xuanzang saw.

On top of the barren mountain where the Buddha was supposed to have preached is now the tomb of Maheb Khwoja in a plain white house. In front of it is a courtyard filled with high poles hung with lambskins, which seemed to come alive in the strong wind. In the distance, the oasis of Khotan was just discernible, caressed by the Black Jade River, which shimmered like a mirage. It seems the end of Buddhist Khotan was inevitable. Buddhism was in retreat even in the land of the Buddha. The rise of Islam was so rapid, unstoppable. How could the precarious oasis kingdom stand against the tide? The oases to the west fell one by one; Kashgar surrendered, and did not suffer so much. The Khotanese could have done the same, but they wanted to defend their faith, however slender their chances. Sutras were composed to praise them and boost their courage. A sutra in Tibetan spells out in detail the Buddha's instruction on the Gosringa Mountain. 'This kingdom has received my blessing, which makes it special. In times of war and destruction to come, Sum-pas and its army, the nomads of the north, the Uighurs and other non-believers will come here, bent on destroying this kingdom. The propitious images of the Buddha will descend here, protecting its frontier, and through their miraculous power, Khotan will be saved. The Bodhisattvas, the myriads of heavenly beings and the invincible dragon kings will all follow, and they will drive away the evildoers and save the people from their enemies' harm.' Such passages gave the Khotanese confidence and hope, but it was in vain. Nothing could survive the huge attacking armies. It was remarkable that they held out as long as they did.

I wondered how Xuanzang would have looked at the death of Khotan, the Buddhist kingdom of which he was clearly very fond. Perhaps it would have put him in mind of the destruction of the Sakya people, ruled by the Buddha's own father. The Buddha sat in the middle of the road under the scorching sun. The king who led the attack stopped and asked him why he did not seek shade under a leafy tree nearby. The Buddha replied: 'My clan is like the leaves. Now you are going to cut them off, I have no shade.' Three times he managed to persuade the king to turn back. But the fourth time, the king swept past him. He killed all the men, buried all the women and burned down the capital of Kapilavastu. For all his power, the Buddha was powerless to prevent it. Nothing is permanent, he would say. A thousand years of Buddhism, a thousand years of Islam. The only inevitability is change.

But Xuanzang was fortunate to have known nothing of Khotan's tragic end. After nine months' wait in the Khotan he cherished, his servant came back from Chang'an, bearing the reply from Emperor Taizong:

When I heard that the Master who had gone to far-off countries to search for religious books had now come back, I was filled with boundless joy. I pray you come quickly that we may see each other ... I have ordered the bureaus of Khotan and other places to send with you the best guides they can procure, and conveyances as many as you require. I have commanded the magistrates of Dunhuang to conduct you through the desert of shifting sands and I have desired the government to meet you in Chang'an.

It was the answer he was waiting for. He set off at once.

ELEVEN

Lost Treasures, Lost Souls

THE JOURNEY FROM KHOTAN to Dunhuang, the old Chinese frontier town, was hard. It was the southern route of the Silk Road, and one of its most arduous and perilous stretches. Apart from a few small oases and ruined cities it was one big ocean of shifting sand. The sun beat down on the caravans mercilessly; the winds that blew across the desert felt as if they were coming straight out of a blast furnace, hot and fierce; even the camels groaned their distress. Xuanzang wrote: 'There is absolutely nothing in sight, no water, no vegetation. There is not even a track. Often you hear howling or crying but have no idea where it comes from – many are led astray by it.' The heaps of bones must have reminded him of his narrow escape in the desert on his outward journey. Silently, he raised his hands and pressed them together, murmuring a short prayer. He was relieved to have the imperial escort to accompany him across the Taklamakan, the 'sea of death'.

They reached Dunhuang in two months. One can only imagine how Xuanzang felt when he set foot in the oasis: he had come home after eighteen years, alive and in one piece. Any of the numberless piles of bones in the desert he had seen could have been his own. At last he must have felt the ease of being among his own people, speaking his own language, no longer a foreigner. Most importantly, he had achieved everything he had set out to do, and more. He attributed the success of his journey to the protection of the Buddhas and the Bodhisattvas. Like all the Silk Road merchants and travellers arriving here, he would have decided to visit the Mogao Caves, a great Buddhist centre, and give thanks for his safe passage and the fulfilment of his vow.

I arrived in Dunhuang in the early morning. The so-called city consists of just four streets radiating from a crossroads, with a large concrete statue of an apsara in the middle, modelled from a Mogao painting. A few men were cycling around it on their way to work. Dunhuang was no longer the bustling oasis that Xuanzang knew. I headed straight for the Mogao Caves, twenty-five kilometres outside.

There is plenty of transport to choose from: tourism is the lifeblood of Dunhuang today. The bus followed the same route that Xuanzang would have taken. On the roadside, lush green vegetable fields and fruit orchards ran for several kilometres, with farmhouses dotted here and there. Abruptly the oasis ended and the desert began, with nothing but grit and pebbles and a low mountain range. Just when I was starting to get tired of the monotony of the scenery, we turned right and in the distance I saw trees and a flying rooftop, and then I caught sight of the caves, honeycombing a steep cliff face. They stretch for almost two kilometres, long enough to accommodate a thousand years of spiritual and artistic activity, from the fourth to the fourteenth century. It was said that a wandering monk arrived here at dusk in the year of 366, and rested his weary body on the slope of the Singing Sand Hills. Suddenly he found the whole place bathed in the golden rays of the setting

366

sun, as if a thousand Buddhas had descended from Heaven. He decided then and there to make a cave in the cliff of the mountain to meditate in. This was the first of more than a thousand caves that were hewn from this mountainside in the next thousand years. Four hundred and ninety-two of them have survived, decorated with over 45,000 square metres of wonderful images of the Buddha and his followers and sculptures. If you put all the paintings side by side, they would stretch for thirty kilometres, making Mogao, the Peerless Caves, indeed peerless in the history of Buddhist art.

But at the ticket window I was informed that I could visit only ten caves with a guided tour. The rest were not open to the public. If I were really keen, I could see them for thirty or forty pounds a cave, depending on their state of preservation. I had planned to see at least a dozen particular ones, either directly from Xuanzang's time or with murals illustrating his journey. I told the ticket lady my problem, and also of Xuanzang. She barely heard me out before waving her hand impatiently. 'Xuanzang? Even Bodhisattva Guanyin wouldn't get you a free entry.'

I did not expect free entry but the sum she mentioned was forbidding. I stood aside and pondered for a while. I decided to buy the standard entrance now and worry about the special caves later. I could not help, however, thinking of how Aurel Stein opened the door to the hidden treasures of Dunhuang, all due to Xuanzang.

Stein arrived in Dunhuang in March 1907 on his second expedition to western China, never thinking for a second that this would be the scene of his greatest discovery. He wanted to see the caves, of which he had heard glowing descriptions from an earlier Hungarian explorer. He needed to replenish his supplies of food and water, and then he was to return to the desert for further excavations of the watchtowers of the Great Wall.

But soon he heard vague rumours about the vast hoard of ancient manuscripts discovered in one of the caves by Wang Yuanlu, the self-appointed caretaker of the Mogao Caves. Not much was known about Wang except that he was born in Hubei Province, central China. A severe famine caused him to flee his village to northern China and join the army. But he found life as a soldier equally cruel so he quit and became a Daoist priest. In his wandering, he chanced upon the Mogao Caves and was so enchanted with them, even though they were Buddhist, that he decided to devote the rest of his life to restoring them. He settled down in a dilapidated monastery, and then began work on his life's goal. He collected donations and used them to hire labourers to clear away the sand and repair the caves, many of which had collapsed after being abandoned for more than five hundred years. When they had emptied Cave 16 of sand, one man found the wall of the passage was hollow. Wang opened it up, and was stunned to find a small chamber with a solid mass of manuscript bundles rising to a height of nearly three metres. These were the hidden treasures of Dunhuang that Stein had heard about.

On their first meeting, Stein instantly sized Wang up as a difficult person – shy, nervous but extremely pious and determined. 'To rely on the temptation of money alone as a means of overcoming his scruples was manifestly useless,' wrote Stein in *Desert Cathay*, the record of his second expedition. He thought of Xuanzang, whose name had always won him sympathy and help from the Chinese. He was not sure if it would work on a Daoist priest, but he would give it a try. At once he noticed that 'a gleam of lively interest appeared in the priest's eyes'. He knew instantly what he had to do now to win the priest's confidence, and his way into the cave. He began to elaborate on his devotion to Xuanzang, and explained how he had followed the footsteps of the Chinese monk from India across inhospitable mountains and deserts, and how in the course of this pilgrimage he had come to Dunhuang and the cave. The effect was instant. Wang, bursting with pride, led Stein to a newly-built veranda outside Cave 16 and showed his guest a series of murals he had commissioned depicting the adventures of the famous monk. 'Gladly I let my delightfully credulous cicerone expound in voluble talk the wonderful stories of travel which each fresco panel depicted,' Stein wrote gleefully. When he left the priest, Stein knew he was over the most difficult hurdle.

Late that night, Jiang Xiaowan, Stein's eager and capable Chinese secretary and translator, came to his tent with a bundle of rolls which Wang had brought hidden beneath his cloak. To Stein's amazement, the first roll he opened was the Chinese version of a sutra which, according to the inscriptions at the end of the scroll, had been brought back and translated by none other than Xuanzang himself. He rushed to break the news to Wang. The omen was not lost on the pious priest. Within hours, the door to the secret chamber was opened.

This would be Stein's greatest coup – one of the richest finds in the history of archaeology. Of the fifty thousand items, the majority are Buddhist scriptures written in Chinese, Uighur, Tibetan, Sogdian and Sanskrit, including a printed copy of the *Diamond Sutra*, the earliest known printed book. Equally important are the thousands of pieces of secular documents glued to the back of the sutras to strengthen them, from classic texts, popular ballads, lyric poems, contracts, accounts and private letters, to fragments of Xuanzang's *Record of the Western Regions*, the oldest copy of the book from the eighth century. They present a panoramic picture of Chinese society, spanning almost a millennium. Birth, marriage, love, the delights of sex, the pain of infidelity and divorce, anxiety about old age and death, the comfort of religions, court cases of land disputes and inheritance – just about every aspect of Chinese life is covered in strong and vivid language. For example, in a school of etiquette, a man learned to write a letter of apology to his host for having got drunk at her soiree the night before:

> The next morning, after hearing others speak on the subject, I realized what had happened, whereupon I was overwhelmed with confusion and ready to sink into the earth with shame. It was due to the vessel of my small capacity, on that occasion, being filled too full. I humbly trust that you in your wise benevolence will not condemn me for my transgression. Soon I will come to apologize in person, but meanwhile I beg to send this written communication for your kind inspection. Leaving much unsaid, I am yours respectfully.

Despite Stein's ignorance of Chinese, he was instantly aware of the value of the manuscripts. For the next ten days, he worked his way day and night through the collection with the help of his secretary Jiang, hardly leaving the cave except to eat. Pressed though he was for time, he never forgot the all-important immediate task – to keep the priest in a pliable mood. He engaged the priest, with the help of his secretary, in long talks about their common hero and patron saint, and liberally displayed his affection to the memory of Xuanzang. Time and again, he asked Wang to show him the cherished frescoes on his veranda walls, in particular the panel depicting Xuanzang returning with his elephant heavily laden with sacred manuscripts from India. To Stein it seemed the most plausible reason he could use for his eager interest in the relics that Wang had discovered.

Stein was ambitious: he wanted to carry away all the manuscripts. His secretary did his best to plead his case with the priest in that 'the removal of the collection to a temple of learning in England would in truth be an act which Buddha and his Arhat might approve as pious'. But the prospect of losing all the sacred texts seriously frightened Wang: he had made Mogao his home and its restoration his mission. He felt certain that his patrons would notice any deficiency in the piles of manuscripts, and consequently stop their donations. Then the position he had built up for himself after years of pious labour would be lost for ever. He had been willing to let Stein select a few rolls in exchange for a donation to fund the restoration. But to part with the entire contents of the secret chamber? It was a risk he would not contemplate.

Stein raised his offer of a 'donation' to a sum which he thought the poor priest could not possibly refuse. He reasoned that the money would enable Wang to return to a life of peace and comfort in his home village if he lost his hard-earned position in Dunhuang. Alternatively the priest could allay any scruples by using the money for the benefit of the temple. But Wang refused. Stein then blackmailed him: he had already taken hold of 'loads of valuable manuscripts and antiques' – Stein's own words – and he could threaten to divulge how he had acquired them. The prospect of losing face and forgoing the promised donation finally made Wang give in and yield up to 20,000 manuscripts, paintings and other artefacts. All this, as Stein was proud to record, cost him only a hundred and thirty pounds. He even had the effrontery to say that the priest 'was almost ready to recognize that it was a pious act on my part to rescue for Western scholarship all those relics of ancient Buddhist literature and art which were otherwise bound to get lost sooner or later through local indifference'.

Stein had indeed brought Dunhuang to the attention of the world. Hot on his heels came the young French sinologist Paul Pelliot, whose mastery of Chinese helped him choose six thousand of the most important documents of Dunhuang. He even showed some of them to Chinese officials in Beijing before he shipped them to Paris in 1909. Outraged, the Chinese central government ordered the removal of all the remaining manuscripts to Beijing, but Wang did not relinquish everything. In 1911 he had enough left over to sell to Japanese and Russian expedition teams; three years later when Stein returned to Dunhuang, he bought five more cases of material. When Langdon Warner arrived in the 1920s, there were no documents to be acquired so he simply cut off twelve of the best murals, and shipped them and two beautiful Bodhisattva statues to America. Today the Dunhuang manuscripts are among the treasures of seventy-seven museums and libraries in England, France, Germany, Russia, the United States, Japan, Korea, Denmark, Sweden, Finland, Turkey and China.

The way Stein and the other 'foreign devils' acquired the manuscripts is deeply resented by the Chinese. Even Xuanzang, with all his compassion, could hardly have approved of how Stein used, or abused, his name. Maybe it is for this reason that Stein, knighted by the British government at the time, is now largely ignored by the very institution which funded most of his expeditions – the British Museum. Unlike its other archaeological heroes whose contributions are proudly acknowledged, the British Museum seems keen almost to erase his memory. In the Asia gallery, only a tiny selection of his finds are on display – the rest are in storage. A Buddhist would say this is his bad karma.

Times have changed. Mogao is no longer the dilapidated place where the glory of the Silk Road was totally forgotten, where shepherds sought shelter in the rain, where soldiers stayed during military drills, and where foreign adventurers pillaged the unprotected treasures to their hearts' content. Today it is a World Heritage site, attracting visitors from all over the world to see, to admire and to remember the triumph of faith in the barren desert, the extraordinary beauty that burst out of this lonely frontier post. It is not neglect but overcrowding that now threatens the fragile murals. That is why entrance is strictly controlled and the most precious caves are accessible only to scholars and experts on Dunhuang.

Twenty of us followed our guide like a flock of sheep as she unlocked the gate of one cave after another. She made fast work of each, relating sketchy information in a bored voice. She would flash her torch at some Buddha on the ceiling or the wall and by the time I had made it out in the gloom, she had moved on to something else. I soon drifted away from the crowd and wandered into any cave that was open. Amazingly, nobody stopped me. In one cave a light had been strung up illuminating all the murals. I poked my head in further and made out a figure: a man with his back turned to me, dabbing at a giant canvas.

He was a painter, copying the Western Paradise on the northern wall. He was well into his reproduction. The drawings had been carefully prepared in pencil with each image precisely located on a grid. He was applying colours, blue, jade green, terracotta and dark red, with occasional gold powder. Amitabha, the Buddha of Infinite Light, was sitting on a lotus blossom, flanked by two Bodhisattvas and their heavenly retinues. Infants, representing the souls of those recently reborn into paradise, danced joyously or knelt in reverence. On floors paved with precious stones, several pairs of apsaras danced gracefully to celestial music, played by an orchestra of fair ladies. In the background were lavish palaces, pagodas and pavilions under auspicious clouds. The process was laborious and precise. The copying of classic artworks by artists has a venerable history in China, as in India. It is an act of reverence, a way of becoming imbued not only with the artistic technique but also with its spirit. This man was following the tradition. When I compared his copy with the mural on the wall, I had to admit it was masterly. I wanted to ask him how long he had been working on it. I coughed to attract his attention. He turned around, looking not too unhappy about my intrusion, and just said, 'Seven months.'

I ventured another question. How long did he think the original painter took to decorate the whole cave?

'It was done by more than one painter, perhaps three or four.' He put down his brush. 'You are not a painter.'

'I cannot even draw a circle.'

He laughed and told me that rarely would one painter do a whole cave, because the people who paid for it wanted to see their paradise quickly. This was a medium-sized cave and it would take three painters perhaps two or three years to decorate. I had read that food and an extra allowance of oil for cooking at the completion of their work were what the painters received for these heavenly images. It did not sound like very much recompense for such patient and detailed work, I told him.

'Worse, they were not allowed to put their names on the murals,' he said. 'Of all the murals in all the caves, we know the name of only one painter. In one cave some years ago, scholars found the mummified body of a painter, covered with a sketch of his painting. He had died devoting his life to the depiction of paradise on earth.' I asked him what was the hardest thing for him. 'You can see survival is no problem for me,' he said, pulling a face with some exaggeration. 'But that heavenly expression on the face of the Buddha and the Bodhisattva is so elusive. It is unfathomable.'

I suspected he was not a Buddhist. 'Perhaps you should try to become enlightened,' I joked.

'Are you a Buddhist?' he looked at me in surprise.

'I am looking for the Buddha.'

'How?'

'By following the footsteps of Xuanzang.'

'But he went all the way to India.'

'I just came back from India.'

'Why are you doing this?'

'To figure out what's behind the Buddha's smile,' I replied.

He stared at me. He was probably wondering if I was serious. 'You know Xuanzang came here and there are murals depicting his journey to the West. Have you seen them?'

No, I shook my head. Then I told him my problem.

'Perhaps I can help you,' he said slowly.

'Can you get me special permission?'

'Special permissions I don't have, but I and my colleagues are working in several caves right now.'

I could not believe my luck; I told him the caves I had in mind.

'Just wait here. I'll be back soon.'

When he returned, I told him how grateful I was. He looked at the keys and rattled them uneasily. 'These are priceless treasures. Please do not steal anything, like Stein.'

'I wouldn't mind stealing one of your reproductions,' I joked. He told me I could see them in the museum outside, where the entire murals of the ten best caves have been reproduced. Visitors could experience the total aesthetic of a cave without actually going in there. 'The breathing from coach loads of tourists is damaging the murals. I am painting to keep people out of the caves,' he said seriously. 'But for the time being I'll show you the real ones.' We exchanged names; I will call him Hua.

'Why don't we start at the beginning,' he suggested, leading the way and fingering one key after another until he came to the one he wanted. 'Let me show you some of the early caves. Xuanzang must have seen them. And anyway, they're my personal favourites.'

It was only a short walk to the first one. Hua turned his torch on the wall, illuminating a burst of colour and form. The paintings were very simple, almost modern, with slightly stylized figures, emphasized by blocks of bold colours. The skin tones of the figures had oxidized to a charcoal grey. 'Don't they look like Picassos?' he said. 'I feel much happier copying these. I don't feel imprisoned by the detail like in the Tang figures. With those you have to spend months just doing the jewellery. These are really liberating.'

'Now let me take you to our greatest treasure,' Hua said excitedly. We emerged from the cave into bright sunlight, and climbed up to the second storey from the corridor in front of the caves. 'Your monk could not have missed this. It was finished in 642 just before he came here. I think this cave has the finest of all the murals.'

Cave 220 was small, but its murals were indeed very special. 'I know I said I prefer the simple ones, but this is the Tang style at its very best. See the heavenly face of the Amitabha

Buddha.' He pointed to the centre of the mural on the northern wall. 'And look at this dancer.' His finger moved further down the wall. 'She looks as if she could come off the painting and start dancing for you. They can't be by local painters. The men who painted them must have come from Chang'an, the capital. This is the most beautiful Western Paradise in the Mogao Caves, and the best preserved.'

I had to agree. The scenery was so vivid, the figures so alive, the palaces so magnificent, and the composition so harmonious. The Eastern Paradise on the opposite wall was equally astonishing. 'This was the destination the donor of the cave had in mind for his families,' Hua said, pointing to a row of men painted on the entrance wall.

All six men were wearing the same official robe of the imperial administration, a garment of dark colour and a hat with fins sticking out above both ears. They were standing there with the contented expression of men contemplating the paradise they had created on earth. From the inscription next to the portraits, we know that the donor, Zhai Fengda, was a high official in the local government in the tenth century. His great-great-grandfather had commissioned the cave as a family temple and had it decorated with the most popular murals. 'But Zhai's children or grandchildren could not maintain the family temple. Others took over. There was no shortage of big donors in Dunhuang in those days,' Hua said, leading me to a corner where there were four layers of painting. 'It was only after peeling off the later works that the splendid commission by the Zhai family was revealed.'

On the two walls next to the entrance were murals of Vimalakirti discussing the Dharma with Wenshu, the Bodhisattva of Wisdom. Originally Vimalakirti was an Indian ascetic and highly unconventional – he visited prostitutes and gamblers in order to teach them Buddhism. But in China we demurred at his questionable background and made him a Confucian scholar complete with wife and children. The Chinese liked him because he combined wisdom with worldly life – just what the rich and powerful donors aspired to. He was debating a most profound point with Bodhisattva Wenshu: non-duality, a concept which Xuanzang would have studied and understood well. Everything is relative, changeable, even the Dharma. Without dirt, there is no cleanliness, without laymen, there are no monks, without suffering, there is no enlightenment. Affliction and enlightenment are the same thing, just one thought apart. Once one realizes this, one has achieved the highest wisdom in Buddhism, which is beyond language, beyond concept, beyond any teaching. One could only smile, and sit in silent contemplation, which was just what Vima-lakirti and Wenshu did at the end of their debate. The debate was so penetrating, even the emperor was listening to the discussion with his large retinue of ministers at the feet of the Bodhisattva.

'That could be Emperor Taizong himself, with his ministers, the very people Xuanzang was shortly to meet,' Hua said. 'Xuanzang is probably pondering how he can get the emperor to listen to his preaching, to support him and Buddhism.'

Hua was right: this must have been pressing on Xuanzang's mind. He was deeply moved by the flourishing of Buddhism in Dunhuang. If only this could happen in the whole of China, he thought. To achieve that, he must win the support of the emperor. In fact, as he would notice, the most splendid Mogao Caves had been patronized by the local rulers. Naturally they had left their portraits on the walls like Zhai Fengda or the King of Khotan – tiny images in some obscure corner to start with, but later they were to become bigger and bigger, eclipsing even the Bodhisattvas. Vanity overtook piety. It was just as well that Xuanzang never saw the eighth-century excesses of the ruling local families. They portrayed their entire retinues on the lower walls of the caves, complete with horses and banners flying, flaunting their wealth, power and prestige. The earthly show had squeezed the heavenly host upstairs. Still, without their support, Buddhism could not flourish. Travelling around India, Xuanzang had witnessed the decline of the Dharma in the land of the Buddha; to revive it, and propagate it throughout China – he saw the purpose of his journey even more clearly in the caves of Mogao.

These two caves had only whetted my appetite. I went on to see a dozen of what Hua thought were the best for my purposes. I was completely bowled over. Looking at the murals of the life of the Buddha – his renunciation, his searching, his enlightenment under the Bodhi Tree, his first preaching and his nirvana – I kept thinking how they must have reminded Xuanzang of his pilgrimage to the holy places. And the mural of merchants being ambushed by bandits in Cave 45 would no doubt bring back memories of his own experience of being robbed five times and once almost losing his life at the hands of bandits. Here on the wall, the frightened merchants were at a loss what to do; while they were desperately looking for a place to hide, their heavily loaded donkeys took flight and a camel stumbled over a precipice. The merchants prayed earnestly to the Bodhisattvas, as Xuanzang had done, and the bandits were repelled. They reloaded their goods and set off again on the journey home. But even bandits were thought to be capable of embracing Buddhism. Just as Xuanzang per-suaded the robbers in Peshawar to give up their trade, in Cave 285, five hundred bandits were depicted receiving enlighten-ment after hearing the preaching of the Bodhisattva Guanyin.

The heavenly abodes of the Buddhas and Bodhisattvas are always enlivened with vignettes from real life, giving us a window on the world of Xuanzang's time, and before and after. I saw a farmer and his family leading horses into a stable in their clean and comfortable courtyard, shaded by weeping willows and surrounded by lush green fields. In a walled city guarded by watchtowers, a monk was instructing his two disciples, while an official was hearing petitions from a line of supplicants. The famous Mount Wutai, the worldly abode of the Bodhisattva of Wisdom, was packed with grand temples and monasteries. Pilgrimages, royal processions, religious ceremonies, weddings, funerals, wars, commercial transactions, women putting on their make-up, men brushing their teeth and children playing with dogs and cats – every aspect of life is recorded in colourful, vivid detail, still fresh, evocative and powerful after all this time. I told Hua that many of the scenes were so familiar they could be happening in the villages and towns I had passed through on my journey. I had the sensation that I was no longer just following Xuanzang's footsteps and reading his *Record* but actually inhabiting the world he lived in.

'Just wait till this afternoon when you see the cave with the painting of him in it!' Hua said.

We left the caves and gingerly made our way down the steep stairs. Hua invited me for lunch in the Academy canteen, but I declined. I was keen to take some photos, and I was aware how quickly the day could pass. I asked him if he could join me later near the big Buddha at the centre of the site. After he was gone, I stood surveying the scene in front of me, my hand against my brow for shade against the full blast of the sun. The heat seemed to dissolve people, trees and caves into separate units, hard and transparent, like the residue of evaporated liquid. Perhaps I would be lucky and have the whole place to myself. But in another second my hopes were dashed. Beyond the railing that bars the entrance, and directly opposite the big Buddha, I saw a group of Tibetans. They were alternately standing up and lying down, prostrating themselves, inching slowly towards the Buddha.

I had no idea how long they had been doing this, but I could see sweat running down their weathered faces in thick rivulets, and their long maroon coats were dusty from flinging themselves on the ground; the covers on their hands were shiny. They were poor men who had travelled far to fulfil a promise made many years ago. I suppose this is more what Xuanzang would have seen – the faithful coming here to pray. The caves were not just beautiful things to admire, nor were they merely offerings to ensure their donors' entry into heaven, they were living temples meant as places of worship.

I watched the Tibetans for quite a while until they stood up for the last time, and with their hands pressed together uttered a silent prayer. Then they started chatting volubly and gathered to leave. Maybe they couldn't afford the tickets, I speculated. Maybe they didn't need to see the murals. They were pilgrims; all they wanted was to pay their respects to this holy place. As they walked away into the distance, my thoughts followed them. I had now seen Bezeklik, Qizil and Ajanta, the major Buddhist caves on the Silk Road that Xuanzang had visited in their prime. Much had faded or vanished, which made Mogao even more precious. I saw the power of faith; I saw beauty; I saw the river of history. But Mogao was still a monument. For them, it was a living embodiment of their faith.

The Tibetan pilgrims set me thinking about my grandmother. She would have loved it here. She could have seen for herself all the important stories and messages in the sutras she could not read. She would have particularly liked the murals illustrating the Lotus Sutra. Here the Bodhisattva Guanyin was shown saving merchants lost in the desert and at sea, people trapped in burning houses, soldiers wounded in battle and a man whose head was on the guillotine. Surely the almighty Bodhisattva could have solved her problems, and delivered her to the Western Paradise? She would have taken the mural of the paradise as the real thing, where suffering was unheard of, where no one was sick, where all that was desired would be granted and where she would be reunited with her children and husband and live happily ever after.

For all her wishes to be granted, Grandmother would have offered incense sticks before she prostrated. Then she would start praying. A tenth-century prayer I read by an old woman from the Dunhuang manuscripts reminded me so much of Grandmother:

> I offer this incense to announce the misfortunes that rain down upon me as fast as lightning ... I beg that my prayer will reach the ears of the Star God Rahu, and that he will force the hundred demons that beset me to go far away, that he will strengthen the power of the good spirits, let my illnesses fade away day after day, year after year. I entreat him for happiness and blessing, for the end of my misfortunes and for pardon of my sins.

I wanted to offer a prayer for her, but the words did not come.

When Hua returned from his lunch, with a bottle of water and a steamed bun for me, we headed straight for Cave 103. It is a small one, with the usual layout and decorations in Cave 220, except that the Eastern Paradise does not occupy the entire northern wall. To the right of the paradise is a small oblong mural, the one I had been so looking forward to seeing. It starts at the top with Xuanzang saying goodbye to his host under an Indian pavilion. Then among the undulating green mountains of the Pamirs, he and his companions can be seen travelling, making slow progress. A Sogdian, with a bushy beard and floppy hat, is leading the white elephant laden with a heavy sack, presumably full of sutras and statues. Xuanzang follows on his white horse, wrapped in a long cloak to keep warm and wearing a monk's hat. As he tells us, the upland plains of the Pamirs were surrounded by snowy mountains, and 'the climate was cold and the winds blew constantly'. Close behind our pilgrim are two servants walking. The scene is harmonious and peaceful, with no indication of the disaster to come when they were attacked by the band of robbers. The next scene portrays him giving thanks for his safe arrival.

What fascinated me was not just the painting itself but also the date it was painted, barely a hundred years after Xuanzang returned to China. Because of his epic journey, Xuanzang was already legendary in his own time, and soon appeared on the walls of the Mogao Caves, alongside the Buddha, Bodhisattvas and heavenly kings, worshipped by the faithful and inspiring them to follow his example. They did just that. The dramas, the adventures, the exotic tastes and customs, the wonders of India, so vividly described in his *Record* and Hui Li's biography, created almost a mania in China for India. More Chinese monks left for India in the forty years after Xuanzang's return than during any other time. Many never made it; others loved India so much they decided to settle there; those who came back received heroes' welcomes and encouraged more of the faithful to follow in their footsteps. This fervour continued unabated for at least three hundred years. A delight of the Dunhuang documents is fragments of Xuanzang's *Record of the Western Regions.* What is more, on the back of one page, the monk wrote down his name and the name of his monastery in northern China. He must have been so impressed by Xuanzang that he bought the book and used it to guide his own pilgrimage. For some reason, he did not travel on after his arrival in Dunhuang, and the guidebook was stored in the secret chamber.

As the legends surrounding Xuanzang grew, they soon overwhelmed and replaced the reality. Hua told me there were half a dozen murals featuring my hero painted much later in the Yulin Caves, some 170 kilometres east of Dunhuang. There, he is accompanied by the fictional monkey; and to cross the river after he had lost his elephant, he had to rely on a giant turtle as described in *The Monkey King*. According to the missionary Mildred Cable, who passed through Dunhuang in the 1930s, Priest Wang built a shrine for Xuanzang and 'every pilgrim who would follow his footsteps offered incense at his shrine and craved his protection from the dangers of the way'. Just as Xuanzang had prayed to the Bodhisattva Guanyin for divine intervention or inspiration, later travellers appealed to him for the same reason – an honour which Xuanzang would never have dreamed of.

At the end of a memorable day at the caves, I caught the Research Academy's shuttle bus back to Dunhuang with Hua. A few stops from where he and all his colleagues lived was the other wonder of Dunhuang: a clear spring in the shape of a crescent moon in the middle of sand dunes that make a thundering noise when you slide down them. I wanted to see them. They would make a perfect end to a perfect day. Hua suggested that I visit the Thunderbolt Monastery nearby as well.

I did not know there was a monastery in Dunhuang today.

'It is new, built in the last decade, but the name is an old one,' he explained. 'Xuanzang stayed there when he was in Dunhuang – at least it says so in *The Monkey King*.' He paused. 'Have you stayed in a monastery?' he asked.

I shook my head.

'It will be an experience for you. Perhaps you can understand your monk better,' he said seriously. 'And if it proves too much for you, you can always escape to the caves.'

I had planned to do this and thought I would come to it at the end of my journey, in a big monastery somewhere, where there was a famous master. I knew it was possible: I had seen lay people and nuns doing it. For nuns and monks, it is called *canxue*, or seeking good knowledge of the Dharma by finding the master, the monastery and the regime that suit them best for their awakening. For me it would be part of my own pilgrimage. Six months into my journey, I had seen, as Xuanzang had, how Buddhism once flourished in the most hostile environments, inspired so many people, created the most sublime objects of art and devotion, disappeared in terrible violence, and was embraced again by the most deprived and disillusioned. I had learned how his grasp of the Dharma made Xuanzang fearless and unassailable in the face of all adversities and temptations. In Sarnath, Bodh Gaya and Kushinagar, I had experienced the most profound feelings of devotion and piety, but as an observer, not a believer. I know I cannot be a Buddhist – I cannot yet accept the fundamental law of Buddhism, karma and rebirth; and I still prefer to think and to understand rather than just to believe. But it would be a great help to me if I could spend some time with the monks, to experience the monastic life, to get a clearer idea of Buddhism, and to find out whether I could reach the deep emotion and sense of belonging I so longed for.

I decided that I would like to have my monastic experience here in this ancient centre of Buddhism and pilgrimage, near the caves which had inspired so many people throughout the centuries. But I knew I could not just walk in off the street and ask to stay – I needed an introduction. By now I had met any number of monks. I called one of them and pleaded for help, and eventually my path was cleared. I was admitted to a cell in the Thunderbolt Monastery.

Clack. Clack. A crisp, dry sound, not loud but piercing in the absolute quiet of the monastery in the dark. What could it be? I groaned and tried to go back to sleep. The strange noise penetrated my ears again. Then I realized I was in my cell and it was the wake-up call, a monk clapping two pieces of wood. But my eyes seemed glued shut. I went back to sleep. Suddenly there was a thunderous noise above my head, 'Please get up.' The light was on, so bright that I could not open my eyes. When I finally succeeded, I saw a moon-like face hovering over me. It was Shan Ren, whom I had met yesterday evening. The abbot had told her to look after me during my stay. How did she get in? I remembered that I could not lock the door from inside. Outside my curtainless windows, it was still pitch-dark.

'Hurry up, you are late,' Shan said softly, and tossed my *haiqing* at me, the long ceremonial black robe for Buddhist devotees. She had brought it for me, together with my bed sheet, quilt and thermos. 'Do you know what they say if you are lazy and stay in bed after hearing the wake-up call? You will be born as a snake in your next life.'

'Who cares?' I grumbled.

I threw some cold water from the washbasin on my face, and slipped into my *haiqing*. It was too big – I was almost lost in it. Clack. Clack. Clack. The monk on duty came round again. I should be out of my room by now. I picked up my prayer book and rushed for the shrine hall, all the time rubbing my eyes, touching my *haiqing* here and there to make sure the strings were tied properly. I was totally conscious of my lack of calm and grace in my Buddhist garb. I was supposed to walk gently and slowly, holding my head high and my hands in front of me. Now I was almost running, with my robe billowing out behind me.

The doors of the shrine hall were wide open, with the drum beating loudly like raindrops on a glass pane. It was to drive away any residue of sleepiness we might have. I bowed to the statue of the Sakyamuni Buddha in the centre before I entered and found my place behind Shan Ren and two other women. Facing us were six monks, one in front of the 'wooden-fish', a percussion instrument, another in front of the gong, a third one beating the drum, and the three others standing. We turned to the Buddha and bowed, stood up and then prostrated ourselves three times. I managed to trip on my robe when I stood up from my second prostration. After I had regained more composure, it took me a while to locate the correct line in the prayer book; I had to ask Shan Ren for help. The monks were chanting. We implored 'the most heroic, mightiest and most compassionate one', the Buddha, to help us eliminate our topsy-turvy thoughts and attain enlightenment as soon as possible. Then I found myself reading words that I thought I knew but which did not mean anything at all to me. It was a magic mantra, but what was the magic and what was it supposed to do for the monks? The book did not say. Soon I was totally lost, with no idea which pages the monks were reading from, let alone their meaning. They went on for over thirty minutes before they stopped to regain breath.

Then they began the *Heart Sutra*. This was familiar, and I quickly found the right page again. But I was too confused to concentrate. It was a bad start; it felt like my first day at school.

The monks raised their voices a notch and tilted their heads upwards. They chanted in a resonant drone issuing from the depth of their bodies and, perhaps, hearts. It was monotonous, lulling, hypnotic. The beauty of their chanting reached me at last and dissolved my confusion, surrounding me with calmness, bringing my wandering mind back to holy thoughts. I was not religious, I did not believe chanting some mystic mantras would bring me luck, reduce my sins, avert calamities, protect me from evil spirits and deliver me to the Western Paradise, but I could still appreciate their beauty and how they managed to bring out a yearning deep inside me – perhaps it was the nearest I could come to a spiritual experience. I watched the monks. Their eyes were shut. They looked as if they were expecting the moment of awakening to the truth – everything is indeed empty and there is nothing to be attained by attachment, hatred and delusion. If the illumination did not come, the recitation would no doubt serve them well as they went about their daily life, which was fraught with chores, choices, temptations and irritations, just like ours.

We went straight from the morning service to the dining hall. We bowed to the statue of the Amitabha Buddha facing the entrance and took our bowls and chopsticks from a fridge-like machine where they were kept away from clouds of flies. We sat down at a round table and a woman filled our bowls with millet porridge and fried aubergines. After a short prayer, the serious business of eating began: the monks attacked their food with the same intensity as they recited the *Heart Sutra*. Nobody talked and when they wanted another helping, they made some mysterious signs with their chopsticks. I could not figure out which sign meant what. Luckily I did not have to ask for more: I was struggling to keep up with the rest of the congregation. When they put down their bowls and said another prayer, I just managed to swallow my last mouthful of porridge without choking. If I did not want to starve, I would have to learn a new language.

Shan Ren followed me out. 'You don't know how to ask for more food, do you? I forget to tell you yesterday.' She looked serene and peaceful, her voice gentle and mellow. She had very smooth, delicate hands, as I noticed when she was turning over the pages of the prayer book. She was in her sixties, or perhaps older. The beige wool jacket she wore was simple but well made. She was different from the other devotees in the monastery, more self-possessed, more serious, more contemplative.

She taught me the chopstick sign language – if I wanted more solid food, I should hold the chopsticks upright in the bowl as if they could stand up in the porridge; if I wanted more liquid I should use a scooping motion; if I did not want any more I should push the bowl to the edge of the table and put the chopsticks down beside it, not on top, as you would normally.

I told her what really puzzled me was the way the monks ate. 'Why do they eat so fast? Aren't they worried about indigestion?' I asked.

She smiled, pointed to a passage in my prayer book which described five contemplations for meal times: 'Take food according to how much merit you have earned; consider whether you really deserve what you are eating; keep your mind pure, avoiding greed in particular; food is medicine for the body; and you eat to achieve enlightenment.' 'You are not supposed to linger over your meal as if you were interested in how it tastes,' she said. 'You just bolt it down. Keep your mind on higher things. It's a kind of meditation.'

Before she went off, she said, 'I hope I didn't frighten you this morning. I did knock on your door. You were too sleepy. You must feel like going back to bed now, poor girl. But you will get used to it in a day or two.'

I went back to my cell in the monks' quarters. It was minimal: a hard bed, a stool, a table with a candle on it in case of electricity failure, and a plastic washbasin. It was perhaps not unlike a monk's cell in mediaeval China. But the little it contained was revealed for all the world to see – the two big windows at the front and back had no curtains. I felt a bit uneasy, both for the monks living opposite me and for myself. It had not bothered me last night: I slept with my clothes on. But now I wanted to lie down for a few minutes: getting up at four o'clock in the morning was too much; I could hardly think straight. But to be seen sleeping in on my first day in the monastery was not a good idea. I had to talk to Shan Ren about it.

I decided to struggle to keep awake. I knocked on the abbot's door – I wanted to find out the order of the day and what I was supposed to do. He was in his thirties, with a serious look that made him seem much older than he was. He was very helpful when I had registered with him, as was required of all visitors to the monastery. He inquired how I had managed so far and I told him of my inauspicious start. Then I asked him what all the mantras in the morning service actually meant. I knew they were supposed to protect the monks and their monasteries, and also the country and all sentient beings. But what did the words mean, especially the longest one, which seemed to go on for ever?

He asked if I knew the story of the Sitatapatrosnisa Dharani, or Lengyan Zhou – its name in the prayer book. Obviously I did not. He explained that it came from a tale about Ananda, the Buddha's favourite disciple: he was out begging, and asked a young woman in the street for a jar of water. She fell instantly in love and begged her mother to use her magic powers and cast a spell on Ananda. She was just about to embrace him when Wenshu, the Bodhisattva of Wisdom, arrived, sent by the Buddha who had divined that Ananda was in danger of breaking his vow. The Bodhisattva brought him into the presence of the Buddha. Ananda was ashamed and in tears: 'How did it happen? I've been listening to you preaching all these years. How could I have been carried away so easily?'

The Buddha told Ananda that listening was one thing but to understand was another. Craving was our poison, which must be removed. If he could achieve that, he could do anything. Then he taught Ananda the Lengyan Sutra, one of the most comprehensive sutras in the Chinese Buddhist canon, analysing in great detail how the mind works, the different paths to enlightenment and the obstacles on the way. At the end of the sutra is the spell that is supposed to protect one from all evils, sexual desire included. The sutra is so important that it is said that when it is gone, Buddhism will disappear too.

'Getting rid of sexual desire,' the abbot explained in his slow, deliberate voice, 'is the first commandment for a Mahayana Buddhist monk. We think it is difficult to achieve because it is basic to human nature. But we must succeed. Failing in this, the Buddha said, was like trying to make rice out of sand; one will never become enlightened.' That was what they had been chanting for twenty-five minutes. Most of the monks were young, in the prime of life. Sexual desire was thought to be at its height in the early-morning hours. If the weak could not overcome it by inner strength, the long recital would exhaust them and leave them at peace.

Was it the same in Xuanzang's time? I asked.

'The prohibition must have been the same. But they didn't resort to these long recitations of the mantras. That and the morning and evening services came much later, in the thirteenth century. We know Xuanzang had no problem – didn't he refuse the hand of the beautiful princess? But we have to work hard to follow the Buddha's advice and master our bodies,' the abbot said. 'Meditation also helps,' he added, pointing to three posters of a human skeleton on his walls, two in colour and one in black-and-white. 'When you think about it, we are just a pile of bones, really.'

I was glad to have this long answer to my first question; clearly everything in the monastery had a meaning and a purpose, all designed to help the monks in their quest for enlightenment – I just had to learn what they were. My next question was how I should spend my days. 'Really you should be working to earn your keep. "No work, no food" is the usual rule. In India or Thailand the monks beg for alms; but in China from the very beginning the emperors thought it was a disgrace, so monks must work to ensure their survival. But we don't have land here any more, just a tiny vegetable plot – and a layman looks after that.' I asked whether I could help in the kitchen. He said there were already two women doing that. 'You told me yesterday you had come to find out about the life of the monks. Concentrate on that. We are a tiny monastery, struggling just to keep going as a religious sanctuary. There are no great teachers here. I hope you won't be disappointed. But perhaps you will learn what you need by living among us.' As I got up to go, he said, 'You should spend time with Shan Ren, and the old abbot. They are good people. I think you can learn something from them.'

I took the abbot's advice and went to look for the former abbot, who was taking a stroll in the orchard filled with apricot trees. A thin, robust man in his eighties, he had helped to build the Thunderbolt Monastery from scratch. 'I went from village to village, begging for donations. Money, trees from their back yards, a sack of flour, bricks, offers of free labour – nothing was too small. I don't know what possessed me. Looking back, I can't believe I have done it, and the cuttings we planted in the desert have grown into a little forest,' he said, pointing to the rows of apricot trees.

He turned to the Dunhuang Research Academy for help to decorate the monastery. They told him they had far more important work to do. He had no money to commission painters nor did he have rich and powerful donors as in the old days. But he dreamed of a monastery covered with murals like the Mogao Caves. 'It is the best way to teach people about the Dharma. It is so direct, so vivid and so moving,' he said. He first visited the caves with his parents when he was thirteen and he could never forget the shock: 'It was like entering paradise.' He found refuge in the caves again during the 1930s and the 1940s, hiding himself from conscription. Poverty and the necessity of supporting a big family forced him to seek a livelihood away from Dunhuang, but when he finally retired in 1981 at the age of sixty-three, he decided to become a monk, realizing his childhood dream. There was no monastery in Dunhuang at the time – all had been destroyed during the Cultural Revolution. His mission was to build one and decorate it with murals. Two painters were so moved by him that they offered to help. One spent two years copying the Western and Eastern Paradises from the Mogao Caves, charging him only for the materials. They hang on the two side walls of the shrine hall. In my confusion in the morning service, my mind wandered a lot to them; for a while I even thought I was in the caves. The other painter completed the murals for the Bodhisattva temples and the front walls of the shrine hall, and then became a monk himself.

Having learned the story of the murals, I could not stop looking at them during the evening service. I was captivated; they were so beautiful you could hardly distinguish them from the originals. They are also the theme of the evening prayers: how to reach the Western Paradise and become enlightened through divine intervention, granted in response to prayer. First is the Amitabha Sutra, a detailed description of the wonders of the Western Paradise. Then we repent our sins, repeat our vow of belief in the Buddha, the Dharma and the Sangha, and pledge our sincere wish for enlightenment. We implore the Buddhas and Bodhisattvas to take pity on us. Miraculous mantras, magic spells and the Heart Sutra are also invoked to help us along the way. Out of compassion, we pray not only for ourselves but for everyone, including those imprisoned in hell who are supposed to reach paradise through merit transferred from the monks, and by the mercy of the compassionate Bodhisattvas. As a last reminder of the transience of the world, we recite an admonition from the Bodhisattva of Benevolence: 'The day is done, and life dwindles accordingly. Like fish without water, what joy is there? Endeavour to make good progress, as if fighting a fire burning on one's own head. Remember the impermanence of all things and do not slacken off.'

I went through the motions of the ceremony. But my mind kept wandering off, to the Mogao Caves, to Grandmother who had set her mind on the Western Paradise, and even to the rituals that every Chinese had to go through during the Cultural Revolution – bowing to Chairman Mao every morning and repenting to him every evening, praising him as our saviour, reciting slogans and passages from his Little Red Book, pledging our commitment to the goal of Communism, searching our souls in self-criticism, and repeating 'May our great leader Chairman Mao live in good health for ten thousand years and beyond!' We had to keep a diary to be read out in class recording our transgressions. One entry from my third year in primary school read: 'Our great leader, teacher and helmsman Chairman Mao said that unity was paramount: without it, there would not have been the victory of the Communist Party. But I fought with my brother today over a very trivial matter. If I could not even unite with him, how could I do so with all the people in the motherland? If people do not unite, how are we going to realize the goal of Communism, the paradise on earth? Must read more of Chairman Mao's works, listen to him more attentively, and be his good child.'

For many Chinese Buddhists like Grandmother, rebirth in the Western Paradise is the core of belief, perhaps more than enlightenment, which is too much hard work, often requiring numerous rebirths – that is if you can achieve it at all. The Lotus Sutra even says that true Dharma is beyond understanding and only the Buddha knows all. But the faithful should not despair because there is a vast pantheon of Bodhisattvas ready to give anyone a helping hand. Amitabha, the Buddha of Infinite Light, created the Western Paradise as a way-station for those who proceed to nirvana. Anyone can rest there, even murderers, as long as they repeat their wish to enter it ten times.

I used to have the impression that the Western Paradise was an end in itself, not a means to reach the final goal of nirvana. It was on Grandmother's lips all the time; I never heard her mentioning nirvana at all. Besides, these way-stations as described on the murals were so delightful, why should the faithful bother to strive for nirvana at all, especially as many are not exactly sure what it is? Grandmother's paradise also reminded me of the promise of the Communist utopia where we were told we would have everything we desired. The Communist utopia did not work. For me, be it a Buddhist or a Communist one, an eternal heaven, which provides all forms of pleasures desired by men and women and where they enjoy every happiness is inconceivable. I cannot imagine that such a place could exist, except in our hearts.

'You sound like a Zen Buddhist,' Shan Ren said when I told her my doubts about the Western Paradise. We were taking a walk in the courtyard after dinner. 'You know what the Sixth Patriarch of Zen says about the Western Paradise?' I shook my head. 'Deluded people do not know that the Pure Land is within themselves. They recite the Buddha's name and look for rebirth in the Western Paradise. But if they do not rid the mind of evil thoughts, what Buddha will welcome them? The wise purify their own minds. A pure mind *is* the Western Paradise.'

I had always liked Zen poetry, Zen gardens, the purity and simplicity that Zen seems to stand for. But I associated Zen Buddhism with the mind-boggling *koans*, or public cases, which were supposed to break conventional mindsets and make you see your true nature. Many of them did not make any sense to me. I said as much to Shan Ren. She smiled. 'You have no problem understanding the Zen Paradise, do you? You will like the Sixth Patriarch's Sutra. It's very much about the cultivation of the mind.'

She was right. The more I learned about Zen Buddhism, the more appealing I found it. There is no belief in an intervening deity, no Amitabha. It is concerned with what one can do oneself: gaining insight into how things really are, achieving inner freedom and abandoning attachment to worldly pleasures. It does not rely on performing rituals or on books, but calls for self-discipline and constant meditation. I suppose it was unrealistic to expect that someone like Grandmother could adopt it. She needed the simpler comforts of the Pure Land. I think I will find it difficult myself but it is the sort of direction I would want to take.

But I was intrigued by Shan Ren. She was very knowledgeable about Buddhism and was obviously well educated. How did she become a Buddhist? After all, she belonged to my parents' generation, who were usually either devout Communists or total atheists. But in a monastery you do not ask people about their past, certainly not on the first day. I was half-dead as well. If I wanted to do better the next day, I had better catch up on my sleep. So I said goodnight to Shan Ren. 'You've done well to stay up this long,' she said. 'Let me get you some hot water and you go to your room.'

She brought me a thermos full of hot water. I poured myself a cup. But then I decided not to drink it: the toilet was a hole in the ground in a shed at the far corner of the monastery, near the orchard, with no lights, and I wanted to minimize my visits there. I brushed my teeth with the water, had a quick wash, and lay down, with my clothes on. I had forgotten about the curtains. I would have to ask for them tomorrow. Within seconds, I was asleep.

I soon fell into the routine life of the monastery: two services; three meals; a little bit of work in the morning, sharing Shan Ren's tasks dusting and cleaning the shrine hall and watering flowers and plants; taking a siesta; learning about Buddhism from the old and young abbots, and from simply being in the monastery. The abbot said that in Xuanzang's time, monks would spend more hours on learning the sutras and meditating and less on the ceremonies, otherwise monastic life then and now was not very different. It seemed to suit me. I liked the structured days. Nothing was rushed, except for taking food. The monks were cheerful, gentle and considerate. I even began to enjoy the impenetrable mantras and their chanting. I learned so much every day about Buddhism and its history. I found out why my *haiqing* is so big: it is supposed to be like the shape of a giant wave, absorbing a sea of wisdom. I discovered why monks had to work even if they had enough donations to live on: the self-reliance of the Zen monks ensured their survival in the mountains after many other sects perished in the most deadly persecutions of Buddhism in 845 A D. I began to see how much Buddhism has enriched our lives and opened us to sympathy and compassion. Its promise of salvation for everybody has given countless people hope; its emphasis on devotion, self-restraint and tolerance has helped us to live with each other; its rituals and festivities have over the centuries provided relief for, and given colour to, an existence that was often grey and humdrum.

In return for all the things I had learned, I was glad I could be of some use to others: on two occasions I was actually useful making up the numbers for the ceremonies for the dead. In Buddhism, everyone becomes a *preta*, literally a departed person, after death and they will remain in the intermediate state until the funeral rites are completed. Then depending on one's karma, the reincarnation may be as gods, humans again, animals or creatures in hell where King Yama hands out appropriate punishments. Unlike those in Dante's *Inferno*, King Yama's damned are not beyond redemption. *Pretas* can be helped: by reciting penances, the monks can draw on the inexhaustible store of merit of Buddhas and Bodhisattvas and their own good karma to cancel out the bad karma of the dead.

I prayed, bowed, prostrated, chanted sutras and walked around the shrine hall twenty times invoking the name of Amitabha Buddha a thousand times. I was not sure, however, that my participation in the ceremony contributed anything to 'delivering the dead' to a good destination. My mind was full of impure thoughts. It looked to me as though rebirth was not simply a matter of karma. If monks could transfer their merit to the dead, where was the incentive for people to lead a good life and be virtuous? Whatever they did, they would be saved in the end. I could not figure out the logic of this.

But the real problem I had in the monastery was the daily meditation in the evening. I had no difficulty sitting with my legs crossed in the lotus position for an hour but I found it extremely hard to concentrate. My thoughts darted about like butterflies, coming and going as they pleased. Memories from my past intertwined effortlessly with impressions from the present: the beatific smile of the Buddha, the subtle blue of the sky, a camel in the desert, a friend from work, my father on his hospital bed, my grandmother praying in the dark – they arrived unbidden from some deep recess, as if trying to defeat the very clarity I wanted to achieve. These subterranean thoughts may have a purpose that we do not understand, as our dreams have, but what is certain is that they distract us from total concentration.

The poster on the door of the meditation hall reminded me that I was supposed to be contemplating who the Buddha was. Was he a god, as my grandmother would have me believe? Was he our very being but hidden from us by our worldly desires and ignorance? Was he the wind that made a banner ripple in the air? Or was he simply nothingness, the void? Meditation is an exercise that focuses the mind on an object or an idea. When the sea is rough and throws up the sediments at the bottom, the water becomes murky and we cannot see clearly. The same is true of the mind. The stream of thoughts and associations clouds our perceptions and prevents us from seeing the object or the idea as it really is. Through learning to meditate, a process as long and painful as psychoanalysis, the restless stream of one's consciousness is brought under control. A mind with enough training can perform extraordinary feats, just like a ballet dancer, whose leaps seem astonishing to the untrained. Totally emptying the mind of distracting thoughts would be just one of them. Ultimately one can reach another realm; this is what the monks aspire to. Meditation is a very important part of their training; in fact it is one of the three pillars of Buddhism. It is how the Buddha became enlightened under the Bodhi Tree. Only by combining discipline, meditation and wisdom can a monk begin to hope for awakening. As for me, I have a long way to go to achieve this state, a virtual Himalaya to climb.

Quite a few times I found myself dozing off during meditation. I confessed as much to Shan Ren. She smiled. 'Do you know what people say about meditators?' she asked. 'Eat their fill, sit down, shut their eyes and go to sleep!' I laughed. 'But it does help you to think,' she added.

Did she find it difficult? What went through her mind? I asked her.

'It is not easy. Things you've done do come back to haunt you,' she said slowly. 'For our generation, so much harm has been done in the name of good causes, so many people wronged. Looking back, I cannot believe how we could have been so cruel, so merciless, so inhuman.'

I asked her about karma.

'It's tempting to believe it,' she said slowly, 'but it's too easy to say everything is fate. We did some mad things and we have to hold ourselves responsible. I am living with the consequences of my actions. I denounced and divorced my husband in the Cultural Revolution. How could I do such a thing? That's difficult to live with.' She paused for a long moment. 'But what is done is done,' she said gently, looking me in the eye. 'It's no use mulling over the past. Do good and no evil and live each day as it comes – that is my motto.'

I hope that she will find inner peace. I only wish my father had found some resource to enable him to cope with his bitterness. If he had, he might still be alive today.

As the days went by, I found out more and more about the monastery. It really was tiny, but still the abbot had a lot to cope with. The Chinese say if you plant a tree, the phoenix will come. The old abbot had built the monastery but it could not attract enough monks or enough money. Dunhuang is no longer the metropolitan city of the Silk Road. It is isolated and poor, in one of the most impoverished regions of China. The oasis used to boast seventeen monasteries and the Peerless Caves; one-fifth of its population were monks and nuns. Today the donations barely cover the basic bills of the Thunderbolt Monastery, the only one in Dunhuang. Life is austere. I had been eating the same food every day since I arrived: porridge, noodles, steamed buns and aubergines from the vegetable plot, or cabbage, the cheapest vegetable in the market. Shan Ren could not find me a curtain – the monks' had been donated by their followers – so I had to do without. I did not have a shower for five days. There was only enough hot water to make tea – the monks washed themselves with cold. It was no surprise that few wanted to come here. If they went to the better-off regions, the monasteries would have far more creature comforts.

The monastery seemed to have only three resident monks – the abbot, the retired abbot and a young monk. Fortunately there were three itinerant monks while I was there, and another waiting to be ordained. Otherwise I could not imagine how they would conduct morning and evening services, which require at least four people. One day the young monk came into the abbot's office with a form, asking for leave to study in another monastery near Shanghai.

'You're a commander without any soldiers now,' I joked with the abbot.

He laughed wearily. 'You know I was told that in Xuanzang's time the Thunderbolt Monastery was so popular they had to devise ingenious ways to keep people out, such as making the applicants memorize an entire sutra of tens of thousands of words. We cannot make any demands now.' I asked him what he would do if the itinerant monks left. 'That has happened before. I had to do a one-man show; the show must go on!' he said resolutely.

The Thunderbolt Monastery is not a spiritual haven with great teachers ready to impart wisdom and truth. When I asked the young abbot about Yogacara, he said, 'I'd be glad if you could tell me what it means.' But as Zen Buddhists say, you can find Buddha nature anywhere. I certainly had a most memorable experience at lunch one day. As usual I took my seat next to Shan Ren. The lunch that day was overcooked noodles with a few cabbage leaves on top. For some curious reason they put soda in it, so much that I felt sick after the first mouthful. But to leave anything uneaten was not an option. I had been told off at breakfast for leaving two grains of rice in my bowl. I struggled on, morsel by morsel, feeling as if I was going to throw up at any minute. I looked desperately at Shan Ren, pointing my chopsticks at the bowl and my mouth. She nodded. Yes, I'd better not leave anything behind. But there was no way I could finish it, so I pushed my bowl to the edge of the table with my chopsticks next to it, indicating my lunch was over. Shan Ren, who had already finished, reached out, took my bowl and poured my leftovers down her throat. She wiped her mouth, said a short prayer and then we stood up to go.

Shan Ren's gesture preoccupied me. The truth was, I was shocked at her finishing my meal. When I was young, my brother and I sometimes left food in our bowls in protest – not often, because there was never enough to eat, but when for example we had to eat noodles made of sweet potato flour for five days in a row. My brother could get away with it but my father would insist that I finish mine. I would play with my food until he left the table. By then the food in my bowl was cold and watery. It was always my grandmother who ate it. She was my grandmother after all. But Shan Ren had no idea whether I had some disease. Perhaps she even saw me spit my last mouthful of noodles back into the bowl. What made her do it?

Was Shan Ren simply following the example of the ever-compassionate Bodhisattvas who love all beings as a mother loves her children? Her love is boundless: she gives and expects nothing in return. The happiness of the child is hers and so are the tears, pains and sorrows. For Bodhisattvas, other and self are identical. A selfless life, like that of the Bodhisattva, said the Buddha, would lead men and women to nirvana. In Mahayana Buddhism, there are supposed to be tens of thousands of Bodhisattvas taking care of the faithful, and the Chinese are particularly fond of four: Dizang, the Bodhisattva who vows to save all beings from hell; Puxian, the Bodhisattva of Universal Worth on his white elephant, which stands for weightiness, thoroughness and perfection in propagation; Wenshu, the Bodhisattva of Wisdom, without whose guidance enlightenment is impossible; and of course, Guanyin, the Bodhisattva of Compassion who listens to and understands all our sufferings. You find them in all the temples and monasteries – the four most beautiful mountains in China are dedicated to them as their earthly abodes.

When I looked at the murals or read the stories of the miraculous Bodhisattvas, I used to think of them as mere fantasies, like Grandmother's paradise. But Shan Ren had made me see them in a different light: the scenes of paradise and the compassion of the Bodhisattvas have not only comforted countless followers but also instilled in them the very virtues the Bodhisattvas possess. Xuanzang was the best example. He prayed to them, he was guided by them, and above all, he aspired to become one. His determination to reach the true Buddhism at whatever cost, his compassionate wish to bring it back for the faithful in China, his calm presence that soothed even the most vicious enemies, his equilibrium that made him indifferent to the flattery of kings and worldly fame, his skilful ways that won him the hearts of beggars and emperors alike and his wisdom that illuminated others – he is, in the eyes of many Buddhists, a Bodhisattva, who devoted his life to the service of others.

In the dim light of the meditation hall, the image of the Buddha on the altar seemed to blur and turn into Xuanzang, the old abbot, Shan Ren or my grandmother – without all the trappings and offerings but somehow each a holy figure. I felt I had come to a certain realization. I could not be a believer like my grandmother, with total faith in divine intervention and final deliverance from the pain and suffering of life. But I had come to understand the core of the Bodhisattva way, as they had showed me. To try to live it was to become a Buddhist.

TWELVE

Journey's End

O N T H E E I G H T H D A Y of the first month of 645, Red
Bird Street in Chang'an was a sea of people. 'All the
monasteries vie with one another in preparing their best
banners, tapestries, umbrellas, precious tables and palanquins.
They send monks and nuns in their ceremonial robes for the
occasion,' Hui Li tells us proudly. The lavish preparations in
the capital's thoroughfare caught people's attention, and the
news spread by word of mouth: Xuanzang, the intrepid monk
who had travelled to India, was coming back after eighteen
years. Everyone wanted to set eyes on him.

Fearing they might crush one another in their eagerness to
greet him, the authorities forbade the crowds to move. Standing still, they chanted prayers, burned incense, scattered
flowers, blew conches, clashed cymbals and broke out again
and again into cries of wonder and delight. Slowly the grand
procession went past them, carrying Xuanzang's collection of
657 books, relics of the Buddha, and seven gold, silver and
sandalwood images. 'It is the most splendid event since the
death of the Buddha,' Hui Li exclaimed.

Red Bird Street in those days was a grand boulevard 150
metres wide. Today it has shrunk from its river-like breadth

to a mere two traffic lanes, flanked by characterless office buildings and shabby restaurants, and crammed in at the end, a makeshift market selling cheap housewares. The only reminder of its former glory is the Gate of the Red Bird itself, an impressive arch presiding anachronistically over the rush hour flow of cars, buses and bicycles. This big arch, according to my guidebook, is in fact only one of four that made up the original gateway with an even bigger fifth one in the centre. Standing there, honked at by cars, looking up at the old characters for 'Red Bird Gate' above the arch, I tried to put myself in Xuanzang's frame of mind as he came through the gate and was confronted by the huge crowds.

He was probably taken aback. He did not expect the court to organize such a sumptuous welcome for him – there could not have been a greater contrast with his hurried, furtive departure eighteen years before. The emperor was away in the eastern capital Luoyang, preparing for a major campaign against Korea. But he had deputed none other than his prime minister to welcome this distinguished monk, whose reputation had grown and grown, and who might be invaluable to the realization of his grandest ambition yet. Besides, it would be a wonderful occasion to gratify his subjects, most of them devout Buddhists.

Xuanzang rode in on his white horse. He waved to the crowd, amid deafening cheers, and then looked pointedly at the officials who had made the lavish arrangements. He knew they were only there because the emperor had ordered them to attend, and deep down they were lukewarm about Buddhism. The emperor's advisor in these matters, the Confucian scholar Fu Yi, was positively anti-Buddhist. He had made his views crystal clear in his famous memorandum when Taizong came to the throne eighteen years ago: 'The doctrine of the

Buddha is full of extravagances and absurdities. The fidelity of subjects to their prince and filial piety are duties that Buddhism does not recognize. Its disciples pass their life in idleness, making no effort whatever ... By their vain dreams they induce simple souls to pursue an illusory felicity, and inspire them with scorn for our laws and for the wise teaching of the ancients.' Fu Yi proposed that the state should force monks and nuns to marry; they would contribute to the general good by bearing children and providing manpower for the army.

Taizong did not go that far, but he had another reason for not endorsing Buddhism. 'The Emperor Liang Wuti,' he remarked one day, 'preached Buddhism so successfully to his officers that they were unable to mount their horses to defend him against the rebels. Such facts speak volumes to one who is able to interpret them!' He also believed that the imperial family was descended from Li Er, the legendary founder of Daoism, because they shared the surname Li. 'One is bound to honour one's ancestors and kindred,' he said, 'they are the roots of life. That is why I have to give the Daoists precedence.' A monk who dared to challenge this fanciful pedigree was whipped at court and then exiled; the rest kept a grudging silence.

Nevertheless, his splendid reception gave Xuanzang a slim hope that Taizong could be persuaded to change his attitude, and even to support him in translating and propagating the sutras. When he was taken to the imperial monastery after the parade and invited to stay, he was in no mood to linger. He had a brief rest, barely enough time, as the Chinese say, to wash off the dust and grime of his journey, and set off again to see the emperor in Luoyang, seven hundred miles away.

*   *   *

Taizong was delighted when Xuanzang was ushered into the throne room. He had not expected the monk to come so soon. For Xuanzang it was something of a surprise to be granted an audience so quickly. He had been told the emperor was preoccupied with planning a military campaign, so he expected a long wait and a short meeting. When he was brought before Taizong, the man he had disobeyed eighteen years earlier, he was a little nervous, despite having been the guest of honour in so many royal courts.

The emperor put him at ease immediately. 'Why did you leave without letting me know?' he greeted him, as if asking an old friend.

'I know that I was guilty of great presumption, and am ashamed and frightened,' Xuanzang replied.

'I am very glad that you went; you certainly did nothing to be ashamed of,' Taizong told him. 'But when I think of the huge distance you covered, all the mountains and rivers that lay between, and the differences of customs and ideas, what surprises me is that you managed to get there.'

'I have heard that it is not far to reach the Heavenly Lake for those who can ride on a speedy wind, and it is not difficult to cross a stormy river, if one sails in a dragon-boat. Since Your Majesty ascended the throne, your virtue and benevolence have prevailed in all areas, with the wind of morality blowing to the hot countries in the south and your political influence reaching as far as beyond the Pamirs. That is why when the princes and chiefs of the barbarian tribes perceive a bird arriving from the east, borne on the wings of the clouds, they imagine that it has come from your empire, and greet it with respect. Xuanzang, whom the Celestial Power protected, could likewise come and go without difficulty.'

Xuanzang of course knew he had never had any support

from the emperor until now. These were flowery words, or skilful means as the Buddhists would say, but this was how it had to be done. His eighteen-year journey and everything he had undertaken would not bear fruit unless he could persuade the emperor to support him. He wanted others to see the light as he had done. On his own he could not do even a fraction of the work. He needed a large team to translate, to check, to polish – and to transcribe: printing was still two hundred years in the future. His great predecessor Kumarajiva had hundreds of monks assisting him – prior to Xuanzang he had translated more sutras than anyone else, under the patronage of an enthusiastic ruler, Yaoxing. Xuanzang just had to find a way to convince Taizong to help him.

Accustomed to flattery as he was, Taizong was still susceptible. His ego was caressed by Xuanzang's praise. He looked at the monk again, only one year younger than himself, softly spoken, quiet of demeanour, but breathing dignity, strength and purposefulness. He spoke of his calamities and finest hours in equally dispassionate tones, as if they had happened to someone else. But beneath the calm he could see there was an iron determination – this was a man who had risked death by defying his wishes, who had braved incredible dangers in unknown lands, who had completed a gigantic task that took eighteen years to fulfil and who had spread the influence of the Tang dynasty where his armies could not reach – and all of these on his own. This was no ordinary monk; this was a man of wisdom and accomplishment. Taizong began to feel a genuine admiration for him.

Just then officials came in to remind the emperor of his next appointment. But Taizong was engrossed in the conversation and wanted to find out more about Xuanzang's travels. He waved his hand impatiently and sent them away. The meeting, scheduled for only a few minutes, went on for a whole day.

What was the weather like? Were the roads to the West difficult? What did the barbarians eat and what languages did they speak? What did their countries produce? How different were they from the Chinese? Were the peoples happy and were the rulers benevolent? Taizong interrogated him about the smallest details of the countries he had passed through.

The emperor had his reasons, which soon became clear to Xuanzang. He was no longer the young prince struggling to establish his authority after usurping the throne. The country was firmly in his grip; the old frontier town of Dunhuang had been replaced by a new one, Turfan. King Qu Wentai, who had given Xuanzang so much help, died of shock when the Chinese army took his oasis kingdom. Now the emperor's ambition was to build the greatest empire China had ever seen, extending his influence over the vast territory of the Eurasian steppes. Nobody knew the Western Region as well as this monk; once in his service Xuanzang would be the perfect man to help him achieve his grand design. He asked Xuanzang then and there to join his government.

Xuanzang knew that Taizong loved to use talented people, no matter what their origins were. Since he had returned, he had heard nothing but praise for the emperor and stories of his enlightened rule through a group of capable, dedicated and diligent ministers. He had met most of them in Chang'an and Luoyang, and the one who impressed him most was Wei Zheng, Taizong's chief advisor, who exemplified, more than anyone else, Taizong's penchant for spotting talent. Originally the head of staff to the crown prince, Wei saw his indecisive master beheaded by Taizong. When he was questioned by the new emperor, he had only this to say: 'If the heir apparent had listened to my advice long ago to get rid of you, he would have been spared his fate.' Everyone was shocked by his impudence and thought he would lose his head too. To their amazement, Taizong asked Wei if he would consider working for him, advising him about the rights and wrongs of his policies. Such humility was rare for an emperor, as the Chinese say, 'as difficult to find as the feather of the phoenix or the horn of the unicorn'.

It dawned on Xuanzang why he had been given such a warm welcome, and he was conscious that Taizong did not ask him a single question on Buddhism throughout their conversation. The emperor's real interest was in the Western Region. But Xuanzang had no intention to serve in the court – he had renounced it all; he was trying to transcend such things. How could he come back to them, even for the sake of fulfilling his mission? He declined, but with his usual eloquence.

Having chosen the monastic life from infancy, and having embraced with ardour the Law of Buddha, Xuanzang has never learned the doctrine of Confucius which is the heart of the administration. If he were to relinquish the principles of the Buddha in order to follow the world, he would be like a vessel in full sail, leaving the sea to travel on solid ground; it could not possibly succeed, it would be shattered and destroyed.

Taizong was dismayed by Xuanzang's refusal. Just when he was about to lose his temper, his brother-in-law intervened on Xuanzang's behalf. If he could write down what he had seen and heard on his journey, the emperor would have the wealth of his information at his disposal. Xuanzang was relieved when Taizong reluctantly agreed.

So they made their agreement. Xuanzang would write the record of his journey, and Taizong would support his translation work. Xuanzang returned to Chang'an this time with his greatest concern removed from his mind. He could take in the tremendous changes in the capital since he had left it, the great achievements in Taizong's era.

His first impression must have been of the cosmopolitan character of the capital and the number of foreigners living there – well over a quarter of a million. 'From ancient times, we have always loved ourselves too much and despised foreigners,' Taizong declared to his officials. 'But I love the two equally.' He welcomed them with open arms, and an open door. Some suspected that he had barbarian blood in him. The truth may be simpler. There is a Chinese saying, the ocean is vast because it has taken in all the rivers; Taizong was confident that foreign influence would only make Chinese culture more splendid.

The richness and diversity of this time is hard to discern today. The carefully laid-out city of old is gone, replaced by many higgledy-piggledy lanes, all enclosed by the city wall. They are quite atmospheric, though: the traditional houses have been turned into souvenir and antique shops, restaurants and teahouses, resembling a film set – all the more so because of the shopkeepers themselves, mostly old men, dressed in traditional Chinese jackets or Mao suits, who sit on stools, peering through their black-rimmed glasses at newspapers that seem to take them the whole day to read.

Fortunately, Xian has the largest number of historians of the Tang dynasty, and I found a professor from my old university who was teaching here. He brought with him Li, a young woman in the last year of her master's degree, writing on the food and social life of the Tang. We met in a restaurant that specialized in reproducing Tang cuisine. For three hours, from the foreign origins of the food on our table to their influence on Chinese tastes, from the elaborate ways of their preparation to their medicinal value, I was given a tour of Tang culinary culture with seemingly endless courses, some of whose authenticity I doubted – turtle soup in the Tang dynasty? I did not touch it. I could not help thinking of the Buddhist custom of putting baby turtles into temple ponds as a symbol of respect for life. But I was yearning for more information about the era in which Xuanzang lived. 'This is an appetizer,' the professor said to me. 'The real feast is in the museum.'

Li and I went next day to the history museum near the Big Wild Goose Pagoda. It is one of the biggest in China, with an unrivalled collection of treasures from the Qin, Han and Tang, the three main Chinese dynasties, all of which had their capitals in and around Xian in the first millennium. I saw terracotta soldiers, gilded dragons, an elaborate silver dinner service from Persia, a Roman glass vase, jade belts from Khotan, figurines of a whole chamber orchestra from Central Asia and glazed ceramic camels with their riders, perhaps fifteen of them in a string, like the old caravans. They were all from the tombs of the rich and powerful: colourful reminders of the exotic life they were so fond of and wanted to take with them into the afterlife. I said to Li that I could just begin to imagine the cosmopolitan lifestyle of the Tang.

'Wait till you see what Xuanzang saw with his own eyes,' Li enthused. 'This will really make your trip worthwhile. You're very lucky. The professor doesn't arrange it for most people.' We went down into the vault built to house the great Tang dynasty murals. I was hit by the chill, as if it were really a tomb. The vault was kept below freezing – but within seconds I forgot how cold it was. At the touch of a button, the first mural slid out on a rail, framed in aluminium and covered by a crimson velvet curtain.

The curtain was drawn back and my jaw fell. There was a group of men, galloping on horseback, playing polo in a field. The horses ran so fast their manes streamed out in the wind. The men raised their sticks high, their eyes fixed on the polo ball. The painting was over three metres long and part of a triptych. Its sheer size as well as the motion it depicted exuded a powerful sense of urgency and movement.

'You must be familiar with the sport. I've heard it is very popular in England,' Li said.

'The Queen's son and grandsons love it.' That's all I knew about it.

'This mural is from the tomb of Prince Zhanghuai, one of Taizong's grandsons.'

The polo players slid back into darkness, replaced by another panel. This one showed the imperial honour guard mounted on horseback, carrying red and black banners; others walked on foot, each one bearing a sword and a long feather. The mural is huge, the colours so alive, each face so clearly painted, the figures so present – you feel you are right there, witnessing what the emperor wanted you to see: the full panoply of the Son of Heaven. The curator pressed another button. Another mural slid out, 'Receiving Foreign Guests'. The honour guard could have been for them; now Chinese protocol officers were working out how to arrange their stay. I noticed that the guests – one Japanese, one from the Byzantine empire, one with a fur hat and fur trousers from the north – looked somehow nervous, as if they were uncertain of the outcome of their visit to the powerful court.

'China was like America is today; Chang'an was like New York. Everyone wanted to be here,' Li explained. 'They came from every country in Asia, as far as Syria – envoys to make alliances, merchants seeking their fortune, missionaries hoping for conversions and adventurers looking for fame.' The Japanese were the most determined, sending shipload after shipload of students to learn every aspect of Tang culture; some of them even studied with Xuanzang. They had to wait up to six months to see the emperor, who would receive them with the most pompous formality, just as the mural showed, with the guard of honour displaying the grandeur and power of the Middle Kingdom in all its finery. The nervous envoys would bow humbly to him, and present their tributes, symbols of their submission: rice that was supposed to restore youthful vigour and prolong life, a bird that was immune to fire, rhinoceros horn that could keep the cold away, ice that would never melt, blood-sweating horses, lions or women of unmatched beauty. The emperor seldom granted their wishes, but they were always rewarded with honorary titles and gifts – often better than the ones they had brought. They returned home with a taste of Chang'an's opulence and sophistication, the memory of the fabulous Middle Kingdom and the glory of the Tang culture. Much of what they imbibed here is preserved to this day in Japan and Korea.

Many loved Chang'an too much to leave; they were welcome to serve the emperor. 'The imperial honour guards were almost entirely foreigners,' Li said, 'because Taizong thought them strong and handsome. But it wasn't just their looks. He would appoint anyone who was competent and would serve him loyally. You know in the Tang dynasty, when the court was in session, all officials had to wear their own national costumes, and half of those present in Taizong's court were foreigners. His generals were mostly Turks and Koreans; an Indian was put in charge of making the calendars; a Japanese monk became a minister responsible for canals; another Japanese held the post of chief librarian; the painters, bodyguards, horsemen, musicians, singers and dancers at the court – they were all foreigners.'

As I listened I thought how different was the time when I grew up. Whatever was foreign had been bourgeois and insidious. Anyone educated in the West was immediately suspected as a traitor. All letters from abroad were censored, and you could be in trouble just for receiving one. A pianist had his fingers broken because he refused to give up playing Mozart. The whole nation was a sea of four colours, blue for workers, green for soldiers, grey Mao suits for cadres and black for peasants. Cosmetics were unheard of; women all had the same hairstyle, designed by Mao's wife. For some reason, my mother was born with curly hair – Chinese hair was straight. In the early days of the revolution, when people were still relaxed and could enjoy life, women used to be envious of her. But as everything became more politicized, they began to shun her. Officials asked questions about her family, going back several generations. Could it be that she had foreign ancestor? Her home town was near the sea, where any number of ships used to dock and foreign merchants and sailors came ashore. My mother desperately tried to straighten her hair; she used industrial acid to rid herself of her dangerous curls. Even when she adopted Madam Mao's style, the curls were still there. In the end she cut them back so hard, she almost looked like a man. But at least she felt safe.

Foreign influence could corrupt us and lead to 'peaceful transformation' of China by the capitalist West, and the triumph of capitalism over socialism. The capitalist revival, we were warned, 'would throw us back into the deep abyss and burning fire and we would suffer again'. When I went to

Beijing University to read English literature in 1982, China had already opened up to the outside world. We had a big, bubbly woman called Jane teaching us colloquial English. I was eager for practice after class and Jane was keen to find out more about China. Every time I went to see her in her dormitory, a building specially reserved for foreigners, I had to fill in a form stating who I was and which department I belonged to. The guards at the entrance examined the form carefully and then asked more questions, as if I was not a student, but a secret spy on a rendezvous with a foreign agent; only when they were fully satisfied would they call Jane to come and collect me. It was such an ordeal, and I soon gave it up. The suspicion is still there. Even on this journey, when I talked to scholars and touched on a sensitive topic like religious freedom in China today, they would invariably say: 'Little Sun, you're a Chinese. We don't think of you as a foreigner, so we can tell you what we really think.'

Taking in the murals and what Li said, I thought back to what I learned about Taizong at school. He was a wise emperor, one of the five whom Mao admired, although he considered them all inferior to him. Taizong did not have his literary talents, Mao declared in a famous poem, which we all memorized. But in a feudal society, an enlightened emperor like him came only once in a thousand years, even if he was the overlord of the ruling classes which exploited the proletariat. I had not realized that under his reign we were so open, so confident, so assured of our own greatness and strength, and so welcoming – what was foreign was a benefit, not a threat. It was the source of the wonder of the Tang, never experienced before or since. It was the time that made Xuanzang. Now I understand why Chinese living abroad call themselves the People of the Tang – the Chinese word for Chinatown actually means 'Town of the Tang People'. Of China's five thousand years of history, they chose the Tang– and they are proud of it to this day.

The Tang's cosmopolitan character also found its expression in Chang'an's spiritual riches. Nestorian Christians, who were regarded as heretics by the orthodox church of Byzantium, were granted a hearing at court; Taizong was impressed, and issued an edict saying it was right that their teaching should spread freely, and ordered their church to be built in the capital. Zoroastrian believers who had fled their homes in Persia were allowed to practise their faith in their 'fire temples'. Daoist priests went around the city, performing rituals for the living and the dead. There were Buddhist temples too, and the monasteries were filled with foreign as well as Chinese monks. Churches, temples, monasteries, pagodas and even one or two synagogues – all religions of the Silk Road found a place in Chang'an. Xuanzang respected other religions, but there had always been competition for the emperor's favour between Buddhists and Daoists. From historical precedent, he was well aware of the consequences of this preference, and having gained Taizong's support for his translation project, he hoped he would persuade him to show more interest in Buddhism, and even to propagate it throughout the empire.

But first Xuanzang had to assemble his team. Two dozen monks were selected from all over China, including Hui Li, whose task was to see that the translations were smooth and easy to understand. They were installed in the Monastery of the Great Happiness, built by Taizong for his late mother. The daily routine Xuanzang set in motion was a gruelling one. He would be up at two o'clock in the morning, meditating and praying, and reading through the Sanskrit text to be translated that day, thinking over each word and phrase. When the team was ready, he would dictate his translations to them. While they worked on them, checking with the originals and making sure they read smoothly in Chinese, he would either be giving talks, twice a day, on the new scriptures and treatises, or answering questions from monks from all over the country and those in his own monastery – he had over a hundred pupils who thronged the cloisters and corridors waiting to obtain instruction and advice. When he had made them all happy, he would sit down with Bienji, a bright young monk from his team of translators, and dictate to him information about the countries he had travelled through for the promised book of the journey – facts, figures and legends, but not a word of his extraordinary personal experiences.

However, everyone wanted to know what the journey had been like and how he had managed it. So on occasion, after a day's hard work and when he was pleased with the progress of the translations, he would satisfy their curiosity by telling them a few bedtime stories about his adventures: his encounters with the bandits, going on hunger strike in order to continue his pilgrimage, the fatal avalanche, or getting lost in the desert. Hui Li wrote down all these reminiscences and then filled them in with details of Xuanzang's early life and what he had told Bienji. The result was the biography which gave the most vivid account of Xuanzang's epic journey – dramatic tales of strange people and stranger customs, Buddhist legends and luminary masters, things never heard or seen before, adversity, temptation, determination and triumph.

Xuanzang was willing to tell the world of his extraordinary experiences, perhaps because he wanted people to treasure the scriptures that he had risked his life to bring back. But to spread the scriptures throughout the country, he would need one thing more from the emperor – a preface: then everyone reading his work would know that it had been blessed by the

Son of Heaven. As soon as he started the translations, he had asked Taizong if he would provide one. But the emperor knew this would indicate a change of religious allegiance; he was not ready to consent.

Xuanzang decided to speed up the completion of his *Record* even at the expense of delaying the translation. So, barely fourteen months after his return from India, he finished the account of his journey. The full title he gave it was 'Record of the Western Regions of the Great Tang', although much of his journey was well beyond the borders of the empire. And he made no mention of his secretive departure; instead he attributed his success to the protection of Taizong's mantle. He deployed his full skill in flattery in his own preface to the *Record*.

> All sentient beings benefit from the Great Tang; all mankind sings its praises. I started from China and travelled through the five kingdoms of India. Even the remotest regions pledge their loyalty to the Tang and come under its influence. Everywhere I have been, people praise in unison the unparalleled virtues and achievements of the Great Tang. I have checked all historical records, and none has mentioned this fact; I have read all the relevant books, and none carries any such description. If I do not write down what I have seen and heard, how can we demonstrate the scope of our influence on the world?

Taizong read the manuscript at once, and the very next day sent Xuanzang a letter of congratulation. Xuanzang took this as another opportunity to request a preface for his translations. Taizong again declined, professing ignorance. 'I am not a clever man,' he said, 'nor very learned. Even in matters of state I feel confused sometimes, let alone understanding the unfathomable teachings of the Buddha. A preface is simply beyond my capacity.'

But a further chance came in the summer of 648 when Taizong summoned Xuanzang to his summer retreat in the mountains outside the capital. 'I found that I missed you badly,' Taizong confided in him when he arrived after riding nearly three days without a stop. 'That is why I have given you this long and fatiguing journey.'

'That a humble individual like myself should receive such an invitation is so unique an honour, I was far too delighted to be aware of any fatigue,' Xuanzang replied in his self-effacing way.

Xuanzang knew the emperor would enquire about his work and he was fully prepared. Remembering Taizong's excuse about how 'unfathomable' Buddhism was, he chose a section of volume sixty-one of the Yogacara Sutra. Although the entire sutra itself, one hundred volumes in total, would indeed be difficult for Taizong to grasp, this volume could not have been more appropriate. It was about how to be a good king: the ten mistakes to avoid, and the ten virtues to practise to guarantee a long, peaceful reign. For example, the seventh virtue of a king is to feel the pulse of the time, to select the right people to run the country, to punish the bad and reward the good; following these rules, the king would be invincible. This was what Taizong had tried to do. When he heard what Xuanzang had to say, he was pleasantly surprised. He wanted to know more about the sutra and sent a messenger to the capital to fetch it. Having read it, he was reported to have said to the attending ministers: 'Reading it is like gazing at the sky or sea. It is so lofty that one cannot measure its height, and so profound that one cannot plumb its depths . . . It is absurd to say that Confucianism, Daoism and Buddhism are of equal

425

value. Confucianism, Daoism and our other teachings are like mere puddles measured against a mighty ocean.'

Two months later Taizong's preface was written, expressing unreserved admiration for Xuanzang in equally flowery language. He called Xuanzang 'Leader of the Dharma'. 'The wind in the forest and the moon on the water cannot compare to the purity of his virtue,' the emperor wrote. 'The morning dew and shiny pearls cannot compare to the clearness of his complexion. He sees through all and is burdened by nothing. He transcends the mundane and the suffering. He is the one and only in history, without equal . . . I hope the sutras he has translated will spread far and wide, bringing benefits to the believers as infinite as the Sun and the Moon, as lasting as Heaven and Earth.'

This was exactly what Xuanzang had hoped for: the preface was the seal of imperial approval for Buddhism and its propagation throughout the country. Soon, the suppression of Buddhism that marked the early years of the Tang dynasty was lifted. And in the fierce competition for the favour of the emperor, Buddhism finally triumphed over Daoism. Buddhism was to enter its golden age, as never before or after in Chinese history. Taizong instructed the imperial secretariat to make copies of Xuanzang's translations of the sutras and to dispatch them to the far corners of the country. At his suggestion, Taizong allowed the ordination of 17,000 monks, filling the monasteries that mushroomed throughout the empire. With generous donations from every part of society, from the imperial family down to ordinary people, monasteries were built on a monumental scale, 'surpassing even the imperial palaces in design, embodying the last word in extravagance, splendour, artistry and fineness', a contemporary writer complained. Xuanzang's own temple was among the greatest, with ten courts, four thousand rooms, and pavilions and pagodas reaching to the clouds. The most telling example of how greatly Buddhism flourished came from an unlikely source, the imperial mint – it almost ran out of copper for coins because of the vast number of Buddhist images and ritual objects being made. Xuanzang's mission was fulfilled.

The emperor, like the whole nation, was more and more drawn to Buddhism, in particular its ceremonies and rituals. Perhaps he was aware of his declining health and the inevitable end. He would not let Xuanzang out of his sight – he even gave him a room in the palace. What would he have talked to Xuanzang about? No records were kept, and we can only imagine. Taizong must have reflected on his life. The campaigns for building the biggest empire in Chinese history had left millions of people dead. He had nightmares of their souls coming to haunt him, and his two favourite generals guarded his chamber every night. This began a tradition that continues today: the Chinese still put the portraits of these two generals on their doors to guard against evil spirits.

Although Taizong had proved one of the greatest of Chinese emperors, his people did not forget his ruthless climb on to the throne. The fragments of a novel discovered in Dunhuang portrayed him descending into hell after his death for the crime of killing his brothers and forcing his father to abdicate – he even had to bribe his way into hell. To make things worse, Taizong was now faced with the same problem: he had twelve sons, some hopeless, others ruthless, still others timid; the crown prince had even made an attempt on his life and was promptly put to death. In the end, he chose the weakest of his sons to succeed him. The whole process reminded him of his own feud. Before he died, he told his chosen son not to look up to him as an example of the ideal sovereign, but to turn to the ancient wise rulers. This was extraordinary; no emperor could admit to such a thing, least of all one who brought about the golden era of Chinese history.

Taizong could hardly have discussed these matters with any of his ministers and advisors, for that would have nullified his legitimacy. Xuanzang spent a great deal of time with him, day and night. Although he could not comment directly, he could have guessed what troubled the emperor. He must have told him about King Asoka. The parallel was striking. Asoka usurped the throne, killed all his brothers, reputedly ninety-nine of them, and began his reign as a tyrant; but after his conversion, he was remembered as the greatest defender of Buddhism in history. Taizong would be equally exalted by virtue of what he had done for the country and for Buddhism. The accumulated merit of all the monks in the country and the ever-compassionate Bodhisattvas would come to his aid. With the teachings of the Buddha, Xuanzang soothed the pain in Taizong's mind. 'Oh why did I not meet you sooner,' the emperor often asked with a sigh, 'so that I could really do something to promote the Faith?'

With these regrets Taizong died in 649, with Xuanzang at his side.

Taizong is buried in the Jiuzong Mountains, ninety miles outside Xian. On a bright, sunny day Li and I set off. There was no direct public transport. We took a bus most of the way and covered the last ten miles in a local minivan, packed with farmers' wives taking their produce to market. The road was narrow and the countryside flat, dotted with carefully tended orchards of apple and pear trees. Suddenly out of nowhere a steep mountain appeared, its pointed peak reaching up into the sky. 'Somewhere up there is Taizong's tomb,' Li said. 'It is the biggest imperial burial ground in China. It's not the most lavish, like the First Emperor's with its Terracotta Army. Taizong didn't want to go to the expense of a gigantic building, or to be buried with gold, jade, pearls and the usual treasures – they would only attract grave robbers. But there are an amazing number of people buried there, maybe two hundred wives, concubines, children and grandchildren, ministers, generals and Confucian scholars. They were devoted to him, in death as in life.'

As we climbed, we passed the tombs of Taizong's favourite concubine at the top of a huge flight of steps and of one of his daughters behind a brick wall. Then we came to an open space littered with fallen steles and layers of grey oblong bricks. These are all that remains of the altar at the northern gate, where offerings were made. Until a century ago, the famous sculptures of the emperor's six horses were still standing on this spot. Two of them were scandalously removed to the United States and are now in the University of Pennsylvania Museum, and the other four were taken for safe-keeping to the Museum of Stone Steles in Xian. But there is no trace of Taizong's tomb. Even the entrance has vanished. This was the greatest man in Chinese history, but as the Buddha said, everything has to pass. At least the mountain is a monument to him, and he lives on in our memories as the ideal ruler.

As we wandered on, we came across a middle-aged farmer gathering grass for his goats. I asked him what he knew of Taizong. 'Of course everyone knows about him. He was a great emperor,' he said, putting down his sickle. 'But why did he choose this place for his next life? It is terrible here. It has not rained for over a year. We don't even have drinking water. I fetch it from four miles away. I haven't washed for two months. My mother and the old ladies in our village think he could help us. They make him offerings of steamed buns and

boiled eggs. Still we have no rain and the crops are pitiful.'
He sighed.

'Not only the locals complain. Very few visitors come here,'
Li said sadly. 'It seems being great is not enough. They expect
a mammoth edifice, and there is nothing to see here. So they
all visit Qian Ling, where Taizong's son, Emperor Gaozong,
and his Empress Wu, are buried. You must see it too. They
supported Xuanzang as much as Taizong did, if not more.'

Emperor Gaozong was as impressed by Xuanzang as his
father had been. He continued the imperial patronage, but he
also made equally strenuous demands on the monk – the
blessing of his family members, the consecration of monasteries and palaces, or accompanying the emperor and the
empress to their summer retreats. Xuanzang was willing to
oblige. Before the empress gave birth, he prayed fervently for
her and forecast that she would have a son. When the crown
prince was born, he chose the name of Fo Guangzi, Buddha-
Light Son, for the boy. After a month, he sent a delegation of
monks to the palace, congratulating the empress again and
bearing auspicious presents for the child: the Heart Sutra written in gold letters, the Sutra on Gratitude to Parents, a cassock,
an incense-burner, a sandalwood desk, a wash-jug, a bookcase,
a rosary, a monk's staff and a toilet-box. He even proposed
to the emperor and empress that their son and heir follow the
example of the Buddha, renouncing the crown for a monastic
life. This was very bold of Xuanzang – he was obviously trying
every possible means to fortify Buddhism in China. It would
have been something unheard of in Chinese history; and
indeed the emperor thought it was going too far.

Xuanzang came up with another suggestion. He proposed
that Gaozong should build a pagoda to house the sutras he
had brought back from India and all his translations. It would

be a grand monument for the achievements of the emperor, including his support for Buddhism. Gaozong agreed, though to a pagoda smaller than Xuanzang had in mind. On the day of construction, Xuanzang instructed that two stone steles bearing Taizong's and Gaozong's prefaces for his translations be built into the pagoda's lower walls. He wanted the most permanent possible protection for Buddhism. History has proved the good sense of Xuanzang's foresight. The Big Wild Goose Pagoda survived two further persecutions during the Tang dynasty, when most monasteries in the country were destroyed, numerous wars and, last but not least, the Cultural Revolution. All these years later, it is still with us.

Gaozong's and Empress Wu's tomb has survived too, in truly imperial style. A broad avenue of grey flagstones sweeps up to the remains of the entrance pavilions, past giant stone statues placed opposite each other – first, exotic tributes of lions and ostriches, then Heavenly Horses with their riders, and lastly the irreplaceable Confucian scholars who are supposed to advise the Son of Heaven even in death. Behind the entrance a steep hill rises with the tomb on its pinnacle. In a separate enclosure to the right is an honour guard of sixty-one foreign kings – life-size statues, as if the emperor was saying, 'You received my protection. Now stand vigil over my grave.' In fact their vigil was long over: they have been headless for centuries.

Both Li and I were more interested in the stele opposite that of Emperor Gaozong, erected by Empress Wu for herself. It is a straight-sided obelisk, with a curved top carved into dragons, but no inscription. Yet no other figure in Chinese history has attracted so much controversy as Empress Wu. And understandably so – ever since Confucius's time, women had been regarded as inferior, 'long in hair but short on wisdom'. A boy was a blessing for the family and a girl a curse. A daughter, a wife and a mother – that was all women were allowed to be. There were precedents of other empresses and concubines drawn into palace politics, but they never managed to push their husbands or sons totally aside and occupy the throne themselves. *Shang Shu*, one of the Chinese moral classics, says, 'If a hen replaces the cock to crow, the household will suffer; if a woman usurp her husband's power, the country will fall.'

Empress Wu broke all the rules. Originally one of Taizong's concubines, she was banished to a nunnery after the emperor's death. Her striking looks caught the eye of Emperor Gaozong when he came to the nunnery to pray for his late father. She was called into the palace as a concubine again, used all her charm and skill to win Gaozong's heart and her rank rose rapidly. She smothered one of her daughters and put the blame on the empress, who had already lost favour because she bore no children. Wu got her wish: the empress was deposed and she was crowned in her place. To remove any threat once and for all, she had the former empress thrown in a barrel of liquor and drowned. When Gaozong died after a long illness, Wu put two of her sons on the throne and then deposed both of them – one died in exile. At the age of sixty-seven, she ascended the throne herself, the first and only woman in Chinese history to do so. She was well aware of her historical importance. The emperors were the Sons of Heaven; she gave herself a new name, Zetian, the Equal of Heaven.

Li told me that Empress Wu's reign was remarkable. She stopped the expansion of the empire because it imposed too heavy a burden on the people. Taxes were lowered and the bureaucracy was made meritocratic. When a Confucian scholar wrote a pamphlet calling for rebellion against her, she said she could use his talent and courage in the court. Ordained by Xuanzang, she became a lay Buddhist devotee before the birth of her first son, and went on to become a great patron of Buddhism: some of the most beautiful statues and Buddhist caves in China date from her time; at least Buddhism did not rule out the possibility of a woman becoming a ruler. She repaired the Big Wild Goose Pagoda and left it as we see it today. She reigned supreme for fifteen years until she was eighty-two, when her prime minister led a military coup and installed her deposed son. Barely ten months later, she died.

I asked Li why we never heard those good things about Wu. 'Just think who writes our history,' she said. 'Men!' Throughout the centuries, Wu has been called all kinds of names: she was a whore who usurped the throne; she was the most ruthless dictator in Chinese history, killing her own children or anyone in her way; and she ruled the country by the only means she knew – by secret police and informers. 'What infuriated them most,' Li went on, 'was that she openly asked men for sexual services. The story goes that all over the country men joked about the size of their penises and wondered if theirs was big enough to satisfy her. I am not sure whether it was a historical fact or whether the historians made it up to prove she was a bad woman.' She paused to get her breath back. 'But even if the story is true, it couldn't begin to compare with the thousands of concubines the emperors had. Women had to be chaste; men did not – because men made the rules.'

Whatever historians would say about her, Empress Wu knew her place in history was guaranteed. Unlike all Chinese emperors who left elaborate accounts of their achievements, she needed no inscription for herself. Just this empty stone stele – it asks us, and history, to make our own judgement.

It suddenly occurred to me why Empress Wu was possible only in the Tang dynasty. I had never thought of it before. This was a time when a girl child was treasured as much as a boy, when women could put on men's clothes and go hunting with them, when they could marry and remarry, even three times, when an emperor could take on his father's concubine. Grandmother had to have her feet bound to please men, and to make them feel safe – she could not run away; she was forced to remain a widow for almost half a century after Grandfather's death. In the Tang dynasty women were taught to read and write for their own good; in Grandmother's day, and in my mother's youth, ignorance was a virtue in a woman, and education was supposed to put wrong ideas in their heads. In the Tang, women could take pride in their beauty and wear tantalizing clothes – when I saw the first Tang drama, the costumes were so revealing I thought they were a director's ploy to please the audience. My mother had to hide her femininity completely. In the Tang, if a woman fell in love with a foreigner, no one blinked an eyelid. When I did, my father nearly disowned me.

How are the mighty fallen. On the way back into the city, we saw huge billboards advertising new housing developments in the Tang style, with slogans such as 'We are the descendants of the Great Tang and must live accordingly.' There were more serious posters, calling on every citizen to learn the Tang spirit and make Xian a metropolis of the world again. I asked Li whether she thought it would happen.

She smiled and shook her head. 'Everyone talks about the Tang spirit,' she said dismissively. 'It's in the papers, on TV and radio. But people haven't the faintest clue what it is, still less how we are going to get it back. The spirit of the Tang was its openness and its ability to borrow what suited it best.

The ethos of Xian today is still Communist self-reliance. As the Chinese say, the cart is heading south, but on an east–west track. How can we catch up with the world if we are not looking forwards, but backwards?'

I thought about what Li had said after I dropped her off at her university and headed back to my hotel, a simple concrete box above a small restaurant on Red Bird Street. The people in Xian obviously wanted very much to revive this ancient city. Some scholars even advocated studying and applying the spirit of Xuanzang to achieve the goal. If everyone, they argued, had a little bit of Xuanzang's willingness to bear hardship, and his indomitable will to remove all obstacles, Xian would be its glorious self once more. But perhaps another Taizong is closer to what is needed, I thought to myself. No doubt Xuanzang would have wished the best for Xian: peace, prosperity and being the centre of the world, as he had experienced himself in this ancient city, his second home, his final resting place.

On the outskirts of Xian, in a beautiful valley, is the temple where Xuanzang is buried. It was the last place on my journey in his footsteps. In the receding morning mist, the pale terracotta colour of its walls stood out from the lush green of the trees and the fields surrounding it. Inside all was peace. The bell and drum towers stood silent. Nothing stirred, except for the wind murmuring through the trees that nestled in among the temple buildings. No tourists, not even a monk, were to be seen. An old man in a Mao jacket was sitting on a stool in the courtyard, reading a booklet. He asked me to buy a ticket. 'I'm glad to see you,' he said warmly, 'so few people come here. Today is quieter than usual, all the monks have gone. They are off somewhere, performing Buddhist rituals.'

He asked me if I was a Buddhist. I shook my head. He then

asked what I was here for. When I told him about my journey, his eyes brightened.

'You mean you have seen everything the Master saw?'

'Quite a bit.' I nodded.

'How lucky you are! You must have accumulated a lot of merit.'

I had definitely acquired some understanding of Buddhism, I told him.

He was happy to show me round. He stood up and closed his booklet, a compilation of extracts from various sutras. 'Some of these are the Master's translations.' He waved it proudly. 'Wasn't he wonderful? He turned down two emperors. That takes a lot of strength. He just wanted to get on with his work so people like you and me could read these sutras and benefit from them. You know some of the actual palm-leaf sutras the Master brought back from India are in our library,' he went on excitedly. 'They are the most precious objects in the temple, perhaps next only to the Master's remains.' Unfortunately, we could not go in – the monks had taken the keys with them. Still I wanted to have a peek. He took me through a semi-circular gate to the east of the main shrine hall and told me to look up. Above the huge groves of bamboo appeared the flying eaves of the library, and turning around a corner I saw a two-storey building right in front of me.

It was big, perhaps spacious enough to hold all the sutras Xuanzang had acquired in India, and his translations. He managed, despite his onerous official duties, to translate more scriptures than anyone else in Chinese history, surpassing even Kumarajiva with his army of helpers – seventy-five sutras and commentaries in a total of 1,346 volumes. They encompassed a variety of Mahayana texts. The most important for Chinese

Buddhism was *Prajnaparamita* Sutra, the Wisdom Sutra. Together with commentaries, Xuanzang's translation of it occupied six hundred volumes, nearly half his work. The core of it was the Heart Sutra, which Chinese monks recite daily in their prayers, to remind themselves of the transience of the world. He didn't start on it until 660, when his health was failing and Gaozong had finally allowed him to retreat from the world, to the Jade Flower Monastery, the late Taizong's summer palace. He never left it. The sutra was so long, he feared he might die before he finished it; he worked frantically on it, day and night, probably accelerating his end. When he completed it at the beginning of 664, he knew his time had come. 'What makes you mention such a thing? You look just as usual,' his disciples asked. 'You may see no difference,' he told them, 'but I know it is time for me to go.'

He stopped translating and gave himself up entirely to meditation and prayer. The instructions for his funeral were simple and precise: he wanted to be buried rolled in a reed mat by a mountain stream, far away from the monastery – 'Let the elk and deer be my companions; let me follow the mallard and the crane.' Then he set about preparing for his passage to the next life. He paid his last respects to the Buddhist statues he had erected around the monastery, and gave away all his possessions to his disciples. He had a list made of all the books he had translated, the images he had commissioned, the poor people he had supported, and the faithful he had guided. He also commissioned a statue of the Buddha under the Bodhi Tree and asked for it to be placed in the hall where he was to die. Finally, knowing the hour was near, he sent for his disciples and all the monks who had been working with him, and bade them a happy farewell:

I am weary of the body now. My work is finished and there is no point in my staying longer. May the good works I have done benefit all living beings. May they and I be reborn in the Tushita Heaven of Maitreya, and serve him there. When Maitreya at last becomes a Buddha, may I go down with him into the world, promote the Faith in all lands and attain the highest enlightenment.

At midnight on March 8, 664, he passed away, at the age of sixty-five.

Emperor Gaozong was heartbroken. He said sadly to his ministers, 'Xuanzang was the boat ferrying the faithful over the sea of suffering. The sea is so vast, and now the boat is sunk.' He adjourned his court for days while the nation mourned the 'Leader of the Dharma'. When Xuanzang's body was brought to the Big Wild Goose Pagoda, records say a million people lined the road along which the coffin travelled. As he lay in state, thousands poured into the monastery and filed past his body each day. And when he was finally buried by the river as he had wished, three hundred thousand people kept vigil for three days and nights, as was the Chinese custom. But Gaozong could see the grave from his palace every morning when he looked out and it upset him so much that he decided to have this temple built for Xuanzang's remains.

The temple has been destroyed and rebuilt many times throughout the centuries. But the pagoda that holds Xuanzang's remains is standing after more than 1,300 years. Turning left from the shrine hall, through another semi-circular gate, I saw Xuanzang's pagoda beyond a bed of flowering roses, accompanied by those of his two disciples, Kuiji and Yuance, who carried on the Yogacara School. There is a memorial hall, a barn-like, simple room, with a wooden statue of Xuanzang, a stone stele showing him travelling on the road, a map of his journey and a painting of him writing his translations. On his birthday, the monks gather here to commemorate him. I asked the old man what they do. 'Oh, not much. We offer the Master a few simple dishes and then recite some sutras he translated,' he said sadly. 'We want to remember him properly. We want to hold big ceremonies on his anniversaries, as they do in the Big Wild Goose Pagoda. But we can't afford it. There are so few visitors and we have little income. Perhaps if you write up your visit, more people will know about our monastery and the Master.' He paused. 'Surely the Master deserves more than this?'

I looked at the pagoda. It is a small version of the Big Wild Goose Pagoda, worn and battered by the centuries, with grass growing out of the top. So modest for a man who did more for Buddhism than anyone else in Chinese history, especially after the grand and imposing tombs of the emperors. I sat down opposite it, feeling sad and disappointed at first. Then I thought Xuanzang would even have regarded this as a luxury. He had asked only to be rolled in a mat and buried under a mound of earth.

Xuanzang embodied Buddhism and the Buddhist message to the very end. Battered though it is, the temple bears witness to his achievements: it is rightly called the Temple of Raising the Faith. This told me as much as all the extraordinary things I had found on my journey. I began to ask myself, had I found the Xuanzang I was looking for? In many ways, yes. After two years of intensive reading about him and travelling in his footsteps, I finally came to see the size of the man and his achievements.

I realized that contrasting this pagoda with the emperors' tombs was wrong. But they set me thinking. Taizong and

Gaozong were among the greatest Chinese emperors, bringing in the golden age. At Ak-beshem in Kyrgyzstan, I had seen the ruined palace of their arch-enemy, the Great Khan of the Western Turks, who built one of the biggest empires in history in such a few years. From King Harsha's biography, I had learned about this benign monarch who unified India for one of the few times in Indian history. These powerful men between them ruled the whole world east of Persia. They had only one thing in common: they all treated Xuanzang with respect, almost deference. Taizong asked for Xuanzang to be beside him at his death-bed. Gaozong could not bear to look at his humble burial place. The Great Khan, instead of arresting him as an 'enemy alien', honoured him by making sure he reached India safely. King Harsha's admiration for Xuanzang and the favour he showed the Chinese monk so enraged the Brahmin priests, they attempted to assassinate him.

What was it about Xuanzang, what was in him? One thing was his presence. This tall, serene and handsome man inspired in people who met him the feelings I experienced when looking at the great images of the Buddha in Sarnath and Peshawar. We have a Chinese phrase for it, the 'Dharma look', the look of someone destined to spread the Dharma. But when he spoke, it was the wisdom on the lips of so young a man that impressed everyone. He had an intuitive grasp of character and knew what to say to each person; kings and commoners all felt he was addressing them individually, their lives, their concerns. His preaching was profound, as was his understanding of Buddhism, but always clear. And perhaps above everything, people recognized his indomitable determination – it set him apart. He intended to achieve his goals, and nothing would prevent him.

I realized that others had done the same things before and

after Xuanzang. Fa Xian had shown the way to India, and written an account of his journey. Kumarajiva, whose statue I saw in Kucha, made large numbers of translations, still preferred by many Buddhists for their simple language and their lucidity – he also inspired Xuanzang. Other great monks set up Buddhist schools which enriched Buddhism in China and beyond. Xuanzang was only one branch of a big tree. But he still stands out uniquely in the history of Buddhism. Through his journey, his *Record*, his translations and the inspiration he gave to generations of Chinese, he did the utmost to spread the teachings of the Buddha in China and elsewhere. If there were a special place in the pantheon of propagators of Buddhism, it must belong to him. Arthur Waley, the English biographer of Xuanzang, summed him up with this apt tribute: 'His kindred, in the world of our imagination, are not the great travellers, not Marco Polo, or Vambery, nor the great theologians such as Saint Augustine or Saint Thomas, but rather Aeneas, King Arthur, Cuchulain. He is the hero of a sort of spiritual epic, as they of their knightly sagas.'

He had his regrets. He would have liked to have translated more of the 657 sutras he brought back – he managed only seventy-five of them – although that was more than anyone else in Chinese history. He hoped others would finish what he had left behind. He would have had more regret if he had lived to know the fate of his Yogacara School, the form of Buddhism to which he devoted his life. At the time, from the emperor to ordinary believers, everyone read about it; it was very popular. But Buddhism itself declined and lost its intellectual vigour in China after the persecution of 845, less than two hundred years after Xuanzang's death. Yogacara came to be considered too abstruse; his translations of the texts were lost, only to be restored in the nineteenth century after being retrieved from Japan, where the School still flourishes today.

I was reasonably happy with what I had been able to discover about Xuanzang, although I am still struggling to make sense of his Yogacara. But had I found what I was looking for myself? If I had, it was mainly through the inspirational people I met: Duan in Xian, the monk who had left his robes and married, but was still a monk to my mind; the dalits in Kushinagar, whose lives were unspeakable but who had found their way to dignity; and Shan Ren, the woman who befriended me in the Dunhuang monastery, who had suffered like my father and had come through, and showed me genuine selflessness: these, and of course my grandmother, about whom I have learned so much. They followed different kinds of Buddhism – but they exemplified one truth common to most Buddhists: the idea that you can change your life by changing the way you look at it. Your mind is what matters, and you can transform it. As the Indian philosopher Shantideva put it, you can either cover the world with leather, or wear sandals.

My education concealed from me this whole side of Buddhism, leaving me with the false view that it had only to do with gods, prayer and paradise, superstition. Of course that is a large part of Chinese Buddhism; we were taught it was an opiate for the poor. What we were not told about was everything else, and in particular the Buddhism that stresses self-reliance. Frequently there are things beyond our control – what could Duan do against the hurricane of the Cultural Revolution? What could Grandmother do when seven of her children died? They could have despaired, but they found their peace of mind. Before, I thought Grandmother was just resigned to her fate; now I knew she had overcome it.

If I ever heard about the mind and Buddhism during my upbringing, it was being lectured that existence determines our mind, our material conditions determine what we believe, not vice-versa. This was another strong attack on Buddhism. I could just imagine the Red Guards shouting at Xuanzang, how can the mind determine the world? If we do not have enough to eat, how can we think about anything else? We were told that when everyone's material wants were satisfied, we would all be happy. It did not occur to me to doubt it; we were lucky if we were not hungry. I did not know the Buddha's path is called 'the Middle Way', avoiding the extremes of luxury and deprivation; and when his disciple asked him to preach to a beggar, he said, 'He does not need my teaching, he needs food.'

When I think about what my family and the whole country went through, I can hardly imagine a clearer demonstration of mind over matter. There were relentless political campaigns to cleanse our thoughts and to make us conform to the ideas of one man. Contrary to what was drilled into us about dialectical materialism, Mao clearly believed as much as any Buddhist in the primacy of the mind. During the Great Leap the laws of science and nature were flouted. One of the most popular slogans was, 'however much we can dream, the land will yield'; newspapers plastered us with news that farmers were producing twenty tons of rice from one acre of land. In the hysteria of the Cultural Revolution, we started every day singing 'East is Red': the sun had risen and Mao had descended to the Middle Kingdom; he brought us happiness and he was our saviour. We prayed for his longevity for ten thousand years and beyond, and we believed his thoughts were the Dharma which could solve any problem. He was revered as a god, in all but name. I swallowed all this – my indoctrination was very successful. But then the god died and our faith in him was dashed, leaving us lost and angry. The goal of the revolution was to satisfy everyone's needs; instead it drove us to starvation and the brink of the abyss. If this was not the power of the mind to change the world, what was?

From Xian I went home. I had one thing left to do: to go back to my grandmother's village. It was eight years since her death. In the midst of a field of peanuts and potatoes I found her grave, a little swelling in the earth, with a wooden stick in front bearing a few Chinese characters: 'The tomb of the woman of the Liu and Wang families'. She had not even been buried with her own name. As was the custom she was identified as the daughter of the Wang family who married into the Liu family. They were there, buried with her – her father, her husband and her two brothers.

Like all Buddhists, my grandmother believed that death was not the end of life but the beginning of rebirth. She began to prepare for her afterlife when I was in my teens. The unknown was frightening and she wanted to make sure that she would not lack anything in the next life. First and foremost, she needed to be buried with clothing for all seasons. Her needs were not extravagant, but in the 1970s when everything was rationed, from rice, flour, meat and oil, to cloth, each of us had just enough coupons for one outfit for the Chinese New Year. Where could we get the cloth for Grandmother's four outfits and a coat, which all had to be cut generously? To our surprise, Father, who did not even believe in the afterlife, told Grandmother not to worry. She would have everything she desired for her next life.

Grandmother lived until 1992. During the intervening decades, one fixture in my summer vacation was to help her

444

get out the 'death wear' from drawers under our bed and air them on hot summer days, one at a time so that nobody would accuse my parents of being superstitious. The whole thing was bizarre and I would make fun of her by putting on the back quilted jacket and hat, pretending to be a ghost. Grandmother would get very upset. But otherwise, the expression on her face was no different from mine on New Year's Day with my new clothes on, showing the whole world that I would start my new year completely afresh. While we were sitting in the shade, keeping an eye on her precious outfits, she told me again and again that I must make sure my mother put on all the clothes for her while she was still breathing, otherwise she would be going to the next world naked.

She also listed other things she must have for her new life: a house, tables, chairs and cupboards, a cow, a cart, a boat to travel with and of course a large sum of money, not only for her own use but for incidental expenses like bribing infernal officials. Everything would be made of paper, of course. She even taught me how to make ingots. The rich and powerful could put real money, or even real people, in their tombs. Apart from his Terracotta Army, the first emperor had his wives, concubines and children buried with him. But my grandmother was happy with paper offerings. To complete our annual ritual, I would write to my uncle in the village and check that the wood my father had bought for her coffin was not rotting away. When everything was confirmed to be in order, Grandmother would announce to us, with a big smile on her face, that she was ready to go.

But in fact Grandmother did not enter her next life as she planned. By the time she died, burial had long been forbidden in China because of the pressure on land. Cremation, which would be like burning in hell in her eyes, awaited her. All her meticulous preparations went up in flames. It was good that she did not know.

Many people would consider hers such a harsh life, a life of suffering till the very end. She had only two comforts: her family and her faith. We loved her and she knew that; but we ridiculed her beliefs, and must have made her feel so lonely and insecure. This tiny fragile woman lived in her own world. I did not know then how much pain we caused her; nor that it was her faith that helped her endure. She never complained. And despite everything, she loved us very much, me especially, the unwanted daughter. I did not understand her faith when I was a child, and although I have begun to learn about it now, I still cannot enter her world entirely. She deserved better of us, and of me – the understanding, respect and tolerance due to anyone. My greatest regret is that we failed to give them to her.

Standing there by her grave, the memories of her rushed back to me like a film. I could see them so clearly. I remembered all those years sleeping in her bed, washing her feet. I seemed to hear again the click of the red beans in the night as she recited her Amitabhas. I thought of the magical stories she told me. I recalled the last time I saw her, half-blind and barely able to recognize me. If she were in Heaven as she had prayed for all her life, she might be comforted that she had set me off on my journey of discovery, and that what I had learned about her faith would be with me for the rest of my life.

I placed on her grave bananas, oranges and grapes that I had bought her, the simple things she never tasted in life.

Softly, I said Amitabha for her.

SELECTED READINGS

IN ENGLISH

Allen, Charles, *The Buddha and the Sahibs: The Men Who Discovered India's Lost Religion*, London: John Murray, 2002.

Almond, Philip C., *The British Discovery of Buddhism*, Cambridge: Cambridge University Press, 1988.

Armstrong, Karen, *Buddha*, London: Weidenfeld & Nicolson, 2000.

Bagchi, P. C., *India and China: A Thousand Years of Cultural Relations*, Bombay, 1950, Westport, CT.: Greenwood Press, reprint, 1971.

Basham, A. L., *The Wonder That was India*, New Delhi: Rupa & Co., by arrangement with Macmillan, 3rd revised edn (1967), 34th impression, 1999.

Bayly, Susan, *Caste, Society and Politics in India: From the Eighteenth Century to the Modern Age*, New Cambridge History of India, Vol. 4, No. 3, Cambridge: Cambridge University Press, 1999.

Beal, Samuel, trans., *Si-yu-ki, Buddhist Records of the Western World, Translated from the Chinese of Hiuen Tsiang (A.D. 629)*, 1884, Delhi: Oriental Books Reprint Corp., 2 vols, 1969.

Beal, Samuel, trans., *Hui Li: The Life of Hiuen-Tsiang*, 1911, Delhi: Munshiram Manoharlal, 2nd edn, 1973.

Buddhist Association of Canada, *The Buddhist Liturgy*, Ontario, 1983

Buddhist Text Translation Society, *The Sixth Patriarch's Sutra*,

San Francisco, CA: Sino-American Buddhist Association, 2nd edn, 1977.

Ch'en, K., *Buddhism in China: A Historical Survey* Princeton, NJ: Princeton University Press, 1973.

Ch'en, K., *The Chinese Transformation of Buddhism* Princeton, NJ: Princeton University Press, 1973.

Cleary, Thomas (trans.) *The Dhammapada: Sayings of Buddha*, London: Thorsons (HarperCollins), 1995.

Conze, Edward, *Buddhism: Its Essence and Development* (1951), New York: Harper and Row, reprint, 1975.

Conze, Edward (ed. and trans.), *Buddhist Texts through the Ages*, Oxford: Oneworld, 1995.

Coomaraswamy, A., *History of Indian and Indonesian Art*, 1927, Delhi: Munshiram Manoharlal, reprint, 1972.

Das, Arvind, *The Republic of Bihar*, New Delhi: Penguin Books, 1992.

Eck, Diana L., *Banaras: City of Light*, London/New Delhi: Penguin Books, 1993.

Errington, Elizabeth, and Joe Cribb with Maggie Claringbull (eds), *The Crossroads of Asia*, Cambridge: Ancient India and Iran Trust, 1992.

Fitzgerald, C. P., *The Empress Wu*, London: Cresset Press, 1956.

Frank, Irene M., and David M. Brownstone, *The Silk Road: A History*. New York: Facts on File, 1986.

Gaulier, S., R. Jera-Bezard and M. Maillard, *Buddhism in Afghanistan and Central Asia*. 2 vols. Leiden: Brill, 1976.

Gopal, Sarvepalli, *Jawaharlal Nehru: A Biography*, 1989, Delhi: Oxford India Paperbacks, abr. edn, 1993.

Grousset, René, *In the Footsteps of the Buddha*, trans. Mariette Leion, 1932, London: Routledge and Kegan Paul, reprint, 1972.

Harle, J., *The Art and Architecture of the Indian Subcontinent*, Harmondsworth: Penguin Books, 1986.

Hedin, Sven, *The Silk Road*, trans. F. H. Lyon, New York: Dutton, 1938.

Hopkirk, Peter, *Foreign Devils on the Silk Road*, London: John Murray, 1980.

Huntington, John, 'Sowing the Seeds of the Lotus: A Journey to the Great Pilgrimage Sites of Buddhism', *Orientations*, Nov. 1985, pt 1 (pp. 46–62); Feb. 1986, pt 2 (pp. 28–44); March 1986, pt 3 (pp. 32–47); July 1986, pt 4 (pp. 28–41); Sept. 1986, pt 5 (pp. 46–59).

Huntington, Susan, and John Huntington, *The Art of Ancient India*, Tokyo: Weatherhill, 1985.

Imam, Abu, *Sir Alexander Cunningham and the Beginnings of Indian Archaeology*, Dacca: Asiatic Society of Pakistan, 1966.

Joshi, L. M., *Studies in the Buddhistic Culture of India During the Seventh and Eighth Centuries*, Delhi: Motilal Banarsidass, 2nd ed., 1967.

Keay, John, *India Discovered: The Achievement of the British Raj*, Leicester: Windward, 1981.

Klimburg-Salter, Deborah, *The Kingdom of Bamiyan: Buddhist Art and Culture of the Hindu Kush*, Rome: Istituto italiano per il medio ed estremo oriente, 1989.

Lamotte, E., *History of Indian Buddhism*, trans. from the French by Sara Webb, Louvain-la-Neuve: Université Catholique de Louvain, 1988.

Le Coq, Albert von, *Buried Treasures of Chinese Turkestan*, trans. Anna Barwell, New York: Longmans and Green, 1929.

Liu Xinru, *Ancient India and Ancient China: Trade and Religious Exchanges*, Delhi: Oxford University Press, 1988.

Mallory, J. P. and Victor H. Mair, *The Tarim Mummies: Ancient China and the Mystery of the Earliest Peoples from the West*, London/New York: Thames & Hudson, 2000.

Mitra, Swati (ed.), *Walking with the Buddha: Buddhist Pilgrimages in India*, Eicher Guide, New Delhi: Eicher Goodearth Ltd, 1999.

Narada, Maha Thera, *The Buddha and His Teachings*, reprint,

Taipei: Corporate Body of the Buddha Educational
Foundation, 2nd ed., 1973.

Nickel, Lucas, *Return of the Buddha*, exhibition catalogue,
London: Royal Academy Publications, 2002.

Rashid, Ahmed, *Taliban: Islam, Oil and the New Great Game in
Central Asia*, London: I.B. Tauris, 2000.

Sangharakshita, *Ambedkar and Buddhism*, London: Windhorse
Publications, 1986.

Schafer, Edward H., *The Golden Peaches of Samarkand*,
Berkeley, CA: University of California Press, 1963.

Sherring, M. A., *Benares: The Sacred City of the Hindus in
Ancient and Modern Times*, New Delhi: Rupa & Co., 2001.

Srinivas, M. N. (ed.), *Caste: Its Twentieth Century Avatar*, New
Delhi: Penguin Books, 1996.

Stein, Aurel, 'The Desert Crossing of Hsuan Tsang 630 A.D.',
Indian Antiquary 50 (1921), pp. 15–25.

Stein, Aurel, *Ruins of Desert Cathay*, 2 vols, 1912, New York:
Dover, reprint, 1987.

Stein, Aurel, *Sand-buried Ruins of Khotan*, London: Hurst and
Blackett, 1904.

Tan, Chung, *China and the Brave New World: A Study of the
Origins of the Opium War (1840–42)*, Durham, NC: Carolina
Academic Press, 1978.

Tan, Chung (ed.), *Across the Himalayan Gap: An Indian Quest
for Understanding China*, New Delhi: Gyan Publishing House
for the Indira Gandhi National Centre for the Arts, 1998.

Tan, Chung (ed.), *India and China: Special Issue*, New Delhi:
Indian Council for Cultural Relations, 1994.

Thakur, S., *The Making of Laloo Yadav*, New Delhi:
HarperCollins, 1978.

Thapar, Romila, *Early India: From the Origins to AD 1300*,
Berkeley, CA: University of California Press, 2003.

Tissot, Francine, *The Art of Gandhara: Buddhist Monks' Art on the
North-West Frontier of Pakistan*, Paris: J. Maisonneuve, 1986.

Waley, Arthur, *The Real Tripitaka*, London: Allen & Unwin, 1952.

Watson, Burton (trans.), *The Lotus Sutra*, New York: Columbia University Press, 1993.

Weinstein, Stanley, *Buddhism Under the T'ang*, Cambridge: Cambridge University Press, 1987.

Welch, Holmes, *Buddhism Under Mao*, Cambridge, MA: Harvard University Press, 1972.

Welch, Holmes, *The Practice of Chinese Buddhism 1900–1950*, Cambridge, MA: Harvard University Press, 2nd impression, 1973.

Whitfield, Roderick, Susan Whitfield and Neville Agnew, *Cave Temples of Dunhuang*, London: British Library, 2000.

Whitfield, Susan, *Life Along the Silk Road*, London: John Murray, 1999.

Williams, Paul, *Mahayana Buddhism: The Doctrinal Foundation*, London: Routledge, 1989.

Wriggins, Sally Hovey, *Xuanzang: A Buddhist Pilgrim on the Silk Road*, Boulder, CO: Westview Press, 1996.

Wright, Arthur, *Buddhism in Chinese History*, 1959, Stanford: Stanford University Press, reprint, 1971.

Wright, Arthur R., and D. Twitchett, *Perspectives on the T'ang*, New Haven CT: Yale University Press, 1973.

Wu, Ch'eng-En, *Monkey [a.k.a. The Monkey King]* c. 1550, trans. Arthur Waley 1942 (abridged), London: Penguin, 1961.

Zhang, Guangda, *History of Civilizations of Central Asia*, Paris: UNESCO Publishing, 1992–1996.

Zurcher, Erik, *The Buddhist Conquest of China: The Spread and Adaptation of Buddhism in Early Mediaeval China*, Leiden: E. J. Brill, reprint, 1st edn, 1959.

IN CHINESE

Fang, Litian, *Chinese Buddhism and Traditional Culture*, Shanghai: People's Publishing House 1998 (3rd impression).

Han, Xiang and Zhu, Rongying, *Kizil Caves*, Urumqi: Xinjiang University Press, 1990.

Li, Bingcheng et al. (eds), *A History of Social Life During the Sui, Tang and the Five Dynasties*, Beijing: Chinese Academy of Social Sciences Publishing House, 1998.

Li, Yinping, *Buddhist Khotan*, Xingjiang: People's Publishing House, 1991.

Rong, Xinjiang, *Eighteen Lectures on Dunhuang Studies*, Beijing: Beijing University Press, 2001.

Rong, Xinjiang, and Guangda Zhang, *Studies of the History of Khotan*, Beijing: Beijing University Press, 1993.

Wang, Guojie, *History of the Donggan People*, Shanxi: People's Publishing House, 2nd edn, 1999.

Wang, Shuying, *Sino-Indian Cultural Exchanges*, Beijing: Overseas Publishing House, 1994.

Xuanzang, *Record of the Western Regions*, with commentary by Rui Chuanming, Guiyang: Guizhou People's Publishing House, 1990.

Yang, Tinfu, *Xuanzang: A Chronology of His Life*, Beijing: Zhonghua Publishing Bureau, 1980.

Zhang, Gong, *A History of Monastic Culture During the Han and Tang Dynasties* (2 vols), Beijing: Chinese Academy of Social Sciences Publishing House, 2000.

Zhao, Keqiao and Daoqiun Xu, *Biography of Tang Taizong*, Beijing: People's Publishing House, 2nd edn, 1996.

INDEX

Afghanistan 43, 150, 154, 156, 176, 185, 191, 193, 224
  Buddhism in 188–90, 196, 206, 289
  Taliban in 187–8, 197–8, 204–6
Afghans 318
Afrasiab, Samarkand 176
Africa 225
Agrawal, Dr 219–20, 222–3, 228
Ajanta, India 319–21, 381
Akayev, President of Kyrgyzstan 151
Akbar, Emperor 202
Ak-beshim, Kyrgyzstan 157, 169–71, 440
Alexander the Great 193–4, 339
Ambedkar (Babasaheb) 306–11
  The Buddha and his Dharma 312
Ambedkar, Ramtirath 306, 308–11
Amitabha Buddha 14, 27, 65, 373, 376, 395
Amrapali 277
Ananda 201, 274, 302, 304, 312, 391
Andrew (American pilgrim) 271–6
antique-smuggling 203–4
Anxi (Guazhou) 82–3, 87, 93
Arabs 175, 357
Archaeological Survey of India (ASI) 219–20, 224, 226, 266
archaeology 170–1, 202, 266, 302–3, 354–5 368–9
  thefts 101–2, 124, 371–2
Asanga 182, 243
Asiatic Society, Calcutta 224–5
Asoka (Bodh Gaya guide) 276–80, 284
Asoka, King 201, 227, 233–5, 266, 267, 284, 299–300, 313, 359, 428
Assam, King of 324, 325
Aurangzeb, Emperor 292

Babur, Emperor 202
Bactria 194
Bamiyan, Afghanistan 176, 188, 190, 204–7
  King of 205
Basham, A. L. 321
Baykal, Lake 150
Bedal Pass 148–9
Begram treasures 203
Beijing 50, 60, 220
  University 35–7, 41, 143, 421
Benares, India 224, 289–93, 296, 298, 316
  King of 358
Bengal, Governor-General of 265
Berlin Ethnographic Museum 102, 103, 124
Bezeklik 99–103, 381
Bienji 423
Big Wild Goose Pagoda 51–72, 236, 247, 417, 431, 433, 438, 439
  Xuanzang Memorial Hall 69, 253
Bihar, India 229–30, 238–41, 262, 265, 278–80, 285, 301, 313
  Governor of 249–50
Bimaran, Afghanistan 190
Bishkek, Kyrgyzstan 149, 151–3, 154, 168–9, 177
Black Jade river 340, 360
Bodh Gaya, Bihar 227, 259, 261–72, 276, 284, 385
Bodhi Tree 189, 192, 232, 262, 266–72, 277, 304, 315
Bodhisattvas 48, 127–8, 248, 295, 359, 395, 403–5
  attributes of 65, 149, 323
  Deva Bodhisattva 294

455

Bodhisattvas – *cont.*
  Guanyin, Bodhisattva of
    Compassion 14, 22, 24, 27, 33–4,
    89–90, 108, 199, 274, 324, 379,
    382, 404
  images of 99, 133, 200, 202, 204,
    221, 321–2, 354, 372, 377–80, 382
  Wenshu, Bodhisattva of Wisdom
    244, 377–8, 380, 404
Brahmadatta, King of Benares 291
Britain 237
British Museum 190, 372
Buchanan, Dr 265
Buddha 8, 31, 52, 211, 399–400
  death and nirvana of 301–3
  disciples of 188, 201, 243, 274, 275,
    277, 289, 291
  enlightenment 15, 87, 127, 188, 201,
    227, 229, 251, 260–1, 266, 268,
    400
  as historical figure 192, 223, 225,
    265
  images of 99, 191–3, 195–6, 202,
    204–6, 220–1, 300, 302–4, 320,
    341
  incarnations of 127, 181–2, 201
  Jataka stories 127, 289, 291, 295–6,
    299
  life events 61, 225–7, 229, 233, 235,
    241, 260–1, 276–7, 289, 291,
    298–9, 356, 361
  relics of 63, 189–90, 194, 201, 202,
    235
  sayings of 62, 67, 71, 97, 125, 143,
    192, 219, 273, 326–7, 443
  teachings of 52, 61, 68, 80, 90–1,
    212, 251, 262, 268, 275, 276–8,
    285, 305, 310, 311, 359
Buddhism 123, 158, 175, 221, 442
  in Afghanistan 188–90
  Chinese form of 14, 17–18, 250–2,
    273–4, 295, 310
  death in 91, 219, 398–9
  Dharma 52, 66, 247, 310, 312, 337,
    356, 395
  enlightenment 13–15, 97, 127–8,
    193, 194, 196, 199, 273, 310
  five precepts of 291
  good government in174

  in India 16, 211–12, 221–8, 251, 270,
    278, 306–10, 312, 315–16, 318, 379
  karma 18, 61–2, 65, 91, 309–11, 399,
    401
  meditation 13, 54–5, 195, 196, 251,
    268, 273, 392, 399–400
  miracles 295–6
  monks and nuns 40, 52–8, 62–3,
    70–1, 194, 211–12, 267–8, 318,
    384, 391–2, 398, 411, 426
  new Buddhists 311–12
  nirvana 194–5, 304–5, 395–6
  non-duality in 378
  non-violence 5, 358–9
  paradise 15, 18, 28, 48, 67, 69, 248,
    273, 274, 382, 394–6
  persecutions 70, 398, 431, 441
  pilgrims 201, 212, 234, 267–71
  rebirth 91, 232, 309–11, 395, 399,
    444
  Sangha 52, 277–8, 318
  schools of 13–16, 127–8, 247, 250–2
  spread of 79, 189, 211–12, 269,
    332–3
  suicide in 66–8
  three jewels of 52, 188
  three pillars of 400
  women in 199
  yoga 260
  see also sutras
Buddhist art 92, 269, 303
  apsaras 125–6, 135, 374
  carvings 320–1
  cave paintings 100, 125–7, 133, 135,
    303, 321–2, 367, 372–83, 433
  Gandhara-style 191–3, 195–6, 197,
    203, 339, 354
  sculpture 191–3, 195–6, 202, 204–6,
    220, 227, 300, 320, 433
Burma 56, 127, 225, 265–6

Cable, Mildred 384
Cambodia 56
Carlleyle, Archibald 302
Caucasians 109, 131–2, 360
Cen Sen 87
Central Asian Republics 140, 151–4
  hostage crisis 152–3, 155–6, 162
Ceylon, *see* Sri Lanka

456

Chan, see Zen
Chang'an 50–1, 81, 95, 120–2, 123,
    150, 362
  religion in 422
  Tang court 418–19
  Xuanzang in 15, 50–1, 75, 409–10,
    416
  see also Big Wild Goose Pagoda;
    Xian
China 150
  army 119, 121, 123, 125, 165, 170
  Buddhism in 24, 71, 212, 250, 252,
    254–5, 282–3, 410–11, 422,
    426–7, 433, 441
  family in 139
  famine 19, 21, 62, 282
  foot-binding 18, 23–4, 198–9, 434
  foreigners in 419–22, 434
  history in 222–3
  literature 254–5
  opium trade 237–9
  peasant rebellions 283
  religion in 17–20, 40, 64, 70,
    165–6, 222, 350, 422
  tea trade 237
  women in 198–9, 432, 434
  see also China, Communist
China, Communist 3–9, 17–23, 31–5,
    280–3, 443–4
  Buddhism in 39–40, 55–61, 64,
    67–8, 70, 275, 393, 431
  Constitution 20
  economic reforms 39, 215–16
  fiftieth anniversary celebrations
    335–6, 348
  labour camps 115
  Land Reform 34, 53, 55
  political campaigns 20, 115, 141, 443
  relations with India 212–13, 216–17,
    235–6, 253–4
  struggle meetings 4–5, 20, 23, 56,
    64–5, 281
  see also Communist Party of China
Chinese Buddhist Seminary, Beijing
    56
'Chinese Buddhist' (fighter plane) 67
Chinese New Year 3, 24–5, 117
Christianity 40, 172, 422
Chunda (blacksmith) 301–2

Communism 17, 151, 153–4, 199, 280
Communist Party of China 17, 19–20,
    31, 35–6, 335–6
  Youth League 35
Communist Party of India 283
Confucianism 17, 254, 341
Confucius 21, 222
Congress Party of India 230, 307
Construction and Production
    Corporation 139, 140
Cultural Relics Bureau, China 59
Cultural Revolution 4–7, 9, 31–2,
    35–6, 62, 143, 156, 394–5, 401,
    443
Cunningham, Alexander 202, 224–5,
    226–8, 245, 266, 299, 302–3

Dalai Lama 235
Daoan 337
Daoism 17–18, 411, 422, 426
Darra arms bazaar 185
Deer Park, Sarnath 298–9
Delhi, India 214, 215, 220–1, 228
Dhammapada 97
Dharmapala 315
Dharmarajika stupa 299–300
Dharmaraksha 211
Dictionary of the Turkic Language 359
Dima (driver) 169–70
Dongan Pagoda, Karakul 158
Dongans 158, 164–7
Dravida kingdom 315
drugs 191, 237–8
Duan, Mr 53–63, 64, 70, 71, 236, 442
Du Huaibao 175
Dunhuang, Western China 358, 362,
    365–9, 377, 378, 384–5, 414
  manuscripts 369–72, 382, 383, 427
  monastery 386–405

East India Company 237, 265
Eastern Turkestan, Islamic Republic
    of 154, 334
Eastern Turks 150–1

Fa Xian: Record of Buddhist Countries
    212, 225, 441
Fat Ma (guide) 92–5, 98–101, 103–6,
    109, 336, 339, 343

Ferghana valley 81
Flaming Mountain 104–6
Flying Horses of Wuwei 80–1
Foucher, Alfred 183
Fu Yi 410–11
Fo Guangzi, Crown Prince 430

Galina (hostel manager) 158–64, 167
Gandhara, Kingdom of 181, 183, 193,
    200–2
Gandhara Buddhas 191–3, 195–6,
    197
Gandhi, Mahatma 307
Ganges river 232, 233, 290, 292–4,
    296–8, 325
Gansu province 164, 166
Gaochang 93, 94–100, 105, 110, 114,
    150, 172, 332
    King of, see Qu Wentai
Gaozong, Emperor 430–2, 437, 438,
    440
Gaya, Bihar 279
Genghis Khan 150, 205, 221
Gobi Desert 87, 89, 91, 94, 132, 150
Gosringa Mountain 355–6, 360
Great Khan 107, 157, 169, 171–6, 185,
    440
Great Wall of China 85, 150, 201, 368
Greeks 193–4, 196, 200
Grousset, René 132
Guazhou, see Anxi
Guljan (interpreter) 157, 164–5,
    167–70

Hadda, Afghanistan 189, 190
Han Chinese 118, 120, 131, 140, 165
Han dynasty 76, 84, 85
Handan, China 31, 143, 341
Hanuman, monkey god 297
Harbin 31
Harsha, King 324–7, 331, 332, 440
Heavenly Mountains 11, 147–50, 156,
    159, 160, 162, 166, 171, 176, 181,
    271
Henan Province 12
Himalayas 212, 217
Hinayana Buddhism 127, 128
Hindu art 220–1
Hindu Kush 331

Hinduism 222–4, 242, 246, 263, 265,
    290, 292–4, 296, 307, 310, 315–19
horses 80–1, 92, 120–1, 125, 171
Hua (painter) 376–80, 382, 384
Hui Li 422, 423
    see also Life of Xuanzang
Huineng 310
Huns 76, 131, 182

India 49, 77, 174, 194, 211–13, 222, 383
    British 101, 224, 226, 237–8, 306
    Buddhism in 16, 211–12, 221–8, 251,
        270, 278, 284, 306–12, 315–16,
        318–19, 379
    caste system 229, 262–3, 277–80,
        282–3, 306–10
    constitution 300, 307
    corruption in 215–16
    movies 213
    relations with China 212–13,
        216–17, 235–6, 253–4
    reputation of Xuanzang in 10, 220,
        222, 228, 247, 253–4, 284
    revolutionary groups 279–80, 283
    tea trade 237
    violence in 229–30, 239, 264,
        278–80, 309, 313
    Xuanzang in 232–5, 240–1, 243–7,
        252, 259, 261
Indus river 322, 331
Iran 154
Islam 167–8, 175, 191, 197, 292, 335
    Chinese 165–6
    crusaders 355, 357–61
    fundamentalist 140, 151, 153–4, 156,
        184, 188
    in Western Region 92, 99
    women in 198–9
Islamabad 182
Islamic Movement of Uzbekistan
    (IMU) 152–3, 154, 155, 168
Islamic Renaissance Party
    (Tajikistan) 154
Issyk-Kul, Lake 157, 162–3

jade 340–1
Jade Flower Monastery 437
Jade Gate 71, 82, 83–6
Japan 56, 70, 196, 419, 442

Jayasena 247
Jia (guide) 123–6, 129–30
Jiang Qing 420
Jiang Xiaowan 369, 370–1
Jiuzong Mountains 428
John (host in Bishkek) 151–5, 168, 169

Kabul 187, 189–90, 203, 206
Kalidasa 322
Kalinga, see Orissa
Kamakshi Temple, Kanchipuram 317, 318
Kanauj, India 324
Kanchipuram, South India 314–15, 317
Kanishka, King 201–2, 206
Kapilavastu 260, 361
Karakul, Kyrgyzstan 156, 157–9
Karamov, President of Uzbekistan 154
Kashgar, Muhammad 359
Kashgar, Xinjiang 162, 357, 360
Kashmir 123, 243
Kasyapa Matanga 211
Kathiawar Peninsula 322
Kazakhstan 166
Keay, John: India Discovered 227
Keewar (Pashtun bodyguard) 184–7, 190–1, 198–200, 203
Khotan 332–4, 335–49, 352–3, 417
  King of 332–4, 338, 342, 353, 357–9, 378
  Muslim crusade against 355, 357–61
  silk-making 341–7
Khwoja, Maheb 356–7, 360
Khyber Pass 185, 186–7
King Milinder's Questions 194–5
Kizil Caves 122–7, 129–30, 132, 133, 135, 140, 381
Kizil Research Institute 122, 123
Kohmari Mazar, see Gosringa Mountain
Korea 17, 196, 410, 419
Korean War 67, 282
Korla, Xinjiang 113, 117, 136, 334
Kucha (Qiuzi), Xinjiang 98, 102, 113, 117–35, 147, 150, 189, 441
  caves 122–30, 132–4, 196, 303
  King and Queen of 124–5, 147

monks 126–8
  music in 125–6, 135
Kuiji 438
Kukkutamara Monastery 235
Kumarajiva 123, 413, 436, 441
Kumutura Caves 132–3
Kushan empire 201–2, 333
Kushinagar, India 227, 301–4, 312–13, 385, 442
Kyrgyzstan 149, 151–6, 159–62, 166, 168–70, 440

Landi Khotal 186
Lang Zhao 66–8
Laos 56
Le Coq, Albert von 101, 102, 124, 131, 160
  Buried Treasures of Chinese Turkistan 102, 124
Li (history student) 416–19, 421, 428, 430, 431–5
Li Bai 175–6
Li Yuan, Emperor 15
Liang Wuti, Emperor 411
Liangzhou (Wuwei) 79–82, 95, 123
Life of Xuanzang (Hui Li) 11, 12, 223, 241, 270
  on Bodhi Tree 269
  on Great Khan 171, 173
  on journey to India 110, 115, 123, 148, 205
  on public debates 246
  on religious beliefs 15, 16, 232
  on return to China 323, 409
  writing of 423
Liuyuan (Willow Station) 82, 89
Loulan Beauty 130–1
Lumbini, Nepal 227, 313
Luoyang 211, 410, 411

Macaulay, Thomas Babington 226
McMahon Line 217
Mahabharata 242
Mahabodhi Temple, Bodh Gaya 264–6, 277, 284
Maharashtra 306
Mahayana Buddhism 127, 128, 181, 189, 246, 247, 255, 275, 326, 391, 403, 436

Maitreya Buddha 69, 128, 193, 232, 262, 283, 356, 438
Malava (Malwa) 322
Mao, Madam, *see* Jiang Qing
Mao Zedong 3–4, 19, 22, 34, 57, 283, 394–5, 421, 443–4
  as Buddhist 17
  education 35
  Little Red Book 3, 395
  and Red Guards 67
  sayings of 21, 32, 37, 61, 141
  verses written by 8, 29–30, 421
  wars 212
Mara, army of 87
Masson, Charles 190
Mathura, India 195, 227
Menander (Milinder), King of Bactria 194–5
Mishra, Dr 249–50, 252
Mishra, V. P. 296–8
Mogao Caves, Dunhuang 366–83, 393
Moguls 237
Mokshagupta 128
monasteries 40, 51–3, 55, 60, 61, 62, 70–1, 385–405, 426–7
Monastery of Great Benevolence, Xian 51–3
Monastery of the Great Happiness, Chang'an 422
Monkey King, The 7–10, 12, 28, 43, 49, 89, 91, 104–8, 384–5
  theme park 104, 110
mummies 109–10, 131

Nagarjuna 243
Nagpur, India 307
Nairanjana (Phalgu) river 259, 261, 289
Nalanda, Bihar 16, 239, 242–50, 313, 322–3, 325
  New Mahavihara 248–50
  Xuanzang Memorial Hall 252–3, 255
Nagasena 194–5
Naxalites 279, 283
Nayaka (monk in Nalanda) 249
Nehru, Jawaharlal 212, 216–17, 300
Nepal 318

Ningrong Cave Monastery 100
Nirvana Temple, Kushinagar 303–4

Ode on Filial Piety, The 223
Omar, Mullah Mohammed 204, 205
opium 237–9
Opium War 238, 334
Orissa, India 313
Oxford University 37, 143

Pakistan 185, 214, 322
Pali canon 193
Pamir Mountains 77, 91, 331, 343, 383
Panjikent 176
Pantuo 83, 86–8
Pashtuns 182, 184–7, 191, 197
Patna, Bihar 227, 231–7, 243
Pelliot, Paul 372
People's Liberation Army 17, 138, 281
Persia 77, 150, 172, 193, 422
Peshawar, Pakistan 181–5, 191, 193, 198–204, 379
  bazaar 200–4
  Museum 191–2, 196, 204
  pipal tree 201–2
Peter (host in Peshawar) 183–4, 197–8
Phalgu (Nairanjana) River 259–60
Pliny 76–7
Polo, Marco 163, 172, 221
Prem (host in Delhi) 215–17, 229–30
Przhevalsky, N. M. 158, 163
Pu Ci 64–6, 68, 71
Punjab 331
Puranas 223
Pure Land School 14

Qian Ling 430
Qing dynasty 334
Qiuzi, *see* Kucha
Qu Wentai, King 95–7, 106–7, 109, 110, 114, 174, 189, 332, 414

Rajgir, India 227
Rajiv (hotelier) 261–4, 278
Rambhar Stupa, Kushinagar 312
Rawak, Khotan 353–5
Red Guards 4–5, 7, 9, 31, 32, 59–60, 64, 67, 443

Record of the Western Regions
    (Xuanzang)11, 220, 270–1, 339
    on Ajanta 319–20
    on Bodh Gaya 266–7, 277
    on Ceylon 314, 319
    on death of Buddha 302
    fragments of 109, 369, 383–4
    on Gandhara 200
    on Hinduism 290, 294–5
    on India 211, 217–19, 246, 296,
        299–300, 302–4, 314, 322
    on Karakul 158, 163
    on Khotan 332, 338–9, 341–2, 347,
        352–3, 356
    on King Harsha 324–5
    on Kucha 122, 127, 131
    on miracles 294–5, 355
    on Nalandra 245
    preface 424
    and rediscovery of Buddhist sites
        222, 224–5, 227–8, 253–4, 299,
        303, 313
    on teachers 247
    writing of 119, 416, 423–4
Religious Bureau, China 56, 70
Richthofen Ferdinand von 76
Romans 76–7, 171–2, 201
Russia 101, 166

Salim (guide) 117–24, 126, 128–32,
        134–7, 155, 173
Samarkand 99, 170, 176
    King of 176
Sanskrit language 246
Santarakshita 243
Sariputra 243
Sarnath, India 224–5, 226, 298, 304,
        385
Savarna Liberation Army 279
Scar Literature 36
Seleucus Nicator 194
Sere 76–7, 172
Shan Ren 386–7, 389, 396–7, 400–4,
        442
Shandong 24
Shang Shu 432
Shankar, Ajay 219–20
Shankara 315–18
Shantideva 442

Shanxi 164, 165–6
Shilabhadra, Venerable 243–4, 247,
        250, 315, 323–4
Si Maqian: *Record of History* 81
Sichuan 13
silk 76–8, 121, 171–2, 201, 214, 314,
        341–7
Silk Road 76–9, 92, 94, 105, 109, 162,
        175, 201, 214, 365
    archaeology 101–2, 170
    caravans 98–9, 114, 147, 160–1, 169,
        171, 176, 200, 332
    merchants 16, 342
    spread of Buddhism via 79, 189,
        269, 332–3
Singh, Dr 249–50, 252
Singh, Ramadhar 279
Singing Sand Hills 366
Sogdians 76, 83, 176
Soviet Union 158, 187, 335
Sravasti, India 227
Sri Lanka 56, 127, 225, 234, 267, 313,
        314, 319
State Slavonic University, Kyrgyzstan
        170
Stein, Aurel 160, 339, 342, 354–5,
        367–73
    Desert Cathay 368
stupas 63–4, 65–6, 68, 188, 202, 234,
        235, 312, 314, 353–4
Suiye 175–6
Sumeru, Mount 16
Sun family
    aunts and uncles 26, 116–17,
        136–43, 155
    Father 3, 8, 21–4, 29, 31–4, 37–8,
        139, 281, 401, 442, 444
        army career 17, 18, 31, 281–2
        as Communist 17, 18–21, 34–5,
        38
        death 38–9, 41, 140, 219
    grandfathers 18, 25–6, 281
    Grandmother 3, 7, 21, 32, 37, 77–8,
        107–8, 142–3, 381–2, 442
        bound feet 18, 23–4, 434
        as Buddhist 9–10, 17–19, 22–3,
        28–9, 33–5, 52, 60, 274, 444, 446
        death 444–6
        life 24–7, 281

Sun family – *cont.*
    story-telling 30–1
    Mother 3, 5, 17, 18, 19, 21–2, 26,
        32–3, 39, 42, 78, 116–17, 213
    Si Cong (nephew) 43
    sisters 3, 6, 29, 35, 142
    Zhaodong (brother) 32–4, 403
Sun Shuyun
    birth 21–3
    childhood 3–11, 23–4, 29–31, 77–8,
        116, 142, 395, 403
    Chinese identity of 167
    education 6, 29, 35, 37, 41, 142–3
    and religion 5, 29, 40–2, 52, 385,
        388, 405, 442
Sunita 277
sutras 8, 10, 40–1, 90, 181, 189, 194,
        201, 430–1
    Amitabha Sutra 394
    Diamond Sutra 250, 369
    Gosringa-Vyakarana Sutra 356,
        360–1
    Great Nirvana Sutra 302
    Heart Sutra 71, 90, 108, 387, 394,
        430, 437
    Lengyan Sutra 390–1
    Lotus Sutra 14, 22, 356, 382, 395
    Sutra Nipata 193
    Sutra on Gratitude to Parents 430
    translat ions 14–15, 84, 123, 128,
        189, 212, 369, 413, 422–6, 436–7,
        441
    Wisdom Sutra 437
    Yogacara Sutra 232, 244, 247, 425
Sutras of the Sage and the Fool 333

Tagore, Rabindranath 228
Taizong, Emperor 125, 174, 214, 333,
        419, 421, 432
    assumes throne 16
    military conquests 150–1, 332, 410
    and religion 411, 414, 422, 423–4,
        425–8
    sons of 170, 427
    tomb 428–30
    and translation work 416, 423–6,
        431
    and Xuanzang 119, 337–8, 361–2,
        378, 410–16, 425–8, 439–40

Tajikistan 153–4
Taklamakan Desert 77, 92, 102, 109,
        132, 333, 365
    oases 91, 92, 102, 201, 338, 357
Taliban 187–8, 190, 197–8, 204–6
Tang Annals 121, 173, 176
Tang dynasty 15, 50, 121, 416–22, 426,
        431, 434
Temple of Raising the Faith 438–9
Thailand 127, 225
Theravada Buddhism 128, 189, 246,
        274–5, 313
Thunderbolt Monastery, Dunhuang
        384–5, 386–405
Tiananmen Square, Beijing 67, 220
Tiantai School 14
Tiberius, Emperor 76
Tibet 60, 243, 318, 360
Tibetans 120, 121
Tocharian language 130, 132
Tokmak 157
Tokyo: National Museum 126
treasure hunters 354–5
Tumshuq 102
Turfan, Xinjiang 92–3, 102, 104–6,
        108–10, 131, 349, 414
Turkestan 102
Turks 150–1, 158, 171, 333, 419
Tushita 69, 193

Uighurs 92, 120–2, 126, 131–2, 140–1,
        350
    Islamic fundamentalists 154, 155,
        334
    separatist movement 154, 334,
        348–9
    uprisings 334–5
United Nations 197–8
Upali 277
Urumqi, Xinjiang 109, 131, 149, 155
Uzbekistan 152–3, 154, 156, 166, 177

Vaisali, Bihar 235, 277
Valentina (archaeologist) 170–3,
        175
Vasubandhu 182, 183, 243
Vietnam 56
Vimalakirti 377–8
Vinaya 67

Waley, Arthur 441
Wang Yuanlu 368–72, 384
Warner, Langdon 372
Wei Zheng 415
Weigan river 132
Western Region 91, 99, 114, 118, 131, 135, 150, 332–3, 414
Western Turks 150–1, 170–2
  Khan of, *see* Great Khan
White Horse Monastery 211
White Huns 182, 197, 233
White Jade river 340, 351–3
Wild Horse Spring 88, 91
Wilford, Francis 221
Wu, Empress 430, 431–4
Wuwei, *see* Liangzhou

Xian 13, 47, 49–72, 409–10, 416–18, 429, 434–5
  see also Chang'an
Xian Buddhist Association 66, 67
Xian Municipal Cultural Bureau 56
Xinjiang 92–3, 101, 115–16, 120, 122, 130–1, 135, 139–41
  Islamic fundamentalism 154, 155, 156
  uprisings 334–5
Xinjiang Airline 149
Xuanzang 10–11, 41–3, 47–8
  appearance 13
  in Benares 290, 292
  in Bihar 232–5, 240–7, 252, 269–70, 284, 322–6
  character of 12, 13, 17, 48, 91, 108, 149, 155, 271, 440
  death and burial place 435–9
  disciples of 438
  Doctrine of Mere Consciousness 315
  and emperors 75, 337–8, 361–2, 378, 412–16, 423–8, 430–1
  and Empress Wu 433
  ill health 148
  journey to India 75, 79–80, 82–4, 86–91, 95–8, 106–7, 110, 114–15, 117, 119–20, 124–5, 147–51, 162–3, 181–3, 205
  legends surrounding 384
  life of 12–17
  life threatened by pirates 232–3, 270–1
  love for India 211, 217–18
  as Mahayana Buddhist 127–8, 181–2
  meeting with Khan 157, 169, 171–5
  monastery of 51–3, 61, 63, 66, 69, 71
  portraits of 72, 159, 383, 384
  presence of 440
  public debates 246, 325–6
  remains of 63, 235–6, 438
  reputation of 159–60, 220, 222, 228, 247, 253, 284, 383–4, 410
  return journey 327, 331, 336–7, 351, 361, 365, 379, 385
  return to China 409–11
  reverence for history 223
  shrine of 384
  in South India 313–15, 319
  studies 12, 189, 246–7, 250, 255
  teachings of 63
  translations 48, 57, 71, 128, 212, 246, 337, 369, 422–6, 436–7, 441
  and Yogacara Buddhism 247–8, 250–2, 441
  see also Life of Xuanzang; Record of the Western Regions

Yadav, Laloo 239
Yagabhu Khan, *see* Western Turks, Great Khan of
Yakshis 220
Yang Weijiang 336, 339–40, 343–4, 346–51, 353
Yangzi River 13, 158
Yaoxing, Emperor 413
Yasa 291
Yashkar (Uighur in Khotan) 351–7
Yellow River 79, 158
Yogacara School 15–16, 182, 183, 243, 250–2, 271, 315, 316, 338, 402, 438, 441–2
  Chinese (*Faxiang*) 250, 252
  Sutra 232, 244, 247, 425
Yogasastra 128
Yogendra (driver in Bihar) 231, 235–6, 239–42, 252–3, 261, 292–3

Yuance 438
Yuechi tribe 201
Yulin Caves 384
Yusupov, Hamid 165–6

Zen Buddhism 13–14, 15, 219, 310,
    396–7, 398, 402

Zhai Fengda 377, 378
Zhang Qian 76
Zhanghuai, Prince 418
Zhangxiong, Gen. 109–10
Zhou Bapi 280–1
Zoroastrians 422
Zuo Zongtang, Gen. 335